Additional praise for *Derrida's Bible*:

"This valuable volume represents a helpful shift of focus of current discussions of 'Derrida and religion' to 'Derrida and the Bible,' to the way in which this scrupulously close micro-reader of texts reads and helps us read Biblical texts, the assembled conglomerate of which is what is meant by 'Derrida's Bible.' The collection shows superbly how 'the Bible' (like 'Plato'), as a single overarching theological unity or an enabling ecclesiastical authorization, is exploded by a close—even 'literalist'— reading which releases an avalanche of metaphors, puns, competing theologies, heterogeneities, multiple layers of cut and paste authorship, good news and bad, awash in problems of interpretation and translation—in short, everything that Derrida predicts a 'text' (a 'scripture') would be. Yvonne Sherwood has produced an important collection for which everyone, readers of Derrida and readers of the Bible, will be grateful."

—John D. Caputo, Watson Professor of Religion, Syracuse University

"Readers who imagine they already know what 'Derrida's Bible' amounts to—a transcendental signified cast down to earth, Lucifer-like, here; gleeful greasing of the higher rungs of a Jacob's ladder there—will be pleasantly surprised by this collection. The Derrida of the title is, for the most part, 'later' Derrida, increasingly irreducible to deconstruction, and certainly to deconstruction-by-numbers; and the readings of biblical texts showcased within are, at their best, correspondingly nuanced, surprising, and consequential."

—Stephen D. Moore, author of *Mark and Luke in Poststructuralist Perspectives: Jesus Begins to Write and Poststructuralism and the New Testament: Derrida and Foucault at the Foot of the Cross*

RELIGION/CULTURE/CRITIQUE
Series editor: Elizabeth A. Castelli

DERRIDA'S BIBLE

(READING A PAGE OF SCRIPTURE WITH A LITTLE HELP FROM DERRIDA)

Edited by

YVONNE SHERWOOD

palgrave
macmillan

First published in 2004 by
PALGRAVE MACMILLAN™
175 Fifth Avenue, New York, N.Y. 10010 and
Houndmills, Basingstoke, Hampshire, England RG21 6XS.
Companies and representatives throughout the world.

PALGRAVE MACMILLAN is the global academic imprint of the Palgrave Macmillan division of St. Martin's Press, LLC and of Palgrave Macmillan Ltd. Macmillan® is a registered trademark in the United States, United Kingdom and other countries. Palgrave is a registered trademark in the European Union and other countries.

ISBN 1–4039–6628–1 (hardback)
ISBN 1–4039–6663–X (paperback)

Library of Congress Cataloging-in-Publication Data is available from the Library of Congress.

A catalogue record for this book is available from the British Library.

Design by Newgen Imaging Systems (P) Ltd., Chennai, India.

First edition: November 2004

10 9 8 7 6 5 4 3 2 1

Printed in the United States of America.

For
Jacques Derrida

Contents

Series Editor's Preface

RELIGION/CULTURE/CRITIQUE is a series devoted to publishing work that addresses religion's centrality to a wide range of settings and debates, both contemporary and historical, and that critically engages the category of "religion" itself. This series is conceived as a place where readers will be invited to explore how "religion"—whether embedded in texts, practices, communities, or ideologies—intersects with social and political interests, institutions, and identities.

Derrida's Bible (Reading a Page of Scripture with a Little Help from Derrida) brings together the work of scholars of religion, literature, philosophy, theology, and the Bible to explore two influential canons: the Bible and the *oeuvre* of Jacques Derrida. In the midst of continental philosophy's famous (or, to some, notorious) turn toward religion, Derrida—as a reader of biblical texts, as the name most closely associated with the philosophical and literary practices of deconstruction, as a figure for "theory" as a whole—has inspired renewed attention among readers concerned with the place of religion, theology, and scripture in the current cultural situation. The title of this collection, *Derrida's Bible*, invites us to consider both the character and nature of Derrida's own Bible but also the shape of scriptural reading in a post-Derridean age. In the process of having produced their elegant readings attuned to (and sometimes in tension with) the writings of Jacques Derrida, the contributors to this book have both issued and answered invitations to engage in an ongoing conversation about the Bible as a ghost in the machinery of contemporary culture. *Derrida's Bible* blurs the lines that so often separate different disciplinary enterprises, especially those lines that have (for ambivalent reasons) grown up between biblical studies and philosophy/theology. Thanks to Yvonne Sherwood's deft conceptualizing and careful editorial work, *Derrida's Bible* makes a compelling contribution to the project to which this series is dedicated.

Elizabeth A. Castelli
RELIGION/CULTURE/CRITIQUE Series Editor

New York City
May 2004

Acknowledgments

The glimmer of the idea that became *Derrida's Bible* and the conference *Derrida and Religion: Other Testaments* (Toronto 2002) first occurred to me at a conference held at the University of Luton, England in 1995. (That conference was originally called, rather whimsically, *Applied Derrida* but was later changed, a little pink-facedly, to *Applying to Derrida*.) As the only representative of religion, let alone Bible, I was struck by unexpectedly enthusiastic responses to a little Bible study that I presented on Derrida and Hosea. I was particularly struck by the responses of the late Anthony Easthope (who I had never imagined as former attendee of Sunday School) and I remember with gratitude a bar conversation about the potential of Bible Study for Grown-Ups. Since then I have been deeply fortunate to find such a congenial set of colleagues and friends among whom to rethink what could be meant by 'Bible' and the act of inheriting Bible. To prevent the list sprawling inappropriately like some incontinent Oscar speech, I'll confine myself on this occasion to the current members of the Reading, Theory and the Bible committee at the *Society of Biblical Literature*: Tim Beal, Deb Krause, Tod Linafelt, Stephen Moore, Hugh Pyper, Ken Stone. I am grateful to Elizabeth Castelli for ushering the book so painlessly into the Religion/Culture/Critique series and to Amanda Johnson, Laura Morrison, Erin Ivy, and Newgen for seeing it into print so efficiently. Above all, I want to express my gratitude to Richard Davie for his very underpaid and very patient sub-editing work. Without his assistance, *Derrida's Bible* would probably still be a pile of papers in my office, rather than the book you're holding in your hand.

Contributors

Editor

Yvonne Sherwood is Senior Lecturer in Old Testament/Tanakh and Jewish Studies at the University of Glasgow. Her work to date includes *The Prostitute and the Prophet* (London: Continuum, 1996; 2nd edn 2004), *A Biblical Text and Its Afterlives: The Survival of Jonah in Western Culture* (Cambridge University Press, 2000), and various articles for *Biblical Interpretation*, the *Journal for the Study of the Old Testament*, the *Journal of the American Academy of Religion*, and *Semeia*. She chairs the Reading, Theory and the Bible section of the Society of Biblical Literature, and is currently writing a monograph on the "sacrifice" of Isaac/Ishmael in ancient commentary and contemporary cultures under the working title *Isaac/Ishmael's Scar*.

Contributors and Respondents

John Barton is Oriel & Laing Professor of the Interpretation of Holy Scripture at the University of Oxford. He is the author of *Reading the Old Testament* (1984, 2nd edn., 1996) and coeditor of *The Oxford Bible Commentary*. He is currently working on a book entitled *The Nature of Biblical Criticism*.

Brian M. Britt is Associate Professor and Director of Religious Studies at the Center for Interdisciplinary Studies at Virginia Tech. His research on literary and theoretical approaches to the Bible combines the analysis of biblical texts with questions of contemporary culture. In addition to articles in biblical and religious studies journals, his work includes two books: *Walter Benjamin and the Bible* (Continuum, 1996; 2nd edn., forthcoming), and *Rewriting Moses: The Narrative Eclipse of the Text*, forthcoming with T & T Clark. He is currently working on biblical curses and their modern legacy. He received his Ph.D. from the University of Chicago Divinity School.

Mark Brummitt is Old Testament Teaching Fellow at the Partnership for Theological Education, Manchester, and is completing a Ph.D. thesis titled "Watching Words: Critical Theoretical Readings of Jeremiah" at the University of Glasgow. His main areas of interest are prophecy and performance and, more broadly, the Bible and critical theory.

Lee Danes is a doctoral student in the Department of English at York University, Toronto, where he teaches Shakespeare and Introduction to Literature and Theory.

His work is interdisciplinary in character, interweaving interests in literature, philosophy, and the Bible. His two formal fields of study are the Early Modern Period and Literary Theory and Criticism (with a particular focus on the relationship of the Greek and Biblical traditions from the perspective of theories of textuality and interpretation).

Oona Eisenstadt (or Ajzenstat) is Assistant Professor of Religious Studies at Pomona College, having formerly worked in the Department of Political Science, University of Toronto. She is the author of *Driven Back to the Text: The Premodern Sources of Lévinas's Postmodernism*, and continues to work on contemporary Jewish political philosophy.

R. Christopher Heard teaches biblical studies at Pepperdine University in Malibu, California. He is the author of *Dynamic of Diselection: Ambiguity in Genesis 12–36* and *Ethnic Boundaries in Post-Exilic Judah*, and the webmaster for iTanakh (www.iTanakh.org) and the Society of Biblical Literature's Semiotics and Exgesis section (www.semioticsandexegesis.info). Heard's research and writing focus on the book of Genesis and Jewish literary activity in the Persian period.

Theodore W. Jennings Jr. is Professor of Biblical and Constructive Theology at The Chicago Theological Seminary and is the author of a dozen books including *The Man Jesus Loved: Homoerotic Narratives from the New Testament* (Pilgrim, 2003) and *The Insurrection of the Crucified: The "Gospel of Mark" as Theological Manifesto* (Exploration, 2003).

David Jobling recently retired as Professor of Hebrew Scriptures at St. Andrew's College, Saskatoon. A former President of the Canadian Society of Biblical Studies, he is the author of *1 Samuel* in the *Berit Olam* series and numerous other books and articles. As a member of the Bible and Culture Collective, he cowrote and coedited *The Postmodern Bible* and *The Postmodern Bible Reader*. For some years he was General Editor of the journal *Semeia*.

Jennifer L. Koosed is Assistant Professor of Religious Studies at Albright College in Reading, Pennsylvania. She earned her degree from Vanderbilt University in Hebrew Bible, and also holds a Diploma in Jewish Studies from the University of Oxford (Centre for Hebrew and Jewish Studies). She has published articles in the journal *Semeia*, and various edited volumes such as *Imagining Otherness: Filmic Visions of Community* (Scholars Press, 1999), *Strange Fire: Reading the Bible after the Holocaust* (Sheffield Academic Press, 2000), and *Autobiographical Biblical Criticism: Between Text and Self* (Deo Publishing, 2002).

Francis Landy is Professor in the Department of History and Classics at the University of Alberta. He has published three books and some fifty articles in the area of Hebrew Bible, and is at work on a book on Isaiah.

Mary-Jane Rubenstein is a doctoral candidate in Philosophy of Religion at Columbia University. She has published articles on Kierkegaard, postcolonial Christianity, and poststructuralist retrievals of negative theology, and is writing her dissertation on wonder.

Robert Paul Seesengood is adjunct Lecturer in Classics in the College of Liberal Arts, Drew University, Madison, New Jersey. He is completing a Ph.D. exploring athletic metaphors for endurance in earliest Christian rhetoric.

Dmitri M. Slivniak was born in Kharkov (Ukraine). He holds a Ph.D. in General Linguistics (Yerevan University, Armenia, 1983) and in Biblical Studies (Tel Aviv University, 2001). He works at the Open University (Tel Aviv) and at the Chais Center of the Hebrew University (Jerusalem).

Marie Turner is Lecturer in Biblical Studies at the Flinders University of South Australia. She is a member of the Earth Bible Project Team led by Dr. Norman Habel. She has published "God's Design: the Death of Creation?" in Volume Three of the Earth Bible Series and is currently completing her Ph.D. on deconstructing the theology of creation in the *Wisdom of Solomon*.

Andrew P. Wilson is currently a lecturer in Religious Studies at Mount Allison University. A recent graduate of the University of Sheffield, his Ph.D. dissertation was entitled "Transfigured: A Derridean Re-Reading of the Markan Transfiguration." The Derridean inspired work begun in this dissertation will soon be extended to include various aspects of Paul's letters as part of a SSHRC postdoctoral fellowship to be taken at the University of Alberta in early 2004.

Frank M. Yamada is Instructor of Hebrew Bible/Old Testament at Seabury-Western Theological Seminary. He has written in the area of postmodern ethics, the ethics of biblical interpretation, and cultural hermeneutics, specifically Asian American biblical interpretation. He is a Ph.D. candidate at Princeton Theological Seminary, working on a narrative and cultural analysis of rape texts in the Hebrew Bible.

Introduction: Derrida's Bible

Yvonne Sherwood

Close readers of Derrida may have long suspected that, despite his protests that he knows these "rich and secret texts very badly" (Derrida 1984 [1981], 30), this very itinerant thinker has an acquaintance with the Bible that goes well beyond occasionally flicking through *Gideon Bibles* in hotels. Prooftexts for this suspicion would include the biblical allusions that accumulate thick and fast in the now labyrinthine Derridean archive: an exhausting though not exhaustive list would now have to include (take a deep breath):

> . . . creation and the "fall," Cain and Abel, the flood, the tower of Babel, Abraham's hospitality to the angels, the "sacrifice" of Isaac, the burial of Sarah, the rejection of Esau, the deception of blind Isaac, scenes of circumcision, the burning bush, Moses and Zipporah, Mount Sinai, the Egyptian plagues, the prescriptions regarding fringes, the temple and the tabernacle (particularly its veils and curtains), Samson, "shibboleth," blind Eli and his sons, Elijah, Job, Esther, Jonah's whale, Jeremiah's curse, the dry bones of Ezekiel, Tobit, the tactile synoptics and the relatively touch-phobic fourth gospel, doubting Thomas, Jesus' healings of the blind, the Lord's prayer, the sermon on the mount, the woman who anoints Jesus' feet, the crucifixion and resurrection; the last supper, the conversion of Saul/Paul, the circumcision of the heart and flesh, the debate on head-covering, the Apocalypse of John . . .

Then there are the quasi-biblical idioms that creep into Derrida's acts of writing, as if to mark the haunting of our languages by the Bible. Note his Isaianic "What I heard without hearing, what I understood without understanding" (Derrida 1995a, 31); his Pauline "I do not want what I want" (Caputo 1997a, 25); his quasi-eucharistic "this is my corpus" (Derrida 1993a, 27); and his twisted Jesus-ism *doubting* the dream of new wineskins / cloth on the grounds that "decisive ruptures" and "epistemological breaks" are inevitably inscribed in "old cloth" that must "continually, interminably, be undone" (Derrida 1981, 39). And then there is the accompanying sense of "hyper-punctilious" (Cixous 2004, 9) Bible study: the way in which Derrida usually consults at least two French versions (as if trying to listen as closely as possible through variant translations to the connotations of the Hebrew, Greek, and Aramaic); the way he turns to expert (?) sources such as the *Interpreter's Dictionary of the Bible*, and, in his attention to the micrology of the text, comes rather close to the close-reading practises of the *Society of Biblical Literature*, or S-B-L.[1] It was this penchant for very careful, very risky Bible study, at least as much as his more famous fascination with questions of theology and religion, that prompted me to invite Derrida to the joint annual meeting of the Society of Biblical Literature and the American Academy of

Religion (Toronto, November 2002): this volume, the second compendium of papers provoked by that occasion, is dedicated to some of the disproportionate number of papers submitted for panels called *Reading a Page of Scripture with a Little Help from Derrida*. Although Bible overspills into a separate volume of its own, readers might also like to consult the more explicitly "scriptural" of the essays in the companion conference volume *Derrida and Religion: Other Testaments* (Sherwood and Hart 2004). The possibilities of what might be meant by that curio that we are calling "Derrida's Bible" are also explored in Gil Anidjar's "Hosting," Hugh Pyper's "Reading and Not Reading the Hebrew Scriptures / Old Testament with a Little Help from Derrida and Cixous," Timothy Beal and Tod Linafelt's "To Love the Tallith More than God," Catherine Keller and Stephen Moore's "Derridapocalypse," Yvonne Sherwood and John Caputo's "Otobiographies: Or How a Torn and Disembodied Ear Hears a Promise of Death," Kevin Hart and George Aichele's "Word Becomes Text," and Regina Schwartz's "The Revelation of Justice."

No one that I know has ever seen Derrida's Bible (despite craning my neck as the film *Derrida* [Ziering-Kofman and Dick 2003] panned around his study at Ris Orangis, I still couldn't catch a glimpse of it, and he didn't bring it with him to our conference), but that doesn't prevent us from speculating about what it might look like—or at least attempting a negative theology of "Derrida's Bible" through an oblique assault by way of what it's not. It's probably not one of those big, leather-bound zipped ones: certainly it is not bound by the concept of the "Book" as the "encyclopaedic protection . . . against the disruption of writing" (Derrida 1976, 18). Nor is it watched over by one of those giant eyes that—abstracting from the vantage point of the transcendental over and above the empirical or contingent—seems to assume that the biblical authors were asked to write a little something for a book called *The Bible* (SPCK: forthcoming) and given firm instructions for their contribution in advance. That is to say that, in the Derridean tradition of "placing in the way of the systematic and the programmatic, reminders of the [biblically] idiomatic" (Derrida 1992, 14), Derrida's Bible is probably not so much a Bible as a Bible-contested-by-biblical (lower case).[2] It's not the kind of Bible that sees itself cringingly, apologetically, as philosophy or theology *manqué*: it's not a place where the "I will be who I will be" who "appears" from the midst of the burning bush is already translated into Greek or German as an agent of "revelation" or an actor in an unfolding, progressive narrative of *Heilsgeschichte* (salvation history). Its cover is probably not one of those gold-embossed, white leather ones that seem to suggest not only ethical purity and a virginity of beginnings (an idealised Judeo-Christian as prelapsarian backdrop to our cultures), but also something of what Stephen Moore calls the "paint-stripper" effect in which colour and "hieroglyphic brilliance" are erased by being dipped in big vats of academe[a]se (1992, 82).

Derrida's Bible is, perhaps rather surprisingly, a fundamentalist's, literalist's Bible for, against all the stereotypes, Derrida is something of a literalist and even a material-ist, at least insofar as *matter* can be taken to designate "radical alterity" in relation to philosophical or theological propositions.[3] In his scriptures the transcendental is always held in awkward negotiation with the linguistic material of its production / incarnation: as Derrida's Plato talks in terms of "asses," "blacksmiths," and *khôra* and *pharmakon*, so Derrida's Bible speaks in terms of seeds, deserts, bread, and blood as well as messianism and justice—dreams made of "metaphors" straining to transport language beyond itself (*metaphorein*), trusting to the capacity of language to surpass itself, but also bound over by a sense of the literality and limit of "so many words." As Derrida provocatively puts it: "In truth, language should be in a state of plenitude, fulfilment and actualisation to the point of self-effacement" (1974 [1971], 41), so locating truth as the point at which language is paradoxically so precise *and* so full that it becomes pure, transparent, redundant, ceding absolutely to the purely self-evident reality that lies behind it. (Compare Frank Yamada's gloss, in this volume, that "For Derrida, language is always promising to reach its destination, to lay hold of transcendence," placing language outside promised land without denying the hope of promised land.) This *point* of truth—this point of absolute fullness and absolute precision—is not a point held loosely by "liberals," abandoned by "pomo" anarchists and adhered to faithfully by "fundamentalists," for Derrida is clear that, just as all preservers or conservers of the letter translate the texts before they countersign (accept its word as theirs), so there is something, we could say, "fundamentalist" in all of us. *All* writing—Derrida's writing and scriptural writing (in some sense) alike—aspires towards that acutely desirable and impossible point where language overflows itself *and* contracts to such a precise point that it elides itself, which is why Derrida, like Bible, overreaches to make new revelatory things happen to old languages *and* at the same time pedantically piles up qualifying phrases as if striving for absolute precision and prefect apprehension. (Compare Derrida's stacked clauses telling us that he means precisely *this* and not precisely *that* to Ezekiel's very precise vision of the "*appearance* of the *likeness* of the *glory* of the Lord" [Ezek. 1:28; my italics].)

Derrida is onto something important here, for, like Derrida, those inner-biblical interpreters that we call redactors or editors or authors (Paul would be one such), express devotion to memory *and* the desire for rupture, as for example they turn oracles on the axis of pun and convert curse into blessing, or reweave old cloth in ways that break with tradition on the grounds of tradition, and so make that break traditional / original. (Those who would accuse Derrida of audacious crimes against "the truth" in contrast to the retrojected fidelity of the once-passive-purveyors-of-tradition need to read their Bible one more time.) Indeed, faithfulness-rupture could be taken as the linking theme of the exegeses of Derrida's Bible in this collection. Not only does this Bible seem to create itself, in time, through this tension between fidelity and rupture, but it also generates stark, iconic figures of that tension. It can be seen in the scroll (Jeremiah II) that self-consciously preserves the memory of an old scroll (Jeremiah I) which it replicates *and* displaces; in a Jerusalem and a Davidic line that eradicate where they come from and, at the same time, seem to be the inevitable outcome of where they came from; in the allure of an all-new Melchizedek, assembled from etymological shards and bits and pieces of existing texts but depicted as if coming from nowhere (as if, as the book of Enoch suggests, he were somehow born, fully clothed, from a virgin). And it can be seen in the "paradigmatic" figure set at the head of this collection: Matthew's figure of a messiah who comes from genealogy and virgin birth. (I am referring here to the essays by Mark Brummitt, David Jobling, Alastair Hunter, and Lee Danes.)

Fundamentalism shocks and outrages intellectuals, and Derrida's Bible can seem crude, raw, and unsophisticated, like the Bible that his fellow-Algerian St. Augustine felt so deeply ambiguous about before he learned to theologise, allegorise, translate, and love it purely, in a way that seems to have eradicated all the ambiguity of love-hate.[4] As I've argued elsewhere (for example, 1996, 205–06, 249–50; 2000; 2001; Sherwood and Caputo 2004), read in the "raw," as it were, the biblical prophets can seem more shockingly "Derridean" than Derrida, even more "Derridean" than the exaggerated Derrida-caricatures, as, for example, they place God *sous rature*, picture him inseminating the female-nation-body-land, and assiduously follow the logic of pun (not of concept) through which "writing and hearing . . . pair up and dance" (Cixous 2004, 7).[5] Derrida's Bible is not an *improved* Bible, even less a *new* Bible, like those New International versions, New English Bibles or New Revised Standard versions, but a rather unfashionably old-new Bible—how else to explain Derrida's interest in, of all things, Bible, than through his perversely retro-obsession with old–new languages, synagogues, and texts (Derrida 1995b)? It's a Bible full of marginalia: like those scholarly editions of the Hebrew Bible with all the notes at the bottom, and the notes down the side, it "deconcentrates," focuses on the secondary, eccentric, lateral, parasitic; or, like those medieval manuscripts where colourful figures cavort in the margins, it brings onto the page of a too-white-theology the still stirring, potentially disruptive graphics of still stirring, active, biblical memory (cf. Derrida 1982 [1971]).[6] It's an edition of uncertain date: in one sense ultra-contemporary, constantly thinking the biblical *cum tempus*, with time—that is with change, flux, interpretation, revision—and with the time(s). There are bits of newspapers taped into it, post-it notes stuck in it marked "cf. Hebron," "cf. Iraq" or "cf. nation-state and borders." It anticipates that "new" scholarly move that opens the text up to its "afterlives" and indeed, like all readers outside the Academy, absorbs afterlives without always knowing that they haven't always been there "in" the Bible.[7] It even seems, at times, to be that very timely, previously unthought of thing—something that R. Christopher Heard seems also to have got hold of to aid his reflections on the responsibility of Abraham to Isaac and to Ishmael—a new edition with cross-referencing to the Qur'an. But then the very idea of the contemporary is unsettled by this Bible which is not even its own contemporary: even a seemingly rock solid figure, or time, like "Sinai" cannot, when you look closer, be held together as one, for it is the time of the giving of the tablets and the breaking of the tablets, of the veiling and unveiling of Moses' face, a split figure that evokes *interruptions* in the narrative of self and caesuras and ruptures in time (Derrida 1999, 63–64).

Derrida's Bible seems to have a great deal to do with tracing tangled and interrupted roots (personal and generic): it is concerned with tracking the genealogies of those cultural hauntologies (rather than ontologies) in which we live, move, and have our thinking and being. (As David Jobling puts it in this volume, "I am haunted, therefore I am.") It's also a personal Bible and a family Bible: I can just glimpse the list of names in the front (in a Babel of languages, including, perhaps, Ladino, Hebrew, Berber, Arabic, and French), as grandfathers Abraham or Moses pass on to Georgette Esther, who passes on to sons and daughter René Abraham or Paul Moses, or Jackie Elie, or Janine, or Norbert Pinhas. The curious origins of this particular Bible in a Jewish-Arab-Christian-Latin-Franco-Maghrebian family (a situation at once very singular and very typical of the twentieth century's proliferation of hyphenated, itinerant individuals), and the way in which it is passed between names that seem to pair the biblical and the secular (Jackie Elie, Norbert Pinhas) perhaps explains why this Bible is so denominationally and faithfully undecided; which is not to say it's a project of wide-eyed ecumenism or broadly accommodating "Judeo-Christianity" (for Derrida, Judeo-Christianity is, to say the least, a rather spurious hybrid, and one should never assume that Judaisms, Christianities, and Bibles are one and the same). For Derrida's Bible seems to be something of a mongrel, cut and paste edition which sits uncomfortably alongside too-easy terms like "International" or "Standard," as surely as it questions terms like "New" or "Revised." Some passages seem to be cut out from one of those Christian Protestant cross-referencing editions (his version of the sacrifice of Isaac is headed with cross-references to the New Testament, Kierkegaard, Luther, and Paul), and yet the binding, or rather lack of it, seems to be Catholic or Jewish in that it strategically unravels the Protestant reification of "Bible" and the "Word."[8] Family Bible it may be, but this is no settled legacy passed on, as it were, quasi-genetically, like a meme, as if having the hidden name Elijah, a mother with the hidden name Esther, and grandfathers Abraham and Moses had somehow injected "Bible" in through the bloodstream or the cerebral cortex (as if Derrida had somehow unproblematically received a lump of Bible at the moment when he received an unproblematised lump of "Judaism"). Scrawled in the front, in Derrida's own handwriting is the following:

> "My" Bible—though one never *has* a Bible any more than one has a language. (Reading is as much about dispossession as possession and inheritance is not something we *receive*, but a *task* . . .)

Derrida's Bible is a source of unsettledness that disrupts the at-homeness of all Judaisms, Christianities, mother-religions, mother-tongues, and mother-secularisms—which is not to say that it is something (tediously, predictably) "disruptive," or "radical." It neither legitimates a rather pious, self-righteous secularity by breaking up all Judaisms and Christianities, nor legitimates an easy piety by showing how an ever-predictably-radical-Bible is always ahead of us (as in certain contemporary images of Jesus as quintessential rebel with a cause; see for example, Crossan 1995). Like Derrida's Heidegger, it is a place where thoughts and motifs that challenge the classical canon coexist with the most settled, static and repetitious motifs imaginable; a place where it is impossible to say, for instance, "Paul in general," but where one must constantly work within the very thick, very complicated, Pauline archive and its consequences "terrible and mild" (see for example, Derrida 2002b, 97). It is not the pure bedrock of Western metaphysics (source of all our founding concepts like onto-theological sovereignty and the Logos), nor some solid *arche*, given once and for all (like the image of the Bible epitomised in the 5200 pound granite monument of the ten commandments erected outside an Alabama courthouse),[9] *nor* some newly discovered, exotic (dis-Orientating? Hebrew? Jewish?) other, come to seduce a Greco-Christian West. (This volume is more prone to talk in terms of careful, qualified, micro-analogy—what has Gilead got to do with Algeria?; what have biblical Jerusalems or Hebrons got to do with their twentieth-century "equivalents"?—than in terms of huge Macro-showdowns between Jerusalem and Athens.) It is precisely to resist such easy, complementary antitheses and to intimate a certain lack and restlessness at the heart of the One, that Derrida writes in the front of his Bible that "everything is in the Bible—everything *and the rest.*"[10]

Bible Study with a Différance

Imagine some devoted *Extraskriver* or "supplementary clerk" who, though neither a philosopher nor a philosopher's daughter, decided to put together a "Derridean" Bible study series called, say, *Bible Study with a Différance.*[11] She would have to make it clear that this was not one of those conventional devotional studies called, say, "Daily Bread" or "Daily Light" (nor indeed its opposite: "Daily Stones/Scorpions" or "Daily Darkness"[12]). She would have to say, pseudo-apologetically, that its author had a rather complicating notion of the relation between sight and blindness, light and darkness, and that he had a constitution too small to digest a Bible whole or to wholly spit it out. She would perhaps write a little introduction explaining that the author was a little retro-Rabbinic, perhaps quoting Victor Jankélevitch on excessive, tangential, insolvent midrashic thinking that risks damage to its most cherished premises by "thinking everything that is possible in a question, thoroughly at all costs . . ." (Jankélevitch 1978, 18–19). Or maybe she would claim that the author could best be understood as a modern day Johannes Climacus or Johannes de Silentio (a.k.a. Søren Kierkegaard), and then apologise that these were not *proper*, professional Bible studies, but little, naïve ones, written for those poor existing individuals who have not yet obtained an alibi from existence by virtue of their huge heads.[13] She might add that these were only little, amateur affairs, designed for those who eat, sleep, sneeze, and still have sex and gods and mothers and who (as well as being in love with the big things like messianism, justice, promise) were still rather attached to those little human things like birth, death, eyes, bodies, hands, and prayers. She would perhaps venture that the author seemed to be pushing that new-old Sørenish question of what it might mean to read the Bible *as if* it did not take place in the exotic elsewhere of the "beautiful regions of the East," or a fairytale "Once upon a time" (apart from our time), where everyone had "faith" or was "great" by virtue of owning real estate in the prime moral territory of "the Bible" (cf. Kierkegaard 1985, 44). She might say that he was still harping on that old (yet still barely asked) question of the relationship between the Bible, responsibility and ethics; reanimating those old Kantian and Kierkegaardian anxieties that have been so thoroughly eclipsed by The Battle Between Religion and Science that it's as if this were the only question that the Enlightenments had ever asked. She might say that it seemed to her that Derrida was asking, once again, what it might mean to read the Bible *humanly*, as if it mattered, which does not always mean *humanely*, as if God and all the biblical protagonists could be expected to act as members of the bourgeois middle class.[14] She might suggest that, though less crusading in his relations with the Church and the Guild of Biblical Scholars than Kierkegaard, the author seemed to be, at least implicitly, hunting Biblical Study out of the "nooks and crannies" where scholars go to take cover, and writing to oppose a banalised Bible, touted by mischief-making Bible Societies all-too-prone to reduce it to idealised niceties and "childish peppernuts" (see Kierkegaard 1996, 136; 1992, 598–99). But she might also add that this author seemed to be going further than Kierkegaard into complex realms where theology, ethics, and politics cross. For whereas *Fear and Trembling* thinks responsibility and secrecy using examples from fairytale and bourgeois life (stories of princesses and princes or a burgher's faith in his roast lamb dinner), *The Gift of Death*, written during the so-called "first" Gulf War, begins with the question of European Responsibility and gives as an example of a particular order of "secret," "nuclear arsenal[s] in underground silos, or explosives in a cache . . ." (1993, 90).

In an Upper Room

Those of us gathered in an upper room in Toronto (in fact a set of luxurious hotel conference rooms) awaiting the coming of Elie-Elijah or a new Toronto blessing were not disciples (certainly not, as the media frequently suggests, brainwashed sectarians), although we did modestly look for that once-prophesied, ironically deferred time when, as one early seer proclaimed (back in 1982), "As he becomes better known, Derrida will have his day, even among the biblical texts" (Schneidau 1982, 6). And I had, a little self-mockingly, spoken of that longed-for day when Jeremiah would drip with observations from *A Taste for the Secret*, and when the books of Samuel would lie down with *Specters of Marx*.[15] What we were hoping for was the far more modest achievement of countering the curious fate of "Derrida" and "deconstruction" in Biblical Studies, which in certain senses mirrored that in the Humanities at large. We wanted to combat the nullification that came from two fronts: the reification of "deconstructionism" as a complex machine, *and* the domestication of "deconstruction" as a mere synonym for critical business as usual. And we wanted at least to provoke reflection on the way in which the name of "Derrida" circulates, detached from all *reading*, as an index of fashionability (a theoretical equivalent of Lacoste™ or K-Mart™, depending on your perspective); as a sign of (commodified, fetishised) "Theory™"; or, irony of ironies, as a truly floating (detached) signifier that signifies cavalier *irresponsibility* towards the text. (For discussion of the functions of Derrida in the marketplace of ideas, see further Sherwood and Hart 2004.) We also wanted to shake the discipline out of some ossified image of Derrida, based on what could be called "vintage Derrida" and certain institutionalised misreadings of vintage Derrida. Without being rude enough to ask, I guess that several of the contributors to this volume were not even born, or at least were barely toddling, when *Of Grammatology* (1976) and *Writing and Difference* (1978) were first launched in the English-speaking world, which is one, but not the only, reason why this collection is distinctly lacking in "floating signifiers" and "transcendental signifieds placed *sous rature*." Indeed, looking back over a disciplinary soap opera into which all of us entered too late (and, as Derrida says, one is always too late, always, in a sense, compensating for a lack of fullness, a lack of justice), we now see the institutionalised misreading of the "Structure Sign and Play" (Derrida 1990 [1978])[16] as *promoting* the "joyful affirmation of the play of signs" and proclaiming a facile neo-Idealism in which "All the world's a text and we are merely players" as no less than catastrophic, for it led to a rejection of Derrida by those who (using a too-easy spatial shorthand that Derrida never uses) work both on the discipline's "right" *and* "left." In the introduction to *Derrida and Religion*, Kevin Hart and I reflect, with the aid of Herman Rappoport's thought-provoking *The Theory Mess* (2001), on how "left" and "right" employ almost identical caricatures to dismiss Derrida: for those whose declared aim is textual conservation/preservation, Derrida represents a "philosophical cloud cuckoo land" (Filmer 1989, 55), while for those who demand *effective* political critique of the Bible he is a noncommitted dealer in spectres, ghosts, and esotericisms, a turner of words that are not *locked on* to politics, context, actuality, and so, as people say, "unengaged." Now is not the time for analysing, in any depth, how these very *useful* Derrida caricatures help us to deal with the fundamental impasses and paradoxes that characterise the "modern," as persuasively diagnosed by Bruno Latour (1993, 35–37), nor to ask how the "straightforward" antithesis to this spurious "Derrida" is posited far too easily without thinking through the philosophical implications. Suffice to ask, acutely desirable though such a situation might be, how one would actually go about setting up an efficient cog mechanism whereby words turn world, and so generate productive scholarship that is, in some *guaranteed* way, "engaged"?[17]

Biblical Studies and Theology has its own supply of Derrida cartoons and pseudo-Derrida-clones: even a careful scholar like John Barton can pronounce, in a deservedly influential student textbook, that "I enjoy deconstruction but do not take it very seriously" and then propagate images of an innocuous retro-hippie Derrida, drawing on his joint and saying "Relax, play with some words, join the party" (Barton 1996 [1984], 231). (This comment comes in a chapter where Derrida is only accessed indirectly, via the much overused Jonathan Culler, and then explained using limericks and extracts from *Alice Through the Looking Glass*, which reinforce a sense of being in the nursery, outside the accountability of the Protestant work ethic and criteria for *productive* research. I cite John Barton because, from the pen of such a habitually careful scholar, this treatment of Derrida seems to be symptomatic of something more than an anomalous lapse of "Barton." John Barton has generously agreed to respond to this collection; for his response, see the "Postscripts" section at the end.) In a well-thumbed introduction to Christian theology, Alister McGrath defines deconstruction as "the critical method which *virtually* declares that the identity and intentions of the author of a text are irrelevant to the interpretation of the text, prior to insisting that no meaning can be found in it" (1995, 114; I highlight that "virtually" because it nicely betrays McGrath's qualifying moment of doubt that anyone could, in fact, be incredulous enough to believe in such a definition, as logically bizarre as defining deconstruction as "the theory that [*virtually?*] proclaims that all the world is made of fish"). The consensus that Derrida is worthy of, at most, tolerant condescension leads us to suspect that the ironic deferral of the day of *différance* within the biblical, prophesied by our seer, was hardly accidental: the none-too-subtle subtext, as if by way of parody on Derrida's work on margins, is clearly "Enter into the *cul de sacs* of play, nascent scholar, at your own risk." But if this sense of secondary, nonessential scholarship feels a little familiar to those who deal in questions of, say, race, gender, and postcolonialism, the response to our call for papers suggested that perceptions of Derrida among these workers on the margins is—irrespective of

Derrida's work on "monolingualism," and his battle against colourless, genderless, contingency-less (as well as "white"-authored) "white mythologies"—prevalently that of the High Parisian "White" Male.[18]

Dictionarying "Derrida" for a *Handbook of Postmodern Biblical Interpretation* a few years ago I ventured that this "headingless writer" could equally be dictionaried under "autobiography," "translation," "gender," or "identity" precisely because he took us beyond a post-code identity politics along the lines of a reductive "Me, White, Caucasian Male; You, Chinese American Female" (Sherwood 2000a, 74–75).[19] The complexity of Derrida's work on "identity" and "monolingualism" is reflected in this volume in Dmitri Slivniak's examination of what it means to "be" a contemporary "Israeli-Russian," or indeed a "Jew" in the book of Esther, and in Frank Yamada's exploration of "crossing-over places" between Ephraimite and Gileadite, Israelite and different-Israelite in "Shibboleth and the Ma(r)king of Culture." Yamada's essay, which could be helpfully read alongside Robert Young's "Deconstruction and the Postcolonial" (2000), makes the important point that the name of Derrida and the language known as Derridean can itself become a shibboleth, a "pass-not word of exclusion," guarded by certain cliques and protocols and surrounded by a keep-out fence of high cultural awe. The purpose of this volume is emphatically *not* to promote a new amalgamating Logo (*Derrida Inc?*) into which all contemporary work on Bible can be incorporated, or to posit an all-supplying, beneficent Derridean paternity under which we can all be gratefully united, but to inject some pause for thought into the increasingly atomized sphere of contemporary biblical studies, where spheres of discussion are subdivided and subsumed under particular names (Homi Bhabha for postcolonialism, Judith Butler for gender), and where names and approaches rapidly decay with ever shorter half-lives and shelf-lives (after doing a little bit of Derrida one should move onto Žižek surely?). It's not an attempt to establish "Derridean" as the new master-language but to show how, within the Derridean corpus, there are supplementary resources for, for example, thinking "apartheid" in relation to "theologico-political-discourse[s]," including Bible, on which such a term depends (Derrida 1985, 292, 296). And, in the spirit of the parable of the great feast, or the story of the hyphenated Syro-Phoenecian woman who outwits Jesus and earns her right to at least the crumbs under the table,[20] it's an attempt to show how the resources of "Derrida" also have the potential to exceed and question the perceived exclusivism of an elitist (?) high table.

Though one can never in advance calculate the effects of acts of writing in advance, this volume will have served an important purpose if it manages to counteract a prevalent sense of "deconstruction" as Sunday-afternoon hobby-scholarship, and to combat dominant images of the "Derrideans" as those who are dazzled by the bright white light of aporia like "deer caught in headlights" (Caputo 1997a, 137), or trapped in the revolving doors of relativism, forever going round and around. And it will have been strategically useful if it manages to at least question the anomalous antagonisms imagined to rage within Biblical Studies between "The Literary" or "The Postmodern" *versus* "The Historical" (note how in this collection the biblical emphatically does not float glibly free of history or context, as if deconstruction were some hyper-advanced "New New Criticism"; note how Derrida speaks of the resources of traditional criticism as an "indispensable guardrail"; note too how, for Derrida, contexts are multiplied rather than negated, as Lee Danes helpfully explains).[21] This volume is inevitably specialist, but not acutely or anomalously so.[22] It comes as an invitation to read, for it would be impossible to understand without at least a little piece of scripture in one hand and a little piece of Derrida in the other. To those who are not bound (confessionally or professionally) to read the Bible, the images of an ancient Judaean court functioning like a "formicarium of worker ants" (Mark Brummitt), of the pastoral epistles as intercepted mail, interrupted by a Pauline-Nietzschean "remember my cloak" / "I have forgotten my umbrella" (Robert Seesengood), of Genesis 14 as a crude bodice-ripping historical yarn and a phantas-magoria of spectres (Alastair Hunter), or of Qoheleth 12:1–8 as a decomposition of book and body, as intimate and poignant as a Bill Viola video installation (Jennifer Koosed) might function as something of an evangelical tract for grown-ups. Though not evangelists, we, like Julia Kristeva, invite you to read the Bible one more time (Kristeva 1995).[23] To those who work within the too-tightly circumscribed discipline of Biblical Studies the collection might just serve to question the divisions of labour that we inherit, unthinkingly, from the Enlightenments (of which, as Derrida says, there is more than one). We would like to pose the question, at least implicitly, "What is the relevance now of the two-century old division between professionalised biblical scholars, toiling in the solid empirical soil, practising a certain fundamental-ism and a devout historicism in their dedication to the question 'Did it happen?,' and the theologians right down the other end of the corridor, occasionally looking to little bits of Bible to support self-evident moral or theological principles before which we can all bow down?" We would like to rudely interrupt the conspiracy of silence per-petuated by a sense that biblical *criticism* can only ever be critical in the euphemistic, professional sense (that the Bible, therefore, is fundamentally good), and also ques-tion the particular atomisation of the Religious Studies academy along the lines of what Rapaport comically calls "the approach approach"? (2001, 155). It is not just that the fields of Religion are divided along the lines of "I'll be a redaction critic of the Bible, you'll be an ancient Jewish historian and he'll be a systematic theologian" in a certain institutionalised hyper-specialised (in)difference, but that these micro-man-aged little fields somehow manage to miss the big questions that undergraduates and outsiders naïvely expect us to be asking, such as "Why read Bible?," "Why does Bible matter?," and "What does Bible have to do with religion, existence, and what is going on in the world today?" To turn the spatial metaphor habitually hurled at Derrida back on the biblical commentators, biblical commentary seems to work at the mar-gins. Ask a biblical commentator what the "sacrifice of Isaac" (Gen. 22) means for religion and the contemporary and you will probably find him drawing on his ciga-rette, looking grim, and saying it's more than his job's worth to tell you anything other than the etymology of the name "Isaac" and the geology of the rock on Mount Moriah.[24] The good thing about the geology of rock is that it is, well, solid; the bad thing is that it is not *interesting*—either in the normal or the Kierkegaardian sense.[25] (For the sake of good conscience, I also need to qualify the all-too-convenient Kierkegaardian cliché of the armchair scholar, whose inadequacies then pave the way for the innovation which is yet to come, and which must then come, like certain Christian clichés of a retrogressive, nonproductive "Old Testament" Jew. Derrida's vision of "tensions, heterogeneity, disruptive volcanoes, sometimes texts . . . which cannot be reduced to an institution, to a corpus, to a system" (Caputo 1997a, 20) also *resonates* with trends in Biblical Studies that seek, in Ernst Käsemann's terms, to disrupt neat, scholarly market gardens laid out on "petrified lava" (1971, 70). Biblical Studies does not lack its own "vulcanologists" (Barclay 2003)[26] or dreamers of the seismic biblical.)

Without absurdly proclaiming Derrida as Messiah, or the One And Only Come To Save Us, I do believe that (in an ironic twist that sounds like one of those gospel sayings about the first and the last) the guild of biblical scholars may have something to learn from this little Arab Jew. The caricature-defying popularity of Derrida (and, with him, that particular mode of philosophy that we demarcate, or dismiss, as "Continental") has, I suspect, much to do with a stubborn refusal to relinquish the big-naïve questions and the vacillations of human being. Derrida is interesting because he writes, as Cixous puts it, as ". . . a man of his word, a man of heart, last analyst of the soul's aching, of the soul's suffering" (2004, 1), and a disarming "Derrider" of eloquence and "stodginess" (2004, ix). The promise, and risk, of Derridean Bible study might be that instead of allowing us to automatically translate the biblical into the same old constative propositions, it might also make us think about the *performative* aspect of language: how words *do* things and how the Word wants to *do* things (note how Derrida's reading of the Apocalypse of John dwells on that final "Even so, *come* Lord Jesus," and the praying, hoping, reaching, and fragility of that "come"; see Derrida 1984 [1981], 31–35).[27] It might lead us to think about those acts of speech and writing that J. L. Austen and his followers would class as performative, such as "curses," but also about the performative dimensions of genres usually thought of as purely constative, such as Law. We might ask whether the legal texts of Old Testament/Tanakh describe or *produce* (dream of?) the state of affairs they articulate, just as Derrida asks whether independence is stated or produced (quasi-messianically invited?) by the U.S. Declaration of Independence (Derrida 1986). And it might lead us to explore what Derrida calls the *perverformative,* that is, the potential of the act of speaking or writing to fail or go beyond, even against our intentions (just as a promise can be disbelieved/unfulfilled and an invitation can be refused, so there is something intrinsically precarious about what happens to and in "our" words). Writing can never be underwritten with guarantees of perfect, efficacious performances: how can one, as Brian Britt asks, totally "blot out" a name or remember to forget by way of curse? Or, one could ask, how could one keep a word about sword-bringing messiahs purely (safely) metaphorical, or a deeply resonant word like "sacrifice" purely positive in its effects? How can one do effective surgery on language so that the dream of the very best is firmly separated from the danger of the very worst?[28]

The promise, and threat, of Derridean Bible study is that it may make the divided disciplines of religion, theology, and biblical studies more permeable to one another (questioning clearly demarcated terrains, methodologies and self-definitions in the process) by inviting *difficult* negotiations between philosophy and theology, and the physical material of the text.[29] Rather than reinforcing familiar divisions between philosophy and theology, and down-to-earth, down-to-the-empirical, "theory-free" Biblical Studies, it might entice us to do some joined-up thinking between Bible and theology and philosophy (something that we tried to provoke in three joint papers between biblical scholars and theologians, published in the companion volume),[30] and it might show how philosophy- and theory-free Biblical Studies has in fact been implicitly (anachronistically) Kantian or Hegelian by default.[31] This may involve holding systematic theologies accountable to the minutiae of biblical vocabularies and grammars: vast concepts such as "the Passion" and "the Abrahamic" might be affected by a little Markan particle "for" [*gar*] or a seemingly innocuous "and"—in Hebrew a single line called *waw* (see "Trembling in the Dark" and "And Sarah Died"). It might involve pluralising settled terms like "messianism" or "Jerusalem" in ways that go beyond the "history" classroom and affect contemporary reflections on theology and politics. When we speak of messianism do we mean "Davidic" messianism, the spectral messianism of Melchizedek, or Abrahamic messianism (and why is Abraham *not* a messianic figure?)? Does "Jerusalem" refer to a secure bastion of monarchy and temple over and against the vicissitudes of history, or the Jerusalem of Lamentations and the midrashim where the temple "turns deadly" and annihilates sacral and social order with rivers of blood? (See "The Missing /Mystical Messiah," "Jerusalem and Memory" and "The End of the World.") It might involve thinking through biblical texts in ways that stay with, without prematurely liquidating, the question. How, as Theodore Jennings asks, can Paul *think* grace in relation to justice and the aporia of pure giving (beyond all remuneration, economy, obligation); or how, as Marie Turner asks, can the Wisdom of Solomon think absolute monotheism and at the same time circumscribe and limit God as pure giver exonerated from responsibility for *das Gift* (the poison) that is death? Or how, as those who gather, transfixed, with Derrida around the *akedah* / "the 'sacrifice' of Isaac" ask, can one *think* the responsibility of Abraham between Isaac and Ishmael, ethics and religion, the equally devoted glosses of Lévinas and Kierkegaard, and the accusing (?) figures of dying Sarah and expelled Hagar? (See "Triangulating Responsibility", "Preferring not Preferring" and "And Sarah Died.")

Thinking Bible-and-theology (also Bible-but-theology and theology-but-Bible) promises and threatens to generate new-old gods and new-old theologies that refuse to take their place in advance, *either* under the gigantic "Derridean" figures of God as the figurehead of religion without religion (or Bible without the more retrogressive features of Bible) as disseminated by John Caputo, *or* under the equal and opposite (?) heading of Mark C. Taylor's "Derridean" divine sponsor of atheology or the "death of God" (Caputo 1997b; Taylor 1984).[32] Instead, taking its cue from the (as yet?) far less well-known (also Derridean) figures of God[s]-in-scripture and God-in-the-process-of-becoming-Scripture, it may produce smaller, different gods, gods in relation to time and language who have not committed themselves to "religion without religion" or atheology in advance. Derridean Bible studies seem particularly intrigued by divine figures such as the God who repents or regrets in Gen. 6:6 and who then regrets his regretting (Gen. 8:20), or the God of Gen. 2:19 who "*wants to see what the man calls the animals*," as if he were somehow defined by the tension between authority and curiosity, ". . . wanting to oversee but also abandon himself to his curiosity, even allow himself to be surprised and outflanked by the radical novelty of what is to occur" (Derrida 2001a, 385–86).[33] (It's as if this god who doesn't yet know what will happen to him in language does not know of the New Testament end that is coming, where the moment at which God-definitively-becomes-man paradoxically inaugurates a new time when these gods, in retrospect, will have to be translated out of all vulnerability, anthropomorphism and subjection to the vacillations of time and language, and converted into the impermeable language of systematic abstraction.[34]) Gods like this, together with a Jesus who does not return from on high in glory offering promises of pure presence (but who also does not fall into the opposite mode of a purely mournful, tragic, clichéd absence), or Qohelet's creator separated by a mere *aleph*, or breath, from dying (as if living, believing, hoping were close to dying), resonate powerfully with contemporary turns in theology as represented by, say, Kathryn Tanner or Rowan Williams (Tanner 1997; Williams 2000; for Mark's Jesus and Qohelet's creator, see "Decomposing Qohelet" and "Trembling in the Dark"). They have something of vulnerability, even humanity, about them, a sense of theology not done from the vantage point of a divine all-overseeing eye. Opening the "divine" and the "human" to one another and to an uncertain future, Derridean biblical criticism would be a new kind of permissive criticism in which a concern with the human is not just regarded (perversely) as narcissism or scholarly bad manners. Note for example, how Derrida reads the biblical creation story as an inaugural scene of the making of the idea of "man," locating "him" in relation to the inhuman/a-human (the animal) and the so-much-more-than-human (God)—"God" being, from the beginning, the *end* (in the sense of the goal *and* definitional limit) of "man" (2001a).[35]

Thus Derridean Bible study might just help us to think the macrocosm in which we think and work differently, in ways that take account of *différance* within the biblical corpus and within God(s). If taken seriously, it may help us to actively think about questions of time, interpretation and the *necessity* of translation: for Derrida, famously, the story of Babel performs the suspension of the human condition between the *necessity* and *impossibility* of perfect translation (and the attendant extremes of absolute confusion and absolute fidelity), and so performs the imperative of translation in which *all* acts of reading are caught (Derrida 1991). Whereas the commentary tradition tends to combine detailed excavations of the biblical languages and contexts with strange leaps in which the text suddenly speaks fluent contemporary theology; whereas it often seems that Amos, or Genesis, or Mark are at the same time[36] both ancient historical artefacts to which only a devoutly focussed historical fundamentalism can do justice *and* our unproblematised Christian/Jewish contemporaries, Derrida raises the inevitability and impossibility of perfect cultural *translation*, which has in turn to do with questions of inheritance *as a task*. Perhaps the most enduring contribution of Derrida's Bible may be the questions it provokes concerning inheritance—questions that could keep us going for several Sundays, or Sabbaths, but that I can only hint at here by way of two quotations from *Spectres of Marx*:

> Inheritance is never a given, it is always a task. It remains before us, as incontestably as the fact that, before even wanting it, or refusing it, we are inheritors, and inheritors in mourning, like all inheritors . . . To be . . . means to inherit. There is no backward-looking

fervour involved in recalling this fact, no traditionalist fervour. Reaction, reactionary, or reactive are only interpretations of the same structure of inheritance. We are inheritors, which does not mean that we *have* or that we *receive* this or that, that a given inheritance enriches us one day with this or that, but that the *being* we are *is* first of all inheritance, like it or not, know it or not. (1994, 54 following the translation in Bennington 2000, 66–67)

An inheritance is never gathered, it is never one with itself. Its presumed unity, if there is one, can only consist in the injunction to reaffirm by choosing. You must . . . filter, select, criticise, you must sort out among several of the possibilities which inhabit the same injunction . . . If the legibility of a legacy were given, natural, transparent, univocal, if it did not simultaneously call for and defy interpretation, one would never have to inherit from it. One would be affected by it as a cause—natural or genetic. One always inherits a secret, which says "Read me, will you ever be up to it." (1994, 16; again following Bennington 2000)

These provocative passages suggest a new kind of slow motion biblical interpretation, foregrounding the acts of choice and negotiation by which we sift the spirits. They open up the possibility of a new narrative of reading that, like so many strands of the Bible on which it comments, is caught up in complex relationships of exultation-mourning, gratitude-disappointment, fidelity-betrayal—rather than wholesale appropriation and pure unadulterated love. They suggest a mode of interpretation that, instead of dividing the world into those who accept or reject a given religious inheritance (in a large act of choice that seemingly exonerates us from the intricacies of inheritance thereafter), implicates us all in little acts of micro-choosing and micro-decision. They place us all in the midst of acts of reading and inheriting that are not yet complete—or just—enough.

Notes

I have deliberately not attempted anything like an introduction to Derrida, as there are some very good ones currently in existence (e.g., Royle 2003) and it may well be better to start, as these essays do, by reading little bits of scripture and little bits of "first-hand" Derrida. Those disappointed by the lack of whistle-stop tour of the essays should turn to the appendix of abstracts. As I explain in the companion volume, I'm just a little resistant to the typical fiction of the modest-masterful editor and his/her omnihospitable pen. Besides conscripting them into my introductory agenda, and my table of contents, I'm going to leave the authors to abridge themselves by themselves.

1. For a reading of Esther with a little help from *The Interpreter's Dictionary of the Bible*, see Derrida, 1987, 73–75. For a proleptic joining of Derrida and "SBL" long before he came there, see Taylor 1990, 158–60.
2. Cf. Timothy Beal's important critique of the idea of the "Bible without Bible" by which Caputo means Bible as the idea of generalised "justice," "faith" or "religion without religion" purged of "Bible" in the sense of its more oppressive, monstrous, difficult texts. (Beal 2002, 185–87.) Derrida's Bible-contested-by-biblical, in contrast, indicates conceptualisations of Bible held hostage to the fabric of the text, where "biblical" is far too complex and diverse to be pre-judged in advance (hence much closer to what Beal is asking for: fidelity to the diversity and "monstrosity" of scripture).

3. Note Cixous's observation that "*Literally* [*à la lettre*] is what concerns our poet, a caller of language and the unconscious to account, hyperpunctilious, a hyperformalizer, a surreptitious mathematician of moods" (2004, 9). Note too (in a less than beautiful sentence, at least in English, that can be taken as something of a symptom of this hyper-formalised pedantry) Derrida's confession of his devotion to matter: "It follows that if, and in the extent to which, *matter* in this general economy designates, as you said, radical alterity (I will specify: in relation to philosophical presuppositions), then what I write can be considered 'materialist' " (Derrida 1981, 64).

4. Cf. Augustine: "Accordingly I turned my attention to the holy scriptures to find out what they were like. What I see in them today is something not accessible to the scrutiny of the proud nor exposed to the gaze of the immature, something lowly as one enters but lofty as one advances further, something veiled in mystery. At that time, though, I was in no state to enter, nor prepared to bow my head and accommodate myself to its ways. My approach then was quite different to the one I am suggesting now: when I studied the Bible and compared it with Cicero's dignified prose, it seemed to me unworthy" (*Confessions* 3.5 or 9, translated in Boulding 1997).

5. For how writing and hearing pair and dance in Derrida and the Prophets, see further Cixous 2004, 7, vii.

6. "White mythology—metaphysics has erased within itself the fabulous scene that has produced it, the scene that nevertheless remains active and stirring, inscribed in white ink, an invisible design covered over the palimpsest" (1982 [1971], 213). For Derrida's reflections on a deconcentrating reading that prioritises the "eccentric" see for example 1988, 44.

7. For example, when he writes of "a kind of opening—as the Bible puts it—of a place vacant for who is to come, for the arrivant, maybe Elijah" (2001b, 30), or when he identifies the woman sinner who anoints the feet of Jesus in Luke 7 as Mary Magdalen (2000, 120), Derrida is using an expansive view of Bible in which later developments are absorbed back into "the text."

8. Derrida's important and timely contestation of the Book, which is scarcely detached from his sense of being *jewish* or *ifnotjewish* (as Cixous puts it [2004]) is also argued by Jewish scholars who have never, presumably, read *Of Grammatology*; see Greenspahn 2000, 1–12.

9. I am referring, of course, to the monument erected on August 1, 2001 by Chief Justice Moore, and recently removed as a result of lawsuits (to scenes of public wailing and lament). This very public confrontation between "democracy" and theocracy, the Decalogue and the Universal Declaration of Human Rights, would hardly be a simple one in Derrida's view. Compare what he has said, repeatedly, about the complex relationship between Revelation and Enlightenments (Enlightenments which *also* have their messianic faith in democracy-to-come, justice-to-come), for example in Borradori 2003, 121, 131–32.

10. Though I am putting the literal words into Derrida's mouth, or writing them in for him on the front of "his" Bible, this is not at all far from Derrida's own comments on the volcanic Bible in Caputo 1997, 20.

11. Cf. the way in which the Kierkegaardian pseudonym, Johannes de Silentio, describes his role in *Fear and Trembling* as an *Extraskriver*, or "freelancer" (1985, 43). Compare too the prophet Amos' disavowal "I am not a prophet nor a prophet's son" (Amos 7:14).

12. Cf. Matthew 7:9–10 [NRSV] "Is there anyone among you who, if your child asks for bread, will give a stone? Or if the child asks for a fish, will give a snake?" and Luke 11:11–12 "Is there anyone among you who, if your child asks for a fish, will give him a snake instead of a fish? Or if the child asks for an egg, will give a scorpion?"

13. Cf. Kierkegaard's scathing denunciations of those who find an excuse to sneak out of the business of life by means of a sick note or a lame excuse that they have "forgotten

something," or those who use their huge heads to exit the business of life, leaving the rest of us (who still eat, sleep, and blow our noses) to "put up with the worst" (1983, 131; 1992, 301, 303, 306).

14. Cf. Kierkegaard: "No human being reads the Bible humanly any more," and "The humane and the Christian [and the biblical] are not one and the same" (1996, 344, 525).

15. Cf., for example, Joel 3:18 [NRSV]: "In that day the mountains shall drip sweet wine, the hills shall flow with milk and all the stream beds of Judah shall flow with water" and Isaiah 11:6: "The wolf shall lie down with the lamb" (bearing in mind Woody Allen's quip that the lamb is unlikely to sleep; 1980, 25). Which is "wolf" and which is "lamb" in the conjunction "Derrida and the Bible" remains to be seen, though the result of the conjunction is definitely sleeplessness.

16. I discuss misreadings of vintage Derrida further in Sherwood 2000a, 69–70.

17. For Derrida's counterblast against the myth of straightforwardness, and his anger at the "Franco-Britannic" decorum that effaces the "labour of theory," see 1993a, 62–63.

18. To use over-reductive ciphers of identity, which Derrida stubbornly resists, we should at least observe that the majority of the respondents to the initial call for papers were overwhelmingly "white" and "Caucasian," though not overwhelmingly male. Frank Yamada's paper was invited as a necessary supplement, in every sense.

19. For parallel qualifications of identity politics within Biblical Studies, see, for example, Moore 1995.

20. The parable of the great feast can be found in Luke 14:15–24, though I am perhaps exceeding it by implying that "the poor, the crippled, the blind and the lame" would still have been invited if the original guests had not made excuses and stayed away. The story of the "Syro-Phoenecian woman" can be found in Mark 7:24–30. Notice how, like the Franco-Maghrebian or Israeli-Russian or Israelite-Israelite (Ephraimite-Gileadite), "she" is divided by a hyphen that subverts the self-identity of the subject, but how, as foreigner-female-gentile-"dog," she also pushes Jesus and the reader to further interrogate the ends and definitions of "man" in ways that would resonate provocatively with Ellen Armour's analysis in note 35 below.

21. Cf. Geoffrey Bennington: "the point is not at all to claim the liberty to read out of context, which would be meaningless (one always reads in several contexts)" (Bennington and Derrida 1993, 85). For the "indispensable guardrail" of traditional criticism, see Derrida 1976, 158; for a careful delineation of what Derrida does and does not say about sign and context, see Danes, "Between Genealogy and Virgin Birth," note 4, in this volume. Those in Biblical Studies who see Derrida as, in effect, a hyper New Critic should bear in mind the interesting fact that caricatures of deconstruction as a solipsistic echo-chamber were perpetuated by those associated *with* the New Critical reification of the text-in-itself (see for example, Wellek 1993).

22. One of the reflex-criticisms of so-called "postmodern" work in Biblical Studies is that it is too complex, difficult or specialised, as if specialisation, in this unique case, constituted a reason for rejection. Those who use such dismissive tactics seem blithely unaware of say the hyper-formalised, hyper-punctilious languages of, say, systematic theology or redaction criticism.

23. See Julia Kristeva's "We should read the Bible one more time. To interpret it, of course, but also to let it carve out a space for our interpretative delirium" (Kristeva, 126)—everything apart, perhaps, from that phrase "interpretative delirium," could have been written by Derrida.

24. The caricature is perhaps a little cruel and misses the way in which many biblical scholars still manage to be more interesting than their methods and their genres. I also need to confess that, while I know of similar discussions of botany, geology, and biology in reference to other passages of Bible (e.g., Jonah's fish and Jonah's plant), I have as yet found no

actual discussion of the geology of the rock of Mount Moriah. I'm using it here with a little poetic licence, as an expression of the fundamental preference for the solid.

25. Kierkegaard uses the term *inter-esse* to evoke being in the midst of the project of being—
life, as it were, as lived, *in medias res*.

26. I am grateful to John Barclay for sharing this paper with me prior to publication.

27. Those who deal in images of Apocalyptic Derrida should note his amusing denunciation
of apocalyptic hysteria, with its boringly repetitious rhetoric of ends and edges and limits
and post-modernisms: ". . . the end of the subject, the end of man, the end of the
West . . . the end of the earth, Apocalypse Now, I tell you, in the cataclysm, the fire, the
fundamental earthquake, the napalm descending from the sky by helicopters . . ." (1984
[1981], 20–21).

28. I need to elaborate lest this sound like a throwaway Derrideanism about the best and the
worst being bound up together for no other reason than that opposites, in Derrida, habitually hang out together. "Sacrifice," for example, inspires radical acts of altruism (loosing
oneself and one's own interest for the greater good) but is also, *by the very same logic*, dangerous insofar as it implies that life should be given up for that which is more than one's
own, mere, physical, life. How could one disentangle the liberating, world-making possibilities of sacrifice from its dark side? How could one purge sacrifice of any perverformative risk without losing all that is powerful and alluring about sacrifice? A related point
vis à vis the perverformative is made in the Glaswegian poet Edwin Morgan's play *AD*
(2000), where a rather *ingénue* Jesus, dictating the word to John, talks of putting swords in
the midst of families, but then clarifies that this is "just a metaphor," and asks John to
write that down. A rather more savvy John has to warn him to be aware of the things that
words do and that people *do* with words—particularly, one could add, capitalized ones.

29. As a biblical scholar, Stephen Moore tenaciously holds the idea of 'the biblical' hostage to
the material of its incarnation while, as a philosopher of religion, John Caputo is most at
home in discussing implications of the biblical for transcendental questions and histories
of philosophy, while tending to bracket out the more unhelpful, complicating nuances of
the biblical text (for a critique of Caputo in this respect see Beal 2002). Is it possible, I
wonder, to do one without losing the other, in an ongoing and relentlessly awkward act of
negotiation? Similar questions about the relationship between the empirical and the transcendental are posed in Jobling's "Jerusalem and Memory: On a Long Parenthesis in
Derrida's *Specters of Marx*" in this volume.

30. See the joint papers by Keller and Moore, Sherwood and Caputo, and Aichele and Hart in
Sherwood and Hart (2004).

31. It goes against the spirits of Derrida to invoke a huge generalising adjective like "Kantian"
or "Hegelian" (particularly by way of a sonorous name-drop with little content or
nuance). Here, for the sake of time, I am using them as shorthand for a sense of evolutionary philosophy, which has in turn to do with evolutionary Christian theology, and a
strongly policed sense of Religion/Bible within the Limits of Reason and Morality Alone.

32. While I am uncomfortable with reducing Caputo and Taylor to slogans like this (their
work is far more nuanced than these trite summaries suggest), these slogans do represent
the way in which these two names have come to stand for equal and opposite receptions of
Derrida in Religion and Theology.

33. For discussion of divine repentance and confession see Derrida 2004; 2001a, 385–86;
and 1999b, especially 185–202.

34. I want to remark, at least in passing, on the curious consequence of the Christian incarnation,
whereby God becomes increasingly (systematically) immune to the human and to time. Is
there any space here for a new Kierkegaard, who, instead of converting the Old Testament
into a retrojected shadow of the New, in a modern theological equivalent of allegoresis,

would use Old Testament and Jewish theologies to interrogate Christianities "from
behind"? (from behind is taken from one of Kierkegaard's titles, and frequently used
motifs: see Kierkegaard 1848).

35. Note Ellen Armour's important extension of this argument in the direction of God,
woman, animal, and raced others, in which she argues against the popular conception that
feminism/womanism and Derrida are mutually allergic to one another (Armour 1999).

36. For Derrida's comments on the phrase "at the same time," see 2002a, esp. 93. The "at the
same time" is, of course, particularly strained here, as commentators claim the biblical as
remote artifact and unproblematized contemporary.

Works Consulted

Allen, Woody. 1980. *Without Feathers*. London: Sphere Books.

Armour, Ellen. 1999. *Deconstruction, Feminist Theology and the Problem of Difference:
Subverting the Race/Gender Divide*. Chicago: University of Chicago Press.

Barclay, John. 2003. "Living on the Fault-Line: Paul, Judaism and Subversion by Grace."
Unpublished paper. The Clark Lectures, Duke Divinity School, April 2003.

Barton, John. 1996 [1984]. *Reading the Old Testament: Method in Biblical Study*. London:
Darton, Longman and Todd.

Beal, Timothy K. 2002. "Specters of Moses: Overtures to Biblical Hauntology." In
*"Imagining" Biblical Worlds: Studies in Spatial, Social and Historical Constructs in Honor of
James W. Flanagan*, ed. David M. Gunn and Paula M. McNutt, 171–87. Journal for the
Study of the Old Testament Supplement Series 359. London: Continuum.

Bennington, Geoffrey. 2000. "Deconstruction and Ethics." In *Deconstructions: A User's Guide*,
ed. Nicholas Royle, 64–82. Basingstoke and New York: Palgrave.

Bennington, Geoffrey and Derrida, Jacques. 1993. *Jacques Derrida*. Chicago: University of
Chicago Press.

Borradori, Giovanni. 2003. *Philosophy in a Time of Terror: Dialogues with Jürgen Habermas and
Jacques Derrida*. Chicago and London: University of Chicago Press.

Boulding, Maria (trans.). 1997. *The Confessions of St Augustine*. London, Sydney, Auckland:
Hodder and Stoughton.

Caputo, John D. (ed.). 1997a. *Deconstruction in a Nutshell: A Conversation with Jacques
Derrida*. New York: Fordham University Press.

———. 1997b. *The Prayers and Tears of Jacques Derrida: Religion without Religion*.
Bloomington and Indianapolis. Indiana University Press.

Cixous, Hélène. 2004. *Portrait of Jacques Derrida as a Young Jewish Saint*. New York: Columbia
University Press.

Crossan, John Dominic. 1995. *Jesus: A Revolutionary Biography*. San Francisco: Harper.

Derrida, Jacques. 1974 [1971]. "White Mythology: Metaphor in the Text of Philosophy."
Trans. F. C. T. Moore. *New Literary History* 6, no. 1.

———. 1976. *Of Grammatology*. Trans. Gayatri Spivak. Baltimore: Johns Hopkins University
Press.

———. 1981. *Positions*. Trans. Alan Bass. London: Athlone Press.

———. 1982 [1971]. "White Mythology: Metaphor in the Text of Philosophy." In *Margins of
Philosophy*, trans. Alan Bass, 209–29. Chicago and London: University of Chicago Press.

———. 1984 [1981]. "Of An Apocalyptic Tone Recently Adopted in Philosophy." Trans.
John P. Leavey. *Oxford Literary Review* 6, no. 2:3–37.

———. 1985. "Racism's Last Word." Trans. Peggy Kamuf. *Critical Inquiry* 21, no. 1:290–99.

————. 1986. "Declarations of Independence." Trans. Tom Keenan and Tom Pepper. *New Political Science* 15:7–15.

————. 1987. *The Postcard: From Socrates to Freud and Beyond.* Chicago and London: University of Chicago Press.

————. 1988. "Limited Inc. a b c." In *Limited Inc.,* trans. Samuel Weber and Jeffrey Mehlman, 29–110. Evanston, IL: Northwestern University Press.

————. 1990 [1st English edn. 1978]. "Structure, Sign and Play in the Discourse of the Human Sciences." In *Writing and Difference,* trans. Alan Bass, 278–93. London: Routledge and Kegan Paul.

————. 1991. "Des Tours de Babel." Trans. J. F. Graham. In *Poststructuralism as Exegesis,* ed. Stephen Moore and David Jobling, 3–34. Semeia 54. Atlanta: Scholars Press.

————. 1992. *Acts of Literature.* Ed. Derek Attridge. London and New York: Routledge.

————. 1993a. "Circumfession." In Geoffrey Bennington and Jacques Derrida, *Jacques Derrida.* Chicago: University of Chicago Press.

————. 1993b. *The Gift of Death.* Trans. David Wills. Chicago and London: University of Chicago Press.

————. 1994. *Specters of Marx.* Trans. Peggy Kamuf. New York and London: Routledge.

————. 1995a. *Archive Fever: A Freudian Impression.* Trans. Eric Prenowitz. Chicago: University of Chicago Press.

————. 1995b. "Unsealing ('the old new language')." In *Points . . . Interviews, 1974–1994,* ed. Elizabeth Weber, 115–31. Trans. Peggy Kamuf et al. Stanford: Stanford University Press.

————. 1999a. *Adieu, To Emmanuel Levinas.* Trans. Pascale-Anne Brault and Michael Naas. Stanford: Stanford University Press.

————. 1999b (second edition). *Donner la Mort.* Paris: Editions Galilée.

————. 2000. *Le Toucher, Jean-Luc Nancy.* Paris: Editions Galilée.

————. 2001a. "The Animal That Therefore I Am (More to Follow)." Trans. David Wills. *Critical Inquiry* 28, no. 2:385–86.

————. 2001b. "I Have a Taste for the Secret." In Jacques Derrida and Maurizio Ferraris, *A Taste for the Secret,* 1–92. Trans. Giacomo Donis. Oxford: Polity.

————. 2002a. "The Deconstruction of Actuality." In *Negotiations: Interventions and Interviews 1971–2001,* ed. and trans. Elizabeth Rottenberg, 85–116. Stanford: Stanford University Press.

———— 2002b. "Typewriter Ribbon: Limited Ink (2)." In *Without Alibi,* trans. Peggy Kamuf, 71–160. Stanford: Stanford University Press.

————. 2004. "Epoché and Faith." In *Derrida and Religion: Other Testaments,* ed. Yvonne Sherwood and Kevin Hart. New York and London: Routledge.

Filmer, Kath. 1989. "Of Lunacy and Laundry Trucks: Deconstruction and Mythopoesis." In *Literature and Belief,* ed. Bruce L. Edwards, Jr, 55–64. Provo: Brigham Young Press.

Greenspahn, Fredrick E. 2000. "Does Judaism Have a Bible?" In *Sacred Text, Secular Times: The Hebrew Bible in the Modern World,* ed. Leonard Jay Greenspoon and Bryan F. Le Beau, 1–12. Studies in Jewish Civilization 10. Omaha, NB: Creighton University Press.

Jankélevitch, Victor. 1978. *Quelque part dans l'inachevé.* Paris: Gallimard.

Käsemann, Ernst. 1971. "Justification and Salvation History in the Epistle to the Romans." In *Perspectives on Paul,* 60–78. London: SCM.

Kierkegaard, Søren. 1848. *Thoughts that Wound from Behind—for Upbuilding: Christian Addresses.* Copenhagen: C. A. Reitzel.

————. 1983. "Repetition: A Venture in Experimenting Psychology." In *Fear and Trembling and Repetition,* ed. and trans. Howard V. Hong and Edna H. Hong. Princeton: Princeton University Press.

Kierkegaard, Søren. 1985. *Fear and Trembling*. Trans. Alastair Hannay. Harmondsworth: Penguin.

———. 1992. *Concluding Unscientific Postscript to Philosophical Fragments* vol. 1, ed. and trans. Howard V. Hong and Edna H. Hong. Princeton: Princeton University Press.

———. 1996. *Papers and Journals: A Selection*. Trans. Alastair Hannay. Harmondsworth: Penguin.

Kristeva, Julia. 1995. *New Maladies of the Soul*. Trans. R. Guberman. New York: Columbia University Press.

Latour, Bruno. 1993. *We Have Never Been Modern*. Trans. Catherine Porter. Cambridge, MA: Harvard University Press.

McGrath, Alister E. 1995 [1994]. *Christian Theology: An Introduction*. Oxford: Basil Blackwell.

Moore, Stephen D. 1992. *Mark and Luke in Poststructuralist Perspectives: Jesus Begins to Write*. New Haven and London: Yale University Press.

———. 1995. "True Confessions and Weird Obsessions: Autobiographical Interventions in Literary and Biblical Studies." In *Taking it Personally: Autobiographical Biblical Criticism*, ed. Janice Capel Anderson and Jeffrey L. Staley, 19–50. Semeia 72. Atlanta: Scholars Press.

Morgan, Edwin. 2001. *A.D.: A Trilogy of Plays on the Life of Jesus*. Manchester: Carcanet.

Rapaport, Herman. 2001. *The Theory Mess: Deconstruction in Eclipse*. New York: Columbia University Press.

Royle, Nicholas. 2003. *Jacques Derrida*. New York and London. Routledge.

Schneidau, H. N. 1982. "The Word Against the Word: Derrida on Textuality." In *Derrida and Biblical Studies*, ed. Robert Detweiler, 5–28. Semeia 23. Atlanta: Society of Biblical Literature.

Sherwood, Yvonne. 1996 (second edition 2004). *The Prostitute and the Prophet: Hosea 1–3 in Literary-Theoretical Perspective*. Journal for the Study of the Old Testament Supplement Series 212. Gender, Culture, Theory 2. London: Continuum.

———. 2000a. "Derrida." In *Handbook of Postmodern Biblical Interpretation*, ed. A. K. M. Adam, 69–75. St Louis: Chalice.

———. 2000b. "Prophetic Scatology: Prophecy and the Art of Sensation." In *In Search of the Present: The Bible Through Cultural Studies*, ed. Stephen D. Moore, 183–224. Semeia 82. Atlanta: Scholars Press.

———. 2001. "Of Fruit and Corpses and Wordplay Visions: Picturing Amos 8:1–3." *Journal for the Study of the Old Testament* 92:5–27.

Sherwood, Yvonne and Caputo, John D. 2004. "Otobiographies: Or How a Torn and Disembodied Ear Hears a Promise of Death." In *Derrida and Religion: Other Testaments*, ed. Yvonne Sherwood and Kevin Hart. New York: Routledge.

Sherwood, Yvonne and Hart, Kevin. 2004. "Other Testaments." In *Derrida and Religion: Other Testaments*, ed. Yvonne Sherwood and Kevin Hart. New York: Routledge.

Tanner, Kathyrn. 1997. *Theories of Culture*. Minneapolis: Fortress.

Taylor, Mark C. 1990. *Tears*. New York: State University of New York Press.

Wellek, René. 1993. "Destroying Literary Studies." *The New Criterion* 2, no. 4 (December):3–7.

Williams, Rowan. 2000. *On Christian Theology*. Oxford: Blackwell.

Young, Robert. 2000. "Deconstruction and the Postcolonial." In *Deconstructions: A User's Guide*, ed. Nicholas Royle, 187–210. Basingstoke and New York: Palgrave.

Ziering-Kofman, Amy and Dick, Kirby. 2003. *Derrida*. Zeitgeist films.

beginnings

Chapter 1

Between Genealogy and Virgin Birth: Origin and Originality in Matthew

Lee Danes[1]

Authority? What is it? Who has it? How is it to be established? For Matthew, Jesus teaches as "one who has authority" and not as a scribe (7:29) and, after the resurrection, Jesus says to his disciples: "All authority in heaven and on earth has been given to me" (28:18).[2] The resurrected Jesus claims all authority as a gift. Is all authority, then, (a) given? Given that authority preexists us, how do we stand before it?[3] If one is to begin with the authority of the given, the gift of authority, must one always authoritatively cite the father of all authority, the son for whom all authority in heaven and on earth is a gift? What would such citation mean? Must all authority be resurrected from the dead? Would not such authority reek of authoritarianism? What sort of living space would it provide for you and me? Or, rather, is it the case that all authority is dead until it has died and been resurrected? To adapt John 12:24, "Truly, Truly, I say to you, unless a grain of authority falls into the earth and dies, it remains alone; but if it dies, it bears much fruit." Is there a sense in which all authority is an authority of death and resurrection—the coming of a spirit that, as always already prophetically fulfilled, is always fulfilling and is at all times in the offing, but as such can be neither fully present nor wholly absent? Yet, have not we, the living, been commanded to let the dead bury the dead: to let sleeping gods lie? How, then, are we the living to appropriate this gift of authority and this gift of death (always en/crypted, always scriptural, always silent, and always secret and thus revelatory) in a way that is not dead or deadening? To transpose the lesson of the Jesus of John's Gospel: is it not true that "before authority is, I am"? (John 8:58).

Perhaps we have started too quickly with the heart and soul and mind of Matthew's Gospel, the problematic of authority: "he who finds his authority (too quickly) will lose it, and he who loses his authority for my sake will find it"? (Matt. 10:39). Merely citing the authority of the gift, have we not cut it out of its proper place—the Gospel's conclusion—and thus corrupted the Gospel and alienated its authority (murdered it in its sleep)? Is not the gift of authority always site specific? But as site specific, must it not, if it is to ground both itself and us, be subject to (the subject of) each of our perspectives? It must somehow demand that each of us sight it, take a closer look at it, be incited by it, insight it, excise it, cite it, recite it, resite it, resight it and ourselves again and again, revising its vision by becoming visionary ourselves.[4] But how, and on whose authority and on what ground, is all this to happen? Let us begin again. Let us begin with the opening of Matthew's Gospel.

Matthew's opening genealogy (1:1–17) provides a human lineage for Jesus. It begins with Abraham and, after fourteen generations, begins again with the house of David. Then, after another fourteen generations, it begins yet again with the Babylonian deportation and ends after another fourteen generations with "Joseph the husband of Mary, of whom Jesus was born, who is called Christ" (1:16).

What are we to make of the genealogy of Jesus "who is called Christ" (Matt. 1:16)? Why does the Gospel begin with it? What does it do? Matthew is clearly concerned not only to establish Jesus as a Jew but also to tie him back through the genealogy's main branches to the house of David and then to the fundamental root of Israel, Abraham (father of the chosen seed). Why? The simplest answer is that, by deriving Jesus from Abraham, but also from the house of David, Jesus is given the perfect credentials for that messianic job posting so long in the offing in ancient Israel. For Matthew, Jesus is a Jew first and foremost—his authority is Jewish and scriptural. The genealogy establishes this.

Genealogies typically establish a connection with the past that lends the product of the genealogical lineage—assuming it is a good lineage—authority.[5] To put it at its crudest level, a genealogy, like a pet's pedigree, establishes that one is of good stock and probably well bred. In the ancient world, in general, those who claimed and proved their priority in time (well born, first born, of the best family, of the best line) were typically given first place in any chain of authority (social, military, political, and economic).[6] The fundamental theme here is the relationship of history (the past) and its authority to the individual and his/her authority. In our case, the individual is both a text and a person: Matthew's Gospel and Jesus.

Yet, there is something problematic about Matthew's genealogy of Jesus. It is followed by the Virgin Birth, which establishes a divine origin for Jesus in contrast to his human and genealogical origin through Joseph. Matthew's genealogy goes to great lengths (in fact, three times fourteen generations) to establish Jesus' scriptural and messianic credentials through Joseph's lineage, but then implicitly discredits their authority, at least on the immediate level, because Jesus is not, because of the virgin birth, of Joseph's seed. Matthew is careful to note and reinforce this. Matthew indicates that Joseph did not "know"—he did not have sexual intercourse with—Mary until *after* the birth of Jesus (1:25). Thus the genealogy that establishes Jesus through Joseph to be of the house of David and the seed of Abraham is, *prima facie*, invalid.

From the beginning, then, we see that there is something uncanny about the way in which Matthew undertakes the establishment of authority. Equally, we might speculate, there must be something strange about the character of an authority so established. At the very least, it is reasonable to say that there seems to be something about Jesus' authority and its character, according to Matthew, that cannot be located immediately either in the usual manner of genealogy or the unusual manner of a supernatural impregnation.[7]

Matthew presents two contrary accounts of Christ's origin—the genealogy—immanent, yet only as an expression of God's intervention in human history—and the Virgin Birth—divine, deriving directly from the Holy Spirit, yet only as written and known in human language and expressed through the birth of a human being.[8]

Could it be that, like the beginning of the Gospel of John, Matthew is also revisiting and rearticulating the opening of Genesis?[9] Could it be that Matthew is subtly, but powerfully, rethinking the relationship of the two creation narratives of Genesis, transcendental (a cosmological God speaking existence into being) and immanent (an anthropomorphic God fashioning the human from the dust of the ground), in order to pose and perform the problematic unique to biblical origins and their authority?[10] As in the Genesis story, Matthew says nothing about, and provides no commentary on, the enormous gap and contradiction, undecidability and aporia, between two differing ways of establishing origins and authority.

What is the economy inhering in the Gospel's juxtaposition of its two contrary accounts of Jesus' origin? The Gospel gives its reader no direct indication that either it is aware of the gap between the two origins of Jesus or that we, its readers, should be aware of it. Yet, does this juxtaposition, particularly in light of the Gospel's ongoing thematic concern with authority, speak secretly and thus openly?

On the one hand, we have the genealogy, an origin through the father, through the patriarchal seed, but not, we learn, through the biological seed. On the other hand, we have the Virgin Birth and the origin through the mother and the Holy Spirit, a feminine and spiritual, or perhaps mythical (or at least supernatural) origin. Could one say that it is the case that all authority having originality is, even as it cites origins, in fact, singularly in the act of authoritative citation, virginal? Virginal in the sense that Derrida—commenting in *The Gift of Death* on the notion in *Fear and Trembling*'s epilogue that each generation must begin again from the beginning— articulates as the "non-history of absolute beginnings" (1995, 80)? Must authority be both historical (have a past, a genealogy) and unique (individually appropriated, virginal or without prior historical cause)? Or once again, in Derrida's terms, is it that biblical authority, in this case Matthew, involves and expresses a "historicity that presupposes a tradition to be reinvented each step of the way, in . . . [an] incessant repetition of the absolute beginning" (1995, 80)? Is originary authority, then, virginal because, as an authority of absolute beginning, it is an authority whose birth has no other origin or cause but itself alone?[11] Does Matthew's opening raise, once again, the biblical problematic of origin and originality, yet now formulated with a difference— an invocation of absolute beginning within the nonstructure of the historical trace (the Hebrew God, his covenant, and justice)?

I shall be returning to the Derrida cited above, but, before going further, let us look more closely at Matthew's passage on the Virgin Birth. The biblical text gives only the barest statement of the Holy Spirit's impregnation of Mary. The biblical text is laconic. All we are told is the following: "When his mother Mary had been betrothed to Joseph, before they came together she was found to be with child of the Holy Spirit" (1:18). Matthew gives us one brief sentence of enormous but compressed drama.[12]

Why the lack of details of the Holy Spirit's and Mary's liaison? How are we (readers or, for that matter, Mary or Joseph) to understand the seemingly mythological or at least supernatural impregnation of Mary by the Holy Spirit? Such a pregnancy is not directly or immediately comprehensible by Mary, Joseph or us. The modern reader might ask, "Did God, like Zeus, inspired by the comeliness of a mortal woman, descend from the heavens and rape her?" Is God another Zeus? Is Mary another Leda (or Io, or Europa, or Danae)?[13] Is Mary perhaps but one more woman in a long line of women raped and impregnated by a god? The Bible is silent about such a possibility. Unlike Homer, Ovid or other mythic systems, it does not give the human details of a divine rape or lingam.To my knowledge the Holy Spirit's lingam has not been a regular feature of Christian worship or liturgy.[14] And I am also not aware of any cult of the Virgin carrying around phalluses, hoping to be rendered if not spontaneously pregnant then at least fertile.[15]

There is no immediately empirical or immediately rational way to understand Jesus' origin and authority either through the genealogy or the Virgin Birth. On the one hand, Jesus is neither a Jew nor the Messiah by genealogy. His Jewishness and messianic credentials, as presented, cannot be directly based on genealogy or biology: he is not a direct product of either Joseph's seed and patriarchal lineage or biological sperm. Thus, like every Jew, having a non-gender specific and a non-race specific "circumcised heart" (Deuteronomy 30:6), his truth as a Jew is not an immediate or automatic product of the biblical tradition in terms of race, culture, or convention.[16] On the other hand, a Virgin Birth is, empirically and rationally, impossible.

Thus, the Gospel presents us with a secret, a mystery, and a parable: a communication about the concealed and non-representable origin and authority of its secret messiah. In *The Gift of Death*, Derrida whispers softly to us, "[t]o share a secret is not to know or to reveal the secret, it is to share we know not what: nothing that can be determined" (1995, 80). A secret must be shared (for unless shared between and among, a secret cannot be [a] secret), but since the secret of the Gospel is infinite (both divine and human), not finitely self-enclosed and self-identical, it is always revealed as a secret, an ineffable trace, a parable, a paradox without either empirical or rational determination. Yet in the Bible, the ineffable and mysterious are intimately linked to revelation, not to ignorance. They are edifying and transformative, always unexpected and surprising, yet not mystifying and unchanging. The biblical secret is openly parabolic (he who has the ears to hear, let him hear, interpretively). The biblical secret is, then, never merely opaque or hermetically closed (as, in my judgment, is the secret in a classical Greek text such as *Oedipus at Colonus*, where the secret represents the impenetrability of fate). A secret must be a secret, but for a secret to be a secret it cannot be secret (unthought or unshared), "for nothing," Matthew's Jesus tells his disciples, "is covered that will not be revealed, or hidden that will not be known" (Matt. 10:26).[17]

Jesus' birth belongs to biblical "myth" or "supernaturalism," a structure of origin that does not impute the human-all-too-human lust and organ of generation to a god. If the myth were Homeric or Ovidian, we would easily understand what was happening between the god and the mortal woman. The god would be enflamed with a human lust and the mortal woman, generally speaking, would be running away in order to prevent the god from raping her.[18] Here, there are no secrets, only mythic and fatal opacity.

An all-too-human lust is not attributed to the Holy Spirit. Raymond Brown puts it simply: "there is nothing sexual in Matt[hew]'s or Luke's account [of the virginal conception of Jesus]" (1997, 219). The Holy Spirit's insemination is dissemination, a trace structure, always already written, a sowing of the Word, an absolute origin yet an origin having no immediate or full presence (no graven image and no name).

Yet, biblical myth or supernaturalism is not about a disembodied spirit. Biblical "myth" involves and expresses the spiritual *and* the carnal: each the other of the other, to be neither identified nor separated. It always expresses a spirit in the flesh, that is, a God in history, and thus a spirit that is carnal—enfleshed historically and implicated in mortality (erring and dying humans).[19] Biblical myth also and equally expresses a flesh (humanity) spiritualized (fertilized by the spirit) and thus ensouled, or rather, enspirited.[20] I say enspirited rather than ensouled because the "soul" of the biblical believer cannot immediately or literally be separated from his/her body (as it can according to both Homeric and Platonic myth as well as to Aristotelian philosophy).[21] The Holy Spirit of Matthew, like the God of Genesis, again and again, hovers over what is vacant, empty or barren and renders it creative: fertile and pregnant.

How do we read the Gospel such that we embrace the genealogy *and* the Virgin Birth *as well as* the gap and contradictory tension or even collision between these two disparate ways of establishing origins and authority? How do we embrace such an aporia? I would like to propose a way in which to read the gap and embrace the contradiction (as undecidable, as paradox).

Before proceeding, however, I would like to make three general points about Matthew's genealogy and the Virgin Birth. First, the Gospel of Matthew stands in relationship to a tradition (Hebrew scripture), an origin and source of authority, which it both negates and reconstitutes (or resurrects) in and through its own originality and authority. Second, the reader must stand in relationship to Matthew—an authority and origin—that she ought both to negate and reconstitute in and through her own authority and originality. An authority cannot be established as an authority until and unless one establishes it authoritatively. Third, each figure in Matthew's genealogical tree must also have broken and reconstituted an authority (God) in such a way as to have recognized both the tradition's authority (out of which s/he emerges) and the singularity of his/her own authority.[22] The four women (Tamar, Rahab, Ruth, and Uriah's wife, Bathsheba) in Matthew's genealogy, of whom, as Brown comments, three are non-Israelite and the fourth was not married to an Israelite, can be seen to exemplify the absolute discontinuity and yet reconstitution of radical originality within the Hebrew tradition that Matthew repeats within his genealogy.

We are now prepared to look more carefully at Derrida's comments on the epilogue of Kierkegaard's *Fear and Trembling*. Derrida notes that the epilogue

> repeats, in sentence after sentence, that [the] highest passion that is faith must be started over by each generation. Each generation must begin again to involve itself in [faith] without counting on the generation before. [The highest passion of faith] thus describes the *nonhistory of absolute beginnings* which are repeated, and the very *historicity that presupposes a tradition to be reinvented each step of the way*, in this *incessant repetition of the absolute beginning*. (1995, 80; italics added)

Biblical faith repeats a nonhistory of absolute beginning that presupposes the historicity of a tradition of absolute beginning. This faith, then, involving and expressing an "incessant repetition of the absolute beginning," stands within, upon and comes out of the "non-history of absolute" beginning initiated by Abraham.

In the case of Abraham, however, there is a radical break with the past (his "historical" context, that is, from the biblical perspective, the non-historicity of so-called paganism). This radical break negates all previous origins and authority, rendering them a desert or a wilderness (a nothing nothing, a nothing in which there is nothing historical, nothing original or creative, a nothing that bears no trace of God's creative call) out of which Abraham emerges and which he then reconstitutes as a desert and wilderness (a nothing now created, a creative nothing, a nothing responsive to God's call, the desert and wilderness of his sojourn). This break from and reconstitution of the past occurs through Abraham's absolutely new and radical concept of self, other, God, and their relatedness. Abraham, in effect, claims "here I am, God is my unexampled origin, an origin without origin, a historical origin that is utterly singular and yet through whose singularity a universality is to be willed into being (a chosenness in which there is no other choice but choice)." Abraham comes from nothing, from the wilderness of paganism (a nothing or nonhistory that, because it bears no trace of God's creative call, is to be distinguished from the nonhistory that belongs to absolute beginnings). His coming to be is, then, a type of Virgin Birth, a claim to an originality whose origin is solely of God (the Holy Spirit) and, as such, has singular and new implications for all the nations.[23]

It is in and through an origin that is at once historical and yet utterly unexampled and singular—it is in and through the gap and the tension produced by the contradiction or conflict between genealogy and Virgin Birth, as two competing origins of authority—that the Gospel constructs and arises from and with its own unique authority, a third authority. Such an authority is in itself neither genealogical nor mythological and yet signifies (in excess) the authority of both. But this authority only truly comes to be, when and if it comes to be, howsoever it comes to be, if the reader authoritatively enters the opening or textual gap/blockage (aporia) between the two competing origins and authorities: genealogy and Virgin Birth. This (non-hierarchical) authority (textual, interpretive, and historical) only comes to be when and if the reader freely enters this fertile and virginal space and, hovering above it like the creator God of Genesis (both male and female in 1:26–27), renders it pregnant (and thus him/herself pregnant).[24] It is thus that the God-child authority, the resurrected Jesus, who possesses all of heaven and earth as a gift, comes to be: "And Jesus came and said to them, 'All authority in heaven and on earth has been given to me' " (Matt. 28:18, cited at the beginning of this essay).

Just as Matthew (and Matthew's Jesus) incessantly cite Hebrew scripture—it is written, it fulfills prophecy—each reader must authoritatively cite, repeat, rewrite, recontextualize, reduplicate, exceed, transform, subvert, radicalize, justify, be justified by, insert into, dialogue with, address and be addressed by, or, in a word, interpret, the authority of the Hebrew Bible, the Christian Bible and indeed their mutual authority. In the following passage from "Force of Law," Derrida articulates the same aporetic and dialogical structure of origin and originality, negation and reconstitution that I have been arguing for, although in slightly different terms:

> To be just, the decision of a judge, for example, must not only follow a rule of law but must . . . confirm its value, by a reinstituting act of interpretation, as if ultimately *nothing* previously existed of the law, as if the judge himself *invented* the law in every

case . . . In short, for a decision to be just and *responsible*, it must, in its proper moment if there is one, be both regulated and without regulation: *it must conserve the law and also destroy it or suspend it enough to have to reinvent it* in each case, rejustify it, at least reinvent it in the reaffirmation and the new and free confirmation of its principle. (1990, 961; italics added)

For a decision to be just, Derrida tells us, a judge must reduce the law to nothing and yet reinvent it according to the law's own principle. The judge conserves the law by destroying it, yet in such a way that the law (the old) is reinstituted in and through a "new and free confirmation of its principle."

To put the problem of a (doubly broken) authority in terms of the reader and text—whether the reader be Jesus and the text Hebrew scripture, or the reader be a reader of Jesus and the text be the Christian Bible—gives us the following: on the one hand, the interpreter of the biblical tradition must break with tradition, and yet, on the other hand, s/he must in the very process of breaking with the tradition, rediscover and be transformed by that tradition (and in being transformed by the tradition, transform it). Breaking with biblical tradition is problematical and paradoxical because the very ground on which and by which one breaks the ground of the biblical tradition is the tradition. At the very instant that one breaks the original ground, the ground of origin—the tradition, but neither the merely traditional nor the simply conventional—one must become, in, through and on that ground, a ground (the ground) of interpretation and thus original.

Here Matthew is once again paradigmatic. As he breaks with the authority of Hebrew scripture, positing the origin of the Virgin Birth in a radical discontinuity with Hebrew genealogy, Matthew is nonetheless scrupulous to base his break on the very ground of Hebrew scriptural authority, citing Isaiah 7:14 as the prophetic justification of the Virgin Birth: " 'Behold, a virgin shall conceive and bear a son, and his name shall be called Emmanuel' (which means, God with us)" (Matt. 1:23). Yet, here again, Matthew shows his originality. Matthew follows the Septuagint, which translates the Hebrew word *almah* from Isaiah 7:14, meaning "young woman," with the Greek word *parthenos*, which can mean either "young woman" or "virgin." In applying the Greek translation to the story of Mary, Matthew reinterprets *parthenos* specifically and originally as "virgin."

From the beginning, Matthew shows us that his authority comes from the biblical tradition yet also that he in turn is the authority and author of the tradition. Authority here means that one reinvents the tradition by affirming its principles yet, paradoxically, its principles not only reinvent the tradition but also provide a critique of both the self (inventing) and the tradition (invented). As previously cited, this is what Derrida calls the "incessant repetition of the absolute beginning" (1995, 80).

In summary, the Gospel of Matthew opens with a sophisticated restaging of the biblical problematic of authority. Using the scriptural strategy of genealogy, Matthew establishes Jesus' and the Gospel's continuity with and through Hebrew scripture (the origin and original). Yet, equally, the Gospel interrupts that continuity in and through the Virgin Birth, an origin and originality radically separate and other than scriptural genealogy. The Virgin Birth removes Jesus from the scriptural tradition of genealogy. As a consequence, the place of genealogy, as placed in the Gospel, is under erasure. The first place is no longer first.[25] The beginning of the Gospel is not a beginning. Jesus, the Gospel tells us, comes from a radically divine origin and thus is to be conceived in himself as the origin and originality of divine authority (the Holy Spirit). Thus, with the Virgin Birth, an absolute interruption or disruption of authority is posited and the nonhistory of an absolute beginning is asserted. Yet this interruption or disruption is uniquely and wholly biblical.

I would like to make six brief points in regard to this interruption or disruption of authority. First, it restages the double origin of biblical authority, reengaging, for instance, the opening of Genesis, as noted previously. But, as a double origin, it is no origin at all. And as a doubly posited authority, it is no authority at all. Second, in carefully grounding the originality of Christ on Isaiah's biblical prophecy, Matthew shows that his break from tradition occurs on the very ground of the tradition, on prophetic ground. His break is thus a reduplication of scripture's "incessant [yet critical] repetition of the absolute beginning." Matthew's break from tradition is a break by means of tradition. Third, the very assertion of continuity and yet simultaneous interruption of continuity, the singularity of the individual bearing the implications of a truth to be universally willed, is in itself unique to biblical genealogy as well as biblical prophecy. Fourth, Matthew's radical interruption and yet continuity with (and of) the tradition's authority is consistent with the biblical principle of the second son usurping the place of the first son (and we might note here, Paul connects Jesus with the second son, the son of resurrection not the flesh [Romans 1:1–6]). Fifth, the Virgin Birth is, in a strong sense, already a figuration of the Christian notion of rebirth: "That which is born of the flesh is flesh, and that which is born of the Spirit is spirit" (John 3:6). Jesus' birth, as the birth of the Christ, is not merely a birth but always already a rebirth (a birth within a birth and thus virginal, since the being that is born is of "the spirit" not of the flesh [John 3:5]). Sixth, in establishing its authority as an authority of silence and secrecy, of aporia and undecidability, the Gospel is self-negating, and requires supplementation: the singularity of interpretative authority, a reader (whose authority must be irreducibly other, neither his/her own nor the Gospel's own).

One must always recreate the tradition from nothing. Yet it is the biblical tradition that is itself always already the nothing that contains the principle, the absolute infinite and nonrepresentable demand (here the silent, secret, and invisible aporia between the genealogy and the Virgin Birth) that each individual must negate and reinstantiate the tradition from nothing (from nothing that is not authoritatively both Jewish and Christian, both the individual's and the tradition's, both human and divine). The biblical tradition locates its authority in and through the logic of the supplement: the reader who adds nothing to the text and yet radically, lovingly, recreates and renews the text by reading it authoritatively, critically and affirmatively, as s/he would desire the text read her/him. As Spinoza saw so profoundly in *The Theologico-Political Treatise*,[26] and as Augustine saw so acutely in his *Confessions*,[27] it is the golden rule or love that articulates the fundamental principle of biblical hermeneutics. Love, as the origin and structure of biblical aporia, always faithfully creates, at once, both the space and the obstruction necessary for the originality of a loving reader.[28] The gift of authority, the authority of the given, is always an authority in and through the othering of love. In Derridean terms, self and other (the neighbor but not *one*'s neighbor),[29] are undecidable traces—each neither present nor absent to him/herself or the other. Each is the other of the other, an Other whose desire and recognition are constituted in and as the origin and originality within and through the mutuality of love. Such an other is so wholly other that it is neither one's own nor the other's but the very ground constituting the mutual will to recognize each as one other, but never merely one's own. The authority of an other so placed can never be placed but is always a topos of love, the secret that is not a secret except insofar as it is shared.

Notes

1. I wish to thank the following for critical comments on my paper: Olaf Alksinis, Mark Cauchi, Geri Das Gupta, Mohamed Khimji, Avron Kulak, Terri Kulak, Tom Loebel, Brayton Polka, and Anne-Marie Williams.
2. All biblical citations are from the Revised Standard Version.
3. Both Kant and Montaigne meditate epistemologically on the authority of the given. In the introduction to the *Critique of Pure Reason*, Kant writes, "[s]ince these sciences [mathematics and natural science] actually exist, it is quite proper to ask *how* they are possible; for that they must be possible is proved by the fact that they exist" (1956, B20–21). In other words, given that authoritative knowledge (synthetic *a priori* judgments) actually exists, how is it possible? Philosophically, Kant poses the question as, "[h]ow are *a priori* synthetic judgements possible?" (1956, B19). Yet Kant's fundamental questions are about metaphysics and morality (practical reason): "in a certain sense, this *kind of knowledge* [metaphysical and moral] is to be looked upon as given; that is to say, metaphysics actually exists, if not as a science, yet still as natural disposition" (1956, B21). Similarly, Montaigne, in his "Apology for Raymond Sebond," taking knowledge as a given (our language "is wholly formed of affirmative propositions" [1957, 392]), does not ask if he knows anything, but rather "What do I know?" (1957, 393). This paper, too, begins with authority as given.
4. In "Signature Event Context," Derrida indicates that "citationality" is a fundamental characteristic of the sign: "[e]very sign" can be "*cited*, put between quotation marks; in so doing it can break with every given context, engendering an infinity of new contexts in a manner which is absolutely illimitable" (1988, 12). Citing Derrida in the context of this paper demonstrates his point, yet how this is needs exploration. "[A] written sign carries with it a force that breaks with its context" (1988, 9) and with every "given context," yet it cannot break with the given, with the gift of communication, authority and the spacing of relationship, if it is not to become a mark that cannot be cited, except as that which cannot be cited, that whose "citationality" has been lost or misplaced. Signs can break with every given context, but they cannot break with the context of having a context, with the contextuality of the context. We will see in this paper that Matthew's citation of authority produces the gap/blockage of biblical aporia and that his gospel invites or demands his reader to recite or re-site his authority in this gap/blockage.
5. The genealogies of the Hebrew Bible do not work merely in terms of authority, that is, in terms of the mere authority of finite power. Thomas Cahill indicates in *The Gifts of the Jews* that genealogies in the Hebrew Bible (e.g. Genesis 12:27–32) have some "surprising dissimilarities" from those of ancient Sumer: "the careful preserving of the names and lineages of ancient characters—even of women—who were neither gods nor kings; and the importance placed on what *appear* at least to be exacting genealogical records" (Cahill 1998, 57–58). See Robert Alter's commentary on "the biblical use of genealogies as an intrinsic

element of literary structure" (1996, 22–23). See also Everett Fox's commentary on genealogy in *The Five Books of Moses*: "[s]uperseding these important themes [origins, order/meaning in history, blessing, covenant, God punishing evildoing, sibling conflict with the younger usually emerging as victor, testing], which occur throughout the Bible in various forms, is the dominant one of *continuity*, represented by the unifying word in Genesis *toledot* (begettings)" (1995, 4). Among their many functions, the biblical genealogies give the reader a sense of historicity, including documentation and the enormous passage of time before something significant happens.

6. In the *Odyssey*, when individuals are asked who they are, they are usually asked, and are expected to answer, in terms of their country and parentage. The parentage is given through the line of the father and, if it is a noble and well known house, the answer is usually in terms of the house (the last name of paterfamilias). And, if it is a young man like Telemachus answering, the grandfather's name as well as the father's is given. Odysseus introduces himself to the Phaiakians this way: "I am Odysseus son of Laertes, known before all men for the study of crafty designs, and my fame goes up to the heavens. I am at home in sunny Ithaka" (IX.19–21). Yet in the Bible, the notion of "first" and genealogy is, as we will see in Matthew's gospel, far more complex. So, for instance, the simple hierarchical ordering of primogeniture (and thus genealogy) is overturned through the phenomenon of the younger brother: Cain and Abel, Jacob and Esau, Joseph and his brothers in Genesis; Moses and Aaron in Exodus. The case of Jacob is particularly telling: through deception (his own and his mother's), Jacob subverts the patriarchal law of primogeniture. He suspends the laws of nature and custom—those based on simple priority in space and time. Jacob does not base, then, his action on the priorities assigned by the conventions of nature or custom. Renamed "Israel" by God, Jacob functions to indicate to the reader of scripture that the origin and originality of Israel and God comes to be through a suspension/abrogation/transgression of all normative ethics and conventional authority (as seen on their own terms).

7. In *Philosophical Fragments*, Kierkegaard's pseudonym, Johannes Climacus, argues that Jesus' authority, as historical, can be located neither through simple temporal nor eternal determinants and, thus, neither through chronology and genealogy nor through simple doctrine and supernatural intuition (knowledge): "the historical cannot become the object of sense perception or of immediate cognition" (1985, 81). According to Climacus, Jesus' historical authority is an "absolute fact" not a "simple historical fact" or an "eternal fact" (1985, 99). Similarly, in *The Genealogy of Morals*, Nietzsche claims that "[a]ll terms which semiotically condense a whole process elude definition; only that which has no history can be defined" (1956, 212). Thus, from both the Kierkegaardian and Nietzschean perspectives, neither Matthew's genealogy nor the Virgin Birth can establish Jesus' (historical) authority as the Christ.

8. As the essay's exposition proceeds it will become increasing clear that it is not my intention to reduce biblical genealogy merely to an expression of male patriarchal power and authority. Equally, it will become clear that I do not intend to reduce the mystery of the Virgin Birth to a mythological rape or proto-artificial insemination.

9. Raymond Brown suggests a number of ways that Matthew's opening Greek phrase, *biblos geneseos*, might connect Matthew's genealogy and the Virgin Birth to the book of Genesis (1997, 174).

10. See Robert Alter's excellent account of Genesis' two different creation stories (1981, 141–47). Both the transcendental and the immanent stories of creation are, of course, equally metaphysical: both accounts set the stage for the story of the relationship of the divine and the human. Each account, both separate from and in relationship to the other account, tells the story of the human created in and as the likeness of the divine and is only paradoxically "complete" through division (disobedience). The first story emphasizes

God's creative and affirmative speech acts. The second story focuses on the human as constituted through the interrelationship of good and evil and comprehensible only in the presence, actuality and consciousness of death. The human person is only "complete" (created in God's image) once expelled from the paradise of idolatrous perfection into a world of historical consciousness, interiority, and action (labor). "Creation," as perfect, is imperfect until it has "fallen," for as the speaker of Wallace Stevens' "The Poems of Our Climate" notes: "the imperfect is our paradise" (1972, 158).

11. I am invoking here the formidable opening of Spinoza's *Ethics*: "By cause of itself I understand that whose essence involves existence *or* that whose nature cannot be conceived except as existing" (Book I, Definition 1, 1994, 85).

12. It is useful here to recall Auerbach's incisive comparison of Genesis 22 with the episode of Odysseus' scar in Book 19 of the *Odyssey*. He notes that, whereas Homeric narration constructs an entirely objectified, that is, externalized present devoid of background (history), the narrative of the Genesis text, although laconic, is historically fraught with development and suspense. According to Auerbach the Homeric text can be analyzed but it is the biblical text that calls for interpretation: "Homer can be analyzed . . . but he cannot be interpreted" (1953, 13). Thus, for Auerbach, history and interpretation are correlative concepts, neither of which is to be found in Homer.

13. Io, daughter of Inachus, is raped by Zeus and then turned into a heifer to protect her from Hera's jealousy (Ovid, Book 1, lines 583–611). Europa, king Agenor's daughter, is carried off by Zeus (who has disguised himself as bull in order to abduct her) (Ovid, Book 2–3, lines 834–75 and lines 1–6). Danae, a daughter of the king of Argos, gives birth to her son (Perseus) after having intercourse with Zeus, who, at the time, has disguised himself as a shower of gold (Ovid, Book 4, lines 611–12).

14. The Holy Spirit's lingam is also not represented in the tradition of Christian art. In this regard one might note that in *The Sexuality of Christ in Renaissance Art and in Modern Oblivion* Leon Steinberg indicates that Jesus' penis was often a focal point in medieval and Renaissance painting. Yet, although Jesus' penis is represented in some paintings, it was not represented as an object of worship. One might contrast the representation of Jesus' penis in European painting with the tradition of representation in Hinduism of Shiva's lingam.

15. Perhaps, one might contrast the lack of a cult based on the Virgin's fertility with the tradition within Japanese Shintoism where infertile women do in fact carry and adore the phallus.

16. For the moment I want to emphasize the apparent negation of genealogy in order to prepare for the way the text radically regains genealogy, yet not on the terms of the immediate authority of genealogy that I have spoken about above. The way in which the genealogy is negated and regained is, in my opinion, consistent with the Bible's use of genealogy as an interruption and yet reconstitution of continuity through narrative time. Biblical genealogy is not about immediate authority but historicity: the story of those within its narrative of bondage and freedom, sin and obedience/faith, expulsion/fall and salvation/redemption. Jesus can bear the truth only as a "trace" structure, not as an immediate biological or cultural linkage.

17. Should one make a distinction between the biblical secret, an open secret, and the secret of *Oedipus at Colonus*, whose secret represents the impenetrability of fate? In "Signature Event Context," Derrida poses the following questions: "What would a mark be that could not be cited? Or one whose origins would not get lost along the way?" (1988, 12). Could one say that it is precisely the secret impenetrability of fate that is a mark that could not be cited—except as a mark that cannot be cited—and whose origins do indeed get lost along the way, for fate is always that origin whose account is immediately inside or outside of language and communication? The secret of *Oedipus at Colonus* is so secret that it is not a secret (but rather, the complete and impenetrable opacity of fate, that whose origin is always immediately itself and thus immediately other than itself).

18. Of course, sometimes if she were lucky and another god intervened, she would be turned into a shrub, as in the case of Apollo and Daphne, for example, where Apollo pursues and Daphne is saved when she is turned into a laurel tree (Ovid, Book 1, lines 448–568).

19. In Hebrew scripture, God's embodiment in history is expressed through his covenant with human persons. But one might also call to mind such vivid examples of divine embodiment as God wrestling with Jacob or almost murdering Moses. In the Christian Bible, the incarnation is the fundamental expression of God's involvement in the historical flesh of human lives.

20. I attempt to articulate here a conception of "incarnation" that could be applied equally to both the Hebrew Bible and the Christian Bible. Hence I speak equally and interchangeably of a God (or God's word/Word) in history and a spirit (or God/Word) in the flesh.

21. See the works of Brayton Polka for a programmatic discussion, consistent with this paper's presuppositions, of the distinction between biblical spirit ("dialectic," "thought," and "psychology") and classical Greek—Platonic, Aristotelian, and Homeric—soul. Also see Oscar Cullman's critical distinction between the immortality of the soul in classical Greek literature and philosophy and the resurrection of the body in the Christian Bible (1968).

22. Why negate and reconstitute authority? One has no other choice. One negates and reconstitutes authority in order neither to be enslaved to nor to enslave the authority. Or, put positively, one negates and reconstitutes authority in order to enter into a dialogue of mutual recognition and liberation. The insidious dynamic of the master/slave dialectic makes it equally true that to be enslaved by another is at the same time to enslave that other and that to enslave another is to enslave oneself. Only the person who negates and reconstitutes the text's authority is, then, what Harold Bloom calls the strong reader, the reader who *reads* when she reads.

23. I make these claims about Abraham without being able to provide here an adequate analysis of the Genesis story.

24. The "fertile and virginal space" between the male origin (of genealogy) and the female origin (of virgin birth) is predominantly textual, conceptual and aporetic and thus, in itself, neither male nor female. It seems to me that a female reader might enter this space and make/find it fertile (and herself pregnant) just as a male reader might enter it and become pregnant (and thus be made/found fertile). Thus I have in mind a reader, male and/or female, who both impregnates (the text) and becomes pregnant (by the text) in one and the same act of reading.

25. The place of the first remains God's. And it is another of God's firsts to lodge His/Her/Its authority in the second. This move (both divine and human) deconstructs God's authority (God's authority is deconstructive) but does not remove His/Her/Its authority-granting status. Rather, it highlights how God's authority necessarily comes to be through His/Her/Its creation, the creature, and thus materially (historically). God's authority is always already under erasure—hence the unrelenting biblical critique of idolatry. God renders all authority supplemental. The Christian tradition represents God's historical authority in Jesus' incarnation (the fullness of his humanity) and subtends or circumscribes the divinity of that authority by means of his death and resurrection as well as the temporal displacement of the fulfillment ("presence") of messianic authority through the notion of the second coming. Biblically, authority both always already is and is yet to come.

26. See Spinoza (1951, 172, 176, 183–84; chaps. 12, 13, and 14). According to Spinoza, it is only owing to the cardinal precept of love of God and neighbor that one can constitute and be constituted in and through a relationship of mutual sovereignty such that self and other are mutually liberated, rather than dominating and dominated. Spinoza's interest here is in the hermeneutics of relationship and is simultaneously religious, philosophical, and political. He argues that when the principles of one's hermeneutics operate such that

scripture is made subservient to reason then one dogmatically produces an authoritarian domination of the scriptural text (the reader over the text). Likewise, he argues that where reason is made subservient to scripture then one skeptically produces an authoritarian domination of reason by scripture (the text over the reader). The first position interprets scripture metaphorically but ignores (when it so chooses) the letter of the text. The second claims to interpret literally but ignores (when it so chooses) the spirit of the text. Both, however, operate within a master/slave binary opposition and neither develops an authority (sovereignty) that is liberating (free and loving).

27. See Augustine 1961, 208, 295–96, 302–303 (Books X.3, XII.18, and XII.25).

28. The paper's most critical (practical) presupposition has been that Matthew's aporetic structure self-reflexively reduplicates the problematic of authority central to the gospel's constant negotiation of the authority of Gospel and the authority of Hebrew scripture—authority and authority—such that the gospel faithfully provides the space and obstruction necessary for a reader to bear the figure/trope of the text's authority.

29. See Derrida's discussion of the other in "Hostipitality." To be a *hôte* (host, guest, stranger, and enemy), the human subject must become "hospitable to its other, to an other than itself that is no longer *its* other" (2002, 362). Biblically, then, the human subject must become hospitable to—love—its enemy and its self as its own worst enemy, if it is to cultivate and be cultivated by a self-other, an other-self, that authentically loves, provides a space for, the spacing of, relationship, where self and neighbor can meet in friendship and mutual liberation (support and critique, the diversity of unity and the creativity of opposition). It was, of course, the incomprehensibility of God's command to love his enemy that drove God's incomparable prophet, Jonah, to his whale.

Works Consulted

Alter, Robert. 1981. *The Art of Biblical Narrative*. New York: Basic Books.
———. trans. 1996. *Genesis*. New York: W. W. Norton & Company.
Aristotle. 1941. *The Basic Works of Aristotle*. Ed. Richard McKeon. New York: Random House.
Auerbach, Erich. 1953. "Odysseus' Scar." In *Mimesis: The Representation of Reality in Western Literature*, trans. Willard R. Trask, 3–23. Princeton, NJ: Princeton University Press.
Augustine. 1961. *Confessions*. Trans. R. S. Pine-Coffin. Harmondsworth: Penguin.
Brown, Raymond. 1997. *An Introduction to the New Testament*. New York: Doubleday.
Cahill, Thomas. 1998. *The Gift of the Jews: How a Tribe of Desert Nomads Changed the Way Everyone Thinks and Feels*. New York: Nan A. Talese/Anchor Books.
Cullman, Oscar. 1968. "Immortality of the Soul or Resurrection of the Dead." In *Immortality and Resurrection: Death in the Western World: Two Conflicting Currents of Thought*, ed. K. Stendahl, 9–53. New York: MacMillan.
Derrida, Jacques. 1982. "Différance." In *Margins of Philosophy*, trans. Alan Bass, 1–27. Chicago: University of Chicago Press.
———. 1988. "Signature Event Context." In *Limited Inc.*, 1–23. Evanston, IL: Northwestern University Press.
———. 1990. "Force of Law: The 'Mystical Foundation of Authority.' " *Cardozo Law Review* 11.5–6, 920–1045.
———. 1995. *The Gift of Death*. Trans. David Wills. Chicago: University of Chicago Press.
———. 2002. "Hostipitality." In *Acts of Religion*, ed. Gil Anidjar, 358–420. New York: Routledge.

Fox, Everett, trans. 1995. *The Five Books of Moses*. The Schocken Bible: Volume 1. New York: Schocken Books.

Homer. 1951. *Odyssey*. Trans. Richmond Lattimore. Chicago: Chicago University Press.

Kant, Immanuel. 1956. *Critique of Practical Reason*. Trans. Lewis White Beck. Indianapolis: Bobbs-Merrill.

Kierkegaard, Søren. 1983. *Fear and Trembling*. Trans. Howard V. Hong and Edna H. Hong. Princeton, NJ: Princeton University Press.

———. 1985. *Philosophical Fragments*. Trans. Howard V. Hong and Edna H. Hong. Princeton, NJ: Princeton University Press.

———. 1995. *Works of Love*. Trans. Howard V. Hong and Edna H. Hong. Princeton, NJ: Princeton University Press.

———. 1965. *Critique of Pure Reason*. Trans. N. K. Smith. New York: St. Martin's Press.

Kulak, Avron. 1997. "Origin and Critique: Reading Nietzsche's Genealogy." Dissertation, York University, Toronto.

Montaigne. 1957. "Apology for Raymond Sebond," and "Of the Education of Children." In *The Complete Essays of Montaigne*, Trans. Donald M. Frame. Stanford: Stanford University Press.

Nietzsche, Friedrich. 1956. *The Birth of Tragedy* and *The Genealogy of Morals*. Trans. Francis Golffing. Garden City, NY: Doubleday Anchor Books.

Ovid. 1986. *Metamorphosis*. Trans. A. D. Melville. Oxford: Oxford University Press.

Plato. 1979. *Gorgias*. Trans. W. C. Helmbold. Indianapolis: Bobbs-Merrill.

———. 1981. *Five Dialogues: Euthyphro, Apology, Crito, Meno, Phaedo*. Indianapolis: Hackett.

———. 1989. *Symposium*. Trans. Alexander Nehamas and Paul Woodruff. Indianapolis: Hackett.

———. 1992. *Republic*. Trans. G. M. A. Grube. Revised by C. D. C. Reeve. Indianapolis: Hackett.

Polka, Brayton. 1986. *The Dialectic of Biblical Critique:Interpretation and Existence*. New York: St. Martin's Press.

——— 1990. *Truth and Interpretation: An Essay in Thinking*. New York: St. Martin's Press.

——— 2001. *Depth Psychology, Interpretation, and the Bible: An Ontological Essay on Freud*. Montreal & Kingston: McGill-Queens University Press.

Shakespeare, William. 1990. *Macbeth*. Ed. Nicholas Brooke. Oxford: Oxford University Press.

Sophocles. 1984. *The Three Theban Plays: Antigone, Oedipus the King, Oedipus at Colonus*. Trans. Robert Fagles. New York: Penguin.

Speiser, E. A. 1985. *Genesis*. The Anchor Bible, third edition. New York: Doubleday.

Spinoza, Benedict de. 1951. *A Theologico-Political Treatise*. Trans. R. H. M. Elwes. New York: Dover.

——— 1994. "Ethics." In *A Spinoza Reader*, Trans. Edwin Curley, 85–265. Princeton NJ: Princeton University Press.

Steinberg, Leon. 1996. *The Sexuality of Christ in Renaissance Art and in Modern Oblivion*. Second edition. Chicago: University of Chicago Press.

Stevens, Wallace. 1972. *The Palm at the End of the Mind*. New York: Vintage.

writing, posting, erasing

Chapter 2

Of Secretaries, Secrets, and Scrolls: Jeremiah 36 and the Irritating Word of God

Mark Brummitt

This is an article about writers and writings, about secretaries and scrolls, turning, that is, on the Hebrew סֹפְרִים and סְפָרִים. Derived from the same root, סָפַר, "to count, to recount, to relate," the former, סֹפֵר a participle serving as both job title and job description for one who recounts, relates and so gives account and writes; the latter, סֵפֶר, a noun, denotes the product of these endeavors, namely a writing, an account given.

More specifically, this article is an account of the סֹפְרִים, "secretaries," in Jeremiah 36, and the appearance in that narrative of a מְגִלַּת־סֵפֶר, a "roll of writing," for which they can give no account.

And finally, it is about the opening image in *A Taste For the Secret* (2001) of a secretary who "conceals"—"like Phaedrus himself, who conceals Lysias' speech under his cloak" (Derrida 2001, vii)—and it works with the surprising association of the "secretary" with the "catalogue," "in which one collects, writes or describes *traces*, which are, at bottom, *secrets*" (2001, vii; Derrida's italics).

Is not the secretary as one who recounts and writes, one who accounts *for* rather than conceals? And what has a scroll—a portfolio of prophetic proclamations, oracles, and declarations (36:3, 6–7)—to do with secrets?

Of Economy

The picture, however patchy, of the courtly personnel among whom the scroll of Jeremiah passes, suggests something of the system of שָׂרִים (officials) and סֹפְרִים (secretaries) set up in Jerusalem's Upper Precincts, the site of temple and royal palace. The narrative, like a formicarium in which one observes worker ants in the service of their queen, provides a glimpse of these specialists and trained organizers—the functionaries of state and state religion—as they form a similarly complex network around about their monarch. It is they, constituting a bureaucracy, a civil service if you like, who protect and provide passage to his royal personage, and so make possible the journey of the scroll.

The scroll is first read "to all the people" (36:9) by the secretary Baruch in Gemariah's chamber, "in the upper court, at the entry of the New Gate of the Lord's house" (36:10). Micaiah son of Gemariah then reports "all the words he had heard" (36:13) to the officials sitting in the "secretary's chamber" in the palace: "Elishama the secretary, Delaiah son of Shemaiah, Elnathan son of Achbor, Gemariah son of Shaphan, Zedekiah son of Hananiah, and all the officials" (36:12)—a meeting of "cabinet ministers," suggests Bright (1965, 180). They in turn send Jehudi[1] to bring both secretary and scroll, Baruch and the written words of Jeremiah, to them. After hearing the scroll recited they are "alarmed" and declare in one voice, "We certainly must report all these words to the king" (36:16). Jehudi is again sent to fetch the scroll, this time by King Jehoiakim himself, who, whilst sitting by his fire, listens to the words as Jehudi reads them.[2] The scroll's journey—beginning among "the people thronging the temple at a fast," and continuing "as it moves through the various echelons of Judean society on its way to the king" (Carroll 1986, 663)—thus reads like an ascent through the Jerusalem hierarchy.

The hierarchy can be fairly described as an *economy*—from the Greek *oikos* denoting "house" and its "system of orderly subordination" (Minogue 1995, 12)—a suitable appropriation of a word to describe as it does in this context the disposition of the בית־יהוה (house of Yhwh) and the בית־מלך (house of the king). Appropriate too because this civil service is identified by lists of names and an abundance of patronymics suggesting "orderly subordinations" that are based around kinship ties and dynastic houses. And appropriate again because at the centre of these *oikia* (households)—these interconnected temple- and palace-based systems and hierarchies of secretaries and officials—is the traditional focal point of the house and home: the *hearth*, אח (brazier) of King Jehoiakim (36:22), which also becomes the final resting place of the first scroll.

Of Exchange

The first reading of the scroll takes place on a fast-day (36:9). Whether the fast would have been a fixed, calendrical occasion, which scholarly consensus seems to doubt, or the response to a national emergency—famine maybe, or the approach of Babylon— cannot be gleaned from the narrative alone.[3] Furthermore, whether it was popularly initiated, which consensus once again doubts (despite the statement in 36:9 that "the people proclaimed a fast"),[4] or cultically instigated, again cannot be ascertained simply from the narrative. It is, nevertheless, quite clearly *not* an unusual event. Fasts are to be expected—"you go yourself, and on a fast day," Jeremiah had told Baruch with the presumption that one would come along soon enough (36:6). The fast belongs to the economic world, the world of order and season, succinctly described by Caputo as the sphere of "reasonable rules, the lawful and customary exchanges, the plans and projects, the rites and rituals, the ordinary life and time" (1997, 145).

Alongside the economies of temple and palace—those of the conventional ministrations of secretaries, officials, and king occurring on the horizontal, "worldly" plane—we must now acknowledge the presence of another economy. Indicated by the fast—though already implied by the existence of a temple and its systems—and working as a vertical exchange, it is a transaction based on propitiation between the people and their God. It may be understood generously, as an expression of popular devotion, or more cynically (or reflecting greater urgency), as an exercise in expiation for protection (suggesting that there is a popular belief that Yhwh is poised with a bag stuff full of evils to unleash—a not unreasonable assumption, in the light of that deity's words in 36:7). This is the second, then, of two systems of custom and transaction, of give and take, which together witness to a sphere of reciprocity, circle and so closure.

Beyond Exchange

Preceding this description of reasonable practice and popular devotion are two rationales for the production and proclamation of the scroll: "It may be that when the house of Judah hears of all the disasters that I intend to do to them, all of them may turn from their evil ways, so that I may forgive their iniquity and their sin" (36:3), and "you shall read the words of Yhwh from the scroll . . . in the hearing of all the people of Judah . . . It may be that their plea will come before Yhwh" (36:6–7). The implication is that the people's "evil ways," later described as a wholesale "not heeding" (36:31), will rightfully result in disaster. It is ironic, then, that the day chosen for this plea for a popular response to Yhwh is a day when the temple is thronging with people already *making a popular response to Yhwh*. The scroll, which is to be read in order that the people turn to Yhwh and so avert disaster, is read on a day when, quite possibly, *the people come and fast in order that they might avert disaster*.

Translated formally, 36:9 reads:

And they called (קָרָא) a fast before Yhwh
    all the people in Jerusalem.
And he called (קָרָא) Baruch on the scroll
    the words of Jeremiah
    [in] the house of Yhwh.

The people call a fast and Baruch "calls" from a scroll; they call before Yhwh, and Baruch calls in the house of Yhwh. Baruch's calling is a singular event which stands in relief against the mass response of "all the people," and which sets off a surprising chain of reactions running right through the temple and palace as secretary reports to officials who report to the king. Like a piece of grit in an otherwise smooth-running machine, the scroll, when introduced in the temple, irritates the system, causing it to shudder and creak.

A Gift in Due Season

In *A Taste for the Secret*, Derrida admits to an interest in things that "irritate the system" but which, he notes, represent "the place where the system constitutes itself" (2001, 4). Explaining this a little further, he adds that this "place" is that "subterranean region in which the system constitutes itself by repressing what makes it possible, which is not systematic" (2001, 4–5). Thus, while already and integrally part of a system—whether this be a text, an identity, or an "economy" (in the broadest terms)—the irritant remains that "whose absolute heterogeneity resists all integration, participation and system" (2001, 5). This irritant, being constitutive whilst at the same time resisting constitution itself, is thus caught up in both participation and nonparticipation. It is by definition then, contradictory: an unsystematic moment within a system; a contradiction within the very thing set up to exclude contradiction.

What is it that irritates an economy? It is that which cannot be accounted for, which goes beyond accounts, plans, ledgers, and balances—a gift. However, that which makes possible the gift, an existing economy against which it is marked as *an excess*, "designate[s] simultaneously the conditions of the impossibility of the gift" (1992, 12). For as Caputo succinctly puts it in his commentary on Derrida's discussion of this paradox, "Gifts tend to form a circular economy . . . a ring of generosity and gratitude, which links or binds the donee to the donor by means of a donatum" (1997, 142), the result being that, as Derrida concludes, "The simple identification of the passage of a gift as such . . . would be nothing other than the process of the destruction of the gift" (1992, 14). Recognition of a gift, *as gift*, inevitably results in an immediate return to economy. The gift, defined as that which does not participate in economy, nevertheless is constitutive of economy—economy as the circle of reciprocity and exchange.

The gift, which cannot be present, *a present*, in the "ordinary life and time" of the economic sphere, is therefore also *the impossible*—exceeding, but always immediately being caught up within, and constituting an economy—and so may be suitably appended (and wrapped?), as Derrida and his commentators tend to, with the comment "if there is any" or "if such a thing exists." But while being "an impossible fix, an aporia, a paralysing [*sic*] bind" (Caputo 1997, 144), the gift, *if there is any*, is also, and so contradictorily, that which sets in motion the economy, "the first mover of the circle" (Derrida 1992, 31)—ever preceding, inevitably procuring, exchange. Thus impossible whilst being at the same time integral, the gift fulfils that role of participation and nonparticipation that both irritates and instigates the system, the economy. As such, the gift is that which irritates, or better interrupts, the circle and so prevents closure—the piece of grit that holds the wound open and prevents it from closing in on itself.

The scroll, which on entry into the economies of temple and palace, irritates their systems is, as word of Yhwh, also that heterogeneous element that set the circle of reciprocity and exchange in motion to begin with. A system, set up in response to the word of Yhwh, is then, by nature of its being worked out in time and place—in exchange (fasting for divine protection), and even in discourse—the very system of economy that cannot accommodate an excess such as the coming of the word of Yhwh. The prophet and his word, it seems, are unacceptable in their own hometown and their own home-system.

A Self-De[Con]Structing Scroll

The narrative of Jeremiah 36 leads us eventually to the centre of the house, to the fireside: "Now the king was sitting by in his winter apartment (it was the ninth month), and there was a fire burning in the brazier before him" (36:22).

The destruction of the scroll forms a kind of chiastic inclusio with its formation: it is written by the secretary Baruch, and, if we take the Hebrew of 36:23 literally, it is Jehudi rather than the king who actively destroys it: "And as Jehudi recited three columns and four, the scribe tore it with a knife and he threw it into the fire which was in the brazier" (36:23). However, it is ultimately the king, Jehoiakim, who is held responsible for the destruction of the scroll—"Now, after the king had burned the scroll . . ." (36:27). The allusion encourages us to think, as I suspect the narrators of Jeremiah 36 would like us to, of another scroll found in the temple, as narrated in 2 Kings 22.

In that narrative, set a few years earlier, a disturbing new scroll is found in the temple, which causes general consternation epitomised by the reaction of the king: "When the king heard the words of the book of law, he tore his clothes" (2 Kings 22:11). The same verb, קְרַע (to tear), used of Josiah's pious reaction, is here, in Jeremiah 36:24 found with the prefix לֹא (not), "they did not . . . tear their garments." But the same verb has already been used in the previous verse, as if to drive the point home, "as Jehudi recited three or four columns, he tore them off with his knife and threw them on the fire" (36:23).

We readers of the Old Testament/Tanakh are used to this device: the paradigmatic comparison of good king, bad king. Josiah as good king heeds the scroll and makes an appropriately penitent response. Jehoiakim, as bad king, destroys it. Jehoiakim, here epitomising a wilful refusal to hear/heed the word of Yhwh, gives a final and theatrical confirmation of that fact. But is Jehoiakim the only one who silences the word?

Josiah tears his garments, then the temple, then the whole national religious infrastructure to make room for this new word of Yhwh (2 Kings 23). In response to the scroll, he sets in motion a whole new system, a new economy. But as a new word, another word, an other, the Other, it is annulled: it becomes *another law, a deutero-nomos.*[5] The contours of the already existing system may be altered, recalibrated to embrace a new word, but this will inevitably, unavoidably, destroy the scroll as other or excess. The singular word finds itself answered and so gathered back into the economy of discourse. Nothing, it seems, will silence the excessive event of the coming of the word of Yhwh so effectively as the economy of the house of Yhwh. As irritant, as gift, the scroll is, by its very nature then, impossible and so self-sacrificial, kenotic even, giving itself to an extreme, giving itself impossibly—gone in an instant. Thus its journey through the temple, the place of sacrifice, reads like stages in a passion. Its final destination, on the mount of sacrifice, becomes the cul-de-sac of an aporia where the impossibility of its own existence is confronted. The hearth (not the temple) is the place where it meets its end by "knife and fire, the tools of sacrifice" (Brummitt and Sherwood 2002, 23).

What we might call the scroll's *passion* (Brummitt and Sherwood 2002, 23) dramatises the idea of covenant. Based on the unilateral grace of Yhwh, the divine self-giving, it inevitably leads to reciprocation and so exchange, to contract and so system. Thus the scroll also bespeaks the impossibility of grace: grace that beyond the instant (the impossible moment preceding the immediate and inevitable recognition and so annulment of a gift) is lost in contract and expectation. It speaks not only of the impossibility of grace, but also of the dissymmetry of grace. The excess of self-giving, always already beyond any system and outside the economies of exchange and discourse, renders it ungraspable, inaccessible to those unavoidably caught within the economic sphere. It must, and indeed can only, remain a secret.

In the sphere of the "ordinary life and time," of exchange and reciprocity, the arrival of the scroll transgresses stable borders: it transgresses the possible, the horizons of expectation. As that which is always already beyond the system, it is "a provocation of something calling from afar that calls beyond itself, outside itself" (Caputo 1997, xix) and to that extent, profoundly fulfils its role as prophecy. By interrupting, disrupting even, the complacency of the life and time of the present, it acts "against the pleasure the present takes in itself, to prevent it from closing in on itself" (1997, xx).

Although initiated by, and formed reciprocally with, a moment of excess, a covenant will inevitably domesticate and so destroy that excess. A covenant initiated by a moment of excess, formed reciprocally with that excess, inevitably domesticates and so destroys the excess. But this moment of excess, annulled by the closed circuit of reciprocation and exchange, is also that moment which can interrupt or cut into the circle in a kind of prophetic reopening. Caputo metaphorically configures this irruptive moment of deconstruction as circumcision, referring to the point at which "circumcision cuts open the same to the event of the other, thus constituting a breach that opens the way to the other" (1997, xx). The image—following Derrida—creatively gathers and disrupts the concepts of prophecy, circumcision, covenant, and grace in a way that resonates with much of the material in the book of Jeremiah.

An Open Book

To suggest that the scroll, described in this chapter as a מגלת־ספר, "a roll of writing," is the locus of secrecy seems unreasonable, a nonsense even. The narrative quite clearly states that it contains words—*the word* no less, since these are the utterances of Yhwh—and so represents the very opposite of secrecy: disclosure. The divine command, "Take a scroll (literally: a 'roll of writing') and write on it all the words which I have spoken to you concerning Israel and concerning Judah and concerning all the nations, from the day I spoke to you, from the days of Josiah and until this day" (36:2), suggests a divine commitment to make available a comprehensive communication, requiring that nothing be left out, that not a single utterance given in the designated time period be allowed to slip away. Nothing is to be lost, forgotten or hidden. Furthermore, this narrative, prolix in its anxieties about the transition of spoken word to written word, obsessively watches the progress of speech into writing, ensuring that nothing can go astray, no single utterance go AWOL: "And Baruch wrote from the dictation of Jeremiah, all the words of Yhwh which he spoke to him, upon the scroll" (36:4).[6] This claim about the seal-tight transmission of speech into writing is reiterated in painful detail, again confirming that absolutely nothing could have slipped away in the gap between mouth and pen: "And Baruch said to them, 'He dictated to me all these words from his mouth, and I wrote them upon the scroll in ink' " (36:17–18). There is, then, no claim to secrecy or hiddenness, no suggestion of lost words or forgotten oracles. All is made available.

Though the words are inked-in, need we assume that the ink is indelible? The narrative suggests not. The divine command, "Take a roll of scroll and write on it," (36:2) is supported by the divine justification: "אוּלַי [perhaps] the house of Judah will hear of all הרעה [the evil, the disaster] I am planning to do to them, in order that they will each turn away from their רעה [evil] so that I may forgive them for their iniquity and their sin" (36:3). Yhwh's "perhaps" indicates, if not indecisiveness, a future that remains undecideable, open. Thus, for the present, the list of evils remains just that, a list, and one that can still be erased. Yhwh is something of a Bartleby here: the "perhaps" evokes the "I would prefer not to" of which Derrida makes this comment: "It evokes a future without either predicting or promising; it utters nothing fixed, determinable, positive, or negative . . . The modality of this singularly insignificant statement reminds one of a nonlanguage or a secret language" (1996, 75).

Paradoxically, the scroll's success will effectively erase its contents: the people's return from "their evil ways" will render its "plans" unfulfilled. There will be no need to justify events, no need to give account, nothing to account, and no need for theodicy at all. Conversely, the writing will hold only if its "plans" come to pass. Thus the writing on the scroll, the fixing of the marks, begins only on its journey toward the king. Those who hear, handle, and reject the scroll, at the same time confirm its charge of evil, and ink it in indelibly. And, as they unwittingly "write" the scroll, they are themselves unwittingly "written": marked down for the disasters listed within it. The scroll, then, now monstrous messenger or angel of death, leaves a trail of ink through temple and palace, writing the wrongs it encounters, writing sentences of death. A roll of writing, writing as it rolls toward the king: a rolling corpus, rolling out corpses in its wake.

Other Writing

Taking this further still, is not "otherness" always, potentially, present in writing itself? Derrida speaks of a "paradoxical desire not to be understood" (2001, 30; his rationale?) "because if such a transparency of intelligibility were insured it would destroy the text, it would show that the text has no future [*avenir*], that it does not overflow the present, that it is consumed immediately" (2001, 30). He states that, although he really does try to be clear, there remains "a demand in my writing for this excess even with respect to what I myself can understand of what I say—the demand that a sort of opening, play, indetermination be left, signifying hospitality for what is to come [*l'avenir*] . . . of a place left vacant for who is to come [*pour qui va venir*], for the *arrivant*" (2001, 31).

Writing can thus have a future inscribed in it—an opening to and for the other. The future for Derrida "*is not present*, but *there* is an opening onto it" (2001, 20,

Derrida's italics). As that which is indeterminate, profoundly so, the future is negated by teleology (2001, 20)—teleology understood as a present economy, a preparation for and projection of the future. To grasp at the future in such a way is to omit, to exclude the other, the radically other, and such closure to the future, to the incoming of the other, has a totalising effect. It is in this sense, of an openness to the future and to the one "who is to come," that Derrida speaks of the messianic and the future as a force of disruption (2001, 25)—another irritant.

The secretaries do not share the content of the scroll with us, the readers. We read of readings (36:10, 15–16, 21) and reports of these (13, 20), but we are never allowed a glimpse of the scroll, as if the secretaries turn their backs to the audience whilst reciting its contents. The one glimpse that is given, occurring after this first scroll has been destroyed, lies several citations "down" (36:29–30); the reader must plod through *the word of the narrator,* **the word of Yhwh,** the word of Jeremiah, *the word of Jehoiakim*, before finally reaching ***words from the first scroll***.

> *The word of Yhwh came to Jeremiah* . . . **And concerning King Jehoiakim of Judah you shall say**: Thus says Yhwh, You have dared to burn this scroll saying, *Why have you written in it that the king of Babylon will certainly come and destroy this land, and will cut off from it human beings and animals*? (36:29–30)

These words are to be found nowhere, in fact, within the book of Jeremiah as it has rolled down to us, and their assertion that "the king of Babylon will certainly come and destroy" jars somewhat with the "perhaps" that served as justification for the writing of the first scroll. The remaining judgement, "concerning King Jehoiakim of Judah: he shall have no one to sit upon the throne of David, and his dead body shall be cast out to the heat by day and the frost by night" (36:30), collides with what we know of Jehoiakim's peaceful death, and of his son's successful, though short lived, reign (2 Kings 24:6, 8). We are not privy to the content of the scroll and the words that so disturb their recipients; what we have is not so much a content as "the silhouette of a content," as Derrida describes Bartleby's "I would prefer not to" (1996, 74).

The secretaries, then, are rather like Kierkegaard's Abraham, the Abraham discussed by Derrida in *The Gift of Death*, to whom "God keeps silent about his reasons" (1996, 58)—the Abraham who cannot share what he does not know and who is caught in a double secret, between God and Abraham, and between Abraham and his servants and family. Troubled by what they read, mulling over its implications, transferring its possibility and potency between themselves, knowing and not-knowing, the secretaries transmit and bequeath to us, the readers of this much later scroll, nothing but a secret.

But in fact it is the scroll itself which is more like Abraham, as it incorporates both words and silence, and guards its secret, its "zone of emptiness." The scroll, as word of Yhwh, contains the words of the other and, in witnessing to the other, must remain silent. "God himself is absent," suggests Derrida in reference to the story of Abraham, "hidden and silent, separate, secret, at the moment he has to be obeyed," adding, "if he were to speak to us all the time without any secrets, he wouldn't be the other, we would share a type of homogeneity. Discourse also partakes of that sameness" (1996, 57). Should we not then in some way expect this of the other, the absolute other, a silence, a secret which is quite simply a witness to absolute otherness, the only possible witness to absolute otherness, as in apophasis or negative theology? Those who witness to the absolute other, as Abraham did, expand our concept of witness, taking us beyond the sense "that to witness means to show, teach, illustrate, manifest to others the truth that one can precisely attest to" (1996, 73). Derrida terms Abraham "a witness of the absolute faith that cannot and must not witness before men" (1996, 73). The witness of the scroll, then, is a witness of silence.

The Future in Writing

Jehoiakim, who clearly has not read his Derrida, does not recognize the "other" in this writing. Rather, he consumes it in a moment and considers its function complete. And, true, the scroll does have a contemporary purpose—cursing kings, nations and so on—that is all spent in a moment. It is Bible, and so has its original, intention-filled historical context: the situation of its first reading. But it is Bible and the contemporary does not exhaust it; it has a future beyond the crisis of the moment. It is a roll of writing, full of turning words which form the kernel of a "rolling corpus" (McKane 1986, l) and which, unlike the proverbial stone that gathers no moss, continues to gather more and more words.

What happened when the scroll was burned? Was the prophetic voice silenced? No, for although in hiding, the prophet was at this point still alive. Nevertheless, the burning jeopardized the continuation of that prophetic "voice" after the speaker would finally disappear. The destruction of the scroll, ironically confirming/releasing the destruction of Jerusalem, marks the end of one story of presence: the story of prophets and kings, of temples and palaces and the systems therein. But Jehoiakim's burning brazier sparks off a new scroll—"Take another scroll and write . . ." (36:28). Lighting up again, the irrepressible word of Yhwh sets rolling a new writing; full of cinders from the old, the new scroll adds "many similar words" (36:32). The spoken word now survives only as written word and, with its "zone of emptiness," holds itself open to an incoming, indeterminate, future. This scroll, if it is indeed to be understood as that kernel which set the book of Jeremiah rolling, is there to be opened and read, interpreted and reread; always giving, but ever holding back, never given to be consumed in a moment.

Notes

1. Seemingly a junior minister, probably a secretary (Berridge 1992, 674).
2. At this point we may presume that Baruch has gone into hiding with the prophet (36:19).
3. Although 36:5 indicates a date shortly after the fall of Ashkelon, not all scholars consider the fast-day to be a response to the approach of Babylon. McKane notes the "insouciance attributed to Jehoiakim," and argues that "we have no impression that he was aware of the presence of a sword of Damocles" (1996, 917). McKane lists those scholars who associate the fast with a natural disaster.

4. Holladay laments that "There is no information in the OT with regard to regular fast-days in the pre-exilic period" (1989, 255), while Carroll infers "presumably the cultic authorities called the fast" (1986, 659). Bright reads "proclaimed" in the weakened sense, "observed" (1965, 181).
5. Biblical scholars have traditionally considered Josiah's scroll to be an early form of the law book, Deuteronomy.
6. On the anxiety over potentially losing the word in Jeremiah 36, see further Brummitt and Sherwood (2002).

Works Consulted

Berridge, J. M. 1992. "Jehudi." In *The Anchor Bible Dictionary Vol. 5*, ed. David Noel Freedman. New York: Bantam Doubleday Dell.

Bright, John. 1965. *Jeremiah: A New Translation with Introduction and Commentary*. New York: Doubleday and Company.

Brummitt, Mark and Yvonne Sherwood. 2002. "The Tenacity of the Word: Using Jeremiah 36 to Attempt to Construct an Appropriate Edifice to the Memory of Robert Carroll." In *Sense and Sensitivity: Essays on Reading the Bible in Memory of Robert Carroll*, ed. Alastair Hunter and Philip R. Davies, 3–29. Sheffield: Sheffield Academic Press.

Caputo, D. John. 1997. *The Prayers and Tears of Jacques Derrida: Religion without Religion*. Bloomington: Indiana University Press.

Carroll, Robert P. 1986. *Jeremiah: A Commentary*. Old Testament Library. London: SCM Press.

Clements, Ronald E. 1988. *Jeremiah*. Atlanta: John Knox Press.

Derrida, Jacques. 1987. *Cinders*. Trans. Ned Lukacher. Lincoln: University of Nebraska Press.

———. 1992. "Force of Law: The 'Mystical Foundation of Authority'." Trans. Mary Quaintance. In *Deconstruction and the Possibility of Justice*, ed. Drucilla Cornell, Michel Rosenfeld, ed. David Gray Carlson, 3–67. Routledge: New York.

———. 1992. *Given Time: I. Counterfeit Money*. Trans. Peggy Kamuf. Chicago: University of Chicago Press.

———. 1992. "Passions: 'And Oblique Offering'." Trans. David Wood. In *Derrida: A Critical Reader*, ed. David Wood, 5–35. Oxford: Blackwell.

———. 1996. *The Gift of Death*. Trans. David Wills. Chicago: University of Chicago Press.

———. 2001. *A Taste for the Secret*. Trans. Giacomo Donis. Ed. Giacomo Donis and David Webb. Cambridge: Polity.

Derrida, Jacques and Geoffrey Bennington. 1993. *Jacques Derrida/Circumfessions*. Trans. Geoffrey Bennington. Chicago: University of Chicago Press.

Derrida, Jacques and Caputo, D. John. 1997. *Deconstruction in a Nutshell: A Conversation with Jacques Derrida*. New York: Fordham University Press.

Hart, Kevin. 1989. *The Trespass of the Sign: Deconstruction, Theology and Philosophy*. Cambridge: Cambridge University Press.

Holladay, William. 1989. *Jeremiah 2: A Commentary on the Book of the Prophet Jeremiah Chapters 26–52*. Minneapolis: Fortress Press.

McKane, William. 1986. *A Critical and Exegetical Commentary on Jeremiah: Volume I*. International Critical Commentary. Edinburgh: T & T Clark.

———. 1996. *A Critical and Exegetical Commentary on Jeremiah: Volume II*. International Critical Commentary. Edinburgh: T & T Clark.

Minogue, Kenneth. 1995. *Politics*. Oxford: Oxford University Press.

Chapter 3

Postcards from the (Canon's) Edge: The Pastoral Epistles and Derrida's *The Post Card*

Robert Paul Seesengood

Letters Lost in the Mail

On the surface, the Pastorals seem the most intimate of the writings attributed to Paul; 1 and 2 Timothy are addressed, "to my loyal child in the faith," "to my beloved child"; Titus is penned to "my loyal child." Paul explains his immediate plans (1 Tim. 3:14), requests his books and papers, and inquires about a forgotten cloak (2 Tim. 4:13). Timothy is given personal encouragement (1 Tim. 4:12) and advice about his character, public presentation (1 Tim. 6:11–19), and physical health (1 Tim. 5:23: "Take a little wine for your stomach"). Titus is invited, with the tone of one pained by separation, to "do your best to come to me" (3:12). We might hope to develop from these letters a side of Paul saved for his closest colleagues.

At the same time, however, they are *too* intimate in places, referring to events and people we know nothing about.[1] They refer to conflicts among early Christian leaders of whom we are otherwise ignorant.[2] They reference Paul's travel to places that we have no other record of his visiting and that are nearly impossible to coordinate with accepted Pauline chronology.[3] They display a vocabulary and syntax that differs from Paul's other writings (Harrison 1921). The conclusion to 2 Timothy is replete with unexpected and unidentifiable referents.[4]

The Pastorals offer instructions about the public ordering of the Christian community and faith. The longest series of such "public orders"—for these sections do indeed carry a more formal tone and often have asides (as in 1 Tim. 2:7) which seem to imagine eavesdroppers—explores issues as varied as the appointment of other officers (1 Tim. 2:1–3:10) care of widows (1 Tim. 5:3–22), and the ethics and dynamics of the family/household (1 Tim. 6:1–10; Titus 2:1–15; see Dibelius and Conzelman 1972, 1–2). Leaders are appointed to enforce "sound" teaching (1 Tim. 6:2b–5; Titus 2:2). The Pastorals forbid speculation and quarrels (2 Tim. 2:16, 23–24). They instruct Timothy and Titus to silence opposing voices and all women (1 Tim. 2:11–12).

The ambiguous references along with significant linguistic irregularities have led many to conclude Paul the apostle cannot be the actual author of the Pastorals.[5] Combing through the scholarship on the Pastorals is quickly wearying. Since 1990, no fewer than six major commentaries on the Pastorals have appeared in English; these commentaries combine for a gross weight of about 4000 pages, with more than 300 pages devoted to introductory matters such as author and provenance.[6] The debate over the authorship of 1 & 2 Timothy and Titus has involved meticulous reconstructions of Christian history, painstaking linguistic analysis and powerful ideological argument. Despite the most vigorous and technical efforts of scholarship, there is yet no final consensus as to whether Paul or a student of Paul wrote the Pastorals.

Figuratively throwing up their collective hands, Quinn and Wacker assert

> The P[astoral] E[pistles] tend to resist questions about their background and origin. . . . All scholars . . . draw inferences from practically the same concrete data in and about the letters, analyzing the linguistic, historico-sociological, and theological components of the correspondence. Yet these data have provoked the most dramatically different hypotheses. (2000, 18)

Even the most conservative assessment of Pauline authorship must admit failure when asked to describe the circumstances and setting of the letters' composition in any but hypothetical terms. Further, the problem is not the absence of data, but the abundance of uncontextualized facts. Either Paul, writing here with unique language, is writing from circumstances unaccountable in other Christian literature or the very specific language of the pastorals ("bring me my cloak") masks (albeit poorly) the face of an imposter.

Luke Timothy Johnson offers a provocative thesis:

> The most fundamental category, that of *authorship*, remains largely unexamined. The model of Pauline authorship therefore remains anachronistic. . . . *In writing his letters, Paul also associated others with him* in the form of co-sponsorship. . . . [D]*id co-sponsors also contribute to the thought and style of a letter?* (2001, 58–59; italics added)

Paul's letters may well be, in origin, collaborative compositions. Taking Johnson's proposal further (I suspect much further than he would intend), reading the Pastorals, whatever their method of composition, reveals multiple authors involved in the production of meaning.

Envois

The Post Card is a collection of three essays on Freud and psychoanalysis. The "preface" (titled *envois*), is a collection of fragmentary "letters" sent to an unidentified lover.[7] Derrida describes this unusual text as "the preface to a book I have not written" (1987, 3). The notes are represented as postcards whose obverse image (taken from a

Figure 3.1 "Plato and Socrates." Frontispiece of *Prognostica Socratis basilei*, by Matthew Paris, MS Ashmole 304, fol. 31v (detail) Bod. lib. Oxford; English 13th century.

medieval manuscript) shows Plato standing behind and directing a composing Socrates (figure 3.1).[8] The *envois* explore the problems of writing and identity, noting that written communication is often fragmentary and always mediated by a "post" that conceals, delivers, and occasionally misdirects messages. There are gaps in the correspondence. In some cases, entire letters are missing—some destroyed before being sent. There is a "missing letter" written about a deep disturbance (never clarified) and sent via registered mail yet never received. Within many letters there are blank spaces that interrupt sentences, thoughts, and even individual words.

With so much unknown, we *do* know substantial detail about local postal schedules. We know about train schedules and trips both planned and canceled. Many letters refer to (and quote) bits of conversations from phone calls or visits. The ordinary fabric of daily life is present, yet the particulars (many of them essential to understanding the substance of the letter exchange) are not.[9]

Gregory Ulmer observes:

As a "preface" to a study of Freud and psychoanalysis, "Envois" mimes the famous transferential correspondence Freud carried on with Fliess—the self-analysis marking the

"origin" of psychoanalysis, of which only Freud's letters survive . . . and which ended
with a picture post card . . . inscribed "Cordial greetings from the culminating point of
the journey." (1985, 126)

The letters dated September 8 and 9, 1977, intermingle personal touches with
reports of ongoing work. The letters have a persistent, personal voice ("you just hung
up" [Derrida 1987, 76]; "I am not well this morning" [1987, 78]) that underscores
intimacy, absence, and longing. One letter reveals:

> I have gotten back to work, no, not only to the "big" work as I sometimes say . . . but to
> my little secretariat. Thus I am reading the Letters of Plato and all those admirable
> discussions around the "authenticity" of their belonging, the one says, to the *corpus
> platonicum*. (1987, 83)

Seven letters have been attributed to Plato. The first six are generally conceded
among classicists to be spurious. Opinion on the seventh, which is Plato's autobiography, is divided (see Edelstein 1966). The letter writer reflects:

> The accusation of "plagiarism" was often thrown around. A multiplicity of authors has
> been suspected, more precisely that each letter or all the letters had several authors at once,
> several masked signers under a single name. . . . Concerning the 7th, one of them says,
> paraphrasing the other: "impression of a collection of pat phrases borrowed from the dia-
> logues and whose style unfortunately is ruined by oversights and gross errors." . . . [W]hat
> I cannot succeed in understanding, in holding together, is this cohabitation, the admirable
> patience of these archivists busying themselves around the finest testament, . . . associated
> with that fundamental, ineducable imbecility, and that vulgarity . . . in their imper-
> turbable assurance: they know, they wish to know and to divulge their index cards, they
> have a properly mathematical—and therefore teachable—certainty of what an authentic
> destination is . . . They want to authenticate. As if one could not pretend to write fictive
> letters with multiple authors and addressees! and even oneself to write to oneself! While
> saying that one has never written anything to oneself. (Derrida 1987, 84)

The letter writer continues with several lengthy quotations from scholars, each assert-
ing with confidence the impossibility that Plato's letters could have been salvaged and
saved by disciples.

> They not only allege that they know how to distinguish between the authentic and the
> simulacrum, they do not even want to do the work, the simulacrum should point itself
> out, and say to them: "here I am, look out, I am not authentic!" They also want the
> authentic to be thoroughly authentic, the apocryphal and the bastard also. They would
> like the counterfeiters to have themselves preceded by a *pancarte*: we are the counterfeit-
> ers, this is false currency. As if there were true currency, truly true or truly false currency.
> (Derrida 1987, 89)

The letters recount, in extensive quotation, the form critical readings of
scholarship—attempts to isolate the "kernel" of Platonic authenticity from redacted
texts. Citing John Burnet (who asserts that, 50 years after Plato, no one could so mas-
terfully imitate Plato's language): "listen to him finally, imagine him for example

behind his podium at the University let us say of Manchester: 'I believe that all the letters of some importance are Plato's, and consequently I will make use of them' " (Derrida 1987, 86).

Such scholarship becomes the "guardian" voice (Derrida 1987, 88, note also 62); perhaps to protect later generations from the "deliberately false" as one author is quoted as saying of the Platonic letters (1987, 90). "This, you see, this interests me, the 'deliberately false' which indeed betrays something . . . [W]hat you can no longer tax as deliberately false, can you call it authentic . . . or true?" (1987, 90).

Pastoral Post Cards

In the letters from September 1977 of *The Post Card* we are invited to deconstruct the binary conditions of authenticity and psuedepigraphy. We are invited to refuse to choose *either* that Plato wrote alone *or* that his letters were written by a later hand. We are invited to reject that we can or cannot read and "interpret" a correspondence of unknown origins. Turning back to the Pastorals, can we imagine a composition that could be both collaborative and private in its composition, authentic and pseudepigraphic simultaneously, at once legible and unintelligible? Letters, like all writing, assume the becoming present of absence. An author inscribes, then vanishes; in engagement as critic/reader, we, ourselves, become the texts' author. Texts exist in *différance*, capable, at once, of being both delivered and lost.

A second image comes to my attention, this one from the cover of a recent book on Paul (figure 3.2). Paul, unlike Socrates, faces his interlocutors here, his eyes vivid, his index finger jutting forward in rebuke, his left hand literally flinging a manuscript into the crowd. Paul is met by five critics. Two mimic his pointed finger; the lead figure has his own text open at the ready. Two others carry books; one scholar, in the back, seems by his posture to be pulling to the front of the pack, his hand ready to unveil a new and critical text. No one writes; everyone carries books and argues their various readings.

Reading Derrida alongside Paul (and Paul's would-be interpreters) reveals critical scholarship (and reading in general) failing at the precise point of intersection. In the pastorals, it is the very specificity—the alluded to places and names, the intimate description of Paul's personal circumstances, the unguarded and unique vocabulary and language (where else in Paul is there anything like "bring the manuscripts that I left in Troas" or "bring me my coat?")—which prevents the critic/interpreter from comprehending the origins of the text.

Letters are misdirected, lost, censored, or purloined. The postcard, with its unprotected, permanently disclosed contents is particularly susceptible to such interception. The contents may easily be read by the postal authorities—the secret identities and intentions of the author laid bare to rough hands. But the message still remains, in essence, ciphered by undefined context. If such is true for postcards, can it be any less for Epistles? In a major sense, the Pastorals are intercepted mail which the Post has taken over and over-read.

Ironically, though, it is the presence of concrete data which is the problem. If the Pastorals were less specific, if they used less idiosyncratic language, if they did not

Figure 3.2 "St Paul discussing with Jews and Gentiles." Enamel plaque form a reliquary or altar in England. Victoria and Albert Museum, London; Erich Lessing Art Resource, NY.

address Church structure and order, if they were less prone to use proper names or to discuss itinerary, then we would have letters whose provenance is not hypothetical but ethereal. The specificity needed for accurate historical reconstruction is the problem. The mundane becomes ethereal; like Nietzsche's umbrella, Paul's requests for his winter coat and books reflect a casual assumption about provenance that mocks critics' inability to recover that provenance without descent to the hypothetical. We can no more deny Paul was the author than we can deny the letters are sinister forgeries. We can not even assert they were written, by Paul or by anyone else, as nonfiction.

Reading *Envois*, Ulmer observes:

> Part of the strategy of the experiment conducted in "Envois" may now be recognized. Derrida, tracking down the effects of identity . . . places himself in the position of censor in the psychic economy, thus performing a kind of psychoepistle, the metaphorical description of an Unconscious-Conscious communicatio. (1985, 129–30)

The Pastorals seem, in places, to intimate an individual thinking aloud. Their instructions, however, seem to presume a public audience broader than Timothy or Titus. The insistence upon authority and its "sound" application is integrally connected to the question of authorship. If Paul did not write these epistles, then where is the impetus to take them seriously—indeed, blindly accepting a "word of truth" (and the Pastorals insist often that they reveal "true sayings worthy of every agreement") may well lead to heresy. Here, however, taking the letters seriously and combing through their contents is the very process which awakens questions about authenticity.

What is it, then, that critics regard in such an ambiguous text that so strictly enjoins against "idle speculation," "mindless debates," and "morbid cravings for controversy and disputes?" The specific ambiguity of the Pastorals begs for just such controversy. Criticism, in this case, is reduced to the production of texts which, themselves, are reconstructions of "Paul" and re-craftings of "Pauline" theology. Such a process invites us to revisit the assertion that all scripture (*pasa graphē*, "all writing") is inspired ("God-breathed") and "useful for training and instruction" (2 Tim. 3:17). Devoid of both author and audience, the Pastorals are endlessly in circulation because they are endlessly under the scrutiny and provision of critics/post officers.

Returning to the actual post card itself—Plato standing behind Socrates, the exact reversal of the normal order—deconstructing the binary oppositions of "authentic" and "pseudepigraphic" places us as critics in the role of Plato, standing behind our Socrates, Paul. In one sense, "Paul" remains the author of the Pastorals. In another, however, he can never be: the text remains the product of a Pauline "school," an educational institution like, and indeed equivalent to, our own. Just such a tendency is overwhelmingly present in the current trend toward "commentary Gigantism"— obese books bursting their spines with fat pages densely crammed with all prior scholarship on the subject, digested and supplemented. Single volumes of commentary outweigh the "primary" text exponentially. Paul is rewritten with every new release from Eerdmans, Fortress, Anchor, or Word. Criticism becomes both autobiography and aesthetics.[10]

Post Script(ing)

Is there relevance to the moment of this writing? Is it pertinent that, as I write, I sit on a beautiful September afternoon, a five year old napping on the couch in my office, a border collie curled up beneath the table at my feet, a New York Yankees pennant hanging on the wall by my books? I am listening to *Faust* and drinking tea to wash down the selective serotonin reuptake inhibitor I have just taken. Within an hour or so, my chair will be empty and I will be out—walking the dog, reading a story to the child, watching the game, taking a nap. Within a few years, someone else will be living in this house and I will no longer be here. Present at composition, I am absent already as you read. I am absent even as I edit this paragraph. Alan Bass, the translator of *The Post Card*, asks "Why does a 'translator,' Freud, for example, often have such a difficulty making acknowledgments? Who gave Freud his time, his help, his gift, with the 'translation?' " (Derrida 1987, x). In my way, like Plato, I stand behind my teachers and scholarly predecessors, directing them to write this essay. The Pastorals, in particular, seem to invite collaboration; Schleiermacher and Gass, Conzelmann and Dibelius, Marshall and Towner, Quinn and Wacker; reading the Pastorals is, again and again, an ambiguous intermingling of pupil and teacher, text and scholarship.

Bass also writes "An entire reading of [*The Post Card*] could be organized around Heidegger's sentence, 'A giving which gives only its gift, but in the giving holds itself back and withdraws, such a giving we call sending' " (Derrida 1987, xii). Giving and sending assume Being but also Absence. A text presumes an absent author—a post card, a letter, a solitary footprint that interrupts our isolation. The sending, the thing sent, overwhelms and defines the sender. Presence becomes absence. Signifier, once again, outpaces signified. As readers, we forensically search texts for the remains of the author. We are drawn backwards by the text's undertow; we are, as readers and critics, overwhelmed by the raw potentiality of the text but at the same time obsessed with its specific ambiguity. We are engaged by the almost-there-ness of the absent author.

Who becomes primary in the Pastoral Epistles? Paul is absent from the letters—they presume his absence, indeed, they demand it—but Paul is also not able to precede his letter. He is produced by it. Skeptical critics who deny Paul wrote the Pastorals craft a Pauline style, theology and manner by the negative image the Pastorals cast across the remaining corpus. Advocates of Pauline authorship shade their image of Paul, seeing depth arise from his addresses drawn and sent to complex and varied situations. They trace his developing diction and vocabulary and his chronology with devoted imagination. They glimpse the light of an "original" Pauline voice unfiltered by an amanuensis and reserved for Paul's closest intimates. (The Pastorals bespeak love—love for the church, the True Teaching, for Timothy and Titus; but it is a long-distance relationship inundated with absence.) Paul does not produce the Pastorals but is, himself, produced by them. Author or not, the texts become his self-portrait, his autobiography. Author or not, the texts obscure Paul far more than they reveal him; it is in this exclusion that criticism begins.

Criticism, however, is not a secondary act. Our essays are also Sendings. Like the letters of Paul, the specific ambiguity of our writing presents us while simultaneously removing and hiding us. Our writing, like Paul's, like any letter, is also handed over to the Post. Our criticism, like any other writing, like any letter, is more evocative than restrictive—produces more meanings than it can contain, more perhaps than we intend or understand ourselves. Ironically, we participate in the interpretation of a text only by first superceding the text we critique in order to present a new text for others to supercede in turn. We stand behind Paul, but only for the briefest of instants. We are not overwhelmed by the authority of the author's intent, but neither are we able to speak with any final authority of our own; we have ceased in the same moment we comment on another's absence. Our meanings pass, like an electric current, backwards through an infinite series of absences, each momentarily illuminating another thought which will, in time, precede it.

Notes

1. 1 Tim. 1:18 there is a reference to a time of "prophecy" over Timothy, predicting his future work, which is without other record. There is a reference to the "household of Onesiphorus" in 2 Tim. 4:19; the only other Onesiphorus in the New Testament is a slave.
2. 1 Tim. 1:20 Paul "hands over to Satan" Hymenaeus and Alexander of whom we know nothing. In 2 Tim. 1:15, Phygelos and Hermogenes are described as turning away from Paul but we are told nothing more about the nefarious pair. In 2 Tim. 2:17, Hymenaeus reappears, this time with Philetus—a new companion whose teachings "spread like gangrene."

3. Paul places himself in Nicopolis in Titus 3:12, but we are told nothing about his ever having traveled there, and he mentions a trip to Crete which is equally mysterious (Titus 1:5).

4. We discover that Demas (?) has gone to Thessalonica while Crescens (??) has gone to Galatia and Titus to Dalmatia (4:9–10). Alexander (Hymenaeus's cohort in 1 Tim.) appears to have worked alone at this time, but, nevertheless, "did great harm" (4:14; both the Lord and Timothy are to get even on Paul's behalf). Paul mentions a mysterious "first defense" (4:16) where he did well despite being alone. At first we are refreshed with the familiar names Prisca, Aquila, Onesiphorus, and Erastus; we quickly are left in the dark, however, with the reference to Eubulus, Pudens, Linus, and Claudia (2 Tim. 4:19–21). Titus refers to Artemis and Tycheus and a lawyer named Zenas (3:12–13a) of whom we know nothing and Apollos (3:13) of whom we know very little.

5. Virtually every scholar who has studied the subject has ventured a hypothesis. The modern debate began with an open letter from Schleiermacher to J. C. Gass (Schleiermacher 1807; see Patsch 1999). The "leading" suggestions are that the letters are:

   (1) orthodox forgeries written to refute a Marcionite canon of Paul's writings (Baur 1835);
   (2) an edited compendium of Paul's writings collected together with embellishments by a Pauline student to flesh out Paul's late career and to preserve as far as possible otherwise vanishing traditions (Quinn and Wacker 2000);
   (3) a new composition written by member of a Pauline "school" of thought which addresses new issues in church order and teaching (Eichorn 1812; De Wette 1844);
   (4) an epistolary appendix to Luke-Acts (Quinn 1978);
   (5) a collection of letters to correspond to traditions found in *The Acts of Paul and Theckla* (MacDonald 1983). Each of these hypotheses, however, is answered by a growing number of scholars (Johnson 2001).

6. The six I have in mind are Quinn 1990 (completed by his student, Philip Boelter); Johnson 2001; Marshall 1999 (composed with the aid of Phillip Towner); Quinn and Wacker 2000; Mounce 20000 and Collins 2002. These commentaries add to the existing "major" commentaries of Spicq 1947; Dibelius and Conzelmann 1972; Roloff 1988; and Oberlinner 1994. A search of the American Theological Library Association database of articles in religion scored more than 350 hits in 5 minutes of searching. I'm not even beginning to note the "minor" commentaries, New Testament introductions, and Bible study handbooks. By way of a sample, note the actuarial precision of Harrison 1921 on the unique Pastoral vocabulary:

   The vocabulary of the Pastorals consists of some 902 words, of which 54 are proper names. Of the remaining 848, 306 or over 36 per cent are not to be found in any one of the ten Paulines . . . One hundred and seventy-five, the so-called "Pastoral *Hapax Legomena*," appear in no other N.T. writing outside the Pastorals. Of these 1 Tim. has 96, that is 15.2 per page, 2 Tim. 60 or 12.9 per page, and Titus 43 or 16.1 per page.

   Now Romans has only four such words to the page, 1 Cor. 4:1; 2 Cor. 5:6; Gal. 3:9; Eph. 4:6 Phil. 6:2; Col. 5:5; 1 Thess. 3:6; 2 Thess. 3:3; and Philem. 4.

   We are thus presented with a gradually ascending scale, approximating, though by no means exactly, to the chronological order, the maximum difference, between the two extremes . . . . (1921, 20–21)

7. *The Post Card*, along with *Glas* and *Truth in Painting*, has hardly been heavily utilized by biblical critics (with the notable exception of Moore 1992, esp. 38–47) despite the text's popularity in the humanities in general and the good efforts of Winquist and Caputo 1990

to bring it to the attention of general scholarship in Religion. In my work, I have found Ulmer 1985 and Bennington 1991 of great value as a companion texts. The accompanying "Circumfessions" by Derrida/Bennington and Ulmer's category of "Autography" inspired my final turn toward autobiography.

8. Identified in the book's credits as "Plato and Socrates, the frontispiece of *Prognostica Socratis basilei*, a fortune-telling book. English, thirteenth century, the work of Matthew Paris. MS. Ashmole 304, fol. 31v."

9. Biblical scholars may also wish to note that the letters treat the story of Esther in some detail: see esp. the letters dated September 7.

10. Jeffrey Staley has demonstrated precisely this movement in his *Reading with a Passion*. Staley uses autobiographical criticism (relating his own experiences growing up as a missionary child on the Navajo reservation in Arizona) to explore the gospel of John. Taking seriously critics who suggested the "implied reader" in his first book, *The Print's First Kiss*, was actually himself, Staley, in part two of *Reading*, overtly moves to autobiography as an exegetical device. Perhaps of even more interest, however, is his concluding "Post-Mortem Morality Play." Staley crafts an exegesis on the passion narrative of John which is a dialog between the corpses of the criminals crucified alongside Jesus. Staley (like Kitzberger 1999:5–9; 2002:5–10 and many others) plants autobiographical biblical criticism in Reader-Response soil, though perhaps the method could be more fruitfully grafted onto a "grammatology" root.

Works Consulted

Baur, Ferdinand, C. 1835. *Die sogenannten Pastoralbriefe des Apostels Paulus*. Stuttgart: Cotta.

Bennington, Geoffrey and Jacques Derrida. 1993. *Jacques Derrida*. Religion and Postmodernism. Chicago: University of Chicago Press.

Collins, Raymond F. 2002. *1 & 2 Timothy and Titus: A Commentary*. The New Testament Library. Louisville: Westminster/Knox.

Derrida, Jacques. 1987. *The Post Card: From Socrates to Freud and Beyond*. Trans. Alan Bass. Chicago: University of Chicago Press.

De Wette, Wilhelm M. L. 1844. *Kurze Erklärung der Brief an Titus, Timotheus und die Hebräer*. Kurzgefasstes exegetisches Handbuch zum Neuen Testament 20. Leipzig: Weidmannischen.

Dibelius, Martin and Hans Conzelmann. 1972. *The Pastoral Epistles*. Trans. Philip Buttolph and Adela Yarbro. Ed. Helmut Koester. Hermeneia. Philadelphia: Fortress.

Edelstein, Ludwig. 1966. *Plato's Seventh Letter*. Philosophia Antiqua 14. Leiden: Brill.

Eichorn, Johann G. 1812. *Historisch-kritische Einleitung in das Neue Testament*. Leipzig: Weidmannischen.

Harrison, Percy N. 1921. *The Problem of the Pastoral Epistles*. New York: Oxford.

Johnson, Luke Timothy. 2001. *The First and Second Letters to Timothy: A New Translation with Introduction and Commentary*. The Anchor Bible 35a. New York: Doubleday.

Kitzberger, Ingrid Rosa, ed. 1999. *The Personal Voice in Biblical Interpretation*. New York: Routledge.

———. 2002. *Autobiographical Biblical Criticism: Learning to Read Between Text and Self*. Leiden: Deo.

MacDonald, Dennis R. 1983. *The Legend and the Apostle: The Battle for Paul in Story and Canon*. Philadelphia: Westminster.

Marshall, I. Howard (with Phillip H. Towner). 1999. *A Critical and Exegetical Commentary on the Pastoral Epistles*. International Critical Commentary. Edinburgh: T & T Clark.

Moore, Stephen D. 1992. *Mark and Luke in Poststructuralist Perspectives: Jesus Begins to Write.* New Haven: Yale University Press.

Mounce, William D. 2000. *Pastoral Epistles.* Word Biblical Commentary 46. Nashville: Nelson.

Oberlinner, Lorenz. 1994. *Die Pastoralbriefe. Erste Folge: Kommentar zum Ersten Timotheusbrief.* Herders theologischer Kommentar zum Neuen Testament 11.2. Freiburg: Herder.

Patsch, Hermann. 1999. "The Fear of Deutero-Paulinism: The Reception of Friedrich Schleiermacher's 'Critical Open Letter' Concerning 1 Timothy in the First Quinquenium." Trans. Darrell J. Doughty. *The Journal of Higher Criticism* 6.1:3–31.

Quinn, Jerome D. 1978. "The Last Volume of Luke: The Relation of Luke–Acts to the Pastoral Epistles." In *Perspectives on Luke-Acts*, ed. Charles H. Talbert, 62–75. Danville, VA: Association of Baptist Professors of Religion.

———. 1990. *The Letter to Titus: A New Translation with Notes and Commentary and an Introduction to Titus, 1 and II Timothy, the Pastoral Epistles.* The Anchor Bible 35. New York: Doubleday.

Quinn, Jerome D. and William C. Wacker. 2000. *The First and Second Letters to Timothy: A New Translation with Notes and Commentary.* Eerdmans Critical Commentary. Grand Rapids: Eerdmans.

Roloff, Jürgen. 1988. *Der erste Brief an Timotheus.* Evangelische-Katholischer Kommentar zum Neuen Testament 15. Zürich: Benziger.

Schleiermacher, Friedrich. 1807. *Über den sogennanten ersten Brief des Paulus an den Timotheos. Ein kritisches Sendschreiben an J. C. Gass.* Berlin: Realschulbuchhandlung.

Spicq, Ceslas. 1947. *Saint Paul. Les Épitres Pastoralies.* Études Bibliques. Paris: Gabalda.

Staley, Jeffrey L. 1995. *Reading With a Passion: Rhetoric, Autobiography and the American West in the Gospel of John.* New York: Continuum.

Ulmer, Gregory L. 1985. *Applied Grammatology: Post(e)-Pedagogy from Jacques Derrida to Joseph Beuys.* Baltimore: Johns Hopkins University Press.

Winquist, Charles E. and John D. Caputo. 1990. "Derrida and the Study of Religion." *Religious Studies Review* 16.1:19–25.

Chapter 4

Erasing Amalek: Remembering to Forget with Derrida and Biblical Tradition[1]

Brian M. Britt

אבל אנשל הרי מת אצל הנאצים ימח שמם וזכרם

[B]ut didn't Anshel die by the Nazis, may-their-name-be-blotted-out . . .

(Grossman 1989, 4; Hebrew 1986, 10)

"I will place you sous rature, Professor Humboldt," said Kraljevic, his face flushed, his eyes dark behind the pince-nez trembling on the bridge of his nose. "If my beloved Lorraine Alsace, my sweet contested territory, does not receive tenure by the end of the term . . . I shall erase you, and you will vanish forever, like a face drawn in sand at the edge of the sea."

(Hynes 2001, 258)

The two epigraphs to this essay, both from contemporary novels, invoke the metaphor of erasure to curse a specific enemy. In the first case, from David Grossman's *See Under: Love*, a Jewish survivor of the Holocaust curses the Nazis. The erasure of their name is linked here, as it is in the Bible, to memory. The second curse, from James Hynes's *The Lecturer's Tale*, is uttered by a postmodern literary critic whose curse invokes specific academic discussions of writing indebted above all to the work of Jacques Derrida. Both curses appear in magical realist novels in which cursing can be genuinely efficacious.

By what line of transmission, and through what traditions, do these curses come to the two novelists? Grossman quotes verbatim the biblical curse analyzed in this essay—a millennia-old biblical (and Jewish) tradition, traceable back to Exodus 17: 14–16, which has passed into common parlance in modern Israeli Hebrew.[2] In order to understand the full implications of the curse, one must recognize the idioms of this tradition. And though the number of people who understand it may be small, the tradition is significantly long and robust to afford complex associations—between the Nazis and the Amalekites for instance.

Hynes draws on a much different "tradition" in his curse. When the ultrahip literary theorist Kraljevic places the novel's protagonist "under erasure" (*sous rature*), he alludes to a small number of recent theoretical texts familiar only to a small group of scholars. The meaning and allusion of the phrase *sous rature* are obscure to most of the novel's characters. For these mocked acolytes of high academic fashion, the ability to cite a text unknown to the adversary is seen as an advantage. In the exaggerated world of the novel, obscurity and obscurantism quickly blur. Nevertheless, like Grossman's curse, this poststructuralist curse must be sufficiently recognizable to make sense to the informed reader; in other words, even poststructuralist theory has enough conventional metaphors to subject it to the sort of parody executed by Hynes.[3] But is poststructuralism, by itself, a tradition?

This essay examines the metaphor of erasure in biblical tradition and in the poststructuralist theory of Derrida; and in addition to observing a number of striking homologies and differences, I imagine the interpretative possibilities and dangers of reading the Bible with Derrida and reading Derrida with the Bible. Such an approach explores some of the mixed disciplinary allegiances of those who work at the intersection between biblical, religious, theological, and cultural studies. Along the way, I will also have occasion to reflect on what is meant by biblical tradition and ontology—questions on which I will have recourse to Derrida and also to Emmanuel Lévinas.

The theme of erasure is one of concern to Derrida, especially in his writings on negative or apophatic theology, a tradition usually traced to the sixth-century Pseudo-Dionysius as well as the later figures Meister Eckhart and Angelus Silesius. Affinities between poststructuralism and negative theology have been richly explored in the works of Mark C. Taylor, Mikel Dufrenne, Jean-Luc Marion, John Caputo, Hent DeVries, and Jacques Derrida. But in all this contemporary theological and philosophical work there is relatively little discussion of the Hebrew Bible. This essay draws biblical cursing into the discussion, particularly around the categories of writing and erasure, and asks how cursing traditions in ancient Israel relate to these contemporary discussions of negative theology. To answer this question, I concentrate primarily on the curse against Amalek (Exod. 17:14–16 and Deut. 25:19) and the work of Jacques Derrida.

The command to write Amalek's erasure is the first of a series of narratives in which Moses writes (Exod. 17:14; 24:4; and 34:27; and Deut. 31). These acts of writing connect stories *in* the Torah with the inscription and promulgation *of* the Torah, thus blurring the lines between speech and text, past and present. Moreover, several biblical texts identify religious well-being and even existence itself with writing. In Psalm 40, for example, the psalmist declares, "*Here I am; in the scroll of the book it is written of me.* I delight to do your will, O my God; your law is within my heart" (vv. 7–8), as if being present (הנה באתי) were somehow equivalent to being written (of) (כתוב). In Deuteronomy, Moses exhorts the children of Israel to "Keep these words that I am commanding you today in your heart . . . Bind them as a sign on your hand, fix them as an emblem on your forehead, and write them on the doorposts of your house and on your gates" (Deut. 6:6–9), and later in the book, Moses proclaims the Torah to be the very life of the people (32:47). By contrast, to be erased or blotted out of the book is the worst fate that can befall a person: when Moses intercedes for Israel after the golden calf episode, he says "But now, if you will only forgive their sin—but if not, blot me out of the book you have written" (32:33).[4] The image of erasure appears also in Deuteronomy after the long list of covenant curses: "All the curses written in this book will descend on them, and the Lord will blot out their names from under heaven" (29:19–20). Written curses play a role in a range of episodes, from the trial by bitter waters inflicted by the jealous husband in Numbers 5, to the curse on the foreign enemy Amalek in Exodus 17 (see also Psalms 9:5–6; 69:28; and 109:13). The object of the curse may be the enemy as in Exod. 17:14–16; Deut. 12:3; Ps. 69:28; 109:14, or it may be Israel, whose blotting out or contemplated blotting out is related to the breaking of covenant regulations (see Exod. 32:32–33; Deut. 9:14; 29:19; and 2 Kings 14:27).

Do these biblical images of writing and erasure operate on the level of metaphysics (referring to absolute reality) or ontology (relating to questions of being)? I affirm both alternatives cautiously, without reducing or translating the texts of ancient Israel into philosophical discourses in which questions, narratives, and paradoxes seek paraphrase and resolution. Instead, Exodus 17 represents a process of tradition and interpretation according to which ancient curse practices are taken through new contexts and meanings. What I propose is that biblical texts have philosophical (ontological and metaphysical) implications though they belong to a tradition (or language game) other than philosophy.

Remembering to Forget

In Exodus 17 there is a paradoxical inscription of erasure in which *the command to erase is written down:*

> Then the Lord said to Moses, "Write this as a reminder (זכר) in a book and recite it in the hearing of Joshua: I will utterly blot out (כי־מחה אמחה) the remembrance (זכר) of Amalek from under heaven." And Moses built an altar and called it, The Lord is my banner [term obscure]. He said, "A hand upon the banner of the Lord. The Lord will have war with Amalek from generation to generation." (Exod. 17:14–16; note the concise variant in Deut. 25:19: "[I]n the land that the Lord your God is giving you as an inheritance to possess, you shall blot out the remembrance of Amalek from under heaven; do not forget.")

Why is the erasure of Amalek written and recited, and how can someone remember to forget? To paraphrase Derrida in *The Postcard*, by what force of amnesia can we aim not simply to transform, deform, or confound, but to forget; how can we forget without knowing and how can we know how to forget? (Derrida 1987, 77). Like Derrida, these biblical texts seem to relate the category of writing to questions of being (ontology) and absolute reality (metaphysics), but, like the acts of excision invoked by other ancient inscriptions, they also play a *performative* role—a role that invokes the efficacious power of language in certain situations, and overlaps with recent discussions of hate speech.[5] By reading the biblical texts with help from Derrida, my analysis will suggest some overlooked continuities between biblical tradition and current discussions of negative theology.

The Threat of Erasure

Erasure always presupposes presence: a word must be inscribed before it can be effaced. By the same token, no act of inscription can occur without an acknowledgment, even an anxiety, that it *could* be erased. A similar duality applies to cursing in general: as Derrida observes in one of his many allusions to the Bible: "When Jeremiah curses the day he was born, he must yet—or *already*—affirm" (1992, 99). For Derrida, negation and affirmation are always interconnected, suggesting the possibility that cursing and erasure demand a central position in any theoretical discussion of writing and speech. (Derrida's attention to the connection between curse and affirmation is a far cry from the minimal attention bestowed by biblical scholars on the phenomena of erasure and cursing.)

The subject of erasure arises in Derrida's most extended reflection on apophatic or negative theology: "How To Avoid Speaking." Here, Derrida insists that any apophatic religious discourse must begin with prayer or an address to God that "recognizes, assigns, or insures its destination" (1992, 98),[6] but in order to avoid making any such claim to the signification or destination of his own writing, he is at pains to distinguish himself from negative theology. Yet a spirit of playfulness infuses the essay, particularly on the question whether it will be *possible* for Derrida to dissociate himself from negative theology: "I knew, then, that I could not avoid speaking of negative theology. But how and under what heading would I do it?" (1992, 85). Derrida never resolves this question, but a number of references to Jewish tradition open up suggestive interpretive directions.

Derrida observes that the expressions of negative theology are usually addressed to God, and that mere statements of absence or the inadequacy of language do not make negative theology radically distinct from other kinds of expression, since they are directed *somewhere*, as a prayer is directed to God. The name of God here indicates the "trace of the singular event that will have rendered speech possible" (1992, 98) and in this sense, negative theology inscribes the same ontological and linguistic claims as other theologies. In a more general way, this act of naming God applies to "every reading, every interpretation, every poetics, every literary criticism . . . the 'already-there' (*déjà-là*) of a phrase, the trace of a phrase . . ." (1992, 98). Derrida shows that negative theology shares the same desire for "meaning, the referent, truth" as other kinds of discourse, and that all such discourse is subject to the economy of "différance" and the trace (1992, 98). This trace is inherent in writing and productive of the kind of dissemination and "différance" so thoroughly theorized by Derrida: "Even if the idiomatic quality must necessarily be lost itself or allow itself to be contaminated by the repetition which confers on it a code and an intelligibility, even if it *occurs only to efface itself*, if it arises only in effacing itself, the effacement will have taken place, even if its place is only in the ashes. *Il y a là cendre*," he says (1992, 98).

In Derrida's hands, apophatic theology becomes a means of reflecting on all reading and interpretation, and the sense in which texts hark back to an original singular event immediately raises the specter of erasure. Effacement of the singular event, the naming of God or the "already-there" of a phrase, becomes a necessary part of linguistic economy for apophatic theology and all other kinds of discourse alike. In this sense, negative theology and erasure are just like all other kinds of writing and they are also *symbolic* or *emblematic* of all other kinds of writing.

Derrida links this paradox of erasure, of presence in absence and absence in presence, to the ontological and theological projects of Plato's *Timaeus*, Meister Eckhart, Martin Heidegger, Jean-Luc Marion, and what he admits is a self-defeating attempt to dissociate his own work from negative theology. His problem with negative theology will be that it is in some sense *not negative enough*: every disavowal of language and meaning will be undercut by its address to God. In fact, theologians often resort to apophatic forms of expression in order to raise their religious claims to a level of absolutism or "hyperessentiality" (1992, 78–79). So is Derrida a negative theologian? Derrida himself remains noncommittal on the question, but others, such as Hent De Vries, rush to deny the possibility. Concurring with Derrida and criticizing Mikel Dufrenne's appropriation of Derrida's "différance" as "the unconceptualizable concept in the name of which every positivity is put under erasure [*sous rature*]," De Vries denies the suggestion that Derrida's work reduces to a negative theology of "productive absence" (1992, 46–47). Readers of Derrida struggle to define what his recent "turn to religion" means (see De Vries and Caputo), in an academic tug-of-war not dissimilar to the struggle over Walter Benjamin's debt to, and invocation of, theology.

Uncertain as to whether his disavowal of negative theology can succeed, Derrida refers the question back to Heidegger, who expressed an unfulfilled desire to write a theology without using the word "being." Is Heidegger's text a form of negative theology, since it lacks the address to God that Derrida considers basic to negative theology? The answer to the question is left open. Derrida's essay is itself full of the kind of addresses and apostrophes that he associates with negative theology (1992, 75, 83, 85, and n. 13), so that without saying so, in fact despite saying the opposite, Derrida appears to concede failure in the attempt to dissociate himself from negative theology. What does this contradictory affirmation and denial mean for Derrida? Derrida's affirmation-denial performs the impossibility of fulfilling certain desires in writing; it thus has implications not just for negative theology, but for writing and affirmation (promise) in general, just as biblical curses of erasure perform a paradox that has larger implications for how biblical writing is understood. Thus Derrida's statement resonates with biblical tradition, even though the biblical and the Jewish are but a "trace" in a meditation in which the core texts are German, Greek, and primarily Christian.

In his work on negative theology, Derrida avoids speaking about biblical texts of erasure such as Exodus 17, and says nothing about Jewish texts on writing/invoking God, and instead focuses on Heidegger's attempts "to write Being, the word *being*, under erasure, an erasure in the form of a crossing out" (1992: 125). This focus on the German philosopher who wrote about the "inner truth and greatness" (Heidegger 1995, 199) of National Socialism places Derrida in a strange position relative to his own Jewish identity, a problem he also explores at length in his autobiographical work, "Circumfession." In "How to Avoid Speaking," Derrida comments with a tone of near-embarrassment:

In other words, what of Jewish and Islamic thought in this regard? By example, and in everything that I will say, a certain void, the place of an internal desert, will perhaps allow this question to resonate. The three paradigms that I will quickly have to situate (for a paradigm is often an architectural model) will surround a resonant space of which nothing, almost nothing, will ever be said. (1992, 100)

The question Derrida begs but avoids here is of course, "Why?"[7] Highlighting the bracketing out of Judaism and Islam, Derrida observes that his essay concerns Plato, Christian theology, and Heidegger, all of which stand apart from, or even against, the Jewish and the biblical. The absent center of Jewish tradition is made even more pronounced in Derrida's reference to the fact that his essay was delivered in Jerusalem, where, ambivalent about his promise to speak about negative theology, he quoted from the Jewish Passover Haggadah: "Next year in Jerusalem! I told myself, in order to defer, perhaps indefinitely, the fulfillment of this promise" (1992, 83).

What to make of this aporia? According to Eliot Wolfson, "This comment must give pause to all those involved in the effort to discern Derrida's relationship to Jewish mysticism, not to mention Judaism more generally" (2002, 488). I concur with Wolfson, particularly on the point that Derrida does not offer a specialized analysis of Jewish texts, but I would risk a bolder connection between Derrida and Jewish tradition precisely on the grounds of Derrida's disavowal. This connection, I suggest, draws upon Derrida's acknowledged debt to Lévinas (which Wolfson overlooks) and involves the practices as well as the content of a reading.

One could see Derrida's invocation of Jewish tradition in his "Next year in Jerusalem" either as joke or dismissal of Jewish tradition or, in a more indirect way, as a kind of affirmation by negation, as if the whole Christian and Hellenistic preoccupation with negative theology were beneath or outside the "resonant space" of Judaism. If this were to be understood as Derrida's position, he would then be well-positioned to disavow the negative theology of which he speaks. He also would have done so with rhetorical flourish, by means of a certain kind of "productive silence." I will suspend these two possibilities for the moment and return to them below in the discussion of Derrida and Lévinas.

Blotting out the Name in Exodus 17 and Deuteronomy 25

What significance attaches to the use of "erase" in the curse on Amalek and other parties in the Hebrew Bible; and what relation, if any, is there between negative theology which does not speak the name of God, and the placing "*sous rature*" of the name—and existence (being?) of the enemy? Expressions of erasure are common in curse traditions in the Ancient Near East, where public inscriptions, a sign of status, success, and prestige, were often protected by curses (Crawford 1992; Gevirtz 1983; Gager 1992). Biblical tradition also has the expressions "to be written in the book" (Exod. 32:32–33) and to be blotted out "from under heaven" (Deut. 9:14; 29:19; 2 Kings 14:27), both of which associate writing with existence and erasure with nonexistence. What do curses of erasure suggest about ideas of writing and revelation in ancient Israel? For an ancient culture in which literacy was limited, the prominence of writing metaphors suggest an emerging religion of the book, in which recitation, preservation, and commentary on scripture begin to constitute central practices.

"Write this as a reminder (זכר) in a book and recite it in the hearing of Joshua: I will utterly blot out (כי־מחה אמחה) the remembrance (זכר) of Amalek from under heaven." What is the purpose of this curse? What idea of writing does it intimate? There is no single answer to either question, though drawing in what Derrida calls the "guardrail of context" may help to clarify them both. The curse comes immediately after victory in a holy war, a war of self-defense in which the Amalekites attack Israel just as they complete their exodus from Egypt at the Red Sea. The passage combines two main aporiae: a command to write with a command to recite the erasure of the Amalekites, and a command to remember to forget them. What could be more aporetic than a written and recited declaration of erasure in the preserved canonical text of Exodus, in which the name Amalek is preserved—albeit as A̶m̶a̶l̶e̶k̶—for evermore? Yosef Yerushalmi's *Zakhor* famously tells us that the verb "zakhor" in various forms occurs one hundred and sixty-nine times in the Hebrew Bible along with its obverse—the adjuration not to forget. Remembering seems difficult enough (certainly the Israelites keep forgetting to remember, and keep having to be reminded to remember) but this difficulty is nothing compared with the logical impossibility actively to forget. From the standpoint of contemporary logic and literalism, the passage seems to represent a moment where the Bible, unexpectedly, sounds logically self-defeating, or Derridean. Like the use of the double negative in English, the curse on Amalek is crystal clear but logically flawed; it represents an emphatic curse against Amalek undermined by the very language of writing, recitation and memory with which it reinforces—and underwrites—that emphasis.

But is the text Derridean? Though the ontological, cultural, and linguistic context of Derrida's reflections on silence and erasure lie beyond the ancient world of this curse text, Derrida's interrogation of writing, being, and erasure shares, I suggest, some "biblical tradition" common to him and Exodus. A juxtaposition of Exodus 17 and Derrida shows, unexpectedly, that both are "biblical" *and* "philosophical" in meaningful ways—that the biblical is Derridean, and that Derrida is biblical, in a certain sense. Certainly the biblical and Derridean corpuses share several features: the interdependence of canonical text and commentary; an understanding of writing and speech as authorized discourse; an understanding of textual coherence that includes fragmentation. However, in order to imagine Derrida and Exodus as sharing a biblical tradition, "tradition" would have to mean not only conscious and ratiocinative projects (such as "Shakespearean tradition" or Alasdair MacIntyre's idea of tradition as "embodied argument") but also many unexpected, and following Freud, even unconscious forms of continuity (MacIntyre 1984, 222): it would have to come closer to what Derrida calls the "archive." Reading Exodus 17 alongside, and with a little help from, Derrida we would have to note there is nothing of willful obscurantism about the curse, and indeed it warrants scrutiny for this very reason: how can we speak of a willful forgetting and how can such a paradoxical expression make sense?

The problem applies equally to a common (but very different) expression in English: "Let's forget it,"[8] where the emphasis is in the opposite direction of the eradication of pain/crime (forgiveness) rather than the eradication of the perpetrator of the crime (vengeance). But what can it mean to forget (a crime, or a name) *deliberately?*

Freud and (in a certain Freudian "tradition") Derrida can account for *inadvertent* forgetting and erasure through the death drive, that which destroys the cumulated archive/tradition with *le mal d'archive*, or "archive fever," but it is a much harder task to articulate a forgetting that is fully conscious and deliberate (Derrida 1996, 10). Logic and history both undermine such forgetting, since, of course, Israel and its literature do *not* forget Amalek. This might lead us to question whether this forgetting is possible, and if not, whether the imperative to forget is really something else—something that will return again and again in destructive ways (see Exod. 17; Num. 14:45; 1 Sam. 15, 27, 30). One can imagine a psychoanalytic view of Amalek as a signifier of evil to which tradition irrevocably and compulsively returns. But from the retrospective standpoint of the writing of Exodus, the inscription of Amalek as perennial enemy is a historical and hermeneutical necessity; the curse of erasure will *inscribe* Amalek as an enemy whose threat is ultimately unimportant; over time, through the unfolding of political *and interpretive* history, Amalek will be "erased."

Every solution that we generate for the text is unsatisfactory, in some sense. If we "solve" the logical conundrum by claiming that no rule of logical contradiction applies in the Hebrew Bible, such a solution condemns biblical culture to irrationalism. If we claim that some of the terms in the passage are not literal—that "Erase" and "Write in the book" refer to the public record rather than individual memory; or that the two forms of זכר ("remember") refer to public, ritual expression rather than mental states, as claimed in Yerushalmi's *Zakhor* (5–15)—we still need (in the absence of an ancient biblical poetics) evidence that these terms are nonliteral, and that tradition could easily distinguish public record and ritual from mental states. And if we point out, as William Propp does, that זכר (like the Akkadian *zakaru*) can simply mean name or posterity, the resolution of the problem still relies on insisting that the memory and the ongoing existence of the Amalekites are two different things: "The point, therefore, is that Amalek will never be forgotten, but will survive *only* as a memory, not as a people" (1999, 619). (In a related vein, Manes Kogan suggests that memory in this verse applies only to the death and destruction carried out by Amalek, and that, in other words, the memory of Amalek is nothing other than death and destruction, so that Amalek "is" not [Kogan 2001, 143]. The fourth century midrash the *Mekhilta de Rabbi Ishmael* suggests also that Amalek exists *only* in the memory of the future generations [*Parsha Beshalach, Amalek* 2:186].)

The reiteration of the curse in Deuteronomy (25:17–19) complicates matters further: here, at the culmination of the law code just preceding its ceremonial ratification, with the people of Israel gathered on the plains of Moab, we have an emphatic reiteration of the Exodus curse: "Remember what Amalek did to you on the way as you came out of Egypt" (v. 17). Lest they forget, the people are reminded to blot out the remembrance of what Amalek did. The erasure of Amalek is commanded again, in a book full of reiterated laws (Deuteronomy as "second law"), to take place after Israel has settled the land and defeated its enemies (v. 19). Such a period of stability is usually associated with the writing of chronicles that memorialize the past, but here memory serves to *un*-write the name and remembrance of Amalek. Set off by the commands "remember" and "do not forget," the emphatically remembered curse of erasure and forgetting poses no barrier to rewriting.

It seems that the curse of erasure, a familiar trope in ancient Near Eastern culture, appears in Exodus and Deuteronomy in a new key, transposed as it were into a tradition that prizes writing as memory and memory as a set of actions that make it possible to speak of "Israel" or "Amalek" and be understood. Biblical curses of erasure, in other words, take familiar customs to a new level by incorporating them in a growing biblical tradition constituted largely by recitation, ritual, and commentary. The question is how such speech and writing are understood: is the curse on Amalek an efficacious speech act that somehow *performs* the erasure of this people, and if so, what are its ontological implications? In the context of an ongoing hermeneutical tradition, the curse's proleptic or future orientation will become a basis for subsequent reference and commentary.

With or Beyond the Aporia in Exodus 17

In the biblical passage and the *Mekhilta*, the acts of writing and reciting conclude a story of battle and indicate a future of wars with Amalek. Already marked in Genesis as a rival people descended from Esau (Genesis 25:23; 36:12), the Amalekites will challenge Israel on a perennial basis.

What bearing do past and future rivalries have on the writing of the curse *in* the text and the writing *of* the text, and what is the bearing of the altar, with its own obscure name: "The Lord is my banner." Without lapsing into complete chaos/incoherence, these ambiguities drive an ongoing process of interpretation: the parts of Exodus. 17:14–16 are discrete but clearly interrelated, and the contrasts and repetitions allow more than one interpretation. The question becomes: Given the clear patterning and paradoxical expression, what would account for a *conclusive* interpretation—some kind of dissipation of the tensions of the passage, at the level of physical enmity, and actual sense? With respect to rivalries and time, the problem of interpretation becomes critical. Though most scholars attribute the passage to an early strand of the Pentateuch (the patriarchal source E; Propp 1999, 615), the passage is proleptic with respect to future conflicts with the Amalekites, such as 2 Samuel 1 and the book of Esther. The conflict with Amalek unfolds through time in biblical history.

Exodus 17 demands to be read, then, in the context of a biblical history that extends back to Genesis and forward to Esther. For the Bible, the rabbis, and Emmanuel Lévinas, revelation takes place over the course of history. In an early rabbinic text, the proleptic nature of the passage plays out over the course of the canon as well as the course of time: reading verse 14 lemmatically, the midrash interprets as follows: "*Write this as a memorial in a book*": " 'This': what is written in *this* book; 'Memorial': what is written in the prophets. 'In the book': what is written in the scroll" (*Mekhilta Amalek* 2:182). Later, the midrash divides the two forms of "erase" into "this world" (for מחה) and the "world to come" (for אמחה) (*Mekhilta Amalek* 2:185). What the midrash means by spreading out the terms of the passage into divisions of the canon and phases of history is not exactly clear, but what is clear is that the midrash seems to expand the scope of the writing to include this book, the Mekhilta, and that book, the Torah—in that one is always implicit within the other—and stretches the meaning of the text across all worlds and all time, including the world to come. What we could call the "dissemination" of erasure betokens an act of making the memory of forgetting Amalek, the inscription of erasure, a cornerstone of Israelite tradition. The notion of erasure and memory as a matter of temporal process suggests that the narrative *requires* subsequent interpretations. But if the Amalekites stand for the perennial enemy against which Israel must forever do battle, if the Amalekites are fratricidal enemies, then there is danger in reading the passage ontologically, since that would elevate fratricidal (and in Esther, genocidal) ethnic conflict to a level of ontology (Schwartz 1997, 6–11).

The unfolding revelation under discussion here is a biblical history of violent ethnic conflict underscored by an emphatic curse of erasure. In this case, we might say that the curse works *too well*, that biblical tradition works *too well*, insofar as it perpetuates a bitter hatred between peoples. Elevated to the level of ontology, as the curse of Canaan in Genesis 9 was in the antebellum South, the curse can remain lethal for millennia. "Amalekite" may not have been a common slur in the Middle Ages, but the term for Amalek's ancestor, "Edom," was.[9] How, then, can the ontological reading of fratricidal violence be avoided within the tradition? One strategy is to read the biblical text *very* closely against the grain, as one Hasidic reading does in the case of the curse of Deut. 25:17, which includes the words (in order), "to you Amalek" (qlm(Kl) (Wittenberg 2001, 128). In context, of course, "Amalek" is the subject of the clause that reads "what Amalek did to you"; but for these readers it also suggests that "you" and "Amalek" are the same, that Amalek, in other words, is also *within* Israel, and the struggle described in Exodus 17 and Deuteronomy 25 is partly a struggle against evil within the self and/or community.[10]

Another hermeneutical or midrashic approach to Amalek is to deliteralize the narrative—to call attention to its literary and symbolic character, its status as a story. Consider the fate of the Amalekite rivalry in the book of Esther. Written in a fictionalized form, the *Diasporanovelle*, Esther presents a wildly exaggerated kind of victory that readers (and Purim revelers) know all too well to be unrealistic (Greenstein 1987, 233). The book also parodies patterns of Jewish vulnerability and victory: in the only biblical book that never mentions God, Esther proclaims a victory so improbable that its satisfaction must always be mixed with a bitter realization that it is far-fetched. Esther clearly alludes to Exodus 17 and 1 Samuel 15, where Saul (Mordechai's ancestor) mishandles the conquest of Agag, the Amalekite ancestor of Haman (Berlin 2001, xxxviii), but at the same time, the book's victory falls short of typical biblical aspirations: Esther's success amounts to little more than the survival of the Jews and revenge on their (Amalekite/Agagite) enemies. And at the end of the book none of the three cornerstones of biblical covenant tradition—homeland, king, or temple—is available to the victors.

Esther engages the interpretive tradition of Amalek—the fratricidal struggle between two nations—and raises it to a parodic, bittersweet, and even ludic level (Berlin 2001, xxii). Exod. 17:14–16 seems universal, uncompromising, and steeped in cycles of animosity, and yet tradition proves supple enough to yield another biblical text, Esther, that transforms the conflict by weaving it into a highly stylized narrative in a very different idiom. Though it may not eliminate the danger of universalized conflict, Esther calls attention to its fictional status by fabulous turns of events that defy historical plausibility. While enemies were familiar to Jewish history, their massive defeat through intermarriage and courtly intrigue was unheard of.

In the festival of Purim, at which the Esther scroll is read aloud, the name of the Amalekite villain, Haman, is drowned out by noisemakers called "groggers." In this ritual, the paradox of erasure and memory is brilliantly expressed through carnivalesque action. Tradition also requires celebrants to drink wine until they can no longer distinguish the name "Mordechai" from "Haman" (*B. Megillah* 7b). Purim thus performs the erasure of Amalek through an oral reading of Esther that is compromised (but not eliminated) by noise and alcohol. Spoken but not heard, the Amalekite name is auditorily erased through ritual recitation. Purim remembers to forget.

Of course, no interpretive clues are "foolproof," contrary to what Meir Sternberg has argued (Sternberg 1985, 50), and there are no guarantees that Esther can contain the danger of violence by its parodic engagement with the curse of Amalek. The boundaries between writing and erasure, memory and forgetting, remain fluid in tradition, and so too do those of fantasy and reality. Certainly the story slipped into literality for the right wing Orthodox Jew who gunned down Arabs at the tomb of the patriarchs in Hebron on Purim (see Hunter's 'Denominating Amalek' [2004]). And as Susannah Heschel observes, "[I]n Israel and elsewhere we also hear about Palestinians as *Amalek*—the incorrigible enemy whom we ore obligated to wipe off the face of the earth" (2003, 59).

By sheer coincidence, Esther invokes the erasure of Amalek and also, alone among books of the Bible, fails to mention the name of God. Absence, erasure, and an emphasis on written decrees and chronicles (3:9–15; 6:1–8) would seem to make Esther an ideal illustration of negative theology. But the sort of metaphysical and mystical terms that animate negative theology do not preoccupy Esther. A diaspora story that appropriates the biblical motif of Amalek, Esther seems to be written for an audience more familiar with the exigencies of chance (cf. "lot," גורל, Esther. 3:7; 9:24) than direct divine intervention. Against the dangers of history Esther affirms biblical tradition and group identity by linking an unlikely victory story to popular ritual (9:17–32). The absence of God, which Georg Lukacs regards as definitive of the novel, serves to make the story's danger, and the imperative to erase Amalek, particularly intense (Lukacs 1971, 88).

Perhaps Esther indirectly elucidates Derrida's hesitation to embrace negative theology. In "How to Avoid Speaking," Derrida repeatedly insists on the importance of specific place in reading, writing, and addressing. His concern about the "hyperessentiality" of negative theology suggests a discomfort with universalism in a reader who always attends to the particular. To a reductive reading of Esther as negative theology in which the erasure of Amalek mirrors devout silence toward the name of God, a Derridean reading would reply that such a universalism ignores too much literary texture, and, moreover, could reproduce the danger against which it warns. Esther does indeed perform the erasure of Amalek and silence toward the name of God, but this performance, like Derrida's performance of hesitation toward negative theology, demands sensitive reading of the text *as* performance.

Lévinas and Derrida

What does it mean to speak of erasure on the ontological level? For Derrida and Heidegger, the question of ontology and erasure can be imagined on an abstract and universal level (i.e., Being and its erasure or crossing-out); for Emmanuel Lévinas, the name of God, like the biblical conceptions of erasure, memory, and the idea of revelation, assumes a particular history. A brief discussion of the work of Lévinas on the questions of erasure and biblical tradition will provide context for the question of how to relate biblical and poststructuralist erasure.

For Lévinas, the study of Torah embodies the historical process of revelation. His readings of Torah and Talmud are not incidental ephemera in his work but rather the linchpin of his ethics and philosophy of religion. In his essay on the name of God, Lévinas carefully dissociates Jewish teachings about the name of God from philosophical abstraction (1982: 147–48). The point here is not simply to reinforce the clichéd difference between Athens and Jerusalem, or to say that the Jewish or biblical way of talking about the divine is not the same as the Greek or scholastic philosophical tradition.[11] Lévinas, rather, seems to be urging a uniqueness in Jewish tradition that *matters* to philosophy: "But revelation of the Name itself is not uniquely the corollary of the unity of a being; it leads us even further. Perhaps even beyond being" (1982, 148). For Lévinas, revelation requires a kind of transcendence that is irreducible to any abstract concept such as being.

In the essay on the name of God, Lévinas cites and builds upon three biblical texts that underlie his talmudic and philosophical analysis: Deut. 12:3–4; 6:13; and 1 Kings 8:27 (1982, 146, n. 3, 149). The notion of erasure appears only in the first case, while all three texts insist on the unique transcendence of the God of Israel in terms of the divine name. The name of God here is ineffable: it exceeds the boundaries of ordinary space, time, and human comprehension. Lévinas follows a specific halakhic discussion of which names of God may and may not be erased, but his own philosophical reflections on revelation and tradition emerge from this rabbinic and biblical commentary.

For Lévinas, it is midrash, the ongoing process of interpretation, that constitutes revelation. In this conception of revelation, the complexities and even inconsistencies of biblical and rabbinic texts are not problems to be resolved but basic elements of a tradition that includes future interpretations. According to such a view, questions, perhaps more than answers, constitute the very subject of revelation and "the slightest question put to the schoolmaster by a novice constitutes an ineluctable articulation of the revelation which was heard at Sinai" (1989, 195).

The influence of Lévinas on Derrida is a subject too elaborate to be addressed here, but both make use of the concepts of trace and erasure in ways that inform the subject of biblical erasure. For Lévinas, the trace is an extraordinary sort of sign that "disturbs the order of the world": "To be in the image of God does not mean to be an icon of God, but to find oneself in his trace. . . . He shows himself only by his trace, as is said in Exodus 33" (1998, 104, 106–07). For Derrida, as we have seen, the trace is a kind of absolute difference that precedes signification: "The trace has, properly speaking, no place, for effacement belongs to the very structure of the trace"

(1973, 156).[12] In *Adieu to Emmanuel Lévinas*, Derrida frequently cites Lévinas's understanding of Torah as justice and revelation, yet at the same time, asserts his commitment to a less stable conception of language and text: "Dare I say that I never forego . . . the right to this analysis, indeed, to the discussion of some proposition or other in a text that cannot be homogeneous because it knows how to interrupt itself?" (1999, 118; 66–67, 109, 123). For Derrida, the challenge to affirm the historicity of revelation, the model of interpretation-as-ethics beyond Heideggerian ontology, will merge with a generalized theory of reading and text, one not based on the canons and practices of Judaism, one that goes further, we could say, from the level of historical texts to the level of language itself.

From this one may be tempted to regard Derrida as inherently more universalistic than Lévinas, whose writings on Talmud may be understood as particularistic, perhaps even specifically Jewish. I resist this temptation. Biblical tradition is, by Lévinas's account, inherently universalizing. And according to philosophers like Peter Ochs, biblical tradition offers important resources for contemporary metaphysics. For those traditions that involve a pattern of text and commentary, there is much to be gained from a direct encounter with such texts—the first element of which is the openness to the tradition itself. To behave, for example, as if the academic institutions of literary criticism and canon have no connection to claims of transcendence, to reject institutional religion as obsolete superstition, are the marks of a narrow, not a universalistic worldview. The notion of Torah as a model for an ethical life in which reading, teaching, and learning are constitutive elements of an ever-expanding tradition indicates a practical, historical universalism.

Lévinas embraces the particular world from which the first epigraph (above, from David Grossman's *See Under: Love*) comes—and participates directly and non-ironically in its tradition of Torah and commentary. Derrida is sometimes cast as the evil Demiurge who creates the world of the second epigraph (in which the erudite literati place one another *sous rature*, together, of course, with that other poststructuralist bogeyman Foucault, whose metaphor of a man vanishing like a face drawn in the sand at the edge of the sea appears in *The Order of Things*; Foucault 1973, 387).[13] Yet Derrida's relationship to Jewish and biblical traditions remains close and highly complex: the question that John Caputo and others have posed, "Is deconstruction a Jewish science?" is problematic and interesting in much the same way as the original version of the question asked about the psychoanalysis of Freud, the self-described "godless Jew" (Caputo 1997, 263–73). Outside the preestablished conventions and canons of rabbinic Judaism, Derrida implements a series of brilliant, strategic interventions in established intellectual discourses and debates. His innovative and scrupulously close readings of texts from the intellectual canon are, as Susan Handelman recognized over twenty years ago, recognizably indebted to rabbinic tradition (Handelman 1985, 163–78).

Conclusion

The epigraphs to this essay come from two distinct interpretive "traditions": a Jewish and biblical tradition that finds its way, through various detours, into an Israeli novel invoking the cursing and erasure of the Nazis; and a poststructuralist school of "literary theory" grounded primarily in the work of Derrida. One belongs to a centuries-old human community of families, to scriptures and to rituals that perform those scriptures, whereas the Derridean "canon" and "tradition" are relatively recent, and only available via the readings of an intellectual elite (as well as a more publicly consumable caricature). Yet for both of these texts—and meditations on textuality—erasure is a paradoxical phenomenon, an absence that always assumes a presence, an effacement that always implies something already written.

In Exodus 17, Esther, the *Mekhilta*, and *See Under: Love*, the curse of Amalek seems to function as a *symbolic* expression that points toward suffering, evil, and conflict without imposing strict boundaries on the horizons of interpretation: the curse on Amalek takes on meanings that range from the improbable victory over enemies in exile to the generalized expression of the encounter with evil. And on the surface, it seems that no metaphysical or ontological anxiety haunts the use and interpretation of the biblical curse. But reading the injunction to blot out, and to remember-to-forget, alongside Lévinas and Derrida (as well as the rabbis) enables us to see how the biblical aporia of written erasure is conceptually, and philosophically, rich. With Exodus 17 and other biblical references to erasure, we see an ancient, widespread form of cursing come into an ongoing hermeneutical tradition that performs variations on a theme. The same paradox of writing and erasure arises in the case of the literary scholar who places his rival *sous rature*, and so invokes a more recent "tradition" that already seems robust enough for a popular novel to invoke it playfully.

What does all of this suggest for biblical scholarship? The two epigraphs testify, first of all, to the cultural availability of two conceptually distinct "traditions" of erasure; seeing the differences, similarities, interactions, and implications of each "tradition" is important for future analysis. Poststructuralist theory highlights the conceptual implications of biblical tradition, while, conversely, biblical tradition provides cultural and historical context often neglected by poststructuralist thought. If poststructuralism struggles with ontological and metaphysical anxieties, biblical tradition offers a range of practices and readings supple enough to embrace or negotiate the aporiae of Exodus 17 without suffering a crisis of meaning or endorsing a cycle of violence. The hermeneutical imperative, implicit in the text-and-commentary structure of biblical tradition, lends itself to a convergence of the poststructuralist and biblical traditions: both return to the text with full acceptance of its ambiguities, open to new readings.

Notes

1. I wish to thank Yvonne Sherwood, Jane Aiken, David Burr, Sue Farquhar, Ann-Marie Knoblauch, and Amy Nelson for their comments on this essay. Helpful suggestions came also from Rabbi Manes Kogan and Peter Ochs.
2. Thanks to my colleague Ester Sheinberg for informing me of this. Another iteration of the familiar curse appears in a newspaper account of the 2003 Israeli election campaign: "That ad showed a clip of [Shas party leader] Rabbi Yosef cursing the Meretz leader, Yossi Sarid. 'May his name be erased,' the rabbi declares," *The New York Times*, January 19, 2003, 3.

3. A much more potent use of the literary-theoretical "tradition" of erasure appears in a sardonic essay about the site of the World Trade Center. In "Groundzeroland," Frank Lentricchia and Jody McAuliffe admonish the reader to "Walk up the ramp to the platform without filter and, for a golden fifteen minutes, see the erasure—see what isn't there—and see what cannot be erased: the meeting ground for the producers and consumers of popular culture" (2002, 359).

4. Cf. the variant in Deut. 9:14; cf. also 25:6, which invokes the law of levirate marriage as a way to prevent the erasure of a deceased man's name. A similar use of the term appears in 1 Sam. 24:21.

5. In *Excitable Speech*, for instance, Judith Butler binds language to physical existence, arguing that "If language can sustain the body, it can also threaten its existence" (Butler 1997, 5).

6. See also the discussion of negative theology in the "Post-Scriptum" to *Derrida and Negative Theology* (Derrida 1992), also in *On the Name* (1995, 60–65).

7. The "internal desert" also refers to the experience of being a "little black and very Arab Jew" (*a pied noir*) who grew up in a colonial situation in Algeria where his very understanding of Judaism was subject to a "Christian contamination" (Derrida 1993, 58; 1998, 54. See also "Hostipitality" in Derrida 2002, 358–420. Thanks to Yvonne Sherwood for these references).

8. My thanks to my colleague, Ananda Abeysekara, for this insight.

9. Thanks to Alexandra Cuffel for this observation.

10. A similar reading appears in the contemporary rabbinic collection *Torah Gems*, vol. 2 (Greenberg 1988, 123), in which the author refers to Amalek as the evil inclination within us (the Yetzer Hara, or simply the Yetzer). Thanks to Manes Kogan for this reference.

11. In this way, I wish to avoid the image of Judaism as "an exotic transgressive Other to the edifice of a 'Greek' western rationalism" against which Yvonne Sherwood warns (2000, 101, n. 34).

12. Susan Handelman notes Derrida's dependence on Levinas as well as his tendency to go further in the direction of "pure difference." For Handelman, Derrida's resistance to clear signification is a kind of "mystification" and a "species of via negativa" (1985, 173).

13. My thanks to Yvonne Sherwood for the Foucault reference.

Works Consulted

Berlin, Adele. 2001. *Esther*. The JPS Bible Commentary. Philadelphia: The Jewish Publication Society.

Butler, Judith. 1997. *Excitable Speech: A Politics of the Performative*. New York & London: Routledge.

Caputo, John. 1997. *The Prayers and Tears of Jacques Derrida*. Bloomington: University of Indiana Press.

Crawford, Timothy G. 1992. *Blessing and Curse in Syro-Palestinian Inscriptions of the Iron Age*. New York: Peter Lang.

Derrida, Jacques. "Différance." Trans. David Allison. In *Speech and Phenomena*, 129–60. Evanston, IL: Northwestern University Press.

———. 1987. *The Post Card: From Socrates to Freud and Beyond*. Trans. Alan Bass. Chicago: University of Chicago Press.

———. 1992. "How to Avoid Speaking." Trans. Ken Frieden. In *Derrida and Negative Theology*, ed. Harold Coward and Toby Foshay, 73–142. Albany: State University of New York Press.

Derrida, Jacques. 1993. "Circumfession." *Jacques Derrida*. In Geoffrey Bennington and Jacques Derrida, trans. Geoffrey Bennington. Chicago: University of Chicago Press.

———. 1995. "*Sauf le nom.*" Trans. John P. Leavey, Jr. In *On the Name*, ed. Thomas Dutoit, 35–88. Stanford, CA: Stanford University Press.

———. 1996. *Archive Fever.* Trans. Eric Prenowitz. Chicago: University of Chicago Press.

———. 1998. *Monolingualism of the Other; or, The Prosthesis of Origin.* Trans. Patrick Mensah. Stanford, CA: Stanford University Press.

———. 1999. *Adieu to Emmanuel Lévinas.* Trans. Pascale-Anne Brault and Michael Naas. Stanford, CA: Stanford University Press.

———. 2002. *Acts of Religion.* Ed. and with an Introduction by Gil Anidjar. New York: Routledge.

De Vries, Hent. 1999. *Philosophy and the Turn to Religion.* Baltimore: Johns Hopkins University Press.

Foucault, Michel. 1973. *The Order of Things: An Archaeology of the Human Sciences.* New York: Vintage Books.

Gager, John G. 1992. *Curse Tablets and Binding Spells from the Ancient World.* New York: Oxford University Press.

Gevirtz, Stanley. 1983. "West-Semitic Curses and the Problem of the Origins of Hebrew Law." *Vetus Testamentum* 11:137–58.

Greenberg, Aharon Yaakov, ed. 1988. *Torah Gems*, vol. 2. Trans. Rabbi Shmuel Himelstein. Israel: Yavneh.

Greenstein, Edward L. 1987. "A Jewish Reading of Esther." In *Judaic Perspectives on Ancient Israel*, ed. Jacob Neusner et al., 225–43. Philadelphia: Fortress Press.

Grossman, David. 1989 [1986]. *See Under: Love.* Trans. Betsy Rosenberg. New York: Washington Square Press. (Hebrew, *Ayen erekh-ahavah: roman.* Jerusalem 1986.)

Handelman, Susan. 1985. *The Slayers of Moses.* Albany: State University of New York Press.

Heidegger, Martin. 1959. *An Introduction to Metaphysics.* Trans. Ralph Manheim. New Haven: Yale University Press.

Heschel, Susannah. 2003. "Whither the Zionist Dream?: A Response to Joel Kovel." *Tikkun* 18:58–59.

Hunter, Alastair. 2004. "(De)nominating Amalek: Racist Stereotyping in the Bible and the Justification of Discrimination." In *Sanctified Aggression: Violent Legacies of Biblical and Post-Biblical Vocabularies of Violence*, ed. Jonneke Bekkenkamp and Yvonne Sherwood, 92–108. New York: Continuum.

Hynes, James. 2001. *The Lecturer's Tale.* New York: Picador.

Kogan, Manes. 2001. *Megillat Ester.* Jerusalem: L.B. Publishing.

Lentricchia, Frank and Jody McAuliffe. 2002. "Groundzeroland." *South Atlantic Quarterly* 101:359.

Lévinas, Emmanuel. 1982. *L'au-delà du verset : lectures et discours talmudiques.* Paris: Editions du Minuit.

———. 1989. "Revelation in Jewish Tradition." Trans. Sarah Richmond. In *The Levinas Reader*, 190–210. Oxford: Basil Blackwell.

———. 1998. "Meaning and Sense." Trans. Alphonso Lingis. In *Collected Philosophical Papers*, 75–108. Dordrecht: Martinus Nijhoff.

Lukacs, Georg. 1971. *The Theory of the Novel.* Trans. Anna Bostock. Cambridge: MIT Press.

MacIntyre, Alasdair. 1984. *After Virtue.* Notre Dame: Notre Dame University Press.

Marion, Jean-Luc. 1998. *God Without Being.* Trans. Thomas A. Carlson. Chicago: University of Chicago Press.

Mekhilta de Rabbi Ishmael, ed. H. S. Horovitz. 1970. Jerusalem: Wahrmann Books.

Ochs, Peter. 1995. "Scriptural Logic: Diagrams for a Postcritical Metaphysics." *Modern Theology* 11: 65–92.

Propp, William. 1999. *Exodus* 1–18. Anchor Bible. New York: Doubleday.

Schwartz, Regina. 1997. *The Curse of Cain: The Violent Legacy of Monotheism*. Chicago: University of Chicago Press.

Sherwood, Yvonne. 2000. *A Biblical Text and its Afterlives: The Survival of Jonah in Western Culture*. Cambridge: Cambridge University Press.

Sternberg, Meir. 1985. *The Poetics of Biblical Narrative*. Bloomington: Indiana University Press.

Taylor, Mark C. *Nots*. Chicago: University of Chicago Press.

Wittenberg, Jonathan. 2001. *The Eternal Journey*. London: Temple Fortune.

Wolfson, Eliot. 2002. "Assaulting the Border: Kabbalistic Traces in the Margins of Derrida." *Journal of the American Academy of Religion* 70: 475–514.

Yerushalmi, Yosef. 1996. *Zakhor: Jewish History and Jewish Memory*. Seattle: University of Washington.

specters and messiahs

Chapter 5

The Missing/Mystical Messiah: Melchizedek Among the Specters of Genesis 14

Alastair G. Hunter

It is clear to anyone with a Jewish ear, to anyone with half an ear for the Hebrew and Christian scriptures, that this whole thing called "deconstruction" turns out to have a very messianic ring. The messianic tone that deconstruction has recently adopted (which is not all that recent and not only a tone) is the turn it takes toward the future. . . . The messianic future of which deconstruction dreams, its desire and its passion, is the unforeseeable future to come, absolutely to come, the justice, the democracy, the gift, the hospitality to come. Like Elijah knocking on our door!

(Caputo 1997a, 156)

Introduction: The Litany of Messiahs[1]

"Let us then praise famous men, and our fathers in their generations." These are the messiahs whose names we honor:

Judas, son of Hezekiah	and	Simon of Peraea
Athronges the Shepherd	and	Judas the Galilean
John the Baptist	and	Jesus of Nazareth
The Samaritan Prophet	and	King Herod Agrippa
Theudas	and	The Egyptian Prophet
An Anonymous Prophet	and	Menahem, son of Judas the Galilean
John of Gischala	and	Vespasian
Simon bar Giora	and	Jonathan the Weaver
Lukuas	and	Simon ben Kosiba
Moses of Crete	and	Muhammad
Abu Isa' al-Isfahani	and	Moses al-Dar'i
David Alroy	and	A Yemenite Messiah
Abraham ben Samuel Abu'lafia	and	Asher Lämmlin
Isaac Luria	and	Hayyim Vital

| Sabbathai Zwi | and | Jacob Frank |
| Moses Guibbory | and | Menachem Mendel Schneerson |

And to that list we must add the Mystical Messiah, Melchizedek—the strange disembodied being whose utterly unexplained presence in Genesis legitimates the embodying of the messiah in the form of Jesus.

Prolegomenon

The first, and most obvious remark to make about Genesis 14 is that it intrudes itself suddenly and unexpectedly into the narrative which embraces it. It is parasitic upon that framing narrative, but at the same time curiously detached from it. Many years ago Robert Davidson, my teacher and erstwhile colleague, characterised it as being like an erratic block of glacial material dumped unceremoniously (my word, not his) in the midst of an environment to which it blatantly does not belong (Davidson 1979, 32). To pursue a different metaphor, it is almost certain that the chapter is a very late addition, couched self-consciously in archaising mode: evidence deliberately planted to look older than it is. It reminds the informed reader of nothing so much as those bodice-ripping historical yarns whose only reference to their purported historical milieu is a liberal sprinkling of verbal tics ("gadzooks," "prithee," "milady," etc.) combined with random references to more or less appropriate historical persons and events. Genesis 14 is a remarkably blatant example of the genre, for the following reasons:

1. The names of the four eastern potentates range from the plausible to the highly improbable, and most commentators today eschew any attempt to relate them to actual rulers or kingdoms.
2. Similarly the five local kings bear designations which seem to be more like pejoratives than personal names. (This is spelled out in the section "Names" below.)
3. The degree of apparent dependence on the early chapters of Deuteronomy and other biblical passages is reminiscent of the way that a student plagiarist might inadvertently disclose his or her web source! The previous chapter, for example, ends with a reference to a place, "Mamre," which becomes a character in chapter 14, and the dependence on the Lot–Sodom cycle (Genesis 13, 18–19)[2] is evident.
4. The frequent use of the phrase "X *that is* Y" signals the use of "planted" archaisms. The Hebrew for "that is" uses one of the forms of the third person singular pronoun. Its occurrences (in a number of contexts) in Genesis 14 are as follows: *hi'*, v. 2.; *hu/i'*, vv. 7,8; *hu'*, vv. 3,15,17; *v'hu'*, vv. 12, 13, 18. This frequency of use does seem more than coincidental.
5. It is effectively impossible, even if the states represented by the four eastern kings can be identified as Babylon, Assyria, Elam, and the Hittite realms, that they could ever have been in any kind of alliance in any period known to archaeology, a point made long ago by Van Seters.[3]
6. If we are to fit Abram into any remotely plausible period (presumably earlier than 1400 B.C.E.) a further problem arises in that for most of the second

millennium the most important great power in the region in question was Egypt—the one imperium studiously ignored in the chapter.[4] For the twelth and thirteenth dynasties (ca. 1990–1640 B.C.E.) see Redford (1992, 76–97); for the creation and character of the "Egyptian Empire" in Retenu[5] during the eighteenth dynasty (ca. 1570–1320); see Redford's extensive treatment (1992, 148–213). The intermediate period—which is commonly described as the Hyksos period—appears to reverse the trend, with "Asiatic" dynasties in power in Egypt; this does not, however, imply that any sort of eastern alliance conquered Egypt: indeed, the takeover was in some senses internal to Egypt, and Egyptian interests in the Levant continued roughly as before.

7. Wherever Sodom and Gomorrah appear we can be sure that legendary material is involved. The myth of the terrible destruction of a pair of wicked cities occurs more than once in Tanakh, and is associated also with Admah and Zeboiim (which are also found in the present passage). These four cities are linked together in the table of the nations in Genesis 10:19 and in a version of the destruction by fire found in Deuteronomy 29:23. Hosea 11:8 makes cryptic reference to the unspecified fate of Admah and Zeboiim. The Sodom/Gomorrah version is, of course, referred to frequently in the prophetic books.[6]

These generally accepted facts are of considerable importance for the ways in which we might read Genesis 14 as a whole and the Melchizedek material in particular, widely agreed to be yet a further insertion into the already-intrusive narrative which constitutes this passage. First of all, they imply a rather late provenance for both the portrait of Abram as a warrior king and for the emergence of the mysterious figure of Melchizedek. I have argued elsewhere (Hunter 1986, 15–17) that the Abram traditions may well have themselves no earlier a provenance than the exilic Judaean community in Babylonia; the historically inappropriate focus in Genesis 14 on the empires of Mesopotamia rather tends to confirm this perspective, at least in terms of a late historiographical interest in the events, nations, and rulers of the *first* millennium B.C.E. Secondly, they point to an extensive interest in the appropriation of earlier scriptures in the interests of later concerns. What these precisely are we can only guess at, but there are certain indications both in the passage under consideration and in its *own* afterlife which open up possibilities. I shall explore some of these later in this paper. And third—and most important for the present discussion—they "permit" a generosity of interpretation which is often foreclosed by the more rigidly historical or biblical-critical schools. For if there is compelling evidence of a considerably free use of sources by the authors of Genesis 14, we in turn find ourselves not only *permitted* but indeed *required* to read with a similar openness and freedom.

Names

The single most overwhelming impression given by Genesis 14 is of a text obsessed with names and naming. In its twenty-four verses there are no fewer than fifty different proper designations (of persons, peoples, towns, and geographical locations), and with repetitions the total rises to ninety-three. Thus something like a quarter of the final word count (allowing for the imprecision of such an estimate) is of this kind. To that already impressive total we ought to add the uses of the term *melekh* (king)—quite clearly the single most significant term of address in the chapter. There are twenty seven, so the final tally is one hundred and twenty—roughly one third of the total. It is hard to imagine a narrative passage anywhere else bearing such a burden of denomination,[7] in which (further) such a strange and specialized list of names is deployed. This profusion of the "proper name" presents precisely the kind of challenge to reading to which Derrida, speaking of another strange episode in Genesis, the Babel Tower (a "tower-de-force" through which the Deity scrambles for ever our power to name), refers when he says: "understanding is no longer possible when there are only proper names, and understanding is no longer possible when there are no longer proper names" (2002, 105).

When we look at what these names seem to point to, we enter what can only be described as a kind of fantasy world of biblical nomenclature. Not only Sodom and Gomorrah are present here, but their twins from an alternative tradition of the destruction of two cities—Admah and Zeboiim—and Zoar, which is associated with them in the legends about Lot in Genesis 13 and 19. Three races of giants are listed— the Rephaim, the Zuzim (perhaps the same as the Zamzumim), and the Emim. Giants turn up in a number of places: the story in Genesis 6:1–4 of the sons of the gods sleeping with the daughters of men (there they are called *Nephilim* as also in Numbers 13:33— the passage in which the spies check out the land), the account of the entry into Canaan in Deuteronomy 1–3, and in the conquest narrative in Joshua.[8]

The names of the kings of the five cities[9] of the plain whose territory is invaded are quite improbable. Some believe them to be punning pejoratives rather than genuine personal names,[10] a possibility reinforced by their being linked to the five cities which figure in the legends of their violent destruction by God for their wickedness. Finally the names and countries of the four eastern potentates are, as we have already noted, both largely unparalleled and (as a group) deeply implausible in historical terms. Only one of the four personal names—Arioch—occurs elsewhere, in Daniel where (appropriately) it is the name of an official in the Babylonian court.[11] Of their associated countries, two (Shinar and Elam) are found in Genesis 10–11, a third (Goiim) is simply a word for "nations" and is also found in Genesis 10, and the fourth (Ellasar) has no parallel in Tanakh.

In the discussion of Babel already alluded to, Derrida comments significantly on the "meaning" of the proper/common "name" *babel/babble* in terms which have a striking relevance to the present discussion:

> Babel: today we take it as a proper name. Indeed, but the proper name of what and of whom? At times that of a narrative text recounting a story (mythical, symbolic, allegorical; it matters little for the moment), a story in which the proper name, which is then no longer the title of the narrative, names a tower or a city but a tower or a city that receives its name from an event during which YHWH "proclaims his name."
>
> Now, this proper name, which already names at least three times and three different things, also has, this is the whole point of the story, as proper name the function of a common noun. (2002, 108–09)

These remarks have relevance to the particular concern of this essay: the figure of Melchizedek, to whom/which we must now turn.

Melchizedek: International Man of Mystery

"Babel": first a proper name, granted. But when we say "Babel" today, do we know what we are naming? Do we know whom? If we consider the sur-vival of a text that is a legacy, the narrative or the myth of the tower of Babel, it does not constitute just one figure among others. Telling at least of the inadequation of one tongue to another, of one place in the encyclopaedia to another, of language to itself and to meaning, and so forth, it also tells of the need for figuration, for myth, for tropes, for twists and turns, for translation inadequate to compensate for that which multiplicity denies us. In this sense it would be the myth of the origin of myth, the metaphor of metaphor, the narrative of narrative, the translation of translation, and so on. It would not be the only structure hollowing itself out like that, but would do so in its own way (itself almost untranslatable, like a proper name) and its idiom would have to be saved.(Derrida 2002, 104)[12]

The "proper name" *Melchizedek*, may well (as we shall see) be a name conjured from a cryptic sentence in Psalm 110. Like most Hebrew personal names it can be "translated" ("my king is righteous" or "king of righteousness" being two possibilities), so the possibility is always there of the kind of misconstrual which converts a statement or description into a proper name. Thus *melchizedek*, from having first been a descriptive phrase indicating some kind of meaning in Psalm 110, then becomes a personal name which is in turn applied to the "named messiah," Jesus. (The latter is itself a suspiciously meaningful proper name.)[13] Applied to Jesus, Melchizedek serves a dual purpose: the vindication on the one hand of the Christian messiah by means of a "real" and "properly named" "historical" person, and the characterisation; on the other, of Jesus in terms of the "meaning" of the name.[14] Derrida might well have had this in mind (even though he presumably did not) when he wrote:

> Now, a proper name as such remains forever untranslatable, a fact that may lead one to conclude that it does not strictly belong, for the same reason as the other words, to the language, to the system of language, be it translated or translating. And yet "Babel" [or "Melchizedek"?], an event [a person?] in a single tongue, the one in which it appears so as to form a "text," also has a common meaning, a conceptual generality. (2002, 109, my additions)

I will return to the "meaning" of *Melchizedek*; for the time being, let me go back to the beginning of Genesis 14. It represents an invasion, by a largely invented alliance, of a fantastic territory ruled by the most unlikely kings—truly a tour-de-force of the imagination, the more remarkable for having elicited from scholars and readers an impressive volume of energy devoted to proving or disproving its historicity (and you may well ask which is the more futile exercise!). This noninvasion leads to the kidnapping of a "real" biblical figure (Lot) and his subsequent rescue by the equally "real" Abram (let the reader apply what irony may be desir-ed/able), and it is into this phantasmagoria[15] (literally, a market place—*agora*—of phantoms) that Melchizedek irrupts from whatever hidden realm has previously contained him. We would do well, then, to wonder at the nature of this messianic person, this anointed priest/king of an unknown town, whose encounter with Abram has had such profound echoes in the messianic afterlife of Christianity (and to some extent of Judaism in some of its early stages).[16]

Melchizedek in Tanakh is a fleeting presence. The two references—Psalm 110:4 and Genesis 14:18–20—tantalize far more than they inform, and constitute almost paradigm cases of the phenomenon of *aporia*. Earlier, more literally historical approaches to the problems posed by these texts have speculated[17] that Melchizedek may have been a genuine character associated with some ancient city state antecedent to Judah ("Salem" bears an intriguing similarity to the final two syllables of Jerusalem, but with enough difference to resist any claim of identity), the memory of whom may have informed the story in Genesis 14. Psalm 110 is then taken to be a later poetic and messianic appropriation of the former which alludes elliptically to some now lost speculative interpretation.[18] However, based on a thesis advanced many years ago by Michel Dahood in his magisterial if eccentric commentary on the Psalms (116–18) we may offer an alternative explanation which runs as follows: (1) the Psalms reference is a misunderstanding in which a descriptive phrase was construed as a proper name; (2) this was picked up by the author of Genesis 14 long after the rest of Tanakh had been settled, possibly in the time of the Hasmonean kings of Jerusalem. To explain: the Psalms reference is nothing more than a completely undefined and uncontextualised statement which may or may not be translatable as "a priest after the order of Melchizedek," but could equally have no significance as a proper name. The verse in question reads:

YHWH has sworn	נשבה יהוה
and he will never change his mind.	ולא ינחם
you are	אתה־
a priest for ever	כהן לעולם
in accordance with my purpose	על דברתי[19]
my righteous king	מלכי־צדק
(*or* king of righteousness)	

Taken by itself, it seems unlikely that anyone would ever have identified a proper name in that passage. Parallelism alone would suggest to the reader a pairing of lines 4 and 6 (note that the line division is my own) describing the functions of the subject of the Psalm, and of lines 3 and 5 contrasting "you" and "my will." Only by drawing a box[20] around "malkitsedeq" can we find a proper name here, and inscribe it in the (puzzling and tantalising) context of Psalm 110 where it can be left to do its worst. A natural question which arises is whether the source of Genesis 14:18–20 misread Psalm 110 to inscribe a hitherto unknown person, or (perhaps more likely) used the well-developed eschatology represented by Qumran (see below) to "place" a character in Genesis who was then retrospectively and serendipitously discovered in Psalm 110. A third possibility is that the figure of Melchizedek was current in apocalyptic writings prior to the composition of Psalm 110, and was intentionally deployed in the psalm.

The Genesis passage, as we have seen, represents a clear inter-ruption, an i(nte)rruption, a break-in or act of violence (by someone trying to bury the past or steal the plot?) that succeeds in utterly transforming the significance of the text it bi- or di-sects. What begins life as a sort of boys-own story giving Abram the (unprece-dented) character of a warrior after the manner of Gideon is thus resolved into a claim that, in consequence of his meeting with Melchizedek, Abram has become heir to the priestly-kingship of the mysterious Salem. The terms of this claim are striking: Melchizedek blesses Abram in the name of "El Elyon, Founder (*qnh*) of Heaven and Earth," an expression unique to this passage,[21] then either gives or receives a tithe. The symbolic use of bread and wine, which adds an incontrovertible ritual dimension which no Jewish or Christian reader could possibly miss, can hardly be an accident.[22]

Melchizedek: Messiah of Messiahs

The distinct impression given by the use of Melchizedek in Hebrews is of a text in search of a convincing messianic model for Jesus, one which will combine the central importance of the priestly orders *within Judaism* with the means (through a suitably mysterious and esoteric other) of formulating the claims of Jesus *qua* Messiah in such a way as to *transcend* or *supersede Judaism*.[23]

The importance of Melchizedek is undoubtedly that he permits Hebrews to side-step the really awkward lack of anything even remotely priestly in Jesus' ancestry by introducing a wild card—the undoubtedly scriptural but equally undoubtedly impenetrable Psalm 110:4—which sidesteps the embarrassment (for a deeply tradi-tional view of Judaism) of a fulfilment of the Torah which makes no reference to the cult. The use made in Hebrews of the two Old Testament sources is actually quite subtle: on the one hand making a virtue of the obscurity of the Psalms text (in 5:6, 10; 6:20; 7:11, 15, 17 it is repeated but never elaborated or explained), and on the other hand by overdetermining the Genesis passage in order to make it perfectly clear that Jesus is superior even to Abraham (since Abraham—the inferior—accepted a blessing from Melchizedek—the superior—and gave a tithe to him).[24] Since Jesus is "of the order of Melchizedek" his superiority over Abraham is thus ensured. But the Genesis text is ambiguous at this point, and is open to the interpretation that it was Abram who received a tithe from Melchizedek.[25] The passage in which Melchizedek blesses Abram (vv. 19–20a) continues with the straightforward *vav* consecutive, with-out naming a new subject. This would strongly suggest that the person who gives a tenth (*vayyitten-la maᶜaser mikkol*) to the other is in fact Melchizedek, not Abram. The generalized statement, "a tenth of everything" bears no specific relationship to anything else in the chapter, and so need not have any connection with the booty captured during the earlier raid. Indeed *mikkol* would imply something more numi-nous, more cosmic, and tends to reinforce the suspicion that the giver is Melchizedek: the mysterious priest-king conveys upon Abram both a blessing and a gift. Thus a kind of dynastic inheritance is passed on from one with no ancestry to another equally with no ancestry (Abram is, in an important sense, the first Jew).

The New Testament writer may not have fastened on Melchizedek purely arbitrar-ily. There are signs that the baffling "King of Salem" whom Abram encounters in Genesis 14 had become the focus of interest in fringe circles of pre-rabbinic Judaism. He appears in the Dead Sea Documents[26] and makes an appearance in Philo.[27]

Figure 5.1   Ravenna—Basilica Di S. Vitale. Mosaic showing Abel (on the left) and Melchizedek making their characteristic offerings of, respectively, a lamb and bread and wine. The context appears to be eucharistic, and the recipient (or celebrant?) is God. Photograph Alastair G. Hunter.

A later engagement in 2 Enoch 71–73 confirms him as having more than a walk-on part in the messianic mysticism of the period 100 B.C.E.–100 C.E.[28] The continuing mystical significance of Melchizedek is confirmed in references found at Nag Hammadi, in two of the early church writers who refer to a heretical sect of "Melchizedekians,"[29] and in an intriguing iconographic tradition amongst the Byzantine mosaics at Ravenna.

The earliest evidence of an explicitly eschatological priestly role for Melchizedek is found in the Dead Sea sources, where he is pretty much identified with the archangel Michael. Davila (1998) shows how both are described as at the head of angelic forces in the eschatological battle with the forces of evil, including such characters as Belial and Melchiresha[c],[30] and both are represented as high priestly eschatological redeemers. The matter of a priestly connection is further developed in both 2 Enoch and the rabbinic tradition, which agree in tracing Melchizedek's priestly lineage from that of Noah.[31] In Enoch Melchizedek is presented as Noah's nephew, the result of a miraculous birth in which he appears fully dressed and capable of speech from the body of his recently deceased mother. She, in turn, was both previously barren and (in respect of Melchizedek's birth) a virgin. The (fully clothed) virgin birth of Melchizedek upstages even that of Jesus, and the fact that 2 Enoch may be a first century C.E. product raises the obvious questions as to the source of this legend. Another link which may be important is the formal similarity between the blessing which Noah bestows on Shem in Genesis 9:26a ("Blessed by the Lord my God be Shem") and that of Melchizedek in 14:19a ("Blessed be Abram by God Most High").[32]

Melchizedek's mystical significance appears yet again in the two mosaics from sixth century Byzantine Ravenna referred to above. These portray, respectively, Abel and Melchizedek sacrificing (to God?). In the first (figure 5.1) from the Basilica Di S. Vitale,

Figure 5.2 Ravenna—S. Apollinare in Classe. Abel and Abraham make characteristic offerings (a lamb and Isaac) in a eucharistic setting. Melchizedek's role is ambiguous: he is either priestly celebrant or quasi-divine recipient (compare figure 5.1). Photograph Alastair G. Hunter.

it is clear that Abel and Melchizedek (who are named) are making offerings, with the hand of God indicating acceptance. Abel's lamb and Melchizedek's wine and bread are clearly depicted. Abel—dressed in a sheepskin and a red cloak—stands beside a hut near a tree. Melchizedek, significantly, wears a cassock and behind him is a grand building which may well represent the Temple in Jerusalem. The hand of God is seen appearing from the clouds to accept both offerings. The second (figure 5.2) is more puzzling, and may owe something to the kind of heretical ideas condemned by Hippolytus and Epiphanius (note 30); for here we discern Abel offering a lamb, Abraham offering Isaac and Melchizedek behind the altar on which are placed bread and wine. He wears purple and adopts a Christlike attitude, clearly superior to the others, as if it is *he* who accepts the offerings of the other two. At the very least he is presented as the officiating priest, Christ's *representative*; but what we have already noted suggests the possibility of something more.[33]

This is all very well, and may help to shed light on why the author of Hebrews chose to deploy Melchizedek in attempting to reinvent Jesus as a priestly messiah. There are, however, deeper matters which merit attention before we return to the

Tanakh texts which started the whole thing off. These concern the very idea of "messiah" and how it is to be understood as a working concept in first Jewish and then Christian contexts, and it is to this topic I now turn.

Messianisms

I begin by affirming Derrida's insight that the hope of a messiah has as its very essence the requirement that it remain unfulfilled. This might seem somewhat paradoxical given that my own cultural and religious inheritance is that most messianic of religions, Christianity. But bear with me: even Christians are still waiting for Messiah! The theme of "waiting for Messiah" is found in both Christianity and Judaism, but it takes a somewhat more sceptical form in Judaism, as the following story demonstrates:

> Many Jews have long been skeptical of predictions announcing the imminent arrival of the Messiah. The first-century sage Rabban Yochanan ben Zakkai once said: "If you should happen to be holding a sapling in your hand when they tell you that the Messiah has arrived, first plant the sapling and then go out and greet the Messiah." An old Jewish story tells of a Russian Jew who was paid a rouble a month by the community council to stand at the outskirts of town so that he could be the first person to greet the Messiah upon his arrival. When a friend said to him, "But the pay is so low," the man replied: "True, but the job is permanent."[34]

The unfulfillable character of the messianic hope is seen most painfully, plainly, and poignantly in the historical record. The catalogue of acclaimed and named messiahs with which we began all too quickly and predictably transforms itself into a catalogue of the named and shamed. The story is a depressingly familiar tribute to human folly and gullibility, and of disappointed hopes. John Cleese's character in the film *Clockwise* at one stage exclaims sadly, "It's not the despair . . . I can stand the despair. It's the hope" (Frayn 1986, 68). Even—or especially—the Christian claim for Jesus as messiah foundered on the rock of the perfectly obvious fact that none of the accompanying features of the messianic age had actually been realized. Devices such as the idea of a "hidden" kingdom of God secretly at work, or the silent activity of the spirit within individuals, or (worst of all) the protest that it would have all been infinitely worse had Jesus *not* come only succeed in proving the point. In any event, and despite arguments of that kind, Christianity very quickly came to realize that it too needed the *hope* of a messiah as distinct from the *realized* messiah who was proclaimed in Jesus. Thus Christians (like every other messianic group) wait for the coming (or, face-savingly, the *second* coming) of the messiah. Why should this be so? What is it about the messianic idea that puts it for ever beyond the scope of a concrete event, and real embodiment? There is much that can be said of a general nature. We should first recognise the fundamental principle that ideals can *never* be attained or realized: success in achieving ideals ought never to be complete since, by definition of human imperfection, anything we can fully realise cannot be an ideal. Even if we draw back from using the language of ideals, we can still affirm a common human need: the expectation of a future in which something we may call "messianic" is inscribed. Thus Derrida (1997, 22–23):

> As soon as you address the other, as soon as you are open to the future, as soon as you have a temporal experience of waiting for the future, of waiting for someone to come: that is the opening of experience. Someone is to come, is *now* to come. Justice and peace will have to wait for this coming of the other, with the promise. Each time I open my mouth, I am promising something. When I speak to you, I am telling you that I promise to tell you something, to tell you the truth. Even if I lie, the condition of my lie is that I promise to tell you the truth. So the promise is not just one speech act among others; every speech act is fundamentally a promise. This universal structure of the promise, of the expectation for the future, for the coming, and the fact that this expectation of the coming has to do with justice—that is what I call the messianic structure.

I think, however, that there are stronger arguments for the necessary unattainability of the messianic state based upon the sense that it belongs to the territory of *hope* more than of ideals. Hope is essentially a kind of *supplément* in respect of the everyday: a substitute for our present lack of fulfilment, but at the same time a complement to our lived experience which enlarges our sense of being simultaneously in three time frames—the imagined past, the implacable present, and the idealised future. The role of the messiah (or of the messianic age) for religions which value that concept[35] is to provide a forever deferred difference from our present condition, and yet a *différance* which, however undefinable and elusive, makes a real difference to how we are and what we do. Living in the shadow of the "what if" we behave "as if" and can thus make some sense of what is paradoxically both a period in between, and yet the only time that we will ever live in. The infinite unrealisability of the messianic hope serves to confirm the transience of the present but also infuses it with a passion for that other which we feel is just around a corner, seen out the corner of the eye, glimpsed in the half-light of the moment of waking or in the tantalising dream we feel we ought to be able to recall.

At the same time, we ought to note Derrida's warning/inkling that the coming of Messiah is a matter for what someone else might have described as "fear and trembling" (1997, 24–25):

> But the Messiah might also be the one I expect even while I do not want him to come. There is the possibility that my relation to the Messiah is this: I would like him to come, I hope that he will come, that the other will come, as others, for that would be justice, peace and revolution—because in the concept of messianicity there is revolution—and, at the same time, I am scared. I do not want what I want, and I would like the coming of the Messiah to be infinitely postponed. . . . [A]s long as I ask you the question, "When will you come?", at least you are not coming. . . . So there is some ambiguity in the messianic structure. We wait for something we would not like to wait for. That is another name for death.[36]

Hebrews represents a form of the foolish defiance of *différance* which constantly tempts philosophers and theologians, didacts and preachers, none of whom can (or can afford to) allow their authority to be lessened by the absence of a final resolution, realisation, application, or existential quality in respect of their cherished truths.

By contrast, the pleasing thing about Genesis 14 and Psalm 110 is that, regardless of whatever speculations concerning a Hasmonean source or context we may plausibly bring forward, we simply do not know when or why or for whom these texts came into being. The utterly mysterious "after the order of Melchizedek" of the latter is fully matched by the sudden appearance (and equally abrupt disappearance) of Melchizedek and the archaeologically unknown[37] "Salem" in the former.

The kings in Genesis 14 (up to the point when Melchizedek appears) have no merits to commend them. They engage in all the usual trite activities of their tribe—acquiring territory, squabbling with each other, engaging in fruitless conflict, and leaving the world, on their departure, a generally worse place for their having been in it. This is pretty much in line with the views of the Deuteronomistic school, which tended to be dismissive of the whole experiment in monarchy. They planted their objections at the beginning of the story (in 1 Samuel), repeatedly throughout Kings, and in the post-exilic doctrine of the exile as a punishment. It is more than a little strange, therefore, that by the time of the Chronicler and the later Psalms a royal messianic ideology had developed in Jerusalem which seemed blind to these obvious failings. We do not know why this happened: the most that can be said is that it appeared after all possibility of a real monarchy in Israel seemed to have vanished.[38]

Were it not for the presence of Melchizedek, we might take Genesis 14 to be another sermon on the superiority of the Jewish "democratic" leader who (Gideon-like) gains the victory solely with God's power. But that one "brief encounter" transforms everything. As Melchizedek wanders in from Psalm 110 (a little bemused from his sudden brush with fame) his name and his combination of offices force the reader to look behind the unacceptable face of kingship to see something more positive. And consequently, in the encounter between Abram and Melchizedek, we reevaluate Abram's position. Whether he is the recipient of Melchizedek's benevolence, or is in some sense his equal and more (as we have seen, the detail of vv. 18–20 suggests both), we come to see that Abram is the one *real* king in the whole piece. Melchizedek is a sort of imaginary friend, borrowed from a particular interpretation of Psalm 110:4. The other kings are beneath contempt. But Abram, by laying claim to nothing, comes to embody everything. The *absence* of any formal claim only makes the *reality* the more incontrovertible.

The presence/absence of kingship in respect of Abram mirrors a similar coming together of opposites in the way that the messiah is presented in both Judaism and Christianity. While the predominant reference of *mashiah* in Tanakh is to the anointing of kings, with a minor note in respect of priests (the verb is more frequently used of priests, and once of a prophet),[39] the post-biblical discourse tends to play down that dimension. While both present the messiah as the descendent of David, it is his [*sic*] role in bringing about obedience to torah/the kingdom of love which is brought to the fore. The messiah is the king who does not behave like a king—who brings peace rather than a sword (Isaiah 2, despite the notorious words attributed to Jesus in Matthew 10:34: "Do not think that I have come to bring peace to the earth; I have not come to bring peace, but a sword"), who ensures that there will be abundant prosperity for all (not just the elite at court; thus the visions in Amos 9 and Isa. 11). And it is precisely Abram in Genesis 14 who rises above the selfseeking concerns of those who bear the formal designation "king." They rebel against each other, invade each other's territory, kidnap innocent citizens and demand their property back from Abram who has gone out of his way to rescue them. He on the other hand seeks no reward for his actions.

This crucial ambiguity in the Genesis text as to who gives a tithe to whom opens up a chink in the armour of the New Testament case for Jesus as Melchizedek, because it refuses the argument that Jesus, being "of the order of Melchizedek" is therefore greater than Abram. For if Melchizedek gives a tenth to Abram, then the former is inferior to the latter. From that would follow the superiority of Judaism to Christianity, or more precisely, of Abram to Jesus. For there is a deeper question as to whom Abram "belongs." Three faiths descend from him in some sense, but each also defines itself through people and events long after the time of Abram, who becomes in consequence as sort of meta-founder, one who stands outside and above *all* of the so-called "Abrahamic" religions. Thus the aporia that is constituted by the crucial lack of definition of the subject of "gave" in Genesis 14:20 opens out into a powerful alternative myth/story: Abram as the true role model for the messiah (not something that even Judaism normally works with), superior equally to Judaism, Christianity and Islam—all of which must defer to the non-king, non-messiah Abram who represents by his refusal of these claims a higher truth, a deeper reality. No one, so far as I know, anticipates the second coming of Abraham—yet he "signs" for all three messianic religions. Perhaps in the end it is our shared not-hoping for Abraham that most aptly expresses the messianic principle: the end, as so often, is in the beginning.

Notes

1. See the excellent web site which Jona Lendering has produced giving information about these thirty two messianic claimants from 4 B.C.E. to 1994 (http://www.livius.org/men-mh/messiah/messiah00.html).
2. Note a second reference to Mamre in 18:1; elsewhere in Genesis (23:17, 19; 25:9; 35:27; 49:30; 50:13) this is evidently a place name. For further evidence of dependence on earlier passages, see §3.
3. (1976, 112–20). In particular, "The notion of a coalition between the Hittites, Babylonians, Assyrians, and Elamites is fantastic, and no historian of the early second millennium BC can seriously entertain such a suggestion" (1976, 115).
4. No doubt Egypt confronted both local power bases, such as Hazor, and expanding kingdoms such as those of the Hittites, Hurrians, and Mitannians. None of these, however, had significant influence in the Dead Sea or Negeb regions, and there is certainly no question of the involvement of Elam, Assyria, or Babylon.
5. The Egyptian term for the territories of the Levant.
6. Isaiah 1:9–10; 13:9; Jeremiah 23:14; 49:18; 50:40; Amos 4:11; Zephaniah 2:9. Sodom is mentioned alone in Isaiah 3:9 and Ezekiel 16:46, 48, 49, 53, 55, 56. It is also worth noting that the fifth "city of the plain," Zoar, is a significant place in the Lot traditions.
7. Of course there are genealogies and itineraries which would exceed this percentage; but the present chapter manages to recount no fewer than six dramatic episodes at the same time: the rebellion of the kings of Canaan, the invasion by the eastern potentates, the kidnap of

Lot, Abram's expedition to rescue his nephew, the encounter between Melchizedek and Abram, and the final meeting between Abram and the king of Sodom.

8. Specifically: Emim (Genesis 14:5; Deut. 2:10, 11), Zuzim (Genesis 14:5 =? Zamzumim in Deut. 2:20), Rephaim (Genesis 14:5; 15:20; Deut. 2:11, 20; 3:11, 13; Josh. 12:4; 13:12; 15:8; 17:15; 18:16), Anaqim (Deut. 1:28; 2:10, 11, 21; 9:2; Josh. 11:21, 22; 14:12, 15) and Nephilim (Genesis 6:4; Num. 13:33).

9. Bera, Birsha, Shemeber, and Shinab. One of the cities (Bela) has no named king; it seems likely that the name, by analogy with the others, is more likely to be that of the king than his city (which must presumably have been let slip at some point, leaving only the explanation "that is, Zoar"—see §2 for more on this turn of phrase). Curiously, the name Bela is the only one of the nine royal names which appears elsewhere in Tanakh!

10. בְּרֶע > בְּרַע, "of evil"; בִּרְשַׁע > בִּרְשַׁע, "of wickedness"; שֶׂנֶאָב > שֵׂנָא אָב "hates the father"; שְׁמֵאֶבֶד = שֶׁמְאֶבֶד in some mss (see Speiser 1964, 101) > שֵׁם אָבָד, "the name [God?] has perished"; בֶּלַע > בָּלַע "devour, destroy."

11. Though at a period at least a millennium later than the ostensible date of the contents of Genesis 14; however, in keeping with the more probable period within which the chapter may have been produced.

12. This passage, which opens Derrida's essay, "Des Tours de Babel," speaks both to the general problem of translation and to the special character of the proper name. The conceit of the hollowed-out (translated) narrative like the hollowed-out tower serves to warn those of us in the business of offering readings of the *hollow* nature of what we do. Like a novice translation or a pass-note précis, the story we provide (after careful excavation) turns out to have left the most interesting material on the literary spoil-heap. Our translation of the myth of Melchizedek is itself a myth, at best; a futile gesture at worst; and somewhere in the middle, a contribution to multiplicity.

13. "You shall call his name Jesus [Joshua = "he will save"], for he will save his people from their sins" (Matt. 1:21).

14. "For this Melchizedek, king of Salem, priest of the Most High God . . . is first, by translation of his name, king of righteousness, and then he is also king of Salem, that is, king of peace" (Heb. 7:1–2).

15. "A fantastic series of illusive images or of real forms" (*Chambers English Dictionary*, seventh edition, 1988)—a particularly apt designation given what Derrida has to say about the "hauntology" of post-Marxist messianism (Derrida 1994; cf. Caputo 1997b, 118–34).

16. Of course, familiarity with the afterlife of the texts of the Old Testament and characters from these texts quickly teaches the reader that much of what we take to be rooted in Tanakh is in reality drawn from the vivid imaginations of those who took these often terse sources and gave them dates, places and times, sometimes fleshing them out (quite literally in the case of Sarah who becomes more and more irresistibly beautiful as the tradition advances), and inventing (or recovering?) forgotten legends and fables both to provide childhood stories (Abram in Ur) and to fill in those awkward gaps which the Biblical writers so often and so inconveniently left (a discussion between Isaac and Ishmael, for example, which confers *some* plausibility on the opening of the Akedah).

17. Thus, for example, Fisher, in 1962: "Malkiṣedeq was a Canaanite priest-king, and . . . the encounter between [him] and Abraham could have taken place during the period of Hittite interpenetration (fourteenth and thirteenth centuries), and a written form of this tradition probably existed shortly after the event." Speiser, writing in 1964 (1964, 108–109), is quietly confident: "All this imposes one conclusion above all others which can be of outstanding importance for the study of biblical origins. . . . Abraham was not a nebulous figure but a real person who was attested in contemporary sources." Further, "the notice about

Melchizedek merits a measure of confidence in its own right"; and finally, "The narrative itself has all the ingredients of historicity." Herrmann (1975, 49–50) in his *History of Israel* refers to "Genesis 14 and the traditions which it combines"; and while he stops short of specific dating, clearly assumes a broadly historical context. Thus: "What was originally an account of the defeat of local vassals by the Dead Sea becomes a triumph for Abraham. Even the city-king of Jerusalem, who possibly stands behind Melchizedek of Salem, cannot ignore the new development brought about by the entry of the patriarchs into the land." Westermann (1985, 182–208) provides a useful summary of the literature up to about 1977.

18. This possibility is explored further in the section Melchizedek: Messiah of Messiahs.

19. The word for purpose/design (*dibrah*) is rare: it occurs otherwise three times in Qoheleth (3:18; 7:14; 8:2) and once in Job 5:8—all of which cohere with the sense of a late use of language. Psalm 110 belongs to the section of the Psalter which was last to be formed, and may well be itself as late as the second century B.C.E (see further Hunter [1999, 181–82]). This in turn supports the contention that Melchizedek is a Hasmonean invention, a figure designed to support the ambitions of a short-lived dynasty with aspirations to a grand role in the scheme of things: the priest-kings of Jerusalem.

20. The idea of "boxing in" the proper name is taken from the Egyptian practice of using a *cartouche* to indicate the proper name. This connection comes from the web site http://www.uta.edu/english/hawk/bystory/glas.htm in which Byron Hawk writes: "In *Glas* Derrida takes full advantage of the proper name, the signature. He allows the name the possibility of taking on all possible meanings, using the Egyptians as his stepping stone. In their hieroglyphic writing they could use images for everyday words, but the proper name was problematic. It was necessary to 'invent' the cartouche—to include a frame around the name in order to designate the images as referring to a proper name rather than a common name. For Derrida, the name still harbours these long forgotten common meanings and he uses their chance relationship to the proper name as an inventional device. He brings the sublated proper name back down from its metaphysical position in order to reinscribe it."

21. The closest parallel is in the repeated phrase "Maker (*ʿsh*) of heaven and earth" found in the Psalms of Ascents and in two other late psalms (Hunter 1999, 184).

22. This is illustrated in the next section in terms of the curious and intriguing mosaics from Ravenna.

23. Koosed (2002, 90–95) has some pertinent things to say on this issue from a Jewish perspective.

24. The matter of the blessing is not in itself conclusive, since examples exist of both the blessing of God by humans and of humans by God. Tithes, however, are always given technically to God, even if they are then distributed to priests, Levites, and others.

25. Hamilton (1990, 412–13) admits both the ambiguity and the grammatical point, but adopts the traditional reading (Abram as subject) on the grounds of coherence with the wider narrative. If, however, the passage is from another tradition, this argument fails. Westermann (1985, 187) quotes Schatz's opinion that though "Melchizedek is the grammatical subject, logically Abraham must have paid tithes to the priest-king." Fitzmeyer (1963) argues that Melchizedek gives the tithe, and Emerton (1971) points out that there is a contradiction with vv. 21–23 whichever way the tithe is paid.

26. 11Q13 (Vermes 1997, 500–02); compare 4Q280 (1997, 380) and 4Q544, fr. 2 (1997, 535), which refer to a wicked king Melchireshaᶜ. A further connection with the angel Michael seems likely (see later): Michael is named in 4Q529 (1997, 523) and twice in the War Scroll (1QM) (1997, 181, 189).

27. *Allegorical Interpretations*, III.79–82; *On Abraham*, 235; *The Preliminary Studies*, 99.

28. The date of 2 Enoch is uncertain, since it only survives in a very late manuscript. Estimates vary from as early as the first century B.C.E. to any time prior to the tenth century C.E.; most opt for a date in the first century C.E.

29. NHC IX.1; Hippolytus of Rome (d. ca. 236) *A Refutation of All Heresies*, 7:35–36; Epiphanius of Salamis (d. 403) *Panarion*, 55, 67. It seems, from these accounts, that Melchizedek had become a divine figure in certain quarters, superior even to Christ, and equated sometimes with the Holy Spirit, sometimes with the Son of God.

30. Compare the fragment 4Q280 (Vermes 1997, 380) which speaks of a wicked king Melchiresha^c. Are there echoes here of king Birsha in Genesis 14? Melchiresha^c also appears in one of the fragments of the Testament of Amram (4Q544, fr. 2 [Vermes 1997, 535]). Note also the formal similarity between Belial and three of the five ill-named kings of Canaan: Bera, Birsha', and Bela.

31. *Midrash Rabbah* 44:7 refers to the blessing of Abram in Genesis 14:19. The *name* used is that of Shem, the builder of the Ark, who is thereby identified with Meslchizedek. Similarly, *b.Nedarim* 32b alludes to the belief that God had intended the priesthood to descend from Shem, and quotes Genesis 18:18 at that point, thus confirming the identification of Melchizedek with Shem. The same passage interprets Psalm 110:4 as speaking of Abram.

32. This is in keeping with the sense of a highly eclectic and derivative text which results from a close formal study of the latter Genesis 14. There is very little in that chapter which cannot be traced to other sources.

33. There is a motif here which could be explored further—is there a known Byzantine tradition of the exaggerated importance of Melchizedek?

34. Quoted from Telushkin (1991, 545).

35. And here I note Caputo's discussion of Derrida's uncertainty as to whether "messianism" is some kind on ontological phenomenon awaiting concrete expression, or whether it is defined purely by the exemplars from Judaism, Christianity, and Islam (1997a, 168–70).

36. See also the thought-provoking piece by Sherwood (2002) in which she reads the closing chapter of Qoheleth as a banal, yet poetically powerful reduction of the traditional apocalyptic drama to that of the onset of old age, decay, and death as a small, personal, apocalypse which in many ways typifies the reality of twenty-first-century eschatology.

37. The identification with Jerusalem is *not* indisputable. Contraction of a proper name to its second part is not normal in Hebrew, and there is a nontrivial etymological difference between the forms *shalem* and *yeru-shalaim*. The former can be construed as a *pun* on the latter, but hardly as a simple abbreviation.

38. The messianic or eschatological pieces found appended to Amos and inserted at a couple of places in Isaiah 9 and 11 may seem to run contrary to this claim; however, most commentators see these as later elaborations upon earlier rather bleak texts.

39. Isaiah 61:1, a passage frequently taken to be messianic, which is quoted in the Qumran fragment where Melchizedek appears as messiah.

Bibliography

Anidjar, Gil, ed. 2002. *Jacques Derrida: Acts of Religion*. New York & London: Routledge.
Caputo, John D., ed. 1997a. *Deconstruction in a Nutshell: A Conversation with Jacques Derrida*. New York: Fordham University Press.
———. 1997b. *The Prayers and Tears of Jacques Derrida: Religion without Religion*. Bloomington & Indianapolis: Indiana University Press.

Dahood, Mitchell. 1970. *Psalms III: 101–150.* The Anchor Bible. New York: Doubleday.

Davidson, Robert. 1979. *Genesis 12–50.* Cambridge Bible Commentary: New English Bible. Cambridge: Cambridge University Press.

Davila, James R. 1998 (1996). "Melchizedek, Michael, and War in Heaven." In ttp://www.st-andrews.ac.uk/~www_sd/med_melchizedek_art.html [First published in a slightly different form in *SBL 1996 Seminar Papers*, 259–72. Atlanta, GA: Scholars Press.]

Derrida, Jacques. 1994. *Specters of Marx: the State of the Debt, the Work of Mourning, and the New International.* Trans. Peggy Kamuf with an introduction by Bernd Magnus and Stephen Cullenberg. New York & London: Routledge.

———. 1997. "The Villanova Roundtable: A Conversation with Jacques Derrida." In Caputo, 1997a, 3–28.

———. 2002. "Des Tours de Babel". Trans Joseph F. Graham in Anidjar (ed.), 2002, 102–134.

Emerton, John A. 1971. "The Riddle of Genesis XIV." *Vetus Testamentum* 21:403–39.

Fisher, L. R. 1962. "Abraham and his Priest-King." *Journal of Biblical Literature* 81:264–1270.

Fitzmeyer, J. A. 1963. "Now This Melchizedek . . . (Heb. 7:1)." *Catholic Biblical Quarterly* 25:305–21.

Frayn, Michael. 1986. *Clockwise.* London: Methuen.

Hamilton, Victor P. 1990. *The Book of Genesis.* New International Commentary on the Old Testament. Grand Rapids, Mich.: Eerdmans.

Herrmann, Siegfried. 1975 (1973). *A History of Israel in Old Testament Times.* Trans. John Bowden. London: SCM Press.

Hunter, Alastair G. 1986. "Father Abraham: A Structural and Theological Study of the Yahwist's Presentation of the Abraham Material." *Journal for the Study of the Old Testament* 35:3–27.

———. 1999. *Psalms.* London: Routledge.

Koosed, Jennifer L. 2002. "Sacrifice in the Epistle to the Hebrews." In *A Shadow of Glory*, ed. Tod Linafelt, 89–101. New York & London: Routledge.

Redford, Donald B. 1992. *Egypt, Canaan and Israel in Ancient Times.* Princeton, NJ: Princeton University Press.

Seters, John van. 1975. *Abraham in History and Tradition.* New Haven, NJ: Yale University Press.

Sherwood, Yvonne M. 2002. " 'Not with a Bang but a Whimper': Shrunken Eschatologies of the Twentieth Century—and the Bible." In *Apocalyptic in History and Tradition*, ed. Christopher Rowland and John Barton, 94–116. Sheffield: Sheffield Academic Press.

Speiser, E. A. 1964. *Genesis.* The Anchor Bible. Garden City, NY: Doubleday.

Telushkin, Joseph. 1991. *Jewish Literacy.* New York: William Morrow & Co.

Vermes, Geza. 1997. *The Complete Dead Sea Scrolls in English.* London: Penguin Books.

Westermann, Claus. 1985 (1981). *Genesis 12–26.* Trans. John J. Scullion. Minneapolis: Augsburg Publishing House.

Chapter 6

Jerusalem and Memory: On a Long Parenthesis in Derrida's *Specters of Marx*

David Jobling

Introduction

I have found Derrida's *Specters of Marx* to be a helpful and even an essential book, but it has been mostly neglected by religion and Bible scholars. In the conference sessions on Derrida (at the Society of Biblical Literature Annual Meeting in Toronto, November 2002) from which this volume originates, *Specters* was not covered, and Marx himself was scarcely mentioned in papers other than mine. This fact is perhaps further evidence of that post-Soviet "death of Marx" which is precisely the theme of *Specters*.

But for me Marx remains a name of power. I am a product of the English working class, and have for many years lived in Saskatchewan, a province with deep socialist roots still acknowledged (at least on and off) by its present government. Though my main conversation partners in biblical studies live in the United States, the political discourse to which I am attuned is very different from what flourishes there, and is still somewhat open to some sort of Marxism (though I don't want to exaggerate). My work for the last twenty-five years has been to teach candidates for ordination in the United Church of Canada, a denomination defined by its concern for social justice. My students, though by no means closed, share the common Left skepticism about postmodernism, so it has been challenging to try to get them to take structuralism and its various offspring seriously; to take them seriously precisely as tools for doing theology with social justice in mind. I want to suggest to my students that deconstruction provides essential spectacles through which to look again at the Marxist tradition. In this situation, *Specters* helps. I need only quote what has probably become its best-known sentence: "deconstruction would have been impossible and unthinkable in a pre-Marxist space" (*Specters*, 92).

A few years ago I made substantial use of *Specters* in a biblical commentary (Jobling 1998, 273–81). I found that it helped me say what I needed to say about Israel's relationship to its past. Since that previous work is relevant to what I have to say here, I shall summarize it at some length in the appropriate place. When asked to speak about "Derrida and the Bible" at the conference, I decided to revisit *Specters*. I wanted to bring it, and Marx, into the frame. I wasn't sure how I would approach the book this time, but I anticipated that I would be just as enthusiastic about it as before. I had some recollection of being intrigued by a long parenthesis in the book (*Specters*, 58–61)[1] in which some "biblical figures" (*Specters*, 58) were discussed. Perhaps start there.

I did start there, but the process of producing this essay, both before and after the version I read at the conference, has been very different from what I expected. I have had to come to terms with the fact that *Specters* is not in any overt way a biblical book; biblical texts are not discussed, nor arguments based on them (in contrast with other of Derrida's texts; *The Gift of Death*, on which I had worked for another purpose,[2] comes particularly to mind). (*Specters* is instead an overtly Shakespearean book—full of *Hamlet* and *Timon of Athens*.) What then of the deeply biblical currents that I had previously thought to find in it? I still believe they are deeply *there*, but my new work has led me to think that, at the overt level, Derrida has made the Bible (or suffered it to become) parenthetical to his argument.

Such a situation—the Bible as a presence but somehow an avoided or an *absent* presence in a text—invites and demands deconstruction. I have indeed found myself drawn relentlessly into a work of deconstructing Derrida's text, focusing on the big parenthesis and its biblical figures. I shall propose that the main discourse of *Specters* is somehow parenthetical to this parenthesis, and hence to the Bible. There is nothing ironic or clever in deconstructing Derrida. My model for doing so is precisely Derrida's own practice with the text of Marx, as I will discuss it in the next section. Derrida unpacks Marx's text in ways which sometimes are very hard on Marx. Yet his readings of Marx are always in the end "for Marx" (*Pour Marx*),[3] intended as a continuation of Marx's own project. They are intended to release Marx's texts from themselves, to release (to use a term that Derrida constantly uses and problematizes) the "spirit of Marx." So with my deconstruction of Derrida.

The Main Argument of *Specters*

In this section I shall summarize not the whole of *Specters*, but rather what I shall call its "main line" of argument. This consists of Chapter 1, part of Chapter 3 (from "Let us return," 84), and Chapters 4–5. I shall return later to the bracketed section consisting of Chapter 2 and the first part of Chapter 3.

The book began as Derrida's contribution to a 1993 University of California conference on "Whither Marxism?" (the oral pun on "wither" is exactly to the point), a conference set up to respond to the widely announced "death of communism" after the (then recent) fall of the Soviet empire. Derrida discusses this "death" in Chapter 1. Then, in the latter part of Chapter 3, he powerfully affirms the ongoing necessity of the "event" of Marxism, which is "absolutely unique":

> There is no precedent whatsoever for such an event. In the whole history of humanity . . . such an event . . . has been bound, for the first time and inseparably, to worldwide forms of social organization . . . All of this while proposing a new concept of the human, of society, economy, nation . . . . (*Specters*, 91)

The uniqueness of Marx and communism lies, for Derrida, specifically in their unique testimony to "a day [of justice] belonging no longer to history, a quasi-messianic day" (*Specters*, 21). This "day" is one name for the possibility at the edge of thought to which Derrida refers in a variety of ways (see especially 65–66: "democracy to come," "hospitality without reserve," "alterity that cannot be anticipated"; see also Caputo 1997, 128–31). This "day," this radical possibility, "haunts" all of history (hence the title *Specters*). It haunts in particular the history of western philosophy, the whole ontological tradition. Derrida coins the word "hauntology" (*Specters*, 10 and passim) and makes it to prior to ontology (the words are even closer to being homophones in French than in English). The whole ontological tradition becomes a defense against this haunting. I am haunted, we might say, therefore I am.

The "day of justice" (with "the messianic" and the other synonyms) is the privileged site for deconstruction. It is the "undeconstructible" (*Specters*, 28) for the sake of which the whole project of deconstruction is conceived. "Specter" in fact becomes, in *Specters*, yet another of those words for what deconstruction is after, like "trace" and "*différance*." It is because Marxism is a unique testimony to the day of justice that it stands also in a unique relation to deconstruction. Hence the assertion, already quoted, that "deconstruction would have been impossible and unthinkable in a pre-Marxist space" (*Specters*, 92). Marxism and Marx's texts are therefore not simply to be deconstructed as part of the ontological tradition, since they are one name for what "haunts," in fact deconstructs, that tradition.

Yet the same paragraph makes it clear that there are elements in Marxism which requires deconstruction—"Marxist ontology" or "orthodoxy" (*Specters*, 92). There is need of a deconstruction of Marxism on behalf of Marxism, "for Marx," as I expressed it earlier; a deconstruction of that in Marx which undoes communism's unique testimony to the "day of justice." Marx often gets caught up in the ontological tradition, and this has had tragic consequences in the subsequent history of communism, which has often become a system of defense against the very specter that it began by being. Derrida is not content to see this history merely as a falling away from Marx. He looks (see below) for the origins of the contradictions in Marx's own texts.

One of the ways in which Derrida presents his argument is by distinguishing between "the messianic" and any particular "messianism" (or, sometimes, "messianic eschatology"). The "messianic" is "emancipatory," whereas a "messianism" is a "dogmatics" or a "metaphysico-religious determination" (*Specters*, 89). It is when Marxism turns itself into a particular messianism that it starts off down the disastrous ontological path. The basic difference is that any particular messianism claims to see the end of history from within history, while "the messianic" stands for a radical openness to the future.

It was precisely as a specter that communism was born! Derrida (*Specters*, 37–40) turns to the opening words of *The Communist Manifesto* of 1848: "A specter is haunting Europe—the specter of communism" (1982 [1848], 22). The very first noun in the *Manifesto* is "ghost" or "specter" (*Gespenst*). That of which large parts of the world have recently been celebrating the "death" is—a ghost! This, of course, creates a paradox, which Derrida exploits. A ghost cannot die. A ghost is the result of a death. Derrida deepens the paradox by moving to the immediately following words of the *Manifesto*: "All the powers of old Europe have joined into a holy hunt against this specter." This refers, of course, to the European situation of 1848, but, Derrida suggests, it is just as true in 1993. Again all of Europe (and now one would have to add America and other parts of the world) have joined in the hunt for any remnants that may remain of communism. Europe is as anxious about communism now as in 1848. Is it really dead, might it not find some way of returning, perhaps in some modified form, hard to recognize? The specter of the *Manifesto* still haunts Europe, and beyond. Derrida diagnoses the European response to the fall of the Soviet empire as a manic celebration which cloaks a deep anxiety.

In fact, there is a sense in which the words of the *Manifesto* must be *more* true in 1993. If communism is now dead, it makes sense to be haunted by its specter—being dead is a prerequisite for being a ghost. But how could the Europe of 1848 have been haunted by the specter of a communism not yet born? There is no ultimate difference, says Derrida, since we are speaking not of communism itself, in its particular history, but of that to which it gives its unique testimony, the "day of justice." "And is this day," he asks, "before us, to come, or more ancient than memory itself?" (*Specters*, 21). Europe now and in 1848, but also all of humanity in all its history, is haunted by the day of justice, whether it be conceived as utterly new or unutterably old.

Pursuing his project of deconstructing Marxism "for Marx," Derrida devotes the last part of *Specters*, Chapters 4 and 5, to the deconstruction of a series of Marx's particular texts. His method is to go to some of the many places where Marx himself refers to specters, ghosts, spirits. According to Derrida, Marx does not believe in ghosts; or rather, he wants to not believe in them but is in fact obsessed with them. He is a relentless sniffer-out of the idealist, cultural ghosts which his opponents substitute for real history. He demonstrates the spectrality of many of the key concepts with which his opponents work. In *The German Ideology* Marx actually enumerates ten "specters" conjured up by one of his chief targets in that treatise, Max Stirner (pseudonym of Johann Kaspar Schmidt, 1806–1856); they include "the supreme being," "the spirit of the people," and even (long before Foucault!) "man" (Marx and Engels 1969 [1845–1846], 140–43; see *Specters*, 139–47). But in his attempt to lay all the ghosts, says Derrida, Marx "spooked" himself. In the interests of a "science" of economics, he tried to identify a precise dividing-line between the scientific and anything spectral. In doing so he lost touch with communism as a specter, as that which haunts all of history.

One of the main passages of Marx that Derrida deconstructs is the first part of *The Eighteenth Brumaire of Louis Bonaparte* (1852). Marx discusses the relationship between the communist revolution and earlier revolutions. He gets himself into a muddle by trying to maintain a distinction between the "spirit" of earlier revolutions (good) and their "ghosts" (bad) (Marx 1982 [1852], 118–19). This distinction (Derrida tries to show through his reading) becomes nonsensical. In this work, published a mere four years after the *Manifesto*, Marx seems to have lost touch with the positive force of the *Gespenst* with which the earlier work announced itself. To try to replace it with *Geist* ("spirit of revolution," Marx 1982 [1852], 118) gets him nowhere, and certainly does not serve the aims of Marx the scientist (or "ontologist"). What Marx is really attempting to do in this passage is to deconstruct the French Revolution; but Derrida has to deconstruct Marx's text in order to restore its own deconstructive force.

Developing the same argument, Marx tries to cut himself entirely loose from the past: "The social revolution of the nineteenth century cannot draw its poetry from the past, but only from the future" (Marx 1982 [1852], 119, see *Specters*, 114). "Earlier revolutions required . . . recollections," but the communist revolution "must let the dead bury their dead" (Marx 1982 [1852], 119). These statements represent for Derrida a culminating point in Marx's efforts to exorcize ghosts: they are an attempt to do away with all memory! This, Derrida points out, is exactly what the post-Soviet world would like to do with Marx himself, and with Marxism—lose the memory of them. Keeping the memory of Marxism, keeping it as *Gespenst*, is a major part of the aim of *Specters*.

Derrida's homage to Marx is always palpable, for example in his tribute to Marx's openness to the future and to Marx's writing of *self-critique* into the theory of revolution (*Specters*, 88–89).[4] Derrida critiques Marxism in such a way as to reinvigorate the *self*-critique which belongs to its very nature, but with which it sometimes loses touch.

My Earlier Use of *Specters*

It was upon this main line of argument of *Specters* that I drew in my *1 Samuel*, 1 Samuel is the book of the Bible that tells of Israel's transition to a monarchy; it has become the official, canonical "take" on this transition. But transition from what? This question has exercised me for as long as I can remember. My students know the answer. Before becoming a monarchy, Israel was a radically egalitarian society. For them, the Bible's fundamental teaching is egalitarian. This implies that the Bible is their reliable ally in their quests for social justice. They accept, because they want or need to accept, the picture of a radically egalitarian early Israel presented by Norman Gottwald in *The Tribes of Yahweh*.[5]

My own starting point was Martin Buber's classic *Kingship of God*. Long before Gottwald (and without his sociological insight), Buber argued that Israel before the monarchy had been a theocracy (hence his title), having no human leadership that might set itself up as separate from divine leadership, and hence without significant human hierarchy. For Buber, this was an experiment in human existence of historic importance and its ending was a tragedy: "Something has been attempted, but it has failed" (1967, 83). These haunting words came back to me when I started reading Derrida on the "death" of communism.

A big problem with this picture of earliest Israel is that the Jewish Bible does not—except in a handful of passages—subscribe to it. Gottwald admits this and employs a method he believes capable of handling the contradiction; Buber tends (as also does Pixley) to read the biblical texts selectively. The handful of passages—the Songs of Deborah (Judg. 5) and Hannah (1 Sam. 2:1–10), Jotham's fable (Judg. 9:8–15), and Samuel's prediction of "the ways of the king" (1 Sam. 8:10–18)—say all that Buber or Pixley could wish. But these passages are small islands in a sea of narrative which describes (particularly in Judges) an Israel far from any social ideal, an Israel which might well pine for monarchy as a way of cleaning up the mess (Judg. 21:25, etc.).

If it is really the case that early Israel had and lost an egalitarian order of society, the memory of it has largely disappeared—at least so far as official, canonical memory is concerned. Israel's loss is (to use Maurice Blanchot's words) a "lost loss" (Blanchot 1995, 41): the process of losing has been forgotten along with the thing lost. Hence I reached the conclusion that 1 Samuel records not only a transition, but also a loss of memory, or the suppression of a memory, of what preceded the transition. So great has been the impact of monarchy that it has wiped out most of the traces of that which came before.[6]

Specters very much helped me to think this problem through. It enabled me to see the myth of egalitarianism and theocracy in its origins as that which *haunted* Israel. Recall the haunting words already quoted from *Specters*—"is [the day of justice] before us, to come, or more ancient than memory itself?" (*Specters*, 21). This is a question to ask of the prophets: is the "day of justice" that they demand an appeal to an ancient national memory of which they are the guardians, or is it called into being through their very demand, and then turned into a national "memory"? Did the prophets *remember* an Israel other than the one they lived in, or did they *create* it? Could even they answer such a question?

If there was such a process of forgetting, its trace will surely remain, and a deconstruction of the text will find it. I found that trace above all in the figure of Samuel. Samuel is a judge, and therefore represents the old order. His consecration to service in the temple is announced by a powerful evocation of "the day of justice" (Hannah's song), and he himself on one occasion evokes that day ("the ways of the king"). But this same Samuel must also be the founder of the new order, the maker of kings. It is on account of this impossible dual role, I argued, that Samuel must live on and on. He lives on past two full-dress stagings of his "death": as a judge he ought to die after the announcement of the peace Israel enjoyed throughout his life (1 Sam. 7:12–17); as a patriarch of Israel he ought to die after his valedictory speech (1 Sam. 12). But he lives on, and even after he does finally die, he—uniquely in the Bible—returns as a ghost (1 Sam. 28:3–25)!

In the discussion of Marx's convoluted relationship with the past to which I referred earlier, Derrida says of Marx: "He too has died, let us not forget, and more than once" (*Specters*, 114). This is an uncannily accurate description also of Samuel. The process of "forgetting Marx" in which much of the world is now engaged seemed to me exactly to parallel Israel's forgetting, under the monarchy, of what had preceded it.

The Middle Section of *Specters*

I omitted from my earlier summary of *Specters* a large middle section, consisting of Chapter 2 and most of Chapter 3. In this section Derrida mainly does two related things.

First, he discusses the new "dominant discourse" (keeping and problematizing this Marxist terminology) that announces the death of Marx and communism. He deals with its manic anxiety (see above) and with its relations to politics, academics, and the mass media. His main example is Francis Fukuyama's *The End of History and the Last Man*. As is now well known, Fukuyama sees the "end" of history in the universal acceptance of liberal democracy and market economics. Derrida's main comment here is that Fukuyama fluctuates opportunistically between idealist and empirical discourse. Up to a point, Fukuyama presents the triumph of liberal democracy throughout the world as an established fact. But whenever he comes up against evidence that this triumph has not, in fact, been worldwide, he shifts into an idealist (Hegelian) mode: liberal democracy, as the only political discourse still viable on a global scale, is sure to be universally adopted (sooner rather than later, it seems). In other words, Fukuyama bases his eschatological scenario on "facts" when it seems plausible to do so (fact #1 being precisely the "end" of communism), but resorts to talk of tendencies and inevitabilities when the facts seem bleak.

The second thing Derrida does is to remind us just how bleak the "empirical" facts are, how abundant is the evidence that speaks against Fukuyama's worldview, how peculiarly implausible a historical moment Fukuyama has chosen, in fact, to read a positive promise in what is going on in the world, Europe and America not excepted.

The culmination of the middle section of *Specters* is a litany of ten intractable current world problems, such as foreign debt (*Specters*, 81–84). Derrida calls them "the ten plagues" (*Specters*, 86). These ten plagues surely counterpoint the "ten ghosts" which Marx hunts down (perhaps we may say, busts) in *The German Ideology*, and which Derrida discusses much later in *Specters* (139–47; see above). Derrida actually calls this list a "Decalogue" (*Specters*, 142), and this second biblical term, along with "plagues," heightens the sense of counterpoint between the two groups of ten. In a flight of fancy, Derrida imagines the ghosts as a soccer team with one player missing (*Specters*, 139; "one may well wonder which one it is"). Pursuing this fancy, I find myself imagining a match. It is between the Idealist Ghosts and the Empiricist Plagues. It is surely being keenly contested, since apparently one member of each team has already been red-carded. I assume that it will be fought to a draw. (As you see, the *sports* discourse to which I am attuned is also not an American one!)

It is in the middle section of *Specters* that the Derridean parenthesis occurs to which my title refers, and to the reading of which I will shortly turn. But vis-à-vis the book's main line of argument, this middle section gives the impression of being itself a parenthesis (so that *my* parenthesis would be a parenthesis in a parenthesis). My soccer fantasy highlights an important aspect of the relationship between the middle section and the main line of argument, namely the opposition of ideal to empirical. What is Derrida doing in the middle section? In *my* parenthesis he will say "We will not oppose some vulgarly 'empirical' evidence [to Fukuyama]" (*Specters*, 61, and see below). Yet the whole middle section seems to do precisely that, climaxing, as we have seen, in the "ten plagues." Derrida seems, like Fukuyama himself, to be hung up between ideal and empirical. His main argument in *Specters*, an argument that I find magnificent, is under the rubric of the ideal. He exposes, even going beyond and behind Marx himself, what it is in Marxism that rules out the facile empiricism (in Marxist terms, "reification"; see Bottomore 1983, 411–13), which would adjudge Marxism dead because the Soviet empire has fallen. Yet in the middle section (parenthetically?) he himself falls back on empirical defenses.

This contradiction will follow us into the parenthesis.

The Argument of the Parenthesis

The parenthesis with which I am primarily concerned is enormous, covering nearly four pages (*Specters*, 58–61). It announces itself very emphatically, at both ends, as *being* a parenthesis: ". . . we can only indicate here in parentheses" (*Specters*, 58); "End of this parenthesis" (*Specters*, 61, though oddly these are not the last words of the parenthesis).

The parenthesis begins at the moment when the discussion of Fukuyama has highlighted two "biblical figures" (*Specters*, 58) employed by Fukuyama in his introduction: "good news" (Fukuyama 1992, xiii) and "Promised Land" (1992, xv). Derrida gives two reasons for pursuing (parenthetically) "these biblical figures"; first, that they "play a role that seems to exceed the simple rhetorical cliché they appear to be" (*Specters*, 58); second, that they focus our attention on the Middle East. Derrida latches onto the latter point with extraordinary rhetorical force. Of all the empirical evidence giving the lie to Fukuyama's optimism, the Middle East is the supreme instance. "The war for the 'appropriation of Jerusalem' is today the world war. . . . it is today the singular figure of [the world's] being 'out of joint' " (*Specters*, 58, with reference, of course, to *Hamlet*).

Still within this opening paragraph, Derrida asks what contribution Marxism can make to analyzing the Middle East situation, and concludes: "Marxism remains at once indispensable and structurally insufficient" (*Specters*, 58). To make its contribution it will need to be "transformed and adapted to new conditions" (*Specters*, 58), a self-transformation which would be "in conformity with . . . the *spirit of Marxism*" (*Specters*, 59, his emphasis). Derrida is here clearly alluding to his main line of argument in *Specters*, particularly the radically self-critical and self-transforming impulse he sees in Marx (see above). One of the reasons he gives for Marxism's "structural insufficiency" is of special interest to us. Because the situation in the Middle East focuses on the conflicts among "three *other* messianic eschatologies" (my emphasis), Marxism is insufficient to the extent that it remains itself "a messianic eschatology" (*Specters*, 59). As I indicated earlier, Derrida uses the latter term in a decidedly negative sense. Projecting itself as a messianic eschatology is part of the ontological or scientific error in Marxism (see above, on *Specters*, 88–92).

In the following paragraph (*Specters*, 59) Derrida chooses to place one of his major statements about Marxism and deconstruction. In the face of "ontological Marxism," what is needed is a work of deconstruction. But "we will not claim that this messianic eschatology common both to the religions it criticizes and to the Marxist critique *must be simply deconstructed*" (*Specters*, 59, my emphasis). Why? Because of Marxism's privileged position vis-à-vis the entire project of deconstruction. Derrida puts it this way:

> . . . what remains irreducible to any deconstruction, what remains as undeconstructible as the possibility itself of deconstruction is, perhaps, a certain experience of the emancipatory promise; it is perhaps even the formality of a structural messianism, a messianism without religion, even a messianic without messianism, an idea of justice—which we distinguish from law or right and even from human rights—and an idea of democracy—which we distinguish from its current concept and from its determined predicates today.
>
> (*Specters*, 59)

The thought here is not different from what I tried to expound above (in relation to *Specters*, 88–92): Derrida's whole project of deconstructing Marx *for Marx*. I highlight this paragraph because of where it is located, following the reference to the "religions of the Book" (*Specters*, 58).

There follows a "return" (*Specters*, 59) to Fukuyama (making the far-reaching discussion of Marxism, messianism, and deconstruction into yet another parenthesis?) Derrida discusses the relationship between the two biblical figures of gospel and Promised Land, and now explicitly characterizes them as "Christian" and "Jewish" respectively (*Specters*, 60). He notes that, while for Fukuyama "good news" is an unambiguously positive figure, "Promised Land" is to some extent associated with a negative ("natural science . . . does not deliver us to the Promised Land itself" [Fukuyama 1992, xv]). With a caution to himself that "We must be careful not to overinterpret," he decides that "one can form at least an hypothesis about which angle Fukuyama chooses to privilege in the eschatological triangle [sc. Christianity, Judaism, Islam]" (*Specters*, 60). The combination in Fukuyama of the positive use of a Christian figure, the somewhat negative use of a Jewish one, and the complete neglect of Islam implies for Derrida a Christian bias, and he goes on to suggest that Fukuyama's main inspiration comes from a reading of Hegel which is very heavily Christian. Fukuyama's vision, Derrida concludes, is of just such a "Holy Alliance" (*Specters*, 61) as *The Communist Manifesto* refers to (Derrida even drags in the pope, just as the *Manifesto* [Marx and Engels 1982 (1848), 22] does).

The parenthesis ends with some further remarks along this line, preceded by the statement I have already referred to, that "We will not oppose some vulgarly 'empirical' evidence" to Fukuyama's position, and by a deferral of further discussion of "the problem of empiricity" (*Specters*, 61).

A Critical Reading of the Parenthesis

This is a very weighty parenthesis! It is weighty not only as to length, but also as to the importance of the topics it takes up, particularly the discussion of Marxism, messianism, and deconstruction (almost as substantial as that in 88–92, and, in the present organization of *Specters*, preceding it). It will also transpire that parts of the subsequent main line of argument of *Specters* are critically dependent on what is said within the parenthesis (e.g., the oblique reference to Iraq in 120: "Babylon, that other center of our Middle-Eastern ellipsis [*sic*],[7] still today"). I suggested earlier that the whole middle section of *Specters* may be parenthetical to the main argument. In that case, is the parenthesis in 58–61, as a parenthesis in a parenthesis, functioning like a double negative, and reinserting the main argument into the middle section?

My particular interest in this essay is why the parenthesis comes at just the moment when the Bible is introduced into *Specters*, in any substantial way, for the first time. The parenthesis begins with the "biblical figures," introduced by Fukumaya, of "gospel" and "Promised Land." Even this beginning arouses some suspicion, since in the case of "gospel" it is not at all clear that Fukuyama intends a biblical allusion at all (though he certainly does in the case of "Promised Land"). Fukuyama does not use the term "gospel"; this is Derrida's translation of "good news," which Fukuyama (1992, xiii) may be employing in a more general sense.

It is as if Derrida were looking for an occasion to take up the Bible, but to do so only parenthetically. Be that as it may, once started, he quickly extends the biblical discussion into the larger area of messianism, particularly the "messianic eschatologies" of "the three religions said to be religions of the book" (*Specters*, 58).

This whole dynamic of rendering the Bible important and yet parenthetical will be repeated towards the end of *Specters*. On pages 167–69, Derrida returns to the Bible and its messianisms, and again the discussion is a substantial one. Though it is not this time literally in parentheses, it is in effect so, since it comes under the rubric of that in which "we cannot get involved here" (*Specters*, 167).

Why are the Bible's only substantial contributions to *Specters* parenthetical ones? The question is the more compelling when one considers how central to the book is the concept of "the messianic," which inevitably implicates religion and the Bible. Why is "the messianic" highlighted while the particular biblical messianisms are somehow hidden away?

Any other biblical allusions in *Specters* are passing ones (as I said at the outset, this is not one of Derrida's overtly biblical texts). It is perhaps worth asking, however, whether the fact that he introduces both the ten ghosts and the ten modern disasters (the two sides in my soccer match) under biblical figures (plagues, Decalogue), does not constitute further evidence of a substantial subterranean biblical presence.

The difficulty that Derrida seems to be having with the category of empiricity is very much present in the parenthesis. The words "We will not oppose some vulgarly 'empirical' evidence" (to Fukuyama's position; *Specters*, 61) obviously refer back to Derrida's evincing (*Specters*, 58) of present-day Jerusalem as the supreme instance of the evidence counting against Fukuyama's claims. They seem then, like a throwaway line shrugging off (while admitting) that "opposing empirical evidence" is exactly what he has been doing in the parenthesis (and will go on doing). The modifier "vulgarly" inevitably (and surely consciously) brings to mind "vulgar Marxism," the facile economic determinism with which Marxism is often equated, and which is surely the extreme instance (or even parody) of the "ontological" Marxism which Derrida so determinedly combats in the main argument of *Specters*. Is he not by this throwaway line rather desperately trying to offset the impression that Fukuyama has drawn him onto dangerous empirical ground?

My final problem with the parenthesis carries me onto dangerous ground of my own (it certainly proved so in the conference session; see below). Earlier, I summarized Derrida's argument that Fukuyama privileges Christianity within the "eschatological triangle" of the three religions of the book (*Specters*, 60). In the course of this argument he criticizes Fukuyama's glib exclusion of Islam from the scope of his "end of history" ("But now, outside the Islamic world, there appears to be a general consensus that accepts liberal democracy's claims" [Fukuyama 1992, 211]). But this argument begs to be turned back on Derrida. At least in *Specters*, Fukuyama's neglect of Islam—certainly lamentable—is simply repeated by Derrida himself.[8] And we need to ask Derrida, as he asks Fukuyama, which angle of the "triangle" *he* is privileging. Judging by the neglect of the Islamic angle, and the extremely negative rhetoric about the Christian, evidently the Jewish. Though I perhaps need to recall Derrida's own warning to himself, "We must be careful not to overinterpret" (*Specters*, 60), it seems to me that he implies, in the parenthesis, especially in his discussion of Fukuyama and Hegel (*Specters*, 60–61), a contrast between Christian and Jewish messianisms—favorable to the latter—over the issue of seeing the end from the beginning. The same tendency is clearer in his return, at the end of the book (*Specters*, 167–69) to the biblical discourse of the parenthesis. There he discusses the fundamental question of whether particular messianisms, especially biblical ones, can have anything to contribute to "an atheological hermeneutic of the messianic," especially to its "waiting without horizon of expectation" (*Specters*, 168). Typically, he answers with a "yes and no," but in doing so he seems at least momentarily to privilege "the Old Testament" type of messianism. Shortly after the publication of *Specters*, he writes elsewhere: "Jewishness here comes down, in its minimal essence . . . to the openness to the future" (1995a, 34).

If Derrida does intend such a contrast—if there is a Jewish-Christian thing going on in the parenthesis and in the rest of *Specters*—then he really ought to say more about Marx the Jew and Derrida the Jew, as well as Hegel the Christian and (I assume though I have not been able to obtain information) Fukuyama the Christian.

The Biblical Figures in the Parenthesis

Having thus far pursued a work of deconstruction on Derrida's text, I want now to discuss the issues I have raised in a more constructive way, by examining the "biblical figures" in his parenthesis. But I count three figures, rather than two: in addition to "gospel/good news" and "Promised Land," also "Jerusalem." In fact it is in this third figure that I am most interested. In the parenthesis, Derrida introduces Jerusalem very much in the realm of the empirical. But his wish not to use Jerusalem as "vulgarly 'empirical' evidence" (*Specters*, 61) seems to invite me to explore it as a figure, along with the other two. I was pleased to note that Derrida himself refers later to the "figure of Jerusalem" (*Specters*, 167).

1. *Gospel/good news*. I am content to take these as synonyms. There is a strong tendency recently to reserve the word "gospel" for the literary genre, and to translate *euangelion* in the New Testament as "good news" (so, almost always, the NRSV). "Good news" is certainly very much linked in the New Testament with a messianism that sees the end from the beginning: for example, "the good news . . . will be proclaimed throughout the world, . . . and then the end will come" (Matthew 24:14). On the other hand, "good news" is very often a particular event in the lives of particular people, notably the poor and oppressed, as they live in the vicissitudes of history. This is the case especially in Luke. It is also a theme of Second and Third Isaiah (40:9; 41:27; 52:7; 61:1; see also Nahum 1:15), so that "good news" may not be described as exclusively a New Testament or Christian figure.

The Christian mandate to preach "the gospel" everywhere has certainly had some doleful consequences (see, e.g., Dube 1998), and Derrida's pejorative or parodic reference to Fukuyama's own "gospel" is quite apt (interestingly, *The Communist Manifesto* [Marx and Engels 1982 (148), 58] refers in a similar parodic way to "the gospel" of utopian socialism). But this is only one side of the picture; biblical "good news" has potential for a much more positive relationship to Derrida's "messianic."

2. *Promised Land*. This is not, in so many words, a biblical figure at all. In biblical statements of the promise of a land the verb is active: "the land God promised" (very often, for example, in Deuteronomy). The receiver of the promise of land is much more often "your (or their) *fathers*" than the present generation. This seems to me important in relation to Derrida's argument about Marx; there is promise of land only in relation to a specific past, and the retention of the land (as the biblical statements frequently reiterate) depends on connectedness to that past.

Even more importantly, the land is *always*, in a sense, promised but not yet received. Derrida's reference to the land's being refused to Moses (*Specters*, 60)—and, he should have added, to Moses' entire generation—is a part of this dynamic but not the whole of it. More striking still is the fact that the Torah ends with Israel outside the land, looking in; the entry into the land lies beyond the bounds of this most sacred part of the canon. "Next year in Jerusalem." Derrida is certainly right to see this "always not yet" as closely related to his "messianic" (and it is fascinating that even the eschatologically inclined Fukuyama uses "Promised Land" in a way that signifies delay or doubt). Especially when viewed in this light, the figure of "Promised Land"—as it has functioned in the recent history of Zionism and in the development of the concept of "Greater Israel"—has at least as much to answer for in the way of historical tragedy as ever "gospel" does.

3. *Jerusalem*. This brings me back to my earlier use of *Specters* in *1 Samuel* (see my third section above). Derrida, as we have seen, thinks of Jerusalem first in the empirical sense. My own point of connection is also with empirical Jerusalem, though it is the Jerusalem of long ago. The event, I argued, in which Israel abandons or "loses" its past is the establishment of the Davidic kingship (Jobling 1998, 254–59 and the whole of Chapter 11). And the very center of this event is "the appropriation of Jerusalem" (to use Derrida's words) by David. The gaining of Jerusalem, we might say, is the loss of memory.

Jerusalem is a figure (the singular figure, I might say, à la Derrida) of the loss of historical memory in the Bible. We see this within the Hebrew Bible in the "Jerusalem theology" based on the everlasting covenant, the divine promises of permanence for the temple on Mount Zion and the monarchy of David's line (see the good brief account in Humphreys 1990, 55–64). In this theology (classically expressed in "royal psalms" like 132 or "Zion psalms" like 46), Jerusalem is the place of Yahweh's permanent dwelling, eternally protected by him, a safeguard from vicissitude, from history. Monarchy, as soon as it is founded, *must* appropriate Jerusalem, for it must enter into Jerusalem's timelessness. With David's appropriation of Jerusalem Israel enters into a form of religion where kingship and the royal city are celebrated as part of an eternal and changeless state of affairs, one which not only must "forget" anything that preceded it, but must deny that anything *essentially different* did or could have preceded it. And in the moment of the creation of this ideal,

I argued in *1 Samuel*, Israel loses its other ideal, the day of justice—and canonically loses the loss.

In this process occurs the birth of the concept of "messianism." Anyone concerned with messianisms or even "the messianic" needs to attend to the prototypical messianism of David. It is very much the type of messianism that sees the end from the beginning. The primary work of the text 1 Samuel, I argued, is to establish (in the face of a number of counterindications) the *inevitability* of David's rise to kingship. The characters (Samuel, Jonathan, Abigail, even Saul) vie with each other in signaling where the story is definitely going (Jobling 1998, 235; only David himself seems doubtful—see below).

I may continue this line of thought about the Hebrew Bible a little further by following Derrida. In the section at the end of *Specters* to which I have several times returned, he figures the messianism of the Jewish Bible not in David, but in Abraham's "Abrahamic messianism" (*Specters*, 167). I do not know whether he avoids David because he realizes that David's messianism is of the kind he resists. There is no need for such an explanation, given the prominence of "the Abrahamic" in another work of his (see Anidjar 2002, 3–11 and passim). Here in *Specters*, as in that other work, the point of "Abrahamic" is that it encompasses all three "religions of the Book" (cf. Derrida 2002b, 56, "Abrahamic religion"); the promise to Abraham (more accurately, to Abram) comes before the birth of Ishmael and Isaac. But even if we allow the term "Abrahamic messianism," can we regard it as any different from the Davidic? We should not forget that (also before the birth of his sons) Abram makes his submission to Jerusalem (Genesis 14). (Parenthetically, I recall that in his paper for the conference out of which this volume comes, Gil Anidjar referred to the war in Genesis 14 as "the first world war." What an uncanny comment on Derrida's "The war for the appropriation of Jerusalem is today the world war" [*Specters*, 58]!) Abram makes his submission to "King Melchizedek of Salem," a kind of pre-David (but of course there is no pre- or post- in Davidic theology); Melchizedek, the one "without father, without mother, without genealogy, having neither beginning of days nor end of life" (Heb. 7:3). That is, without memory!

It is thus firmly on the basis of the Hebrew Bible that the New Testament carries this sort of messianism further. In the gospels, Jerusalem is the place where the drama of redemption *must* be enacted. It is also the place whose renewal, New Jerusalem, is the very end of the very end (Revelation 21), the ultimate figure of a future known in advance. Jerusalem in these respects continues to stand for loss of memory. The drama of redemption signals the annulment of memory in a way analogous to what I have said about David's kingship; for memory of the time before the redemption, *as a time that did not know its end*, is lost when the end becomes known (one might pursue this as a contribution to "the quest of the Historical Jesus"!) The end of Revelation presumably signals the end of *all* memory.

The Empirical Middle East

What remains most unresolved in Derrida's parenthesis is the empirical Middle East, the "world war" for the "appropriation of Jerusalem" (*Specters*, 58). Derrida rhetorically creates Jerusalem as neutral, a piece of real estate fought over by the three "religions of the book." He fails to pay due attention, in the parenthesis, to the "*figure* of Jerusalem" (*Specters*, 167, my emphasis; even this later discussion [*Specters*, 167–69] does not remedy the problem in any adequate way). I believe it needs to be said that Derrida's evenhandedness (to put it at its best) fails to foster a "day of justice" for the Middle East. At the session out of which this essay came, I got into considerable trouble for saying this, but I believe it has to be said.[9]

The current dynamics around Jerusalem have been played out before. Biblical scenarios, established millennia ago, continue to be reprised. I do not want to affirm this in the sort of extreme way that makes current history simply a playing out of "biblical prophecy" (and I am most ready to acknowledge, as a context for the following remarks, the profoundly negative effects on the Middle East of Christian messianisms that think along these lines). But neither can we at all underestimate the effects of the biblical scenarios, whether consciously acknowledged and repeated, or internalized at less conscious levels, in various Judaism(s), Christianity/ies, and Islam(s).

"Jerusalem," I have argued, figures a very ancient type of Jewish messianism. It is for me, and has been from its origin, a destructive type of messianism. It has been specifically taken up in Christianity, beginning in the New Testament, with equally negative effects. It is a messianism very much of the type that sees the end from the beginning (see above on the "inevitability" of David's rise to kingship and appropriation of Jerusalem). It figures a loss of memory of the "day of justice." If I am right that Derrida is at some level probing the possibility that Jewish messianism is more usable for the Marxist project than other messianisms, he needs to come clean about the "Jerusalem" messianism. His appeal to "Abrahamic messianism" (*Specters*, 167) seems very much like an avoidance of the prototypical messianism, the Davidic (no one anointed Abraham!). To put it more sharply, and this is the essential point of my essay: does Derrida make the Bible parenthetical, in a book which seems to cry out for deep biblical analysis (given above all the centrality of the category of "the messianic"), because of apprehension over where such analysis might carry him?

Even the Palestinians, in a strange way, figure in the ancient biblical scenarios, via their etymological relationship to the Philistines. In my use of Derrida in *1 Samuel* (1998, 280) I commented on David's first visit to Jerusalem. It comes in 1 Sam. 17:54, long before his kingship, and it is extremely curious. He takes to Jerusalem (and apparently leaves there) the severed head of the Philistine Goliath. This episode seems wholly anachronistic (in exactly the way that Abram's visit to Jerusalem in Genesis 14 does); Jerusalem is not yet an Israelite city (note Judg. 19:10–12). But of course the Jerusalem theology posits its own timelessness; it cannot remember "no Jerusalem." It is in mythic time that there "was" a monarchic Jerusalem where David could deposit his trophy—the dismembered (forgotten) remains of the past.

The ending of the First Book of Samuel is placed, with amazing precision, at a point where David faces a choice—a real choice, within the narrative world the book creates (Jobling 1998, 286–88). Should he move on towards Jerusalem, toward kingship—as every prophecy has told the reader he must do—or should he cast his lot with the Philistines? Is this not the choice of the state of Israel, between a fortress Israel centered on Jerusalem (empirical, figural) and coexistence with those who, by the strange chance of history and etymology, are the new "Philistines," the Palestinians? In the old story, the overcoming of the Philistines becomes the essential condition for David's triumph and appropriation of Jerusalem; the Goliath's head episode establishes this point with brevity and precision. Small wonder that in a certain kind of current "Jerusalem theology" the overcoming of the Palestinians is likewise essential.

The thing I got into most trouble for at the session was quoting Marc Ellis, the controversial Jewish theologian. He said, on a recent trip to Saskatoon, that, in what is now happening in Israel and Palestine, Judaism is dying. What made me want to borrow that particular form of words was the importance in Derrida of a death, the "death of communism," or of Marx. I do not intend to go back on what I said, nor do I expect that a bit of further explanation here is going to change anyone's reaction. But I do believe that I did not make myself adequately clear. What manner of "death" are we talking about here? For Derrida (and, as he says, many in his generation) "a certain (and I emphasize *certain*) end of communist Marxism did not await the recent collapse of the USSR . . . All that started—all that was even *déjà vu*, indubitably—at the beginning of the '50s" (*Specters*, 14, his emphasis). He is speaking of the sort of death that comes not in weakness and defeat, but in a certain kind of triumph. Communism, to put it in an altogether too facile way (Derrida endlessly and rightly hedges his remarks), died in Stalin rather than in the fall of the Soviet empire.

Of this kind of death in "victory," the supreme recent example (though there are a great many from which to choose) is the death of a certain Christianity in the Holocaust. It is in entirely conscious relation to this latter "death" that Ellis speaks of a death of Judaism. It is the death (as Derrida might put it) of *a certain* Judaism, the Judaism which has provided a unique religio-ethical testimony, from earliest times and throughout history, to the "day of justice." The memory of that kind of Judaism is, for Ellis, now being lost in Jerusalem.

It is the Judaism, perhaps, of an Emmanuel Lévinas or, more personally for me, of an Abraham Joshua Heschel. (I am fully aware that both of them espoused some form of Zionism; but neither lived to see the present situation.) I don't know how Heschel's name resonates with a new generation; perhaps simply as the author of a still readable book on the prophets. But I remember, during another war, marching on Washington behind Abraham Joshua Heschel and John Coleman Bennett.[10] I also remember a story about Heschel. Challenged to explain how a religion of history could find a potent symbol in the static Jerusalem, he said, "Ah, but Jerusalem is an event!"[11] In the context of the time (about 1960), Heschel was undoubtedly responding to the powerful emphasis on the Exodus as event in the (mostly Christian) "biblical theology" movement. Well, in the face of Derrida's "world war," we certainly need a Heschel, or someone, to make Jerusalem into an event, into a figure for the remembering, rather than the forgetting, of the "day of justice."

Conclusion

The SBL session to which I contributed had the title "Reading a Page of Scripture (With a Little Help from Derrida)." He has certainly, in the past, helped me to read many pages of scripture, perhaps all the pages. This essay has turned out, rather, to be "Reading Four Pages of Derrida (With a Little Help from the Scripture)."[12] But is not this just the sort of reversal that Derrida has taught us to accept, expect, demand?

Notes

1. For convenience I shall reference Derrida *Specters* in this unconventional way.
2. See the large extract from this work included in Jobling, Pippin, and Schleifer 2001, 334–52.
3. This is my own, not Derrida's expression, borrowed from the title of Louis Althusser's famous work. I believe that in using it I am being true to Derrida.
4. Derrida might at this point have referred to the superb passage just a little later in *The Eighteenth Brumaire*: "Proletarian revolutions . . . criticize themselves constantly, interrupt themselves continually in their own course, come back to the apparently accomplished in order to recommence it afresh . . ." (Marx 1982 [1852], 120).
5. Perhaps of more practical use to them even than Gottwald is another book, *The Kingdom of God* by Jorge Pixley, which, aside from being much shorter and a lot less complicated, comes directly out of Latin America. Accepting Gottwald's picture, Pixley insists that traditions of social justice constitute the center of the whole Bible *because* the Bible had its origin in radical egalitarianism. For him, the coming of the monarchy is the great fall.
6. In this analysis I was helped also by the work of one of my colleagues on the panel out of which this essay comes, Regina Schwartz, on the patterns of remembering and forgetting inscribed in Israel's narratives.
7. "Ellipsis" is surely a translation error. It should be "ellipse," a conic section with two foci (at a pinch, two "centers"). French "ellipse" carries both meanings.
8. Derrida has elsewhere engaged extensively with Islam. At a 1996 colloquium on his thought in relation to religion, he said "No Muslim is among us, alas . . . just at the moment when it is towards Islam, perhaps, that we ought to begin by turning our attention" (2002b, 45). Important references to Islam appear in this essay (see esp. 2002b, 45–46, 51, 58) and in another in the same volume, where he deals extensively with Louis Massignon and the Arabic tradition of hospitality (2002c, 365–80, 402–409). Gil Anidjar, the editor of the volume (whose help I acknowledge in finding these references), has much to say about Derrida and Islam in his introduction, esp. the two sections entitled "Moorings" (Anidjar 2002, 11–20, 32–39).
9. I wish to make this public acknowledgment of how much I value the intervention on my behalf, as I faced hostile questioning, by Daniel Boyarin.
10. When they were presidents of the Jewish Theological Seminary and Union Theological Seminary, respectively.
11. This story was told to me by James A. Sanders.
12. The ways of biblical figuration are complex and strange. I cannot resist mentioning that "a little help" is also a biblical figure. In Daniel, according to a common interpretation of 11:34, the Maccabees—the group which strove to reappropriate Jerusalem from the Seleucids by war, and whose ultimate accomplishment was to make themselves both kings and priests in Jerusalem—were at best "a little help" to those carrying out God's real program.

Works Consulted

Althusser, Louis. 1977 [1966]. *For Marx*. Trans. Ben Brewster. London: NLB.

Anidjar, Gil. 2002. "Introduction: 'Once More, Once More': Derrida, The Arab, The Jew." In Derrida 2002a, 1–39.

Blanchot, Maurice. 1995. *The Writing of the Disaster*. Trans. Ann Smock. Lincoln: University of Nebraska Press.

Bottomore, Tom, ed. 1983. *A Dictionary of Marxist Thought*. Cambridge, MA: Harvard University Press.

Buber, Martin. 1967. *Kingship of God*. Trans. Richard Scheimann. New York: Harper & Row.

Caputo, John D. 1997. *The Prayers and Tears of Jacques Derrida: Religion Without Religion*. Bloomington: Indiana University Press.

Derrida, Jacques. 1994. *Specters of Marx: The State of the Debt, the Work of Mourning, and the New International*. Trans. Peggy Kamuf, with an introduction by Bernd Magnus and Stephen Cullenberg. New York and London: Routledge.

———. 1995a. "Archive Fever: A Freudian Impression." Trans. Eric Prenowitz. *Diacritics* 25:9–63.

———. 1995b. *The Gift of Death*. Trans. David Wills. Chicago and London: University of Chicago Press.

———. 2002a. *Acts of Religion*. Edited and with an introduction by Gil Anidjar. New York: Routledge.

———. 2002b. "Faith and Knowledge: The Two Sources of 'Religion' at the Limits of Reason Alone." Trans. Samuel Weber. In Derrida 2002a [orig. 1996], 42–101.

———. 2002c. "Hostipitality." Trans. Gil Anidjar. In Derrida 2002a. [First publication of seminar notes from 1997], 358–420.

Dube, Musa W. 1998. "Savior of the World but not of This World: A Postcolonial Reading of Spatial Construction in John." In *The Postcolonial Bible*, ed. R. S. Sugirtharajah, 118–35. Sheffield: Sheffield Academic Press.

Fukuyama, Francis. 1992. *The End of History and the Last Man*. New York: The Free Press.

Gottwald, Norman K. 1979. *The Tribes of Yahweh: A Sociology of the Religion of Liberated Israel, 1250–1050 B.C.E.* Maryknoll, NY: Orbis.

Heschel, Abraham J. 1962. *The Prophets*. New York and Evanston: Harper & Row.

Humphreys, W. Lee. 1990. *Crisis and Story: Introduction to the Old Testament*. 2nd ed. Palo Alto, CA: Mayfield.

Jobling, David. 1998. *1 Samuel*. Berit Olam. Collegeville, Minn.: Liturgical Press.

Jobling, David, Tina Pippin, and Ronald Schleifer, eds. 2001. *The Postmodern Bible Reader*. Oxford: Blackwell.

Marx, Karl. 1982 [1852]. *The Eighteenth Brumaire of Louis Bonaparte*. In *The Marxist Reader: The Most Significant and Enduring Works of Marxism*, with commentary and notes by Emile Burns, 116–31. New York: Avenel.

Marx, Karl and Friedrich Engels. 1969 [1845–1846]. *Die deutsche Ideologie*. In *Karl Marx Friedrich Engels Werke*, Vol. 3, 9–530. Berlin: Dietz.

———. 1982 [1848]. *The Communist Manifesto*. In *The Marxist Reader: The Most Significant and Enduring Works of Marxism*, with commentary and notes by Emile Burns, 21–59. New York: Avenel.

Pixley, George V. 1981. *God's Kingdom: A Guide for Biblical Study*. Trans. Donald D. Walsh. Maryknoll, NY: Orbis.

Schwartz, Regina M. 1990. "Joseph's Bones and the Resurrection of the Text." In *The Book and the Text: The Bible and Literary Theory*, ed. Regina M. Schwartz, 40–49. Oxford: Blackwell.

boundaries/hyphens/identity-markers

Chapter 7

Shibboleth and the Ma(r)king of Culture: Judges 12 and the Monolingualism of the Other

Frank M. Yamada

Introduction: Crossing-Over Places (מעברות)
Between Judges and Derrida

In *Monolingualism of the Other; or, the Prosthesis of Origin*, Jacques Derrida begins with an inscription. in it, he is ma(r)king a space to reflect on language, to write about speech. He says, "I only have one language; it is not mine." Within this contradiction, Derrida points to the possession and nonpossession of language. On the one hand, he says that he is "monolingual, "that he lives within this habitat of one language. He inhabits it and it inhabits him. He declares, "It is impassable, *indisputable*: I cannot challenge it except by testifying to its omnipresence in me. it would always have preceded me. It is me. For me, this monolingualism is me" (1998, 1, italics his). On the other hand, this language will never belong to Derrida, nor has it ever belonged to him. Language, for him, is a double-edged sword, causing both suffering and pleasure. It creates him and confines him, and yet, he cannot possess it because it never was his to possess. "Yes, I only have one language, yet it is not mine" (1998, 2). Derrida's confession turns into two propositions: "1. *We only ever speak one language. 2. We never speak only one language*" (1998, 7).[1] The singular has transgressed into the collective, the particular into the general. Thus from Derrida's first move, the reader becomes aware that the demonstration of this text will move between the autobiographical tendencies of metaphysics and the metaphysical inclinations of autobiography. Derrida chooses to address these propositions through a series of reflections on language and culture—the cultural speech of a Franco-Maghrebian.[2] The topic of culture, as will be shown, also proves to cut both ways since Derrida professes his love for "pure French," a language that simultaneously reinforces his cultural alienation as an Algerian Jew (Derrida 1998, 44–58).

Judges 12:1–6, which narrates the story of a conflict between Ephraim and Gilead, is also a text about the double-edged (s)word of culture and language.[3] In this tale, the men of Ephraim confront Jephthah because of his failure to call them to arms against the Ammonites. A battle breaks out between the Ephraimites and the Gileadites, the latter routing the former. The men of Gilead proceed by taking the fords of the Jordan in order to prevent the fleeing enemy from crossing back into the territory of Ephraim. When the Ephraimites attempt to cross the river, the Gileadites make the fugitive say the word, "shibboleth". Since, however, the men of Ephraim cannot say the word correctly, mispronouncing it as "sibboleth", they are easily singled out and put to the sword. A total of forty-two thousand Ephraimites are slain. Nor is this the only example of the use of a word/accent to mark a potentially fatal difference in the context of war, though it is the bloodiest one, with the highest fatalities: Soggin cites at least three other examples including the pronunciation of French at the Sicilian Vespers in 1282; a Flemish accent during a revolt in Flanders, 1302; and the case of fleeing Germans who were made to pronounce "Scheveningen" by the Dutch in the Second World War (Soggin 1981, 222). For the men of Ephraim, life and death is determined by a word, indeed a single phoneme: violence turns on the accent of the other. Judges 12:1–6 provides an illustration of how language writes itself on culture. The cultural implications of Gilead's violent act on Ephraim are more complex when one considers that both groups are Israelite. What does this text say about culture when the very act of creating cultural difference is a violent act of self-differentiation?

The present paper will explore the issue of culture as it appears in the shibboleth incident of Judges 12 and in Derrida's *Monolingualism of the Other*. Derrida's reflections on shibboleth (1986) will also provide an intertext for reading the biblical material. My interpretations of these texts will not attempt to locate a meta-cultural perspective, for to do so would suggest that Derrida's text and/or the biblical text has some unmediated access to culture or its representations. This essay is not offering cultural theory, though it is informed by it. The interpretations in this paper will also try to avoid thinking of culture in essentialist categories such as in the statements "Gileadite culture is X," or "Derrida's discourse is determined by his French-speaking Algerian Jewish culture." Rather, my intention is to read these texts carefully with an eye pointed in the direction of what Homi Bhabha has called the "location of culture."[4] Instead of looking for patterns that constrain cultures into fixed identities, the present essay will press for the emergence of culture through the difficult contradictions and conflicting hybridities within and among the texts. A more compelling reading of Judges 12 and Derrida surfaces when one considers the in-between-ness of cultural identity—the production of culture in the interstices. I will begin by looking again at Derrida's opening proposition that we only speak one language and we never speak only one language.

Derrida: Monolingualism of the Other and Cultural Identity

Monolingualism of the Other is the literary product of what was originally an oral presentation given at the conference, "Echoes from Elsewhere"/ "*Renvois d'ailleurs*." This conference, which was held on the campus of Louisiana State University in April 1992, sought to address the problems of speaking the French language in a context outside of France. Derrida's essay responds to the work of Abdelkebir Khatibi, a French-speaking Moroccan writer, who has discussed the issue of bilingualism and the loss of the mother tongue (Khatibi 1985, 1990). It is within this dialogue with Khatibi that Derrida refers to a necessary and impossible monolingualism where we only speak one language, and we never speak only one language. It is also with reference to Khatibi that Derrida declares that he is Franco-Maghrebian. In fact, in addressing his friend, Derrida declares, "You see, dear Abdelkebir, between the two of us, I consider myself to be the *most* Franco-Maghrebian, and perhaps even the *only* Franco-Maghrebian here" (1998, 12, italics his). Derrida claims this identity by pointing to the contradiction within Franco-Maghrebian. In order to assert such an identity, one must both be a French citizen and must not be a French citizen at the same time (Maghreb is a region not a citizenship). How does this happen? Derrida proceeds to narrate a brief history of Algerian Jews, who were granted citizenship in 1870 under the Crémieux decree. Less than a century later, in 1940, the French government revoked the citizenship of Jews in Algeria, only to reinstate it in 1943. Thus, Derrida claims to be the most Franco-Maghrebian, having been both a citizen and noncitizen *by birth*, that is by virtue of being an Algerian Jew. Derrida does not use the privilege of this identity to characterize some group or ethnicity as Franco-Maghrebian. Instead, he points to a "*precarious, recent, threatened*" citizenship that is based on a prior inclusion and exclusion (1998, 15). Thus, what Derrida finds in this story (his-story) is not solace within a fixed cultural identity, but "a disorder of identity." Toward the end of the third chapter, Derrida touches on the exclusion experienced in this displacement. He suggests that schools that were solely for French citizens left a mark upon those who were not citizens. This exclusion contributed to the latter groups' relationship to language. When the language that one speaks is not one's own, then language reinforces the dislocation of an insecure citizenship.[5] Thus, Derrida as a self-proclaimed Franco-Maghrebian is in exile within language, a language that is not his own, and yet it is the only language that he speaks. In this way, Derrida turns his reflections on identity and culture back into a question of language, the monolanguage of the other. If Derrida's way of ma(r)king culture is emerging, it will be located somewhere in his experience of language.

Before proceeding further with Derrida's discussion of language, it will prove helpful to examine further the significance of the term, Franco-Maghrebian. What does it signify? Derrida is careful to show that he is not talking about "some historical unity of *a* France and *a* Maghreb" (1998, 11, italics his). He even questions the use of the conjunction "and" to connect the two in coherence. The putting together of these two terms represents a promise that such a thing as a Franco-Maghrebian exists as a singularity. Derrida, however, points to the silence of the hyphen, similar to the nonconjunction of the word "and," which is always promising to point to a unity that is not there, and thus remains a promise—a silent promise. He is also clear that the silence of the hyphen cannot keep quiet the tortures and brutalities of the past, in fact, it may exacerbate them. "It could even worsen the terror, the lesions, and the wounds. A hyphen is never enough to conceal protests, cries of anger or suffering, the noise of weapons, airplanes, and bombs" (1998, 11). Thus, though Derrida proclaims himself as a Franco-Maghrebian, indeed the Franco-Maghrebian *par excellence*, this cultural identity is not a fixed or easy unity. Instead, the silence of the hyphen threatens to undo the very connection that the term Franco-Maghrebian assumes. The complexity of this (non)union becomes more apparent through Derrida's further exploration of language, and the purity of a particular language.

One of the more troubling and difficult movements in *Monolingualism of the Other* occurs when Derrida takes up the topic of his love for "pure French" (1998, 44–58). According to Derrida, he developed this taste for a particular accent while encountering French literature as a young student in Algeria. He describes a separation that took place through his education. This division, which Derrida calls a " brutal severance," forged a cut between the culture of French literature and the culture of French-speaking Algerians. As Derrida suggests, "One entered French literature only by losing one's accent" (1998, 45). He is not proud of this taste for pure language, but he admits it all the same. In one of the more striking examples, Derrida describes how a poetry reading by René Char was ruined by the poet's accent, and in the process, a writer whom Derrida admired in his early years became an example of the absurd and comical through a performance of language. Thus, Derrida's love for French reveals a simultaneous intolerance for other dialects.[6] Language, a particular accent in this case, marks a space that Derrida signifies as cultural difference—the difference between French and French Algerian. The irony in this difference is that Derrida identifies with the purity of French, a language that is other to himself and one that marginalizes the otherness of an accent that still dwells within him (1998, 45–46). Since Algerian students were educated in French, they learned a distinction that marks culture. For other Algerian Jews like Derrida, this incision made by language created a community that was "cut up and cut off" (1998, 55). Not only were they alienated from French, the only language that they spoke, but they were severed from Arab and Berber culture, and their own Jewish culture (which had no language). The exile of language is reflected by those who are strangers to their own culture and at the same time find themselves estranged by a language that is not their own—their only language. Thus, the monolingualism of the other threatens the very possibility of self-identification since one must understand oneself in a language that alienates its subjects through the promise of a pure language.

The brief interpretation of Derrida offered above is not comprehensive: rather my intention was to highlight different ways that one could see culture emerging from *Monolingualism of the Other* in conversation with Judges 12. Some themes are worth highlighting at this point. First, one can trace within Derrida's work the idea of *culture as the exclusion of/within language*. Language cuts both ways through what he calls an "essential alienation in language" (1998, 58). As Derrida's reflections on Francophone Algerians suggest, the monolingualism of the other cuts off the self from itself. Derrida describes Algerian Jews as "strangers to Jewish culture: a strangely bottomless alienation of the soul: a catastrophe . . ." (1998, 53). Language also cuts in a different way in that one is alienated *within* a language that is always other. His (self)description of a Franco-Maghrebian Jew is telling, for it portrays one who speaks only the language of the other, and yet this person has no language (Hebrew, Berber, or Arabic) with which to refer to him/herself.

A second theme within *Monolingualism of the Other* can be found in Derrida's discussion of the (non)conjunction between France and Maghreb, or the silence of the hyphen in Franco-Maghrebian. Though he does not acknowledge it, his description of this identity suggests *the ma(r)king of a space in-between cultures, nationalities or ethnic identities*. Within this space, difference is marked and negotiated between that which is French and that which is Maghrebian, even if the two of these are not fixed unities. This negotiation is necessitated by the arbitrary connection assumed by the silence of the hyphen. This silence does not point to a connection or unity between the two terms, for this mark cannot erase the violence and suffering that is represented through the combination of these two particulars. The placement of the hyphen is arbitrary, based on historical contingencies, conflicted subjectivities, individual particularities, and so on. The cultural space that opens up between French and Maghrebian points to the emergence of culture "in-between," where cultural identity requires the negotiation of this nonbinary space.

The third theme points toward the construction of cultural, identity. Identity, cultural, or otherwise—which is located in the (non)space or in-between place of cultures or cultural identities—*is conflicted or at odds with itself*. Derrida suggests that there is a desire for language or culture that is other than oneself (e.g., Derrida's love for pure French). Since, however, this language of the other, which is never one's own, involves exclusion and the intolerance of other accents, it leaves one alienated from oneself with no recourse to self-identification. Thus, identity is conflicted with itself and unresolved, a cultural construction that is always emerging without end. One hears echoes of this emergence in Derrida's confession of a desire for a language that is not his own—a language that simultaneously encourages the intolerance of difference.

The last theme, which is embedded in the first, is one that returns often in Derrida's writing. Since language alienates or excludes, and since we are simultaneously alienated within language, *there is no immediate access to what we might call identity or culture*. The language of autobiography and cultural identity, like language in general, is *always promising* (1998, 67–69). Such speech, however, is bound within the contradiction that we only ever speak one language and we never speak only one language. Put in a biblical idiom, there is no crossing over (עבר) into the land of promise. For Derrida, language is always promising to reach its destination, to lay hold of transcendence. It promises a land that never comes, and thus remains a promise. Language is always pointing beyond itself, while always referring only to itself. We may touch the promise only through the non-touch of a prosthetic extension— the prosthesis of origin. It is what Derrida has called in other places *différance*.[7] Within the context of culture or cultural identity, Derrida is ma(r)king a space in which culture is always differing/deferring, a cultural *différance*.

Judges 12:1–6: What's in a (S)word: Shibboleth and the Creation of Culture

What has Gilead to do with Algeria? What does an ancient Semitic language variation have to do with the monolingualism of the other? At first glance, Judg. 12:1–6 does not seem to have much to do with Derrida's *Monolingualism of the Other*. The shibboleth incident, which closes the Jephthah cycle (Judg. 10:17–12:7), depicts an intra-Israelite war between two groups: the Ephraimites and Gileadites. The last scene in this passage revolves around the (mis)pronunciation of the word, shibboleth. While a cursory read of Judges 12 and Derrida surfaces only a vague connection around the subject of language, a closer reading of the biblical text reveals a more significant series of convergences. When one reads Judges 12 with an eye toward the cultural themes traced above, the text opens itself up to a dialogue with Derrida, an encounter with cultural *différance*. In this dialogue, language cuts like a knife to divide or mark difference between/within Israel in ways that resonate with what Derrida has to say about culture and cultural identity. Before undertaking a close reading of Judges 12:1–6, some context will prove helpful.

The setting for Jephthah's entrance into the book of Judges starts at the end of chapter ten. Jephthah's life begins with Israel in a state of crisis. The Ammonites have encamped around the city of Mizpah of Gilead. This prompts the people of Gilead to say, "Who is the man that will begin to fight against the Ammonites? He shall become head over all the inhabitants of Gilead" (10:18). The narrator responds to this question by alluding to the answer in the next verse, "Now Jephthah, the Gileadite, was a mighty warrior and he was the son of a prostitute" (11:1). The first point of Jephthah's characterization is a regional one. The next two cast Jephthah in an ambivalent light. The description of Jephthah as a "mighty one of strength" (גִּבּוֹר חַיִל) suggests that he would be well suited to take up the battle against the Ammonites. Thus, Jephthah's identity is shaped by his destiny to become a warrior who will deliver Israel from its enemies. His identity, however, is conflicted by the fact that he is the son of a prostitute. This latter aspect results in alienation from his father's house, when his brothers drive him out because he was "the son of another woman" (v. 2). Jephthah settles in the remote land of Tob (טוֹב), which is anything but a good land. He becomes in v. 3 the leader of a group of thugs from the area, and thus his identity as an outsider is reinforced within a large collective of "worthless" men (אֲנָשִׁים רֵיקִים). He is a "marginal figure" who lives on the margins both geographically and socially (Exum 1989, 65). Thus, the reader is introduced to Jephthah as a man whose identity is divided. He is both a mighty warrior and marginal figure who is alienated from his place of origin.

Chapter 11 also depicts Jephthah as a man of words. When the Ammonites begin to wage war against Israel, the elders of Gilead ask Jephthah to return. Jephthah replies to them in a speech that begins with a question: "Did you not hate me and drive me out from my father's house?" (11:7). After he has probed them further on why they have decided to come to him now in their time of distress, Jephthah uses words to negotiate with the elders of Gilead. He agrees to lead them into battle against the Ammonites when the Gileadites propose to make him head (רֹאשׁ) over them. Thus, the stone that was rejected has become the chief stone. The scene ends with Jephthah, the head of Gilead, continuing to be a man of words—a talking head: "Jephthah spoke all his words before the Lord at Mizpah" (11:11).

This initial characterization of Jephthah as a man of words reverberates throughout the tales of this warrior judge. Later, in both his confrontations with the Ammonites (11:12–33) and the men of Ephraim (12:1–6), Jephthah begins with words before proceeding to battle against his foes. Jephthah is a man who argues first with the word and then with the sword. As Mieke Bal has suggested, he is a man of the "s/word" (Bal 199a, 161–68). The most pronounced instance of Jephthah's use of words occurs in 11:29–40, where he makes a vow to the Lord before going up against the Ammonites. He promises that the first person to come out of his house to greet him in victory will be sacrificed as a burnt offering. Jephthah learns that his vow cuts both ways when his daughter, an only child, is the first to come out to congratulate him.[8] Tragically, Jephthah keeps his word, and his daughter is sacrificed. The word of his vow has divided his house against itself. First, Jephthah was alienated from his father's house due to the accident of his birth. Now, through his own word, he is cut off from his house and from succeeding generations of his house. Language is the source of Jephthah's alienation from himself.

The preceding characterization of Jephthah highlights conflicts of identity, *and* constructs him as a man of conflict. Jephthah is characterized at the beginning of the story as a mighty warrior who is destined to be a military leader over his people, and at the same time presents him as alienated from his place of origin and from the very people who would make him head over Gilead. His identity is conflicted and he is a man of conflict; he is a mighty warrior and a man of words. Though he uses his speech to negotiate (e.g., with the elders of Gilead and with God), his words are often a pretext to battle—fighting words, words as s/words. His words lead to violence, not only against his enemies, but also against his own house and family. This characterization, which is developed throughout the Jephthah stories, will prove crucial at the end of the cycle in Judges 12:1–6, where a single word violently divides Israel.

Chapter twelve begins with a call to arms, directed not to Gilead, but to Ephraim. The Ephraimites cross over (ויעבר) to confront Jephthah for not having called them to battle against the Ammonites. The verb, from the root עבר, which means "to cross over, pass over, transgress," is used frequently within the Jephthah cycle to describe the movement of peoples or individuals as they cross dividing lines. Prior to battles or confrontations between groups, the narrator foregrounds boundary issues in the root, עבר.[9] In 12:1, the use of עבר suggests to the reader that Ephraim's dispute with Jephthah is significant enough to warrant a crossing. Indeed, by not calling them out to battle, Jephthah has gone *too far*. The meaning of עבר will take on more significance at the conclusion of this story, where the Ephraimites will not be allowed to cross the Jordan when they ask to return to Ephraim (v. 5). The final use of עבר, which expresses a desire of the Ephraimites to return to their home, in the end, will signify a noncrossing.

After the Ephraimites express their displeasure to Jephthah, they threaten to burn down his house. Jephthah offers words of defense against the claims of Ephraim. He explains that he and his people were involved in a dispute with the Ammonites (v. 2). The phrase used to describe this conflict is איש ריב הייתי, lit. "I was a man of strife." The term ריב often refers to legal disputes, but in the context of the previously narrated war with Ammon it points to both the verbal and military conflict.[10] Jephthah identifies not only himself within this characterization but also makes reference to his own people (עמי). Thus, Jephthah's identity as a man of conflict has found a larger context within what Jephthah calls "my people." The man of conflict has generated a people of conflict. After Jephthah's initial justification, he contradicts the Ephraimites' accusations. The men of Ephraim accuse Jephthah of neglecting to call them to battle. Jephthah, however, contends that he did call them, but that they failed to reply. Only after they neglected to come to his aid, did Jephthah "take his life in his hand" and go up against the Ammonites (v. 3). Thus, Ephraim's initial complaint and threat has become a dispute over words with Jephthah. Earlier in the book of Judges, there is a similar incident involving Ephraim and their complaint of not being called to battle. In Judges 8:1–3, Gideon is able to pacify the angry Ephraimites, talking them out of a violent dispute. In Judges 12, however, Jephthah's words are far from diplomatic. They lead to violence between Gilead and Ephraim, a battle that begins with a dispute over words, or as Ephraim contends, a lack of words (i.e. Jephthah's absent call to battle).[11]

The dispute over words degenerates quickly into violence in v. 4. Jephthah gathers the Gileadites and proceeds to fight against Ephraim. There is a seam in v. 4 between the first part of the verse, "*Jephthah* gathered all the men of Gilead, and fought (וַיִּלָּחֶם) with Ephraim," and what follows, "*the men of Gilead* defeated (וַיַּכּוּ) Ephraim." The verb, וַיִּלָּחֶם, is a third person singular form, "he fought." The next verb, וַיַּכּוּ, "they defeated/smote," is a plural form, corresponding to the subject "men of Gilead" which follows the verb. Syntactically and contextually, the reader can assume that Jephthah and the men of Gilead fought with Ephraim together. However, a closer reading reveals a fold in the text. After the mention of Jephthah in v. 4a, including his action represented with the singular verb וַיִּלָּחֶם, Jephthah disappears from the text. He is not mentioned again until the Deuteronomistic postscript, "Jephthah judged Israel six years" (v. 7). The remainder of the story has the men of Gilead acting as the primary subjects against Ephraim. It is they who take the fords of the Jordan, ask for the password, and slay the fugitives. Jephthah's absence alone is not surprising until it is coupled with the fact that a second rationale is given for the war in the last part of v. 4. The narrator provides motivation for the men of Gilead: "The men of Gilead defeated Ephraim *because* (כִּי) they said, 'You are fugitives of Ephraim, O Gilead, in the midst of Ephraim and Manasseh.' " This taunt suggests that the Ephraimites provoked the men of Gilead into battle by labeling the latter as fugitives. Verse three, however, points to Jephthah's dispute with Ephraim as being the precipitating force behind the conflict. In v. 3, Jephthah's question betrays his astonishment, "Why have you come up to me this day, to fight against me?" Immediately following the question, Jephthah wastes no time and musters his troops to fight against Ephraim. It is possible, even likely, that we are dealing with a seam between two traditions, one describing Jephthah's conflict with Ephraim and one recounting a postwar skirmish between Gileadites and Ephraimites on the banks of the Jordan.[12] In the received text, however, the reader is left to navigate this uneven space between the singular and the plural, where the "he/she" becomes "they," and the "I" becomes "we." This is a negotiation that is familiar to readers of Derrida, where what is presented as autobiographical is always speaking about the general, and where metaphysics always seems to be a reflux to autobiography. In the end, this move from the singular to the plural, from Jephthah to the men of Gilead, suggests identification and assimilation. On the one hand, Gilead becomes Jephthah, on the other, Jephthah's identity is dispersed into a larger collective. One can detect evidence of this blurring between the individual and the collective in the Gileadites' motivation to slay the men of Ephraim. The Ephraimites' taunt, which points to Gilead being a fugitive, hearkens back to the original episode in the Jephthah cycle. In that scene, Jephthah's brothers drive him out for being the son of another woman (11:2). This event seems to have imprinted itself on his memory and identity. When the elders of Gilead ask Jephthah to return, he replies, "Did you not hate me and drive me out of my father's house?" (11:7). As the beginning of the Jephthah cycle suggests, the judge's identity was marked by an alienation from his own land. Thus, in the last episode, when the Ephraimites label the men of Gilead as fugitives of Ephraim, the taunt recalls a collective memory of alienation in Jephthah, the leader of Gilead, and his people. Just as Jephthah was exiled from his father's house through the exclusion of his brothers, the Ephraimites try to inscribe an identity of alienation on Gilead, calling them fugitives, wanderers in land that is not their own. For the men of Gilead, like their head (ראש) Jephthah, these are fighting words. As it was with Jephthah, so it is with Gilead: words lead to war. The Ephraimites' designation of the Gileadites as fugitives will prove to be ironic. After Gilead defeats Ephraim, the narrator characterizes the fleeing Ephraimites as "the fugitives of Ephraim." Thus, in the end, the outcome of the battle will determine who the *true fugitives* will be. For the Ephraimites, violence will shape their identity as outsiders, fleeing toward a home to which they will not return.

The conflict between Ephraim and Jephthah began with words. The post-battle scene between Ephraim and Gilead ends with a word, "shibboleth." The majority of Judges 12:1–6 has been about words that lead to conflict, of words in conflict with other words. In fact, the entire battle scene is glaringly brief. Even after Gilead defeats Ephraim in v. 4b, the narrator quickly adds the reason that motivated Gilead to slay the Ephraimites: the *words* of a taunt, "You are fugitives in Ephraim." Words can start wars and in the final scene the pronunciation or mispronunciation of a single word can kill. Thus, Judges 12:1–6 reflects a theme that resounds throughout the Jephthah cycle—words have the potential to inflict violence. These stories turn on the blade of the Jephthah's identity, an identity that has emphasized conflict in both his internal makeup and speech. Within such an identity, words lead to confrontations; indeed, words can kill. Jephthah has learned from experience the double-edged s/word of his identity, since a word, his vow, brought ruin on his household. As it was for Jephthah, so it is with Gilead on the banks of the Jordan in 12:5–6. Gilead, the community over which Jephthah is head, will kill with language through the (mis)pronunciation of a single word, shibboleth.

The final scene begins in v. 5 with the Gileadites taking the "fords" (מעברות) of the Jordan. By seizing the fords, the Gileadites have taken by force the margin that separates Gileadite from Ephraimite, insider from outsider. They have secured the "crossing-over places" (מעברות, from the root עבר), and thus, have determined how the space in-between cultures will be navigated. As one would expect from this story about language, Gilead controls the borders through an utterance, "shibboleth." Many scholars have focused on the linguistic aspects of this passage, and have attempted to parse out the phonemic or dialectic variation between shibboleth and sibboleth,[13] and to suggest different meanings for shibboleth as "an ear of corn" or "river, stream." But the word signifies more through its exclusion than from its definition. Whether by dialectal difference or the inability of the Ephraimites to pronounce the word correctly, the main force of shibboleth, that is, the power of its rhetoric, lies in its ability to distinguish Ephraimite from Gileadite, to mark who is inside and who is outside. At the point of passage (מעברות), shibboleth is what Derrida has called a "pass-not-word" (1986, 320).[14] It has cut an arbitrary barrier between the Ephraimites and the Gileadites, dividing the two groups from each other through language, and thus, dividing Israel from itself. In the end, the pass-not-word of shibboleth has cut both ways, a violent potential that lies hidden within the word's pronunciation. Derrida, commenting on Paul Celan and "Shibboleth," states,

> . . . at once both secret and readable, mark of membership and of exclusion, the shared wound of division [blessure de partage], reminds us also of what I will call the *double edge* of every *Shibboleth*. The mark of an alliance, it is also an index of exclusion, of discrimination, indeed of extermination. One may, thanks to *Shibboleth*, recognize and be recognized by one's own, for better and for worse, for the sake of partaking [partage] and the ring of alliance *on the one hand*, but also, *on the other hand*, for the purpose of denying the other, of denying him passage or life. One may also, because of the *Shibboleth* and exactly to the extent that one may make use of it, see it turned against oneself . . . . (1986, 346, italics his)

Throughout the Jephthah cycle and at its end, language cuts both ways. For Jephthah, the mighty warrior and man of speech, words have the power to negotiate a rise to the head of Gilead and to assure victory through his vow to Yahweh, but his words bring about war and condemn his daughter to death. In the final scene, the men of Gilead, the socialized body of Jephthah, are able to differentiate themselves from their enemies through the pass-not-word of shibboleth. At the same time, it is shibboleth that cuts off Israel from itself through a violent act of self-definition. In this last episode, language has the power to both define and exclude. It marks a cultural space between Ephraim and Gilead through the difference of a single word, an utterance that divides into different sounds (shibboleth/sibboleth) when it is pronounced. The severance of this culture, however, is spoken in a violent tone, for not only does it divide between Gileadite/Ephraimite, insider/outsider, but it determines life and death.

The interpretation of Judges 12 offered above articulates (stutteringly?) themes from *Monolingualism of the Other* with a similar but distinct accent. Harkening back to our first theme, Judges 12 presents *culture as the exclusion of/within language*, especially through the violent imposition of shibboleth. Throughout the Jephthah cycle, and most prominently in the closing scene, language cuts both ways. In this last setting, shibboleth marks the cultural difference between Gilead and Ephraim, insider from outsider. As Derrida (1986) suggests, shibboleth has the potential to both unify and alienate simultaneously. Shibboleth enables the Gileadites to differentiate themselves from the Ephraimites, marking a space of cultural identity. The imposition of shibboleth, however, violently cuts off Ephraim through exclusion and thus divides Israel against itself. An act of self-definition leads to a killing of the self by the self. In this way, cultural difference, as it is presented in Judges 12, is marked by language— an arbitrary difference in pronunciation. In a word, shibboleth.

The second theme highlights *the ma(r)king of a space in-between cultures, nationalities, or ethnic identities* (as in the nonconjunction, or overstrained hyphen, between France and Maghreb). The Jephthah story suggests that one must negotiate the "crossing-over" (עבר) spaces with care. In a world where words of negotiation can degenerate quickly into war, the space between cultures, tribes, or nations can be a place that differentiates fugitive from inhabitant, alien from resident, even life from death. In Judges. 12:1–6, the Gileadites control the boundary that divides Ephraim and Gilead. This act of force becomes a speech act through the imposition of the pass-not-word, shibboleth. Thus, not only have the Gileadites sought to control the navigating of a geographical boundary (i.e. the Jordan), they also have dominated the discourse of navigation across boundaries through shibboleth. This violent act marks a cultural space between Ephraim and Gilead and between Israel and itself. The unity that is implied in the term, "Israel," deconstructs through the language of Gilead's self-differentiation. The coherence of "Israel" cannot hold together the tensions of difference that threaten to divide it—the tensions "in-between" Ephraim and Gilead.

Harkening back to the third thematic strand from *Monolingualism of the Other,* Judges 12 also suggests that *identity, cultural, or otherwise, is conflicted or at odds with itself.* Jephthah is a man of conflict whose identity is conflicted: as mighty warrior, marginal figure, head, alien, man of strife, אִישׁ רִיב, man of s/words, his words (like the words of the narrator which construct and cut him) negotiate, vow, contest, dispute, and cut—leading to the cutting down of warriors on the battlefield and a radical cut in the future of his own house. The cultural identity of Gilead—the social body which embodies the identity of their head at the end of the Jephthah cycle—is conflicted in a way that mirrors the judge's identity. The Gileadites, provoked by the Ephraimites' labeling of them as "fugitives of Ephraim," force their interpretation on the space between Ephraim and Gilead through speech. They seize the boundary between the two groups that is the Jordan River, and they mark the space with the violence of a word. Shibboleth becomes the language of exclusion, one that divides insider from outsider, native speaker from foreigner, and Israel from itself. Thus, Gilead is a people who are conflicted in identity and speech, whose word of self-definition leads to violence against the other who is also the self.

The fourth theme provides a point of convergence and divergence between *Monolingualism of the Other* and Judges 12. As we saw above, for Derrida *there is no immediate access to what we might call identity or culture.* Culture, like language in general, is always differing from itself and deferring to a horizon that both precedes it and points beyond itself to an unfixed destination. Culture emerges in/through *différance.* In a similar way, the shibboleth drama paints a world in which culture and cultural identity is characterized by difference. The word shibboleth marks a pronounced distinction between shibboleth/sibboleth and Gileadite/Ephraimite. Thus, a person from Ephraim differs from someone in Gilead due to a performance in language, the execution of a consonant. The story, however, describes this phonemic difference as an act of violence on the part of Gilead—a self-mutilation within Israel that threatens the coherence of the *promise* inherent in the term. In the book of Judges, the notion of Israel promises a unity that is always threatening to undo itself; it both differs from itself and defers to a singularity that never coheres. The book as a whole moves toward an increasingly chaotic and violent end, where campaigns against the enemies of Yahweh turn into bloodshed among Israelites. Holy war becomes civil war. Acts of violence against the other become acts against the self. Thus, the culture in the book of Judges is represented through a nation that is violently divided against itself, never making good on the assumed unity inherent within the term, "Israel." While one can find traces of *différance* in Judges 12 and in Judges as a whole, the book characterizes cultural difference in a particularly violent way. This violent pronunciation, while remaining a possibility in Derrida's text, is unmistakably clear in the book of Judges, especially in the shibboleth incident. Shibboleth marks the difference between camaraderie and execution. Thus, while both *Monolingualism of the Other* and Judges 12:1–6 are traced through with *différance*, the book of Judges speaks of the cultural difference in a particularly violent accent.

Derrida as "Shibboleth"?: The Navigation of Difference and the Construction of Culture

Both *Monolingualism of the Other* and Judges 12:1–6 suggest that identity is not one, but is constructed through a negotiation of differences "in-between" groups, in interstitial spaces where over-determined polarities reveal themselves to be complex and conflicted hybridities. Derrida's culture, if he has "one," is marked by *différance* and produced through the *différance* of language: "I only have one language; it is not mine" (1998, 1). Judges 12 performs a defining moment in which cultural identity is marked through the different pronunciation of a single word, as Gilead, the people who control the boundary of cultural negotiation by force, impose a shibboleth to divide Ephraimite from Gileadite and Israel from other Israel(s). In both cases, culture is not a static reality that determines beliefs, values or actions, but is rather "that" which emerges through the navigation of difference; the space that opens up between Franco/Maghrebian or Ephraimite/Gileadite is the location of culture, where culture emerges in the interstitial spaces "in-between"—what Homi Bhabha calls the "Third Space" (Bhabha 1994, 36–39). Culture and cultural identity is always threatening to undo itself, even as it emerges, and the instability which results from the movement and negotiation of difference is both the possibility of culture and the violence inherent within it. Cultural distinctions have the ability to both unite and divide, to rally people around a just cause or to promote genocide in the name of cultural purity; and how one navigates difference, cultural or otherwise, will affect the cultural identity that emerges from the space "in-between." The negotiation of this space has been a constant theme in Derrida, from his meditations on the "double-edge" of shibboleth (1986, 346) to his more recent works on hospitality and *The Politics of Friendship* (Derrida 1997; 2001).

Reading Derrida on "culture" invites us to also reflect on how "Derrida" functions in culture in ways that have implications for the present volume. In a world of textual production and discourse, decisions about how one chooses to use Derrida, who is using Derrida, and with whom you put Derrida in dialogue will make a difference in how Derrida is pronounced or how one speaks the idiom/language that is becoming known as "Derridean." What differences are being navigated and by whom? For example, if those who speak Derridean most fluently, properly, and purely are predominantly of one race, ethnicity, gender, and sexual-orientation, the emergence of that culture will lack a variety of flavors and accents. In this particular cultural construction, Derrida becomes a shibboleth, a pass-not-word of exclusion. Such exclusion is not immune to the violent potential of a shibboleth. Culture as the navigation of difference, however, has the potential to disrupt such privileged spaces, while simultaneously creating a new identity that refuses the totality that would seek to constrain it. This is what Homi Bhabha refers to as the unsettling force of the hybrid:

> Produced through the strategy of disavowal, the *reference* of discrimination is always to a process of splitting as the condition of subjection: a discrimination between the mother culture and its bastards, the self and its doubles, where the trace of what is disavowed is not repressed but repeated as something *different*—a mutation, a hybrid. It is such a partial and double force that is more than the mimetic but less than the symbolic, that disturbs the visibility of the colonial presence and makes the recognition of its authority problematic. (1986, 111, italics his)

The navigation of cultural difference has the potential to disarm the privileged nature of a discourse while producing a hybridity that refuses the path of fixed identities and essentialized cultural distinctions. Derrida as shibboleth? The possibility is always there since shibboleth, like language in general, has the potential to exclude or invite. Let's hope that the crossing-over places (מעברות) are accessible, and that the borders are not too heavily patrolled.[15]

Notes

1. Derrida later elaborates on these propositions saying, "1. *We only ever speak one language—or rather one idiom only. 2. We never speak only one language—or rather there is no pure idiom"* (1998, 8, italics his).
2. In *Monolingualism,* Derrida discusses at length the term Franco-Maghrebian and even identifies himself by this designation (see 1998, 7–18, and discussion below). He reflects on the conflicted displacement of French-speaking Jews who lived in Algeria during the nineteenth and twentieth centuries. This chaotic cultural configuration created what Derrida calls a "disorder of identity" (1998, 17). Thus, when Derrida refers to a language that is not his own, and a language out of which he is compelled to speak, he is talking with a certain cultural accent—the accent of a French-speaking Algerian Jew.
3. For a discussion of Jephthah as a man of the s/word, see Bal 1988, 161–68.
4. Bhabha 1994. See his essay, "The Commitment to Theory" (19–39; esp. 36–39) in which Bhabha describes what he calls, the "Third Space." The Third Space is that critical movement between cultures that refuses sharp dichotomies such as colonized and colonizer. Instead, Bhabha describes this interstitial space as a place of negotiation between conflicting cultural differences rather than an assimilation of one identity into another.
5. Derrida proceeds by suggesting that the possession of language is a myth. Later, he will use this notion to describe colonialism in terms of two tricks. The first trick is the belief of the master who pretends to possess language, and through force or rhetoric persuades others of this mastery. The second trick is that those who seek liberation from this hegemony do so by appropriating the language of the master, though only to a certain point (1998, 23–24).
6. Derrida's confession of intolerance for other dialects is framed within his hyperbolic speech of "more French than French," "more 'purely French'" (1998, 49). The cultural implication of these statements, which will be explored below, point to a conflict in identity where the desire for a pure language alienates the self from itself, since the language of self-identification is always the monolanguage of the other.

7. For a discussion of Derrida's neologism, différance, see "Différance," in Derrida 1982, 1–27.

8. For some of the many fine treatments of the story of Jephthah and his daughter, see esp. Trible 1984, 93–116; Exum 1990b; Day 1989; Bal 1990; and Fuchs 1989.

9. See also 11:29 and 11:32, where Jephthah "passed" or "crossed over" to the Ammonites. Polzin (1980, 181) recognizes the significance of עבר in the Jephthah cycle, arguing that the "crossings" have become confused geographically. This disorientation is reflective of the increasing thematic disorientation that leads to the chaotic end of the book of Judges. One place in the Jephthah cycle where עבר does not seem to have the connotation of encountering others' borders is in 11:29–30. Jephthah "passed through" (ויעבר) Gilead and Manasseh. He then "passed" (ויעבר) on to Mizpah of Gilead before he "passed" (עבר) to the Ammonites (v. 29). This series of "passings," however, sets up the story that follows—the vow of Jephthah. In the vow, he promises to sacrifice one from his own house to Yhwh to ensure victory. Thus, in a figurative way (vowing to offer a member of his house), and also a geographical way (passing through Mizpah in Gilead), the battle must first "pass" through Jephthah's home.

10. Thus, the NRSV translates this verse, "My people and I were engaged in conflict with the Ammonites . . ." (v.2). Boling emphasizes the negotiating aspects of איש ריב. He translates this phrase as, "I was using diplomacy" (1975, 212). ריב, however, can also point to violent confrontation, e.g. Ps 55:10, where ריב occurs parallel to חמס, "violence."

11. See Jobling (1986; 1995), who compares this passage with two other Jordan crossing incidents in Judges (3:27–29 and 7:24–8:3) that involve Ephraim.

12. Burney (1970, 327), Boling (1975, 211–14), and Soggin (1981, 221, following Richter) recognize the tensions in this text. Burney, followed by Boling, suggests that the expression "fugitives of Ephraim" has come into v. 4 by dittography from v. 5. Thus, Ephraim's comments are truncated in v. 4 to "O Gilead, you are in the midst of Ephraim and Manasseh" (Boling 1975, 211). As Burney admits, however, this solution does not make Ephraim's taunt clearer (1970, 327).

13. For discussion on this topic, see Emerton 1985 (including bibliography); Swiggers 1981; Rendsburg 1986; Beeston 1988; Hendel 1996; and Faber 1992.

14. In *Monolingualism of the Other*, Derrida invokes the term "shibboleth" to point to the contradiction inherent in the politics of speech and identity, where one "demands the multiplication of shibboleths" to secure one's place in a language that is not one's own (1998, 57).

15. I would like to thank A. K. M. Adam and Patricia Dailey for reading early drafts of this article and for providing valuable comments and insights on Derrida. Catherine Wallace also was charitable with her time, giving me helpful feedback on the style and presentation of the essay.

Works Consulted

Bal, Mieke. 1988. *Death and Dissymmetry: The Politics and Coherence in the Book of Judges*. Chicago: University of Chicago Press.

———. 1990. "Dealing/With/Women: Daughters in the Book of Judges." In *The Book and the Text: The Bible and Literary Theory*, ed. Regina Schwartz, 16–39. Oxford: Blackwell.

Beeston, A. F. L. 1988. "*Šibbōlet*: A Further Comment." *Journal of Semitic Studies* 33:259–61.

Bhabha, Homi K. 1994. *The Location of Culture*. London: Routledge.

Boling, Robert G. 1975. *Judges: Introduction, Translation, and Commentary*. Anchor Bible 6a. Garden City NJ: Doubleday.

Burney, C. F. 1970. *The Book of Judges: With Introduction and Notes and Notes on the Hebrew Text of the Book of Kings: With an Introduction and Appendix.* Library of Biblical Studies. New York: KTAV.

Brettler, Marc. 1989. "The Book of Judges: Literature as Politics." *Journal of Biblical Literature* 108:395–418.

Day, Peggy L. 1989. "From the Child is Born the Woman: The Story of Jephthah's Daughter." In *Gender and Difference in Ancient Israel*, ed. Peggy L. Day, 58–74. Minneapolis: Fortress.

Derrida, Jacques. 1982. *Margins of Philosophy.* Trans. Alan Bass. Chicago: University of Chicago Press.

———. 1986. "Shibboleth." Trans. Joshua Wilner. In *Midrash and Literature*, ed. Geoffrey H. Hartman and Sanford Budick, 307–47. New Haven: Yale University Press.

———. 1997. *Politics of Friendship.* Trans. George Collins. Phronesis. London: Verso.

———. 1998. *Monolingualism of the Other; or, The Prosthesis of Origin.* Trans. Patrick Mensah. Cultural Memory in the Present. Stanford: Stanford University Press.

———. 2001. *On Cosmopolitanism and Forgiveness.* Trans. Mark Dooley and Michael Hughes, with preface by Simon Critchley and Richard Kearney. London: Routledge.

Emerton, J. A. 1985. "Some Comments on the Shibboleth Incident (Judges 12:6)." In *Mélanges bibliques et orientaux en l'honneur de M. Mathias Delcor*, ed. A. Caquot, S. Légasse and M. Tardieu, 149–57. Alter Orient und Altes Testament. Neukirchen-Vluyn: Neukirchener Verlag.

Exum, J. Cheryl. 1989. "The Tragic Vision and Biblical Narrative: The Case of Jephthah." In *Signs and Wonders: Biblical Texts in Literary Focus*, ed. J. Cheryl Exum, 59–83. Semeia Studies. Atlanta: Scholars Press.

———. 1990a. "The Centre Cannot Hold: Thematic and Textual Instabilities in Judges." *Catholic Biblical Quarterly* 52:410–31.

———. 1990b. "Murder They Wrote: Ideology and the Manipulation of Female Presence in Biblical Narrative." In *The Pleasure of Her Text: Feminist Readings of Biblical and Historical Texts*, ed. Alice Bach, 45–67. Philadelphia: Trinity.

———. 1992. *Tragedy and Biblical Narrative: Arrows of the Almighty.* Cambridge: Cambridge University Press.

Faber, Alice. 1992. "Second Harvest: *šibbōlet* Revisited." *Journal of Semitic Studies* 37:1–10.

Fuchs, Esther. 1989. "Marginalization, Ambiguity, Silencing: The Story of Jephthah's Daughter." *Journal of Feminist Studies in Religion* 5:35–45.

Gunn, David M. and Danna Nolan Fewell. 1993. *Narrative in the Hebrew Bible.* The Oxford Bible Series. Oxford: Oxford University Press.

Hendel, Ronald S. 1996. "Sibilants and *šibbōlet* (Judges 12:6)." *Bulletin of the American Schools of Oriental Research* 301:69–75.

Jobling, David. 1986. *The Sense of Biblical Narrative: Structural Analyses in the Hebrew Bible*, Vol. II. JSOT Supplement Series 39. Sheffield: JSOT Press.

———. 1995. "Structuralist Criticism: The Text's World of Meaning." In *Judges and Method: New Approaches in Biblical Studies*, ed. Gale A. Yee, 91–118. Minneapolis: Fortress.

Khatibi, Abdelkebir. 1985. *Du bilinguisme.* Paris: Deonoël.

———. 1990. *Love in Two Languages.* Trans. Richard Howard. Minneapolis: University of Minnesota Press.

Klein, Lillian R. 1988. *The Triumph of Irony in the Book of Judges.* JSOT Supplement Series 68, Bible and Literature 14. Sheffield: Almond.

Landy, Francis. 1990. "Shibboleth: The Password." In *Proceedings of the Tenth World Congress of Jewish Studies*, 91–98. Jerusalem: World Union of Jewish Studies.

Marais, Jacobus. 1998. *Representation in Old Testament Narrative Texts.* Biblical Interpretation Series. Leiden: Brill.

Polzin, Robert. 1980. *Moses and the Deuteronomist: A Literary Study of the Deuteronomic History, Part One: Deuteronomy, Joshua, Judges.* Bloomington: Indiana University Press.

Rendsburg, Gary A. 1986. "More on Hebrew *šibbōlet*." *Journal of Semitic Studies* 33:255–58.

Soggin, J. Alberto. 1981. *Judges: A Commentary.* Trans. John S. Bowden. Old Testament Library. Philadelphia: Westminster.

Sugirtharajah, R. S. 2001. *The Bible and the Third World: Precolonial, Colonial and Postcolonial Encounters.* Cambridge: Cambridge University Press.

Swiggers, P. 1981. "The Word *šibbōlet* in Jud. 12.6." *Journal of Semitic Studies* 36:205–7.

Trible, Phyllis. 1984. *Texts of Terror: Literary-Feminist Readings of Biblical Narratives.* Overtures to Biblical Theology. Philadelphia: Fortress.

Webb, Barry G. 1987. *The Book of the Judges: An Integrated Reading.* JSOT Supplement Series 46. Sheffield: Sheffield Academic Press.

Chapter 8

The Book of Esther: The Making and Unmaking of Jewish Identity

Dmitri M. Slivniak

The deconstructive reading of the Book of Esther proposed in this paper is related to one of the central themes in the recent work by Derrida—that of collective identity: its paradoxical character, essential instability and violence.[1] Derrida has elaborated, in particular, upon Jewish identity,[2] which in the last two hundred years has become especially paradoxical due to the processes of secularization. I would like to refer especially to *The Monolingualism of the Other or the Prosthesis of Origin* (Derrida 1998), an essay relating to the experience of "hav[ing] only one language [, which] is not [one's own]" (1998, 1–2). For Derrida, the language belongs to the other; it is the other who is perceived as "monolingual" and/or possessing a homogeneous identity. Identity, like God in negative theology, is not what one is but rather what one is not—a "dispossession" of law and language, which are imposed and heteronomous (cf. 1998, 39). Derrida is himself an Algerian Jew, a native speaker of French acculturated into French culture. No one of the three components of this identity (Jewish, Algerian/Maghrebian, French) is self-evident for him: each of them is either hidden, inaccessible, or imposed. At the same time the desire to excavate one's "true" identity, to build "the prosthesis of origin" too easily turns it into another "language, which is not one's own" (1998, 62).

Derrida's reflections echo my own identity concerns. I am a Russian Jew residing in Israel or, as this identity is sometimes defined, a Russian Israeli (a newspaper with this name is published in Israel in Russian). Every component of this complex self-definition refers to "others."

The word "Israeli" defines me in my relation to the outside world (more politically than culturally), and I am recognized as such inside my own group. But for the "monolingual" others in Israel (native speakers of Hebrew) I am a Russian, a Russian immigrant or a Russian Jew, a "foreigner" subject to the laws of hospitality (Derrida 2000, 3–74); they define themselves as "Israelis" in order to distinguish themselves from immigrants like me. Their own identity is in no way simple. It is recognized that a feeling of alienation from "Israeliness," of being a foreigner in one's own country exists in every group of the Hebrew-speaking population. At the same time one can be "more" Israeli or "less" Israeli. According to Elgazi (1992, 29), men are usually perceived as more Israeli than women, secular people—more than religious, and people who have served in the army—much more so than those who have not.[3] There is also a tension between Israeli and Jewish identities—Israeli identity is still viewed by some people as an alternative to the Jewish one (especially to Jewish religious identity).

Being "Russian"[4] means that I am a native speaker of the Russian language (my only language, yet not mine, like French for Derrida) and a carrier of Russian culture. Russian cultural identity is also a confused one—Russians usually feel "Western" in relation to Moslems, Hindus, and others, but "non-Western" in relation to the "genuine" West.

Finally, I am Jewish. I grew up in the Soviet Union, whose leaders attempted to cultivate the identity of the new Soviet person completely devoid of any religious component. Hence the identity of Russian (Soviet)[5] Jews of my generation tends to lack this component even now. Jewish education and traditional rites were completely absent from our life in the Soviet Union; attempts to learn Yiddish, and especially Hebrew—or something from the cultural heritage—were suspect and dangerous. Jewish identity was based on minor cultural differences only (specific Jewish humor, some memories from traditional Jewish life, generally a more "Western" orientation), and to a much larger extent on a set of opportunities different from those of "native" Russians, Ukrainians, and others. The Jews suffered from career restrictions due to antisemitism and feared antisemitic excesses, but at the same time, from the early seventies, they had the possibility to emigrate to such countries as Israel or the United States. The intermarriage rate among Soviet Jews was perhaps the highest among the Jewish communities in the world, yet the feeling of being Jewish and the desire to build for oneself a "prosthesis of origin" (Derrida 1998) was so strong among some of us, that it compelled, for example, a completely acculturated person like me to learn Hebrew, Yiddish, and Aramaic, to come to Israel and to become a Biblical scholar. At the same time I don't want to build this "prosthesis" in ways that certain Jewish "others" would like to impose upon me; this is one of the reasons why I am attracted to postmodern thinking.

The last decade has witnessed a wave of mass immigration to Israel from the former Soviet Union. According to the Law of Return (the core of Israeli "laws of hospitality") not only the Jews, but their first-degree relatives and grandchildren are also allowed to immigrate to the country. Non-Jewish relatives of Jews, initially thought of as a "marginal" and "supplementary" component of the immigration stream, gradually become the majority of the immigrants from the former Soviet Union. Although some consider this to be a threat to the Jewish character of the Israeli society, in fact, one can call it a deconstruction of Zionism. The Law of Return was designed to ensure the Jewish identity of the state by giving immigration rights to Diaspora Jews. In reality it has connected this identity with people of Jewish origin who don't qualify as Jews according to religious law (so-called "social Jews") and with non-Jews. A typically deconstructive situation comes into being, when the "exterior" penetrates into the very core of the "interior."[6] Zionism attempted to resolve the Jewish problem by extracting the Jews from their former environment and resettling them in a new country. One was supposed to know who the Jews were. On the other hand, the non-Jews in the new country were Arabs—people easily distinguishable from the immigrants/settlers. Zionism continued, in fact, the old opposition of Jews-Gentiles, which took the form of the opposition Jews-Arabs (Israelis-Palestinians). Mass immigration from the former Soviet Union has brought to Israel a group for which the difference between "Jews" and "non-Jews," defined by the religious law, is the least important of all the possible differences. ("Non-Jews" are mostly members of Jewish families or children/grandchildren from mixed marriages.) In fact a large segment (nearly 20 percent) of the population of Israel (immigrants from the Former Soviet Union) can be defined today as neither Jewish nor non-Jewish, or as both Jewish and non-Jewish. I view this situation as deconstructive not only for Zionism,[7] but also for a Jewish identity based on the opposition between "us" and "them," which has existed in this form at least since the Persian and Hellenistic periods.[8]

In this article I want to show how traditional Jewish identity is constructed and already deconstructs itself in one of its founding texts—the Book of Esther. This is perhaps the most "Jewish" of all the books of the Hebrew Bible, probably written at the end of the Persian period or at the beginning of the Hellenistic period,[9] which tells a story about the Jews in the Persian Empire. The fundamental opposition underlying it is that of "Jews-Gentiles." Jews succeed not only in preventing genocide, but also in killing their numerous enemies. A (threat of) massacre is the situation where the opposition between "us" and "them" is the most sharply articulated: one group takes the lives of the members of the other.[10] One of the basic problems which the book attempts to resolve is the strategy of Jewish survival in an alien environment.[11] At the same time, the "secular" character of the book, where God and Temple are not mentioned, makes it appealing in modern times to Jews of all backgrounds and worldviews.[12]

On the other hand, Esther is perhaps the only book in the Hebrew Bible that has often been perceived in an antisemitic fashion—it has been intuitively felt as being "too Jewish."[13] This circumstance also highlights an especially close connection between Esther and Jewish identity.

Being a "Jewish" and a "secular" book, Esther at the same time is often considered "carnivalesque" (Craig 1995; Greenstein 1987; Polish 1998 and others): it abounds in feasts and is permeated with the comic, and some of its characters are overtly mocked (Haman, Ahasuerus). Haman displays the evident features of a carnival king, elevated and then thrown down (cf. Polish 1998). The plot of the book is sometimes linked to the Persian New Year feast of Nowrūz and other similar festivals, which display affinities with the European carnival.[14] Finally, the holiday of Purim, for which the Book of Esther is a *Festlegende*, has borne a clearly carnivalesque character, at least since the rabbinic epoch.

All these considerations make it possible to read Esther in dialogue with the conception of carnival developed by Bakhtin in *Rabelais and His World*.[15] One of the possible interpretations of carnival as conceived by Bakhtin is the temporary reversal or neutralization of the binary oppositions of a culture (Ivanov 1998, 744): during the carnival "high" and "low," "good" and "bad" change places or become indistinguishable. Accordingly, at Purim one should get so drunk that one can no longer distinguish between "Cursed be Haman" and "Blessed be Mordecai" (*BT Megillah* 7b). In light of this, Derrida's deconstructive strategy of reading—understood as demonstrating how the text undermines the very oppositions it builds (Culler 1982, 86)—when applied to a carnivalesque book is hardly a "reading against the grain."

One cannot but agree with Greenstein (1987, 233) that "the Esther story is mock serious, and thus homologous with Purim observance." But one should not forget that its concern with the theme of Jewish survival and the threat of annihilation is quite serious, and that alongside the comedy and merrymaking one finds a genuine anxiety (also a point made by Greenstein [1987, 226] and adopted by Berlin [2001, xvi]). Carnivalesque and non-carnivalesque elements in the book penetrate each other, and the message pertaining to Jewish identity and survival in the diaspora is in tension with its tendency to "hide" the realm of the sacred, that very realm which creates Jewish difference from the pagans. Indeed, according to Greenstein (1987, 282–83), the very tendency of such a "hiding" may have roots in the frivolous or "secular" atmosphere of carnival.

Given the double-sided character of the book, I have chosen the following strategy for its interpretation. First I present a "constructive" reading of Esther pertaining to its treatment of the issue of Jewish identity (Reading A) and then I deconstruct this reading (Reading B).[16] At the end of the article conclusions will be drawn from the comparison of these readings. Both the "constructive" and the "deconstructive" interpretations of Esther will use as a departure point various symmetries found in the system of characters and in the plot of the book.[17] Such a double procedure[18] will highlight the complexity and ambivalence of the message of the Book of Esther pertaining to the question of Jewish identity.

Reading A: Wisdom and Folly

One of the central manifestations of the concern for Jewish identity in the Book of Esther is the division of its main characters into Jews (Mordecai, Esther) and Gentiles (Vashti, Haman, Ahasuerus). There is a certain role symmetry between both groups: Esther replaces Vashti, Mordecai replaces Haman. (The last replacement is especially blatant: Haman is impaled on the stake reserved for Mordecai; Mordecai enjoys the marks of honor that Haman expected to enjoy himself.) Thus a structural system for the main characters can be represented as follows:

Ahasuerus
Haman ———➤ Mordecai
Vashti ———➤ Esther

Ahasuerus is the only "invariant" character in this plot: nobody replaces him, he is married first to Vashti and then to Esther, and successively promotes Haman and Mordecai. Yet, being a Gentile, he may be placed in the same column as Haman and Vashti:

Ahasuerus   [God[19]]
Haman   Mordecai
Vashti   Esther

Mordecai and Esther not only replace Haman and Vashti, but are also their very opposites. It is widely accepted[20] that Vashti represents a counterpart to Esther. "Vashti's recalcitrance contrasts with Esther's docility" (Fox 2001, 169; cf. Berg 1979, 73). The confrontation of Vashti's refusal to come when bidden and Esther's coming when not bidden is also widely noted. The contrast between Haman and Mordecai is still more evident. Haman is: "evil," "the adversary and the enemy" (7:6),[21] "the foe of the Jews" (3:10). Mordecai, unlike him, is himself an archetypal Jew "[seeking] the good of his people" (10:3), an ideal figure (Fox 2001, 185–190).

An additional dimension inherent in the characters' system is the opposition "wisdom versus folly." Talmon interprets the Book of Esther as belonging to Wisdom Literature. Although his attempt is not completely convincing,[22] the importance of wisdom for the book cannot be ignored. Niditch (1987, 126–145) sees in the book an "underdog story" containing wisdom motifs. She perceives the Jewish characters of the story as "wise" (wisdom heroes), while other main characters are "foolish." "The wisdom heroes and heroines seek to become a part of the system that threatens them and (. . .) enjoy being a part of the establishment, deriving much benefit from it" (1987, 141). In fact, in order to survive in the Diaspora despite cultural differences (cf. 3:8: "[Jewish] laws are different from those of any other people"), Jews had to be wise like Esther and Mordecai—they had to know how to obtain the protection of the Gentile state, like Mordecai, and learn to act in indirect ways, like Esther. On the other hand, such characters as Haman and Ahasuerus display clear evidence of foolishness. Haman, the "carnival king" looks foolish and ridiculous when he expects to be honored, but will, in fact, be compelled to honor his worst enemy (6:6); he rejoices at the invitation by Esther to the second feast where he will himself be denounced (5:12); and prostrates himself before the queen (7:8). As for Ahasuerus, he is "all surface," without private thoughts or plans that are not obvious to everyone, impulsive and irresponsible (Fox 2001, 171, 173). Not only the king, but the whole Persian empire is, in a certain sense, "foolish": it is enough to mention the probably absurd decree, according to which the husband should "wield authority in his home and speak the language of his people" (1:22; cf. Greenstein 1987, 227–28; Berlin 2001, xix, 20; Fox 2001, 25).[23] An interesting question is whether Vashti can also be considered foolish. On the one hand, if Esther's behavior is wise and Vashti is her counterpart and opposite, her refusal to appear before the king (the only action by which she is characterized in the book) should be regarded as folly. On the other hand, one can understand the reasons for her action, although they are not explicitly named: it seems that "for Vashti to come would be tantamount to reducing herself to a concubine or dancing girl, making herself available to other men. Vashti is in a no-win situation, and must either go against Persian mores (which banned royal women from the drinking party)[24] or disobey the command of the king. She chose the latter in an attempt to preserve her own dignity or that of her husband . . ." (Berlin 2001, 15). A long tradition of sympathy toward, and even glorification of, Vashti exists, especially in feminist circles, beginning with such authors as Charlotte Brontë and Elizabeth Cady Stanton and continuing to contemporary feminist scholarship (see the discussion and bibliography in Berlin 2001, liv and footnote 75, and Fox 2001, 205–11; cf. also Beal 1995; Wyler 1995, 116–18; Butting 1999, 244–46). At the same time, feminist criticism sometimes shows contempt for Esther, virtually

changing the Book of Esther into a Book of Vashti. In fact, readings seeking to present Esther's predecessor as a protofeminist heroine lack sufficient textual support and
are, at best, to be accepted as "readings against the grain": "Vashti's indignation is
probably motivated by sense of rank than any protofeminist ideals" (Fox 2001, 168).

Yet, with all the sympathy for Vashti and understanding of the motives of her
action one must admit that in a certain sense she *is* foolish.[25] As Fox puts it, "Vashti is
an example of how *not* to do things, as well as a demonstration of the dangers of running afoul of the king. Her blatant self-assertion, whether or not it is praiseworthy in
the abstract, is simply not the way to get along in the Persian court . . ." (2001, 169).
Given the scarcity of her presentation in the text and the general carnivalesque atmosphere of the book, perceiving her as just another carnival fool does not seem too great
a mistake: "[Vashti] is probably more suitably read in carnival as a figure of fun"
(Green 2000, 147), a stereotyped "stubborn queen" (Greenstein 1987, 231).
Moreover, her "blatant self-assertion," justified or not, can be compared to the excessive pride of the "carnival king" Haman himself (Fox 2001, 179–82). Both are
dethroned in perfect accord with the laws of the carnival (cf. Bakhtin 1984, 196 ff.).

Summarizing Reading A, one can agree with one of the tenets of Niditch (1987,
140): the main characters of the Book of Esther can be divided into "Jewish" and
"Gentile"—which corresponds to their division into "wise" and "foolish."[26] In order
to survive in the "foolish" Gentile state[27] personified by Ahasuerus, Jews have to be
"wise" like Mordecai and Esther and not "foolish" like Vashti or Haman. At the same
time Vashti's "foolishness" is less evident than Ahasuerus' and Haman's, and she can
even evoke sympathy, especially in the modern reader.

Reading B: Authority and Defiance

Alongside the symmetries described above there is an additional symmetry between
the behavior of Vashti and Mordecai:[28]

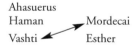

Ahasuerus
Haman ————▶ Mordecai
Vashti ◀———— Esther

Both refuse to do the thing demanded of them and defy thereby an authority
(Vashti that of Ahasuerus, Mordecai that of Haman). In both cases the refusal entails
an edict of general importance: in the first case pertaining to all the women, in the
second to all the Jews. In both cases it destabilizes the situation: Vashti is replaced by
Esther, while Mordecai's refusal to bow before Haman entails a sequence of events
which constitute the bulk of the plot of the book.

Finally, the reasons for both refusals are not fully clear. The case of Vashti has been
discussed above. As for Mordecai, the reason for his refusal to bow before Haman
seems evident: "Jews prostrate only before God."[29] This is explicitly referred to in
Addition C to the Septuagint translation, in Josephus' *Antiquities of the Jews*, in such
Jewish sources as *Targum Sheni* and Rashi's commentary, and even in such a modern
Jewish commentary as Soncino.[30] Yet Jews are not forbidden to prostrate before

human beings (Genesis 23:7; 43:28; Exod. 18:7; 1 Kings 1:23) and there is no mention in the text of Esther that Haman was granted divine honors; moreover, it seems quite improbable since he was the second highest person in the kingdom and not the first. Other Jewish sources (*Targum Rishon, Midrash Esther Rabba, Ibn Ezra,* to name just a few) refer to an idol on his chest, before which Mordecai would prostrate himself ("worship") while bowing to Haman. The very need for such a complicated and blatantly "rabbinic" explanation shows that Jewish commentators felt a problem with the reasons for Mordecai's refusal.

Of course, other reasons can be offered for this behavior—personal ambition or the ancient rivalry between Israel and Amalek.[31] As for the first, it would be too imprudent on Mordecai's part to endanger his people.[32] The second motive, although more "respectable," does not depict Mordecai as particularly wise: the Persian court with Haman the Amalekite as prime-minister was not the most appropriate place for renewing the ancient enmity (as I explore in more detail below).

If so, we stand before a textual gap difficult to fill—in fact, we are left ignorant of the reasons for Mordecai's refusal to prostrate before Haman. The question "Why do you disobey the king's order?" (3:3) receives no answer. Yet, such reasons are extremely important from the perspective of Jewish survival (cf. Reading A)—a behavior endangering the very existence of the Jewish people should be produced by causes leaving no other choice, otherwise it is irresponsible and therefore foolish. The classical cause compelling the Diaspora Jews to disobey the authority of a pagan kingdom is the order to worship idols (cf. Daniel 3, as well as various midrashim and stories from the Hellenistic period). The text skillfully creates the impression that we are dealing here with such a situation for the following reasons:

1. the gesture of "prostrating oneself before . . ." reminds one of the religious setting of worship;
2. Mordecai explains to the king's courtiers that he is a Jew (3:4), enabling one to infer that his refusal to prostrate before Haman has something to do with his being Jewish;
3. Haman's reference in his edict to the " [Jewish] laws" that are "different from those of any other people" (3:8) may seem to indicate, among other things, the Jewish prohibition of idolatry.

It should be noted that it is never explicitly said, either by the narrator or by Mordecai himself, that Mordecai refuses to prostrate before Haman *because* he is a Jew. The very placement of this phrase at the end of v.4 seems peculiar: does the verse mean that Mordecai's being a Jew led the king's courtiers to report the whole thing to the vizier? Berlin (2001, 37) fills the gap by supposing that "it was Mordecai's Jewishness that prevented him from bowing to Haman. The servants wanted to see if Haman would accept Mordecai's explanation of not bowing to him . . ." In fact, as we saw above, it is difficult to establish a causal connection between Mordecai's identity and his refusal. The attempt by Fox (2001, 45–46) and others to explain Mordecai's behavior in terms of his ethnic hostility to Haman seems especially unconvincing: no state (including modern liberal democracies) would accept such a reason for not fulfilling the orders. Mordecai's proclamation to the king's servants: "I do not bow to Haman because I am a Jew and Jews hate Amalekites" would be called anything but wise and responsible.

(One has to add that "Mordecai the racist" would be too precious a gift to the antisemitic readers of the book.) Together with this, one cannot deny that the conflict between Haman and Mordecai is viewed in the book as, among other things, a reflection of the ancient strife between Amalek and Israel (especially between the posterities of Agag and Saul); it therefore has an "ethnic" dimension. This ethnic rivalry is, however, very specific and has nothing to do with the universal source of tension in the relationship between Jews and Gentiles—the cultural specificity of Jewish customs.

Returning to our theme, we have seen that the "religious" explanation of Mordecai's behavior cannot be accepted, and two other explanations are incompatible with Mordecai's wisdom. *The Book of Hiding* (Beal 1997)[33] tries to hide from the reader the truth that there is no substantial difference between the behavior of Vashti and Mordecai.[34] A "wise" Jewish man behaves in the same way as a "foolish"[35] Gentile woman. Reading A, which divides the main characters of the book into Jews and Gentiles, on the one hand, and into "wise" and "foolish" on the other, is thus deconstructed by the parallel Mordecai-Vashti.[36] As has been remarked on several times,[37] this parallel personifies the parallel between women and Jews—two sectors of the population that the empire has difficulty controlling.

It is worth noting that a text that "hides" all the religious issues should also "hide" the essence of the cultural specificity of the Jews, which is religious in its nature (cf. above). This is reduced to background information, and thus the manipulation of the reader is facilitated. (At the same time, as I have tried to show, the book attempts to hide the very act of hiding.) As I have remarked above, Esther is a "secular" book, and the cultural specificity of secular Jews is, at least partly, "hidden" (displaced to the subconscious/archetypal realm), which makes Jewish identity in the secular age especially paradoxical.

A Comparison of the Readings

Reading A turns the Jewish characters of the book into role models for the sort of "wise" behavior that is needed in order to survive in the "foolish" Gentile world and opposes them to "foolish" Gentiles. It is deconstructed by Reading B, drawing a parallel between "wise" Mordechai and "foolish" Vashti. According to Reading A, the Jews need wisdom in order to achieve the almost impossible task "to be Persian citizens while remaining cultural outsiders" (Clines 1998, 17). From Reading B we see that the collision endangering the existence of the Jews lacks a clear cultural motivation. Mordecai can even be opposed to the "wise" Esther: "the Jewish people find themselves under a death sentence because one Jew acts like a Jew and tells his people he is a Jew; they escape through the good offices of another Jew who has pretended she is not a Jew . . ." (Clines 1998, 18; cf. Clines 1984, 294).[38] (One can also compare Mordecai's inexplicable disobedience to the דת [law, royal order] with that of Esther, which is a real act of "no choice," the only possible way for her to save the Jews [4:16]—"if I am to perish, I shall perish.")

The perspective of Reading A is that of the Jews—the book is read as a reflection on their most appropriate behavior in a Gentile empire. In Reading B the perspective is, in an ironic fashion, that of the empire itself: women and Jews may challenge the authority of the state and need to be under control. This shift of perspective can, in itself, be viewed as a kind of carnivalesque reversal: Jews view themselves through the eyes of those who threaten them and to whom they have to accommodate themselves in order to survive.

The very parallel between Mordecai and Vashti discloses its ironic character in the reversal of the book's plot.[39] Let us compare two narrative sequences:

(1) Vashti refuses to appear before Ahasuerus   (2) Vashti is eliminated
(1a) Mordecai refuses to bow before Haman   (2a) Haman is eliminated

As the parallel suggests, in (2a) Mordecai should be eliminated and not Haman (this is the "normal" order of things). Yet, the Great Reversal in the plot of the book also reverses the disastrous consequences of Mordecai's action—Haman is impaled on the stake he prepared for Mordecai. Maybe Mordecai can even be seen as wise "post factum"—finally, whatever he has done, he is the winner.[40]

How does the lack of motivation in Mordecai's refusal influence the treatment of the Jewish identity issue in the book? One can point to three consequences:

(a) the opposition between "wise" Jews and "foolish" Gentiles is deconstructed;
(b) the Mordecai-Vashti parallel shifts the perspective from that of the Jews to that of the empire;
(c) if we accept the "Jewish" character of Mordecai's refusal to prostrate himself before Haman (as I tried to show above, this is what the "implied author" of the book wants the reader to understand in spite of the problematic character of such a reading), one sees that he most closely approximates the "foolish" Gentiles at the moment when he wants to behave in a "Jewish" fashion. Thus a connection can be established with the deconstruction of the book by Clines (1998, 17–21), which emphasizes the need to hide Jewish identity in order to preserve it.

Finally, if Reading A is, to a certain extent, wisdom-oriented, Reading B is more ironic and "carnivalesque." It is more akin to the spirit of Purim—a feast during which "wise" people behave "foolishly" and Jews often dress as Gentiles. The celebration of Jewish collective wisdom has become, in a paradoxical way, the most "foolish" of Jewish holidays. The sober message of Reading A is undermined by the carnivalesque element of reversal and subversion. In other words, Jewish identity in the Book of Esther is both constructed and deconstructed. Even if we fail to eliminate the contrast between cursed Haman and blessed Mordecai, at least the essential difference in behavior between Mordecai and Vashti can be erased by a close reading of the book.

Conclusion

If I wanted to summarize my reading of Esther in one phrase (an operation hardly possible, if not forbidden, for a deconstructive reading), I would formulate it as follows: *it seems to us that we know what the Jewish difference is, but in fact we don't know it.* It seems that the Jews are "wise" unlike the "foolish" Gentiles—but Mordecai's refusal to bow before Haman can hardly be called wise. It appears that the core of the matter is the religious prohibition to worship idols, but Mordecai's refusal to bow before Haman is not determined by this prohibition. In other words, *we know what Jewish difference is not.* I even dare to say that, from the angle of the proposed deconstructive reading, Jewish difference (and therefore Jewish identity) is approached in the Book of Esther *via negativa*—in a way suitable for an entity located in the realm of the sacred

Yet, the book in no way resembles a treatise of negative theology. It is carnivalesque, secular, "earthly." Secularization and acculturation are the ways of hiding Jewish difference without erasing it. Being a "loss," this hiding at the same time represents an opportunity and a challenge to reconstruct Jewish difference/identity in a different way.

Notes

1. See, for example Derrida, 1998, 2000. A postmodern approach to the problem of collective identities can be found, among others, in Bhabha 1990. Among now classical works on national identity one can quote, for example, Anderson 1991.
2. See, for example Derrida 1993, 1998.
3. Military service is an essential component of the Israeli identity, and Israel is perhaps the only country in the world where a disease like asthma—which brings exemption from service on medical grounds—can entail an identity crisis as well (although things have begun to change in this respect over the last decade).
4. Inverted commas around this word are in no way fortuitous and reflect a highly ambivalent relationship. Cf. the advice of a Russian-Jewish writer more than a decade ago: "a Russian Jew should not pretend to be a Russian in Russia and a non-Russian outside Russia."
5. The relationship between such identity markers as "Russian" and "Soviet" is also very complicated and tense, although I will not enter into any details in this article.
6. "Invagination" in Derrida's term (1977, 98; quoted from Leavey 1982, 55), i.e. "inverted reapplication of the outer edge to the inside of a form where the outside then opens a pocket."
7. This situation has little to do with the debate on so-called post-Zionism—an intellectual stream aiming at the revision of the Israeli/Zionist narrative concerning the Israeli–Arab conflict. Yet the situation in contemporary Israel may be qualified as "post-Zionist," even for those who do not belong to this stream, just as the contemporary state of the world may be termed "post-modern" even for those who do not define themselves as "post-modernists."
8. See in detail Slivniak 2001a (in Russian; Hebrew translation in preparation).
9. See Berlin 2001, xli–xliii.
10. Cf. Slivniak 2001b, 42.
11. Fox (2001, 4) enumerates six questions "provoked by the story's own perspectives and emphases." Four among them are related to Jewish identity and/or Jewish survival.
12. Jewish identity according to the book of Esther differs quite significantly from its "main-stream" version as represented, for example, in Deuteronomy. Not only is it a "secular"

identity without emphasis on God and cult, but also a "diasporic" one: the return to Zion is not discussed in the book, which virtually lacks the opposition between "homeland" and "Exile" (with the probable exception of the Exile, mentioned in 2:6).

13. See in detail Beal 1997; Greenstein 1987, 225–26 and footnotes; Fox 2001, 217 and the bibliography there. A recent attempt at an antisemitic interpretation of Esther (this time in Russia) can be found in Kuraev.

14. See the bibliography in Berlin 2001, xlvi, footnotes 52–54.

15. Such an approach has been systematically applied by Craig (1995). For a discussion of his approach see Green 2000, 144–47 and Fox 2001, 291–293.

16. For a different approach to the deconstruction of the Book of Esther, see Clines 1998, 17–21, which also emphasizes the question of Jewish identity.

17. On symmetries in the Book of Esther see Brenner 1995 as well as Berg 1979.

18. Cf. a similar approach to Genesis 1 in Greenstein 2001.

19. Ahasuerus' counterpart in the second column may be the unnamed character behind the scene: God. Cf. Brenner 1995, 76.

20. See, for example, Day 1995, 203 and the bibliography there, as well as Fox 2001, 169–170.

21. Quotations are from the JPS translation.

22. See criticism in Crenshaw 1969; Fox 2001, 142–43.

23. The tradition of viewing this decree as absurd goes back to the rabbinic midrash (*Meg. Esther Rabbah* 4), where Ahasuerus is openly called "stupid" in this connection. (סרחה דעתו של אחשורוש). The demand that the husband should "speak the language of his people" is probably less absurd than it seems at first glance: according to Gordis, "when an intermarriage took place . . . the mother's language would normally prevail . . . . Ahasuerus' edict was designed to make the father's language dominant in the home" (Gordis 1974, 24–25; quoted in Wyler 1995, 116–17).

24. Certain Greek sources indicate that "honorable" women were absent from Persian men's parties. However, in my view, it does not necessarily follow from this that a presentation of the householder's wife to the guests (after which she would return to her place) was contrary to custom. In fact, we do not know who went against Persian mores in this case—Ahasuerus or Vashti.

25. One should not forget that the category of "wise vs. foolish" has a specific meaning in the framework of Reading A with its concern for Jewish survival strategies: "wise" behavior is responsible, rational, well calculated, and indirect, while "foolish" behavior is irresponsible, miscalculated, straightforward, and/or impulsive. Vashti's behavior is impulsive, direct, and miscalculated (she hardly counts on loosing her status as a queen).

26. But one hardly can agree with Niditch's statement that "all the wise and good characters in the book are Jews, the foolish, rash, evil ones non-Jews" (1987, 140). Such second-rank Gentile characters as Hegai, Hathach, and Harvona are not "evil" at all, and even Haman's wife Zeresh sometimes has insights of wisdom (6:13). She is "wiser than her husband" (Brenner 1995, 76, footnote 3).

27. For the fullness of the picture one has to add, that, while being ridiculed, the Persian empire is at the same time respected and even admired—for example in the description of the feast in 1:3–8. With all their circumspection and reserve, the Jews have their pride in participating at the glory and wealth of such magnificent a state. Cf. Clines 1998, 16: ". . . the ideal state of affairs for the Jews of the book of Esther is not that the Persian government should be overthrown, but that a coreligionist of theirs should be 'next in rank' to the king (10:3) and should wield the 'power and might' of the Persian empire (10:2)." This is not to exclude that one is dealing here with the usual carnivalesque ridiculing of a respectable institution. On traditional Jewish interest in the protection of a strong centralized state see Arendt 1958, 23–25.

28. Cf. Greenstein, 1987, 233–234; Levenson 1997, 68–69; Beal 1997, 17 and others.
29. See the discussion of Mordecai's motives in Levenson 1997, 67–68; Fox 2001, 42–46; Berlin 2001, 34–37.
30. Cohen 1946, 210: ". . . *that he was a Jew*. And therefore could not pay Haman divine honor."
31. The last explanation is accepted, among others, by Clines (1984, 294), Fox (2001, 45–46) and partly by Berlin (2001, 35).
32. Cf. Addition C of the Septuagint: "You know, O Lord, that not in arrogance or in haughtiness or in love of glory did I refrain from prostrating myself to the haughty Haman, for I would have agreed to kiss the soles of his feet for the sake of the safety of Israel" (quoted in Fox 2001, 43).
33. The title of the monograph by Beal may point to the rabbinic midrash (*BT Hullin* 139b) connecting the name אסתר with the Torah text ואנכי הסתר אסתיר פני "And I will surely **hide** my face . . ." (Deut. 31:18).
34. In fact, Mordecai's behavior is much worse. While Vashti's refusal to appear before Ahasuerus concerns mainly herself and entails, at worst, the ridiculous edict demanding that every man "wield authority in his home and speak the language of his people" (1:22), Mordecai's refusal endangers the physical existence of the Jews.
35. Although, as I have remarked above, she is less evidently "foolish" than Ahasuerus and Haman.
36. It is worth noting that, while discussing the dismissal of Vashti, Niditch ignores, in her syntagmatic-folkloristic analysis of the plot, Mordecai's refusal to bow before Haman. It seems that the last does not fit the "wisdom tale" morphology postulated by Niditch for the book. If we transfer her treatment of the Vashti issue (1987, 133) to the parallel case of Mordecai, the advice of Zeresh to hang Mordecai (5:14) will be marked as an "exercise of wisdom," while the "resolution" stage will be exactly the opposite of that anticipated in her scheme—not Mordecai but Haman is impaled on the stake.
37. See, e.g., van Hoek 1998; Beal 1997; Butting 1999, 243–45.
38. Cf. also the formulation in Clines 1984: "the triumph of . . . Jewish charm (Esther) over Jewish gaucherie (Mordecai)" (1984, 263). In the context of approaches close to Reading A, "gaucherie" becomes almost a synonym of "foolishness."
39. On reversals in the book of Esther see, e.g., Berg 1979, 106–22.
40. Although the result would not be complete without the "good offices" of Esther and there would be no reversal at all without the assistance of an unnamed character who is wiser than all the "wise" characters of the book taken together.

Works Consulted

Anderson, Benedict R. 1991. *Imagined Communities: Reflections on the Origin and Spread of Nationalism*. Rev. and extended edn London & New York: Verso.

Arendt, Hannah. 1958. *The Origins of Totalitarianism*. Cleveland & New York: World.

Bakhtin, Mikhail M. 1984. *Rabelais and His World*. Trans. Helene Iswolsky. Bloomington: Indiana University Press.

Beal, Timothy K. 1995. "Tracing Esther's Beginnings." In *A Feminist Companion to Esther, Judith and Susanna*, ed. Athalya Brenner, 87–110. Sheffield: Sheffield Academic Press.

———. 1997. *The Book of Hiding: Gender, Ethnicity, Annihilation, and Esther*. London & New York: Routledge.

Berg, Sandra B. 1979. *The Book of Esther: Motifs, Themes and Structures*. SBL Dissertations Series 14. Missoula, MA: Scholars Press.

Berlin, Adele. 2001/5761. *Esther. The Traditional Hebrew Text with the New JPS Translation.* The JPS Bible Commentary. Philadelphia: The Jewish Publication Society.

Bhabha, Homi K., ed. 1990. *Nation and Narration.* London & New York: Routledge.

Brenner, Athalya. 1995. "Looking at Esther Through the Looking Glass." In *A Feminist Companion to Esther, Judith and Susanna*, ed. Athalya Brenner, 71–80. Sheffield: Sheffield Academic Press.

Butting, Klara. 1999. "Esther: A New Interpretation of the Joseph Story in the Fight against Anti-Semitism and Sexism." In *Ruth and Esther. A Feminist Companion to the Bible (Second Series)*, ed. Athalya Brenner, 239–48. Sheffield: Sheffield Academic Press.

Clines, David J. A. 1984. *Ezra, Nehemia, Esther.* New Century Bible Commentary. Grand Rapids: Eerdmans; London: Marshall, Morgan & Scott.

——. 1998. "Reading Esther from Left to Right: Contemporary Strategies for Reading a Biblical Text." In *On the Way to the Postmodern: Old Testament Essays, 1967–1998*, Vol. 1, 3–22. JSOT Supplement Series 292. Sheffield: Sheffield Academic Press.

Cohen, A., ed. 1946. *The Five Megilloth. Hebrew Text, English Translation and Commentary.* Hindhead, Surrey: Soncino.

Craig, Kenneth. 1995. *Reading Esther: A Case for the Literary Carnivalesque.* Louisville, KY: Westminster John Knox.

Crenshaw, James L. 1969. "Method in Determining Wisdom Influence upon 'Historical' Literature". *Journal of Biblical Literature* 88: 129–42.

Culler, Jonathan. 1982. *On Deconstruction: Theory and Criticism After Structuralism.* Ithaca, New York: Cornell University Press.

Day, Linda. 1995. *Three Faces of a Queen. Characterization in the Books of Esther.* JSOT Supplement Series 186. Sheffield: Sheffield Academic Press.

Derrida, Jacques. 1977. "Ja, ou le faux-bond." *Digraphe* 11:83–112.

——. 1993. *Circumfession: Fifty-nine periods and periphrases written in a sort of internal margin, between Geoffrey Bennington's book and work in preparation (January 1989–April 1990).* Trans. Geoffrey Bennington. Chicago: University of Chicago Press.

——. 1998. *Monolingualism of the Other, or, The Prosthesis of Origin.* Trans. Patrick Mensah. Stanford, CA: Stanford University Press.

——. 2000. *Of Hospitality / Anne Dufourmantelle Invites Jacques Derrida to Respond.* Trans. Rachel Bowlby. Stanford, CA: Stanford University Press.

Elgazi, Gadi. 1992. "*Lashav yenase ha-mitstaref* (The newcomer tries in vain . . .)." *Politika* 42/43:28–29 (in Hebrew).

Fox, Michael V. 2001. *Character and Ideology in the Book of Esther. Second Edition with a New Postscript on a Decade of Esther Scholarship.* Columbia, SC: University of South Carolina Press.

Gordis, Robert. 1974. *Megillat Esther with Introduction, New Translation and Commentary.* New York: The Rabbinical Assembly.

Green, Barbara. 2000. *Mikhail Bakhtin and Biblical Studies. An Introduction.* SBL Semeia Studies 38. Atlanta: Society of Biblical Literature.

Greenstein, Edward L. 1987. "A Jewish Reading of Esther." In *Judaic Perspectives on Ancient Israel*, ed. J. Neusner, 225–243. Philadelphia: Fortress.

——. 2001. "Presenting Genesis 1, Constructively and Deconstructively." *Prooftexts* 21:1–22.

Hoek, Karen van. 1998. "Purim: the Limits of Control." *Tikkun* 13:47–48.

Ivanov, Vjacheslav V. 1998. "Ocherki po predystorii i istorii semiotiki (Essays on the Pre-history and History of Semiotics)." In *Izbrannye trudy po semiotike i istorii kul'tury (Selected Works in Semiotics and Cultural History)*, Vol. 1, 605–812. Moscow: Shkola "Jazyki russkoj kul'tury" (in Russian).

Kuraev, Deacon Andrei. 1998. *Kak Delajut Antisemitom (How They Make One Into An Antisemite).* Moscow: Odigitrija (in Russian).

Leavey, John P. Jr. 1982. "Four Protocols: Derrida, His Deconstruction." In *Derrida and Biblical Studies* (*Semeia* 23), ed. Robert Detweiler, 29–41.

Levenson, Jon D. 1997 *Esther. A Commentary.* London: SCM.

Niditch, Susan. 1987. *Underdogs and Tricksters: A Prelude to Biblical Folklore.* San Francisco: Harper & Row.

Polish, Daniel F. 1998. "Aspects of Esther: a Phenomenological Exploration of the *Megillah* of Esther and the Origins of Purim." *Journal for the Study of the Old Testament* 85: 85–106.

Slivniak, Dmitri M. 2001a. "Russkij Manifest (The Russian Manifesto)." *Zerkalo* 15/16: 108–17 (in Russian).

——. 2001b. *The Opposing Helper: Hierarchical Oppositions, Dangerous Assistants and Ambivalence in the Pentateuch.* Doctoral Diss. Tel Aviv (in Hebrew).

Talmon, Shemaryahu. 1963. " 'Wisdom' in the Book of Esther." *Vetus Testamentum* 13: 419–55.

Wyler, Bea. 1995. "Esther: the Incomplete Emancipation of a Queen." In *A Feminist Companion to Esther, Judith and Susanna*, ed. Athalya Brenner, 111–35. Sheffield: Sheffield Academic Press.

responsibilities, secrets, gifts

Chapter 9

Triangulating Responsibility: How and Why Abraham, Isaac, and Ishmael Offer and Refuse the Gift of Death, and to/from Whom

R. Christopher Heard

Two Sons, Two Offerings

To speak of Abraham attempting to sacrifice his beloved son is problematic from the start, for Jewish, Christian, and Islamic tradition all concur that Abraham in fact had *two* sons—Ishmael and Isaac—when God called for the sacrifice. Debates between Jews, Christians, and Muslims over the interpretation of the Offering have often focused on the identity of the intended victim. Jewish tradition, with roots in Genesis 22, identified Isaac as the intended victim. Christian tradition affirmed Jewish tradition with regard to the literal sacrifice, but saw in Isaac a prefiguration of Jesus' death. The Qur'an's version of the Offering (*sura* 37:99–113) does not name the intended victim; some Islamic interpreters understood the story to depict Isaac as the intended victim, while others understood the story to place Ishmael in that position. Jews, Muslims, and—in a different way—Christians all place their ostensible link to Abraham under the patriarch's sacrificial knife. This fact, to which I will return, opens up an intriguing possibility for thinking the gift of death—for knowing, to paraphrase Derrida, to whom to give it, but also from whom not to receive it, and why.

I begin, however, with the biblical text, Genesis 22. Kierkegaard's ruminations in *Fear and Trembling* relate to this form of the story, as do Derrida's in *The Gift of Death*. Although Derrida occasionally uses the compound adjective "Judeo-Christian-Islamic" in connection with Abraham (Derrida 1995, 64), and occasionally switches from the Hebrew-style vocalization "Abraham" to the Arabic-style vocalization "Ibrahim" (Derrida 1995, 69), and may even in one paragraph allude ever so lightly to Islamic traditions identifying Ishmael as the intended victim (Derrida 1995, 69), he nowhere mentions Ishmael *by name* in the 1995 English version of *The Gift of Death*.[1] The Offering remains "the sacrifice of Isaac" throughout.

So too Derrida's conversation partner Kierkegaard, who states baldly that "Abraham had just one, the son he loved" (1985 [1843], 54) even though he had referred in passing to "Hagar and the son whom [Abraham] had driven out into the desert" just a few pages before (1985 [1843], 47). Thus Kierkegaard and Derrida both begin with Isaac on, or at least headed for, the altar.

Perhaps it will prove helpful here to rehearse some important elements of Kierkegaard's reading of Genesis 22. God has placed before Abraham a monstrous demand: "Take your son, your only one, the one you love, Isaac, and go to the land of Moriah; offer him there as a whole burnt offering on one of the mountains that I will tell you" (Genesis 22:1). Abraham, in seeming contradiction to all that is ethical, obeys this command to the letter. Abraham becomes, for Kierkegaard, the "knight of faith," because "he did not doubt, he did not look in anguish to left or right, he did not challenge heaven with his prayers" (1985 [1843], 55). Kierkegaard particularly emphasizes Abraham's "anguish" throughout the affair:

> If I myself were to talk about him, I would first depict the pain of the trial. For that I would suck all the fear, distress, and torment out of the father's suffering, like a leech, in order to be able to describe all that Abraham suffered while still believing. (1985 [1843], 81)

To explain Abraham's ability to sacrifice Isaac despite this fear, distress, and torment, Kierkegaard seems to gaze at Abraham through the lens offered to him by Hebrews 11: Abraham "all along . . . had faith, he believed that God would not demand Isaac from him . . . God could give him a new Isaac, bring the sacrificial offer back to life" (1985 [1843], 65; cf. Hebrews 11:17–19). And thus Abraham's faith defeats his fear and he is ready to draw his knife—the embodiment of his faith—across Isaac's neck until the faith with which this knight is armed is parried at the last moment by a voice from heaven.

In *The Gift of Death*, Derrida transposes certain elements of Kierkegaard's reading into his own vocabulary of "the gift of death," and the elements thus translated lead us toward new ways of thinking this story. In particular, Derrida's casting of the directionality of the gift of Isaac's death has profound implications for interpretation, though some of these remain unrealized in *The Gift of Death* itself. To speak of the "directionality" of the gift of Isaac's death is to raise the question of interest. In whose interest, or for whose sake, was Abraham willing to slaughter Isaac? According to Kierkegaard,

> Then why does Abraham do it? For God's sake, and what is exactly the same, for his own. He does it for the sake of God because God demands this proof of his faith; he does it for his own sake in order to be able to produce the proof. (1985 [1843], 88)

Or, to speak in Derridean tongue, God has "asked Abraham to put Isaac to death, that is, to make a gift of death as a sacrificial offering to himself" (1985 [1843], 65), and "Abraham has already consented *to make a gift of death*, and to give to God the death that he is going to put his son to" (1985 [1843], 75). Kierkegaard's understanding of the offering is represented in figure 9.1.

Yet it is difficult to gaze at Isaac upon the altar without also seeing his older brother, Ishmael, just outside Moriah, somewhere off to the side of the mountain of

Figure 9.1   Genesis 22, typically.

vision—in one's peripheral vision, perhaps. For although God proposes the test using the words "Take your son, your only son, whom you love," readers know full well that Abraham has *two* sons. Those readers whose readings are immortalized in *Genesis Rabbah* certainly took notice of Ishmael's lingering presence in Genesis 22:

> And He Said: Take, I pray thee, thy son, etc. (xxii, 2). Said He to him: "Take, I pray thee—I beg thee—thy son"."Which son?" he asked. "Thine only son," replied He. "But each is the only one of his mother?"—"Whom thou lovest".—"Is there a limit to the affections?" "Even Isaac," said He. And why did he not reveal it to him without delay? In order to make him [Isaac] even more beloved in his eyes and reward him for every word spoken. (*Genesis Rab.* 55:7)

The midrash reveals that the first three items in God's specification—"your son," "your only son," "whom you love"—could at face value apply equally well to Isaac or Ishmael. Thus Ishmael lurks in the margin of Genesis 22. This "trace" of Ishmael in Genesis 22 is highly suggestive. Just one chapter earlier, Abraham had banished Ishmael and his mother, Hagar, from the family camp, after God endorsed Sarah's insistence upon such banishment. Genesis 21 and 22 thus exhibit parallel storylines: in Genesis 21, God commands Abraham to exile Ishmael, which Abraham does; in Genesis 22, God commands Abraham to sacrifice Isaac, which Abraham makes every possible attempt to do. Several smaller plot elements strengthen the impression of a strong parallelism between these two stories. In Genesis 21, Abraham sends Hagar and Ishmael away early in the morning with such meager provisions that the boy is soon at death's door—one might say that by providing only a skin of water and a loaf of bread, Abraham in effect gives death to Ishmael (Hagar seems to be hardier; see Heard 2001, 86–90 for a fuller discussion of these provisions). Only the last-minute intervention of the angel of God preserves Ishmael's life. In Genesis 22, Abraham sets out with Isaac early in the morning to conduct a sacrifice for which provisions— that is, the lamb—are woefully lacking. By taking with them only fire and wood, but no lamb, Abraham shows that his plan is to give death to Isaac. Only the last-minute intervention of the angel of the Lord preserves Isaac's life. The strong correspondences between these stories recommend reading them as a matched pair (cf. Goldingay 1998, 148; Gossai 1997, 7; Leviant 1999; Levenson 1993, 103–10, 123–24; Wenham 1994, 99–100).

Reading Genesis 21 and 22 as a matched pair, however, complicates some aspects of Kierkegaard's—and Derrida's—reading of Genesis 22. Here and there in *The Gift of Death*, Derrida refers to Abraham giving death to Isaac (i.e. "putting Isaac to death") and of Abraham giving Isaac's death to God (e.g., Derrida 1995, 75, 93). The parallels between the expulsion of Ishmael and the sacrifice of Isaac problematize the latter part of this expression. To be sure, when Genesis 22 is read *alone*, it looks as though Abraham's sacrifice of Isaac is solely a response to God's command; it looks as though in giving death to Isaac, Abraham is giving Isaac's death to God. But is he really? If we could penetrate Abraham's own secret reasoning, is that really what we would see?[2]

Genesis 21 itself gives us some clues. In this story, Sarah's demand that Abraham expel Ishmael and Hagar from the household is explicitly an economic issue: Sarah "said to Abraham, 'Disown this slave-woman with her son, for the son of this slave-woman must not inherit along with my son, along with Isaac' " (Genesis 21:8–10). No matter how one interprets the irreducibly ambiguous description of Ishmael's activity at Isaac's weaning-party (see Heard 2001, 82–86 for discussion), Sarah's stated rationale is entirely and exclusively about wealth. She does not want Abraham's wealth to be split between two sons when he dies; all must go to Isaac. And so Abraham, once God has endorsed Sarah's behest, effectively sacrifices Ishmael (and Hagar) for the sake of Isaac (and Sarah). This leads to an alternative sacrificial transaction, represented in figure 9.2.

To put it this way is accurate, but leaves out one very important element in Genesis 21, namely, Abraham's initial reaction to Sarah's demand. The narrator describes Abraham as first being very upset about all this "on account of his son." Only after God has assured Abraham that Ishmael will live, indeed prosper, does Abraham actually follow through with the expulsion of Hagar and Ishmael. Yet in the act of expulsion itself, Abraham in essence gives the exiles death by giving them insufficient food and water. Is Abraham testing God to see whether the latter will deliver on Ishmael's promised prosperity, or is Abraham acting "by faith" (as Kierkegaard, following the author of the book of Hebrews, posits on so many occasions)? In either

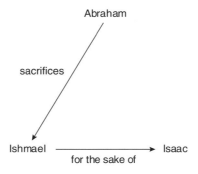

Figure 9.2   Genesis 21, explicitly.

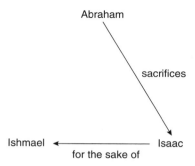

Figure 9.3   Genesis 22, heterodoxically.

event, Sarah will have to blame God rather than Abraham for Ishmael's survival. In her eyes, at least, Abraham will have sacrificed Ishmael for Isaac's sake.

The strong parallels noted above between Genesis 21 and 22 invite reexamination of Genesis 22 to see whether Abraham's actions might be read there as a mirror image of his actions in Genesis 21. Is it possible that Abraham's silent willingness to sacrifice Isaac in Genesis 22 may not be so much because Abraham is a "knight of faith," as Kierkegaard would have it, or that Abraham has "renounced calculation," as Derrida would have it (1995, 95–97), but rather because he finds now an opportunity to "reverse" the "sacrifice" (expulsion) of Ishmael in Genesis 21? In Genesis 21, Abraham "sacrifices" Ishmael for Isaac's sake. Is it possible that in Genesis 22, Abraham is willing to sacrifice Isaac for Ishmael's sake, leading to a more heterodex "sacrifice" along the lines of figure 9.3.

To be sure, this is not the most common or most popular reading. One might even call it heterodox. Nevertheless, prior to chapter 22, Abraham has always acted in a way that suggests he prefers Ishmael to Isaac. When God announces Isaac's imminent birth to Abraham in Genesis 17, Abraham immediately objects, lobbying for God to attend to Ishmael instead. In the same chapter, Abraham circumcises Ishmael, causing Ishmael's body to bear the mark of the covenant to which God has explicitly said that Isaac, and not Ishmael, will be heir. Abraham displays no interest in the unborn Isaac's welfare—or his paternity—in Genesis 20. Even after Isaac's birth, Sarah's demand for the expulsion of Hagar and her son troubles Abraham precisely because of his attachment to Ishmael. Might Abraham's willingness to sacrifice Isaac stem at least in part for a preference for Ishmael?

Most readers probably deny themselves access to this line of reasoning through a too-credulous reading of God's reference to Isaac in Genesis 22:2 as the son that Abraham loves. Derrida's own affirmation of Abraham's love for Isaac lies more in the realm of logical necessity. For Derrida, Abraham *must* love Isaac; otherwise, the Offering is no sacrifice: "If I put to death or grant death to what I hate it is not a sacrifice. I must sacrifice what I love" (1995, 64).[3]

Yet we are faced with the fact that "God is not willing to have the boy killed. But Abraham is. In the final analysis, God says no. Why doesn't Abraham?" (Fewell and

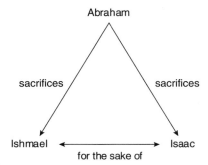

Figure 9.4   Genesis 21 and 22, parallel.

Gunn 1993, 54). Perhaps Abraham does not really love Isaac after all (cf. Davies 1995, 111), or at least loves Ishmael more than Isaac. Perhaps such a preference for Ishmael is the reason that God needs to speak in a manner designed to, in the words of *Genesis Rabbah*, "make [Isaac] even more beloved in [Abraham's] eyes." Abraham may reason that with Isaac gone, Ishmael can once again be his beloved son (which perhaps he, not Isaac, was all along) who inherits both wealth and covenant. Although such a reading is disturbing, it does have the virtue of exposing the "mirror image" quality of Genesis 21 and 22, represented in figure 9.4 above.

Were we to entertain this notion that Abraham might be willing to sacrifice Isaac, not because he has renounced calculation but precisely because he has calculated the advantage to Ishmael in Isaac's death, what ought we say about God? Following Kierkegaard, Derrida posits that "God wouldn't have asked Abraham to put Isaac to death, that is, to make a gift of death as a sacrificial offering to himself, to God, unless Abraham had an absolute, unique, and incommensurable love for his son . . ." (1995, 65; cf. Levenson 1993, 127–28). But is this necessarily so? Might God have other motives in asking for Isaac's death? Clearly, God asks Abraham to do something that God does not really want Abraham to do, namely, to slaughter Isaac. God *asks for* Isaac's death, but God does not *want* Isaac's death. It is worth noting that this is not the first time God has asked Abraham to do something, the successful completion of which will complicate God's stated plans for the genealogical transmission of God's covenant with Abraham. Here in chapter 22, God asks Abraham to kill Isaac, even though God has vehemently specified in 17:19 that God has slated Isaac to inherit the covenant. In that same chapter, God demands that Abraham circumcise himself and all the males in his household. This Abraham does with letter-perfect obedience, just as in chapter 22. However, circumcising all of the males in Abraham's household entails circumcising Ishmael. Yet circumcision is to be the bodily sign of participation in God's covenant with Abraham, and God has explicitly cut Ishmael *out* of that covenant in 17:19. Ishmael thus bears in his flesh the marks of a covenant to which God apparently does not consider him a party; this marking resulted, however, from Abraham following God's commands quite thoroughly. With regard to *both* sons, God's short-term commands are at cross-purposes with God's long-range plans.

Recently, a few interpreters have begun to question whether the traditional understanding of the test God poses in chapter 22 is the most plausible one available. Noticing that Abraham "has shown no difficulties sacrificing members of his family," Danna Nolan Fewell and David Gunn ask whether the test might not be "really designed to see just how far Abraham will go?" (1993, 53; cf. Gunn and Fewell 1993, 98; Trible 1991, 188). Given Abraham's track record of sacrificing his wives (chapters 12; 16; 20; 21) and son (chapter 16, neonatally; 20, neonatally; 21), can God really doubt that Abraham will be willing to sacrifice Isaac, especially if Abraham really does harbor a preference for Ishmael over Isaac even at this late hour? Might God be hoping that Abraham will refuse to sacrifice Isaac, or at least mount some sort of protest against the sacrifice, not unlike the mild protest he raised against Ishmael's exclusion from the covenant when God announced Isaac's birth to him (Genesis 17), his extreme displeasure at Sarah's demand for Ishmael's expulsion (Genesis 21), or his haggling for Sodom's survival (Genesis 18), not to mention his attempt to rescue Lot from Chedorlaomer and his allies (Genesis 14)? Abraham has, on occasion, risked his life or, what may be the same thing, challenged God's plans where Ishmael and Lot are concerned. Might God be trying to learn whether Abraham's attachment to Isaac has come to match (or even exceed) his attachment to Ishmael, hoping for an affirmative result?[4] Derrida himself opens a door ever so slightly to this possibility in a footnote where he quotes Lévinas:

> But one can posit the contrary: the attention Abraham pays to the voice that brings him back to the ethical order by forbidding him to carry out the human sacrifice, is the most intense moment of the drama. . . . It is there, in the ethical, that there is an appeal to the uniqueness of the subject and sense is given to life in defiance of death. (1995, 78; quoting Lévinas 1976, 113)

Lévinas's characterization of the moment Abraham *abandons* his intention to sacrifice Isaac as "the most intense moment of the drama" recalls the visual representations of this scene by Rembrandt (including the engraving featured on the dust jacket of the 1995 English edition of *The Gift of Death*) and Caravaggio, in which the angel is depicted as *physically restraining* Abraham from completing the sacrifice.

From the viewpoint of this alternate reading of God's intentions, Abraham fails this test miserably, showing that his attachment to Ishmael is still strong enough that he will take the opportunity afforded by God's bizarre command to dispatch Isaac so that Ishmael might enjoy God's favor instead. Even readers who are unwilling to impute such dastardly calculation to "father Abraham" must admit, nevertheless, that Ishmael is apt to benefit from Isaac's death, just as Isaac's economic benefit was not only the result but indeed the cause of Ishmael's ousting in chapter 21. And thus even on the mildest possible reading, Abraham's attempted gift of Isaac's death is drawn inexorably toward Ishmael. Abraham "sacrifices" (by expulsion) Ishmael for Isaac's benefit in chapter 21; if he succeeds in sacrificing (by slaughter) Isaac in chapter 22, Ishmael is the likely beneficiary. The triangle is perfectly balanced. Each son stands to benefit from the other's death.

One Offering, Two Sons

Genesis 21 and 22 offer a structurally balanced pair of Abraham's attempts to give each son's death to the other son. The mechanisms of each offer are different in these two texts: banishment (Genesis 21) and slaughter (Genesis 22). Yet Ishmael's and Isaac's mirroring of each other does not stop there. Some strands of Islamic tradition actually identify Ishmael as the intended victim of Abraham's Offering. Such traditions bind the triangle of death-giver and death-receivers even more tightly together, and lead on toward questions of ethics and responsibility.

The Qur'an's version of the Offering appears in *sura* 37:99–113. The Qur'an does not, however, give the victim's name. Differing versions of the story emerged within Islam, some of which identified the victim as Isaac, and some as Ishmael (see Calder 1988 and Firestone 1989 for descriptions and analyses). Reuven Firestone (1989) has traced out the general trend from early Islamic interpreters who proposed Isaac as the victim to later interpreters, and the eventually dominant view, that Ishmael was the intended sacrifice. That historical trend makes it easy to assume that the tradition specifying Isaac, reflected in Genesis 22, is older than the nonspecific tradition reflected in the Qur'an. Firestone cautions, however, against "the glib readiness to read the Qur'an through the eyes of the Bible" over against "[r]eading a biblical narrative through the eyes of the Qur'an" (2000, 182). He goes on to argue, against his own earlier practice, that a version of the story more like that of the Qur'an, in which the sacrificial victim is not explicitly named, might indeed be older than the Isaac-specific version now found in the Tanakh. If Firestone's intriguing reconstruction is allowed to disrupt, even for a brief moment, the more common understanding of the tradition-historical and/or literary links between the biblical and qur'anic versions of the Offering, a scenario of mutual displacement emerges. Readers who allow themselves to think that a version of this story that did not name the sacrificial victim predates the Genesis telling—or who simply examine the Islamic and Judaic traditions side-by-side, synchronically instead of diachronically—may begin to wonder why various groups of Jews and Muslims (or their progenitors) placed their own putative ancestor under Abraham's knife.

Outside of Genesis 22, Jewish accounts of the Offering evince a shift in emphasis from Abraham's obedience toward the image of Isaac as a willing victim, complicit in his own death.[5] Perhaps the earliest indications of this new emphasis are to be found in Josephus (*Antiquities* 1.232), where Isaac joyfully rushes to the altar upon learning of his father's intentions. 4 Maccabees 13:12 briefly alludes to Isaac as one who "would have submitted to being slain for the sake of religion." But it is really in the Targums and among the Amoraim that this emphasis comes into full bloom and the Offering becomes the *aqedah*, "the binding" of Isaac. *Targum Pseudo-Jonathan* to Genesis 22:1 actually casts Isaac's willingness to be sacrificed *prior to*, in fact *the cause of,* God's command to Abraham (Isaac's willingness to be sacrificed emerges, not incidentally, in a dispute between Isaac and Ishmael over who is more submissive to divine demands).

Similarly, in Islamic tradition, accounts of *al-dhabih,* "the intended sacrifice," almost universally include the motif of Abraham's son explicitly accepting and endorsing his fate as sacrificial victim once he learns of Abraham's intentions. No doubt the prominence of the motif should be attributed to its presence in the Qur'an, where Abraham's son says, "Father, do as you are commanded; you will find me, God willing, submissive" (37:102). This element of the story is present both in versions that specify Isaac as the intended victim and those that specify Ishmael as the intended victim.[6] Some post-qur'anic traditions insert Satan, Iblis, or an unnamed "old man" into the story as a tempter who tries to dissuade Abraham, Sarah or Hagar, and Isaac or Ishmael from going through with the sacrifice. In these traditions, the intended victim first learns of his father's intentions from the tempter, but immediately rebuffs the temptation in favor of obedience to God (Firestone 1989, 99–104; note that both Isaac and Ishmael are featured in this role in different sources).

Firestone has shown that Jewish, Christian, and Islamic interpreters have all at various times approached the Offering with a view toward a vicarious appropriation of the merit attaching to their putative ancestor's willingness to submit to the Offering:

> Nowhere is this more apparent than in the motif of Abraham's near-sacrifice of his son, where Judaism, Christianity, and Islam each makes use of the powerful story in order to buttress its own particularity. The interpretive traditions of these religions agree that so much merit is associated with the exceptional willingness of the protagonists to carry out God's command to the last letter and often through personal suffering, that some or much of that merit is considered to have spilled over or is held as credit for the generations who follow them. Those lucky followers, however, are restricted in each separate religious interpretation of the event to the official believers of that religious system. (1998, 93–94)

Firestone's arguments for the role of inherited merit in Jewish, Christian, and Islamic identifications of the sacrificial victim are particularly persuasive because he is able to show how this quest for vicarious merit accounts for the divergence within Islam of Sunni and Shiite identifications of the sacrificial victim as Ishmael and Isaac, respectively (including shifts over time), and how this dynamic operates in Christian typological appropriations of Isaac as a forerunner of Jesus. This self-offering for the sake of descendants is represented in figure 9.5 below.

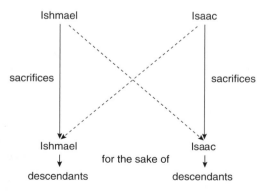

Figure 9.5 *Dhabih* and *aqedah*, vicariously.

Although tradents have emphasized vicarious merit in various versions of the Offering, this interpretive move is only possible in retrospect. That is to say, it is not something that could have been in the mind of Abraham's son (whichever son it might have been) as he waited to feel the sting of his father's knife. Whatever merit for self-sacrifice accrues to the intended victim accrues precisely because the victim (thinks he) is about to die and accepts this fate willingly. But if Abraham's son thinks he is about to die at his father's hands, he cannot possibly have been thinking that his descendants would somehow participate in whatever merit accrues to him as a result of this willingness, *because as yet he has no descendants.* The idea of transmitting merit genealogically could not have occurred to the victim at the time; it can only be a product of hindsight.

The impossibility of Abraham's son calculating that his death will bring merit to his nonexistent descendants does not mean, however, that the more general question of benefit must be far from the victim's mind. The story of the Offering in Pseudo-Philo's *Biblical Antiquities* is suggestive in this connection. Here Isaac makes a short, enigmatic speech upon learning of Abraham's intentions to sacrifice him. In that speech, Isaac declares, "My blessing will be upon all men because there will not be another [sacrifice], and generations will be told about me, and through me nations will realize that God has regarded the soul of a man worthy to be a sacrifice" (*Bibl. Ant.* 32:3; following Davies and Chilton 1978, 524). Here Isaac is thinking in terms of benefit for "all men." But the one man most likely to benefit immediately from Isaac's death is Ishmael, and Isaac can hardly be unaware of this. *Genesis Rabbah* recounts a temptation scene (not unlike those in Islamic tradition) in which the evil angel Samael first criticizes Abraham's willingness to offer Isaac, and then attempts to dissuade Isaac himself: " 'Son of an unhappy mother! He goes to slay thee.' 'I accept my fate,' he replied. 'If so,' said he, 'shall all those fine tunics which thy mother made be a legacy for Ishmael, the hated of her house?' " (*Genesis Rab.* 56:4). Isaac falters for a moment—more out of love for his mother, who hates Ishmael, than for his clothes—but proceeds nevertheless. *Targum Pseudo-Jonathan* to Genesis 22:3 even casts Ishmael as one of the two "servants" who accompany father and son to Moriah. Isaac cannot escape the implications of his own death for Ishmael. If Isaac dies, Ishmael is likely to inherit Abraham's wealth, his name, his blessing, perhaps even his covenant with God. Even so, Isaac willingly takes his place on the altar. The sons' mirror-image qualities hint that Ishmael might do (did) the same thing if (when) the roles were reversed. If Ishmael is the intended victim, he too can hardly escape the implications of his own death for Isaac, yet he goes willingly.

Thus the features of post-biblical and post-qur'anic elaborations of the Offering lead us to a configuration that does not necessarily correspond to the tradents' own motives or desires. The victim's self-sacrifice despite benefits to his potential rival, along with the variations in the identification of the victim, set in place a structure of displacement that transcends the textual or tradition-historical and enters more strongly the realm of ethics. In this structure of displacement, "Abraham," "Isaac," and "Ishmael" cease to be characters in texts and tradition, and become instead theoretical subject positions in a triangulated relationship of death-giving.[7] In this triangulated structure, Abraham gives death to Isaac. The relationship between Isaac and Ishmael is such that Ishmael will benefit from Isaac's death. Because Abraham knows this, he may therefore be said to offer Isaac's death to Ishmael. Isaac also knows that

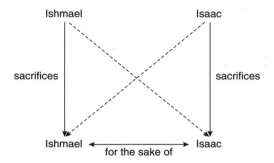

Figure 9.6 *Dhabih* and *aqedah*, ethically.

Ishmael will benefit from his death, yet accepts Abraham's offer of death, and so may be said to offer his own death to Ishmael. The positions of Isaac and Ishmael in this structure are reversible, however; Ishmael and Isaac can swap places throughout. A new vision of the Offering's significance can be established by the fact that in their respective traditions, "Isaac" and "Ishmael" both prefer to be the sacrificial victim, rather than the beneficiary of the other's death. This preference enables us to think of Ishmael's and Isaac's mutual self-sacrificial displacement as *a rejection of the benefits that might otherwise accrue from accepting the gift of another's death*. In Kierkegaardian and Lévinasian terms, Abraham's dilemma can be summed up as a contest between two "absolute duties." The command of God says to Abraham, "Kill Ishmael/Isaac," the face of Ishmael/Isaac compels Abraham, "Do not kill me." The triangulated structure of double displacement produced by the mirroring of *aqedah* and *dhabih* presents Abraham with a third compelling ethical voice: Ishmael/Isaac says, "Kill me *instead of him*, for his good," as in figure 9.6.

Abraham's Sons and Soldiers' Offerings

Had Jesus spoken with a Derridean rather than a Galilean accent, John 15:13 might read, "No one has greater love than this, to give one's own death to one's friends." The foregoing analysis of Isaac's and Ishmael's mutual displacement from Abraham's altar exposes a deep structural complication in this brief saying. Isaac and Ishmael invite us to think the case in which two love one another in accord with the Johannine superlative. If nonpareil love is shown by giving one's death to one's friends, does this not suggest that accepting the gift of another's death, rather than substituting oneself so that the other might live, fails in some measure to heed the call of this love? Yet in their mutual displacement on Abraham's sacrificial altar, Ishmael and Isaac bear witness to this potential ethical structure which, in large measure, neither those claiming affiliation to Abraham through Ishmael nor those claiming affiliation to Abraham through Isaac have actually put into practice. What if, instead of simply seeking vicarious participation in the ancestor's merit (as per the actual history of this story's interpretation), Isaac's and Ishmael's self-identified heirs chose actually to instantiate the protagonists' ethical gesture toward one another by refusing the gift of the other's death? What if their stance toward one another were, to appropriate Isaac's and Ishmael's mutual displacement, "I would rather die than benefit from your death"?

There are many possible repercussions; here only a few implications for the contemporary practice of war will be traced. This choice is not made merely for timeliness or convenience of finding examples. Although Derrida does not dwell on the subject at length in *The Gift of Death*, he does mention war from time to time. Early on, Derrida cites war as an experience of the gift of death (1995, 17). Elsewhere, he specifically alludes to Judeo-Christian-Islamic conflict and connects such conflict thematically with the Offering:

> These three monotheisms fight over [the "temple mount"], it is useless to deny this in terms of some wide-eyed ecumenism; they make war with fire and blood, have always done so and all the more fiercely today, each claiming its particular perspective on this place and claiming an original historical and political interpretation of Messianism and of the sacrifice of Isaac. The reading, interpretation, and tradition of the sacrifice of Isaac are themselves sites of bloody, holocaustic sacrifice. Isaac's sacrifice continues every day. (1995, 70; cf. pp. 86–87)

But as noted above, the "sacrifice" need not be read merely as "Isaac's," for in the interpretive tradition Isaac and Ishmael displace one another from the altar. How might this displacement, understood as each son's rejection of the father's gift of the other son's death, disrupt the practice of war, especially by Ishmael's and Isaac's contemporary, self-described heirs?[8]

North Atlantic culture valorizes individuals who evidence a willingness to risk their lives for others by participation in their nation's armed forces. In the United States, at least, the very vocabulary of "serving" in the military, and the common reference to the combined branches of U.S. armed forces as "the service," participates in this valorization. Public, posthumous commemoration of soldiers who die in war undoubtedly arises, at least in part, from genuine gratitude and/or grief. Nevertheless, speeches memorializing fallen soldiers as "the bravest and best" also promote a "heroic" conceptualization of the military enterprise. In turn, this rhetoric of heroic soldierly self-sacrifice functions, with varying degrees of subtlety, as a recruitment tool (see Goode 1978, 223, 344–45). In effect, the rhetoric of military heroism paints soldiers as practitioners of the Johannine superlative: they are willing to offer their deaths to their fellow citizens. As Derrida puts it, "War is a further experience of the gift of death . . . I give my own life in sacrificing myself 'for my country' " (1995, 17). By valorizing wartime self-sacrifice, the rhetoric of military heroism plays upon potential recruits' altruism and directs that altruism toward those recruits' own deaths. In other words, *the rhetoric of military heroism functions as a technique by which a society persuades some of its members to offer their deaths to other members of that society.*

The coercive dimension of recruiting candidates for self-sacrifice is helpfully illuminated by Claudia Mills's example of a heroic firefighter. In the course of a consideration of "why it often seems morally problematic to get others to act by taking advantage of the motivational lever of their *goodness*" (1995, 485), Mills introduces the scenario of a firefighter rescuing a child from a burning building. In her initial consideration of the scenario, Mills suggests that "heroism is just the willingness to take risks on behalf of others, and that no one ever promised us that no good deeds would ever result in ultimate self-sacrifice" (1995, 489–90). Later, Mills returns to this example and places the firefighter's actions in a broader, and very instructive, context.

> Along these lines, consider a variation on the heroic fire fighter example. Suppose that only one fire fighter is needed for the dangerous mission in question, and I am the fire chief charged with selecting the right person for the job. How should I make my choice? I might ask all the fire fighters to draw straws. I might simply give an order to a fire fighter I particularly dislike. I might tell one fire fighter who has been delinquent in the past: "Accept this assignment and I'll wipe your slate clean." Or I might tell him: "Accept this assignment or you're fired!" I might offer a financial bonus to anyone willing to go. Or I might issue a general call for a volunteer, knowing that I have one exceptionally kind and noble fire fighter, Betsy, who will be sure to step forward. Finally, I might call Betsy aside and say to her: "I hate to ask you to do this, but would you, one more time?" (1995, 496)

One cannot help but notice a curious feature of Mills's scenario: the fire chief has already excluded himself or herself from the category "the right person for the job." Even in Mills's preferred option, that of a general call for a volunteer (1995, 497), her fire chief seeks to extract from one fire fighter the offer of that fire fighter's death—*an offer the fire chief himself or herself has already decided not to make.*

Like soldiers, the "exceptionally kind and noble fire fighter, Betsy," is seen as "heroic" because she offers her death for the benefit of others. It is to those others that attention is drawn by the triangulated double displacement of Isaac and Ishmael on Abraham's sacrificial altar. The image of Isaac attempting to persuade Ishmael to take his place on Mount Moriah, of Isaac saying to Ishmael, "Please die so that I don't have to, so that I can inherit Abraham, so that I can be the child of promise and enjoy father's covenant with God" is preposterous. Yet the rhetoric of heroism leads down this very path, as citizenries and military hierarchies seek to recruit self-sacrificial victims in order to preserve their own lives or, more often, their own "ways of life." In their mutual displacement of one another as sacrificial victim, Ishmael and Isaac suggest an alternative "economy" of self-sacrifice. How different might things be if citizenries and military hierarchies changed their attitude toward actual and potential soldiers from "Please die for my benefit" to "I (we) would rather die than benefit from your death"?

The rhetoric of military heroism that calls forth in soldiers the willingness to give their deaths to their fellow citizens masks a darker summons. Despite the rhetoric, citizenries and military hierarchies do not *really* want soldiers to give their countries *their own deaths*, but rather *the deaths of their "enemies."* Derrida recognizes this when he describes war as "a further experience of the gift of death . . . I put my enemy to death" (1995, 17). Countries do not declare themselves the victors in warfare because their casualty figures are *higher* than their opponents'. It is the side that *kills* most successfully, not the side that *dies* most successfully, that wins a war.

The earlier discussion of self-sacrifice works within the confines of the Johannine Jesus' dictum that "No one has greater love than this, to give one's own death to one's friends" (John 15:3). Yet as Derrida himself is aware (1995, 103–06), the Matthean Jesus calls for a love greater than that which the Johannine superlative imagines: "But I say to you: love your enemies and pray for those who persecute you" (Matt. 5:44). Suppose that, for the purposes of analysis, we place military or paramilitary combatants not in the place of an Ishmael who corresponds to their constituents' Isaac (or vice versa), offering *their own deaths* to their fellow citizens, but in the place of Abraham, who offers to one *the death of another*.[9] Ishmael's and Isaac's mutual displacement from Abraham's altar helps us envision these "fellow citizens" *refusing* the gift of their "enemies' " deaths that their soldiers offer, and offering their own deaths instead. How different might things be if nations followed Isaac and Ishmael in saying to one another, "We would rather die than benefit from your deaths?" Or if they said to their militaries, "Kill *us* instead of *them*?"

Son(s) of Abraham, Son of God

In the final pages of *The Gift of Death*, Derrida touches ever so briefly, through a quotation from Nietzsche, on the Christian concept of Jesus' death as a gift of vicarious atonement. Many Christians understand Jesus' death as a gift given to them by which Jesus' self-sacrificial merit somehow accrues to his followers and/or effects their forgiveness from sins and, hence, spares them from "the second death." For the earliest Christians, vicarious atonement provided only one possible explanation of the metaphysical significance of Jesus' death, and it was by no means the most prominent explanation early on. Yet for much of contemporary Christianity, vicarious atonement has become the primary, if not the only, explanation for the meaning of Jesus's gift of his own death. The triangulation of self-sacrificial responsibility charted above troubles this common Christian notion.

A thorough exploration of this disturbance in Christian understanding of atonement is beyond the scope of this article, which, like *The Gift of Death*, can only brush up against the topic in passing toward its own end. Here only an initial gesture toward that broader conversation can be made, but it is easy to intuit that Ishmael and Isaac model in a certain way the rejection of a gift of death offered for one's own vicarious atonement. Thinking along these lines already finds expression in what might be thought the most unlikely of places, Anselm's *Cur Deus Homo* (2:14):

A[nselm]. If that man were present, and you knew who he was, and it were said to you, "unless you slay that man, the whole world would perish, with all which is not God," would you do it in order to preserve every other creature?
B[oso]. I would not do it, even though an infinite number of worlds were displayed to me.
A. What, if it were said to thee again: "Either kill him, or all the sins of the world shall be laid upon you?"

B. I should answer that I would rather take upon myself all other sins, not only those of this world both past and future, but also all which can be imagined besides these, than that one only. And I consider that I ought to answer the same not only as to the slaying of him, but also as to the smallest hurt which might be done to him.
A. You judge rightly . . .

Anselm goes on, of course, to defend the doctrine of vicarious atonement. Yet this snippet of his dialogue with Boso points, perhaps, to a different economy of self-sacrifice, one in which the gift of another's death to one's own benefit must be refused. By mutually displacing one another from Abraham's sacrificial altar, Ishmael and Isaac bear witness to this alternative order—and, perhaps, beckon their contemporary heirs toward its realization.

Notes

1. I am given to understand that the 1999 French edition of *Donner la mort* does mention Ishmael regularly, but it was the English edition by which I came to know this work—if it is appropriate to think of *Donner la mort* (1993), *The Gift of Death* (1995), and *Donner la mort* (1999) as "this work." All interactions in this paper are with *The Gift of Death* (English 1995).
2. To ask such questions smacks of attempting to read Abraham's mind, and that task is equally difficult whether Abraham is a long-dead historical person or a purely literary construct. Yet Kierkegaard's and Derrida's treatments of Genesis 22 hinge to a significant extent precisely on Abraham's existential, subjective experience of the sacrifice of Isaac (e.g., Kierkegaard 1985 [1843], 81 and passim), so this sort of speculation is an appropriate part of any examination thereof. Not that I have ever shied away from such speculations; my book *Dynamics of Diselection* is full of them, and they are an "occupational hazard" of my frequent focus on characterization. See Gunn and Fewell 1993, 46–51 for a defense of, and suggested limits on, speculating about biblical characters.
3. Cf. Derrida's (1995, 65) quotation of Kierkegaard: "Only *in the instant* when his act is in absolute contradiction to his feelings, only then does he sacrifice Isaac."
4. For more on this line of reasoning see Davies 1995, 111; Fewell and Gunn 1993, 53–54; Gunn and Fewell 1993, 98–99; Heard 2001, 91–95.
5. On the tradition history of the *aqedah* and antecedent readings of the Offering, see Spiegel 1967; Davies and Chilton 1978; and Fitzmeyer 2002.
6. See Calder 1988 for a catalog of both types of sources.
7. This move is, perhaps, not terribly unlike the move Derrida makes in casting himself as Abraham (1995, 68) or in reading Patocka psychoanalytically (1995, 9).
8. It would also be appropriate to investigate the triangulated structure of double displacement in connection with Derrida's (2002) discussion of *substitution* and the *hostage* in the writings and prayers of Louis Massignon, although that investigation is outside the scope of this particular article.
9. See Derrida 1995, 102–05 for Derrida's own argument in favor applying love of enemies to *national* enemies in wartime.

Works Cited

Anselm. *Cur Deus Homo?* 1889. *The Ancient and Modern Library of Theological Literature.* London: Griffith, Farran, Okeden and Welsh.

Calder, Norman. 1988. "From Midrash to Scripture: The Offering of Abraham in Early Islamic Tradition." *Le Museon* 101:375–402.

Clarke, E. G., W. E. Aufrecht, J. C. Hurd, and F. Spitzer, eds. 1984. *Targum Pseudo-Jonathan of the Pentateuch: Text and Concordance.* Hoboken: Ktav.

Davies, Philip R. 1995. *Whose Bible Is It Anyway?* JSOT Supplement Series 204. Sheffield: Sheffield Academic Press.

———, and Bruce D. Chilton. 1978. "The Aqedah: A Revised Tradition History." *Catholic Biblical Quarterly* 40:514–46.

Derrida, Jacques. 1995. *The Gift of Death.* Trans. David Wills. Chicago and London: University of Chicago Press.

Fewell, Danna Nolan and David M. Gunn. 1993. *Gender, Power, and Promise: The Subject of the Bible's First Story.* Nashville: Abingdon.

Firestone, Reuven. 1989. "Abraham's Son as the Intended Offering (*Al-Dhabih*, Qur'an 37:99–113): Issues in Qur'anic Exegesis." *Journal of Semitic Studies* 34:95–131.

———. 1998. "Merit, Mimesis, and Martyrdom: Aspects of Shi'ite Meta-historical Exegesis on Abraham's Offering in Light of Jewish, Christian, and Sunni Muslim Tradition." *Journal of the American Academy of Religion* 66:93–116.

———. 2000. "Comparative Studies in Bible and Qur'an: A Fresh Look at Genesis 22 in Light of Sura 37." In *Judaism and Islam: Boundaries, Communication and Interaction*, ed. Benjamin H. Hary, John L. Hayes, and Fred Astren, 169–84. Leiden: Brill.

Fitzmeyer, Joseph A. 2002. "The Offering of Isaac in Qumran Literature." *Biblica* 83:211–29.

Freedman, H. and Maurice Simon, trans. 1961. *Midrash Rabbah.* 10 vols. London: Soncino.

Goldingay, John E. 1998. "The Place of Ishmael." In *The World of Genesis: Persons, Places, Perspectives*, ed. Philip R. Davies and David J. A. Clines, 146–49. JSOT Supplement Series 257. Sheffield: Sheffield Academic Press.

Goode, William J. 1978. *The Celebration of Heroes: Prestige as a Control System.* Berkeley: University of California Press.

Gossai, Hemchand. 1997. "Divine Vulnerability and Human Marginality in the *Akedah*: Exploring a Tension." *Horizons in Biblical Theology* 19 (June):1–23.

Gunn, David and Danna Nolan Fewell. 1993. *Narrative in the Hebrew Bible.* Oxford Bible Series. Oxford: Oxford University Press.

Heard, R. Christopher. 2001. *Dynamics of Diselection: Ambiguity in Genesis 12–36 and Ethnic Boundaries in Post-Exilic Judah.* Semeia Studies 39. Atlanta: Society of Biblical Literature.

James, M. R., trans. 1917. *The Biblical Antiquities of Philo.* London: SPCK.

Kierkegaard, Søren. 1985 [1843]. *Fear and Trembling.* Trans. Alastair Hannay. London: Penguin.

Levenson, Jon D. 1993. *The Death and Resurrection of the Beloved Son: The Transformation of Child Sacrifice in Judaism and Christianity.* New Haven and London: Yale University Press.

Leviant, Curt. 1999. "Parallel Lives: The Trials and Traumas of Isaac and Ishmael." *Bible Review* 15 (April):20–25, 47.

Lévinas, Emmanuel. 1976. *Noms propres.* Montpelier: Fata Morgana.

Mills, Claudia. 1995. "Goodness As a Weapon." *The Journal of Philosophy* 92:485–99.

Spiegel, Shalom. 1967. *The Last Trial.* Trans. J. Goldin. New York: Random House.

Trible, Phyllis. 1991. "The Offering of Sarah." In *"Not in Heaven": Coherence and Complexity in Biblical Narrative*, ed. Jason P. Rosenblatt and Joseph C. Sitterson, 170–91. Bloomington: Indiana University Press.

Wenham, J. Gordon. 1994. *Genesis 16–50.* Word Biblical Commentary. Dallas: Word.

Chapter 10

Preferring or not Preferring: Derrida on Bartleby as Kierkegaard's Abraham

Oona Eisenstadt

At the end of Chapter Three of *The Gift of Death,* Derrida quotes a passage from Kierkegaard's *Fear and Trembling.* "Anyone who loves God," Kierkegaard writes, "needs no tears, no admiration; he forgets the suffering in the love. Indeed, so completely has [Abraham] forgotten it that there would be not the slightest trace of his suffering left if God himself did not remember it, for he sees in secret and recognizes distress and counts the tears and forgets nothing." Derrida tells us that we find buried in this passage a reference to the Gospels. *He sees in secret:* it is Matthew 6.

Everything in *The Gift of Death* revolves around this phrase, for the book is about the nature of secrecy and its relation to morality. In general, or on the surface, Derrida presents secrecy as a feature of the highest responsibility. The highest responsibility cannot be told, for to tell it would be to share it and so to dilute it; to tell it would be to burden others, irresponsibly. But Derrida also hints at a different idea, whereby to conceal a responsibility is to lose it or repress it; whereby not to tell is also not to converse, and thus not to listen, and so not to discover the needs of others.

Do we keep silent or do we talk? An answer must be affected by many considerations. One involves the extent to which we can bear to stand alone, to count on none of our fellows. Another, more immediately pertinent, involves the relation of responsibility not just to speaking but particularly to naming. Kierkegaard does not set his citation off with quotation marks: he occults Matthew within his text, creating a textual secret. But then, he also occults himself: *Fear and Trembling* is signed by Johannes de Silentio. Derrida discusses the pseudonym earlier in the chapter, pointing out that the name "Kierkegaard" is kept secret by the name "de Silentio"—it is kept silent by speaking silence. But, though a secret, says Derrida, this is not at all a falsification. The names one calls oneself in secret are already truer than one's legal names; how much more true when the secret name is published, voiced, and revealed to be *silence*? In a similar vein, Derrida argues that *he sees in secret* is all the clearer, to those who know their Gospels, by not being set off in quotation marks. *He sees in secret* (a revelation but concealed) is concealed (because not in quotation marks) and thereby revealed (to those who know). In other words, silence talks. Maybe this is the

way to reconcile the two thrusts in *The Gift of Death*, the idea that the highest responsibility must be kept silent and the idea that silence represses responsibility.
Maybe silence does repress. Maybe the truest responsibility exists where what has been
silenced becomes clear, breaking through into speech, albeit perhaps a silent speech.

We will return later to these complicated matters. For now it suffices that they
alert us to the fact that there may well be secrets embedded in Derrida's own text.
Indeed there must, if Derrida is to live up to the highest responsibility—and he
always does. Somewhere in this chapter are quotations not set off, and a silent name
that calls out to those who know. The experiment of this paper is an argument to the
effect that that name is Emmanuel Lévinas, and those quotations are Lévinas's ideas.
To be sure, Derrida mentions the name of Lévinas, but only at irrelevant times and in
odd ways. To a reader familiar with Lévinas's thought, however, the name breaks
through in many places where it is unstated.[1]

John Caputo writes that "Derrida mediates between Lévinas and Kierkegaard: this
is what deconstruction is" (2000, 295). I believe Caputo to be both right and wrong.
Derrida does, at least sometimes, mediate between Lévinas and Kierkegaard.
Certainly this is what he is doing in chapter three of *The Gift of Death*, where the
ostensible subject is Kierkegaard and where, as I claim, Lévinas lurks under the surface. But this mediation is not what deconstruction is; indeed, deconstruction is not
mediation at all. Mediation is a matter of erecting a network of connections, of drawing things together under a paradigm which then becomes the context in which the
things are seen; to mediate is to synthesize under a third term. Deconstruction is
about decontextualizing; it is about pulling things apart to look at what they are, or at
what they were before they were contextualized and synthesized under this or that
paradigm.

But if deconstruction is not mediation, if deconstruction is, as I think, anathema
to mediation, why does Derrida mediate between Lévinas and Kierkegaard in the
chapter in question? Why should he offer us what is in effect a synthesis of the two
thinkers? He does it, I contend, to show us something about the uses and abuses of
history and of text. For what he gets when he puts the two men together is a very
great deal closer to Kierkegaard than it is to Lévinas; Lévinas is swallowed up and
silenced. And this is not all. A mediation between Lévinas and Kierkegaard, as John
Caputo knows, is a mediation between Jew and Christian. And such mediations have
not gone well for Jews in history: it is under such a paradigm that, as Shakespeare
puts it, the Jew turns Christian. The existence of the mediation and its nature (and its
danger) are therefore already flagged not only by the unstated name but also, more
pointedly, in Chapter Two of *The Gift of Death*, where Derrida writes that it is "far
from clear" that Lévinas's general line of thinking is not Christian (1995, 48). They
are also flagged by the use Derrida makes of Herman Melville's story "Bartleby,"
which illustrates and supports the mediation, but does so badly.

The argument on Bartleby will form much of what follows. Before we take it up,
though, we must watch Derrida mediate between the two philosophers and the two
traditions. To do this he takes us to the story of Abraham's sacrifice of Isaac, the
akedah. The *akedah* is already a meeting place not only for Lévinas and Kierkegaard
but also for Judaism and Christianity: surrounding the story there is already
occulting, synthesis, repression, and reclamation, or, in short, a long history of

contextualization, recontextualization, and decontextualization that illuminates both the nature of human responsibility and irresponsibility—which is what the story is about—and also a history of textual responsibility and irresponsibility.

Kierkegaard uses the *akedah* to draw a distinction between two kinds of responsibility, that of ethics and that of faith. The first responsibility is social: it involves meting out resources fairly and applying laws equitably; it rests, moreover, on accountability, on giving reasons for one's actions, and is thus associated with clear, open speech. The second responsibility is private and personal. It has nothing to do with equitability or fairness, but is about infinite attention to a single unique entity, that is, to God. This responsibility knows no law. He who answers to it gives no reasons, for he is beyond reasons. He does not know why he does what he does, and he cannot tell even what little he knows, for to do so would be to share his responsibility with others and thus to impose on them. Where ethics demands speech, faith demands secrecy.

According to Kierkegaard, Abraham's willingness to sacrifice Isaac is, from an ethical perspective, tantamount to murder; but Abraham must also be seen as a "knight of faith," acting on his other responsibility, his duty to God. There is no way to reconcile the two: to act under faith always entails ethical irresponsibility; to act under ethics is to abdicate the responsibility of faith; Abraham's story is thus "a scandal and a paradox" (Derrida 1995, 60). But, for Kierkegaard, the private duty is higher than the public duty, secrecy higher than disclosure, and the service of God higher than the law. This, says Derrida, is Kierkegaard's break with the history of philosophy, as well as with common sense. For Plato, for Hegel—for reason or dialectics—the general or universal must ultimately trump the personal and the singular, and the telos of human existence is the kind of meaning by which all is disclosed, everything accounted for. For Kierkegaard, personal responsibility trumps ethics, and the secret is maintained.

Now, part way through his argument, Derrida begins to shift the Kierkegaardian conception in what I am calling a Lévinasian direction, such that what Kierkegaard calls "ethics" is conflated with what Lévinas calls "justice" or "responsibility to the others," and what Kierkegaard calls "faith" is conflated with what Lévinas calls "ethics" or "responsibility to the other." The semantics are confusing, but the issue itself need not be. We continue to deal with two kinds of responsibility, only now we use one of Lévinas's many sets of terms for them: *responsibility to the others* is appropriate to the social realm where the general good must be considered, and where public accountability and therefore disclosure are fundamental; *responsibility to the other* is infinite, absolute, non-generalizable, and nontransferable. The difference between Kierkegaard's conception and Lévinas's—and the reason Derrida wants to shift or translate the one into the other—is that while Kierkegaard understands the absolute responsibility to obligate us to God and only to God, Lévinas understands it to obligate us to any and every other human being we meet.

Under the now Lévinasized conception, then, Abraham is not torn between God and human beings but between the other and the others, and in this way he becomes a representative of anyone at the instant of moral decision. How, Derrida asks, can I justify feeding the cat who lives with me when so many cats starve? How can I justify being here speaking to this person instead of there speaking to them? How can I justify any action, any movement, any gift, when it implies, as it must, a choice of one over the others, a betrayal of the universal, a betrayal of equality? And yet this is the way we live; all action involves this "paradox, [and this] scandal" (1995, 68). Kierkegaard's analysis of Abraham's predicament expresses the quandary of all the tiny moral decisions we make at every moment. And it is all the more difficult a quandary because "every other (one) is every (bit) other. *Tout autre est tout autre*" (1995, 77–78). That is, even if our responsibility to *each* trumps our responsibility to *all*—and this is essentially the Lévinasian translation of the Kierkegaardian paradigm—every single person out there is *each* in her own right.

Derrida calls Abraham's choice of duty to God over duty to Isaac a "gift of death." Abraham is called to give death both in the sense that he raises the knife and in the more complex sense that he offers this death to God. Extending this into the Lévinasian mode, Derrida suggests that we are offering the gift of death whenever we are responsible to the other and sacrifice the others, that is to say, all the time, every day. Responsibility at its best or highest is always "the sacrifice of love to love" (1995, 64); this is the terrible secret of responsibility, which makes us tremble, and forbids speech. It is at this point, perhaps the high point of Derrida's synthesis, that he turns to Bartleby for a further example of responsibility.

The bones of Melville's story are as follows. The narrator, a lawyer, hires Bartleby as a scrivener, that is, a copyist of documents. Bartleby copies industriously, but when he is asked to proofread his work he says, "I would prefer not to." It soon becomes clear that there are many things Bartleby prefers not to do. He does not run errands; indeed, having concealed the materials for washing and sleeping under various chairs, he hardly leaves the chambers at all. He does not read; he does not speak unless it is to answer; often he does not even answer. The lawyer, from a mixture of amazement, weakness, charity, and superstition, puts up with Bartleby's eccentricity. One day Bartleby announces that he has given up copying altogether, and from that moment on he does nothing at all. The lawyer tries to fire him, to find him another line of work, or to pension him off; eventually he goes so far as to invite Bartleby to come and live in his house. Bartleby prefers none of these. The lawyer moves office, leaving Bartleby standing motionless in the old room. The new tenant and the owner of the building appeal to the lawyer, who, surmounting anguished misgivings, denies all ties to Bartleby; finally they have Bartleby taken to jail, where, despite help provided by the lawyer, he stops eating and dies. A few months later, the lawyer hears a rumour that Bartleby used to work in the dead letter office in Washington. The story ends:

> Dead letters! Does it not sound like dead men? Conceive a man by nature and misfortune prone to a pallid hopelessness, can any business seem more fitted to heighten it than that of continually handling these dead letters, and assorting them for the flames? For by the cart-load they are annually burned. Sometimes from out the folded paper the pale clerk takes a ring—the finger it was meant for, perhaps, moulders in the grave; a bank-note sent in swiftest charity—he whom it would relieve, nor eats nor hungers any more; pardon for those who died despairing; hope for those who died unhoping; good tidings for those who died stifled by unrelieved calamities. On errands of life these letters speed to death.
> Ah Bartleby! Ah humanity!

Derrida begins his account of the story by noting that when the lawyer sees Bartleby lying dead in the courtyard of the jail, he murmurs that Bartleby sleeps "with kings and counsellors" (Job 3:4, cf. 36:7; Melville 1995, 46). The reference is to Job, and with it the lawyer raises the question of whether Bartleby's story has been a matter of a test or trial in the biblical mode. It has indeed, says Derrida, but the test is more like Abraham's than Job's. He then proceeds to unfold his interpretation in the form of a comparison between Abraham's statement that "God will provide a lamb for the holocaust" and what is sometimes called Bartleby's formula, "I would prefer not to" (Deleuze 1997 coins the phrase "Bartleby's formula").

Abraham's line has a complex relationship to secrecy, perhaps best understood by looking at the ways in which it is ironic. Certainly it is a dramatic irony: what he says is true, even though he does not yet know it. But there is a subtler irony in the way he uses the line to hide the truth he does know, namely, that God has called him to sacrifice Isaac. In this subtler sense, the line's irony is Abraham's responsibility. He cannot burden Isaac with what he knows, but neither can he lie; he therefore finds himself "speaking in order not to say anything"; he "responds without responding" (1995, 59): the line conveys his higher responsibility precisely by hiding it. Bartleby's line is similar. It points, albeit vaguely, toward an undefined truth that Bartleby himself does not seem entirely to have grasped. But it is also disingenuous, since Bartleby must know or intend something more, and, if he does, then it is something that the formula both occults and represents. In short, both characters speak the truth in a way they do not understand, and both feign an ignorance different from their real ignorance. In Abraham's case this feigning is his truth-telling: it preserves and represents his higher responsibility. And maybe Bartleby's case is the same.

Abraham "has decided to but he would prefer not to" (1995, 75). Bartleby would prefer not to, and has *not* decided to. Or has he? Bartleby's formula, says Derrida, is haunted by "the silhouette of a content"; it inscribes "a hypothetical reference to some indecipherable providence or prudence" (1995, 75). Both men are being led toward death; both, in a sense, succumb, relinquish control; they give up, or in short *give.* In both cases it may therefore be that the death is not just offered to the victim but also offered up to something greater. The culmination of Derrida's interpretation is that Bartleby is indeed in a critical respect like Abraham: he is another representative of the highest responsibility, responsibility to the other. His responsibility, like Abraham's, acts to call the lower responsibility and its representatives into question; his formula throws the lawyer into the turmoil of doubt and remorse that produces the story. He, like Abraham, offers the gift of death; he is engaged in an illustrative or paradigmatic "sacrificial passion" (1995, 75).

Does Derrida distort the story to make his points? If we accept his interpretation, we must read not only a decision into Bartleby's apparent lassitude, but also a preference into his refusal to prefer—a preference for the singular, the one cat, the absolute, the other, or God. For this is the nature of the difference between the two responsibilities. The absolute, infinite responsibility is to and for a *you*: it prefers. The general, finite responsibility is to and for everybody: it refuses to prefer. Now to make a preference of Bartleby's refusal to prefer is a move that—though perhaps partly justified by the evocation of "some indecipherable providence"—defies the plain sense of the story and the understanding of almost every previous commentator. I believe that Derrida is waving a flag.

In order to begin to see what he is signalling, we must turn back to what is for him the main question—the mediation of Lévinas and Kierkegaard—and ask whether Bartleby sheds any light on the matter. I suggested earlier that a movement of secularization, a shift from God to the other, was the only difference between Kierkegaard's conception and that of Lévinas. In fact, it is neither the only difference nor the most important one. Derrida emphasizes the secularization, pointing out that Kierkegaard might object to it, and then justifying it, adequately in my view, with the claims that there is a bit of God's alterity in every unique being (1995, 78) and, more simply, that the secularized version of the paradigm works forcefully to describe responsibility (1995, 79). But he does not ask the other question, namely, whether Lévinas would object to having his account of responsibility described in terms that make it compatible with Kierkegaard's. Indeed, he does not allow such a question to arise at all, since he does not overtly acknowledge that what I have called the Lévinasian paradigm— the tension between responsibility to the other and responsibility to the others, which is the core of all of Lévinas's philosophy—is Lévinasian, instead presenting it anonymously and placing Lévinas in the sphere of the ironic. But the question is there, unstated.

There is little problem, from a Lévinasian perspective, with the conflation of God and the other. The problem, rather, is that Lévinas disagrees with Kierkegaard about the incommensurability of the two responsibilities and about the rank Kierkegaard accords them; in short, Lévinas does not advocate the sacrifice of the others for the other. This is to say that while he often describes how my responsibility to the others is a betrayal of my responsibility to the other, he does not do so in order to encourage a dialectical reversal in which the other is attended to and social justice overridden. It is, for him, simply not a matter of a choice between polar alternatives. On the contrary, what he encourages is a recollection of my responsibility to the other such that my conceptions of social justice are called into question and made more just; and thus, responsibility to the other, far from operating as a single-minded directive, as it does in Kierkegaard, becomes, for Lévinas, a check on any single-minded directive. This is a fundamental difference: in Lévinas's thought there is and can be no "purity of heart to will one thing." Kierkegaard, or at any rate Derrida's secularized Kierkegaard, overemphasizes the difference between the two responsibilities, between preference and nonpreference. He turns the love of the other, which ought to be the ground of social life, into something that is at odds with social life, something that trumps it.

What is the significance of Bartleby here? Derrida's Kierkegaardian interpretation of the story can be summarized fairly easily. The law refuses to prefer the one over the many and thus represents responsibility to the others. When Bartleby gives up the law, he gives up equality in favor of preference, thus becoming the representative of responsibility to the other. But what happens if we accept for the moment the Kierkegaardian terms in which Derrida mounts his argument while rejecting his interpretation, that Bartleby prefers, in favor of what seems the more tenable interpretation, that Bartleby does not prefer. In this case, far from rising above the law into a higher preference, Bartleby becomes an embodiment of the law's refusal to prefer.

Bartleby, one might argue, has seen the failure of personal, private communication—of the response to the singular other—in the dead-letter office; the dead-letters have taught him the failure of preference. He turns to the law to overcome preference's heartache, forcing himself to prefer less and less until all is equitable, until he prefers nothing, until he has no need to copy the law since he lives it. By this interpretation, Bartleby does indeed believe, with Kierkegaard and against Lévinas, that one must make a choice between responsibility to the other and responsibility to the others; the choice he makes, though, is the opposite of the choice made by Kierkegaard's Abraham. Melville, however, seems to be suggesting that human beings do not and cannot live in this polarized way. Human morality and human love must include dimensions of preference as well as dimensions of equality. Bartleby, having rejected all preference and become the most equitable man—having become, in effect, the law—dies of neglect and despair. For Melville, as for Lévinas, life cannot be a matter of a choice between opposites.[2]

It is worth reflecting on the fact that Derrida never mentions the dead letter office. Reading his account, one could easily get the impression that the story ends with Bartleby's death. One cannot help thinking that by omitting it, he is offering a clear indication of its importance.[3] And it is in the dead letter office that we find the strongest possible sign that Bartleby takes to the law because he has given up preference. We may assume, therefore, that Derrida is conscious of all that I have just said, and indeed is silently pointing to a reversal of the interpretation he offers overtly; such an assumption is in any case suggested by the fact that the reversal works so neatly and, once seen, stands out so obviously. But if Derrida is indeed pointing to a reversal then he is also—tentatively, as always—pointing to the idea that Lévinas and Kierkegaard, like Melville and Kierkegaard, see things in different ways, and that perhaps there is little ground for a mediation between them.[4]

What, then, about the traditions they represent? Melville's story is often seen as a commentary on messianism enacted as a retelling of the passion narrative with Bartleby in the role of the Christ. Bartleby, at least ostensibly, turns away from "the book" and from "the law"; he is given up to the worldly authorities; he refuses to speak in his own defence; he is denied by the one who knows him best; he dies; and finally, after his death a rumour comes to light by which he emerges as a representative of humanity. But Bartleby is also a failure: he accomplishes nothing, and changes nothing. Can one be a Christ and a failure at the same time? Perhaps one can. Perhaps one can only be a Christ if one is a failure.

The commentator who singles out Bartleby's failure as both central to the story and praiseworthy is Maurice Blanchot. Early on in *The Writing of the Disaster*, he describes Bartleby's formula as "the abandonment of the self, a relinquishment of identity, refusal which does not cleave to refusal but opens to failure, to the loss of being, to thought." As he goes on to suggest, failure of Bartleby's kind stands outside the "System." What it means to fail is no longer to be a part of the dialectic of control: to fail is not to control, not to be controlled, and not to defy control. And thus to fail is to *not* participate in the totality: failure is outside, in the place (or nonplace) where thought is possible, the *only* place where thought is possible (1986, 17). Having said this, Blanchot allows Bartleby to drop out of the picture. But he returns to him at the end of the book, in the context of a discussion of messianism. Blanchot's messianism, here as elsewhere, is not at all that of the common conception; it is decontextualized, wrenched out of the confines of history or time, and stripped of any aura of anticipation. Shortly after discussing it, Blanchot returns to Bartleby, describing the formula as "negative preference, the negation that effaces preference and is effaced therein: the neutrality of that which is not among the things there are to do—the restraint, the gentleness that cannot be called obstinate, and that outdoes obstinacy with those few words" (1986, 145). It is all very thin, but it is nevertheless evocative. Blanchot seems to be suggesting that if Bartleby can be seen as a messiah, it is because he offers us nothing to look forward to, nothing we do not already have. Only perhaps he teaches us that we need not look forward, that we need not worry so much about *the things there are to do*, about making changes, or pushing forward in time or history. Bartleby is a messiah to the extent that he is untouched by the inescapable system: he is a messiah insofar and only insofar as he fails.

It must be said, however, that Bartleby does not represent the full Blanchotian understanding of messianism. For while Blanchot's messiah is not involved in the things there are to do, he does take action in one specific way: he comforts. Blanchot calls his messianism Jewish, and contrasts it with several elements of the Christian conception, notably that the Christian messiah is divine and is a single identifiable being. He suggests, in effect, that by divinizing the messiah the Christians contract the messianic role, placing all the responsibility to comfort in one locale (1986, 142). Blanchot's messiah "is a comforter, the most just of the just, but it is not even sure that he is a person—that he is someone in particular. When one commentator says, The Messiah is perhaps I, he is not exalting himself. Anyone might be the messiah—must be he, is not he" (1986, 142).[5] This is to say that the one who provides comfort is "I"—is each of us. Each of us recognizes distress and counts the tears. In short, Blanchot's messianism is not just detemporalized but also delocalized; and it emerges as human responsibility. To expect a temporal, locatable messiah, Blanchot suggests, is to absolve oneself of at least some of the duty to comfort, and thus to lean towards an abdication of responsibility.

Derrida claims to have learned a great deal about messianism from this very passage in Blanchot (1993, 162). Blanchot attributes the understanding, in the body of his text, to Gershom Scholem and also to Lévinas (1986, 142).[6] There exists, thus, a certain conception of messianism with a more or less direct lineage: Lévinas to Blanchot; Blanchot to Derrida. And it is also presumably the case that these pages of Blanchot, over which he has poured and which have taught him so much about the messiah, have given Derrida certain ideas about Bartleby.

What is there to be learned from these pages? At least that it is as difficult to mediate between Christian and Jew as between Lévinas and Kierkegaard. The two traditions, for all their great commonality, appeal to different elements in the human constitution and suggest different ways of thinking and reading, ways that emerge in different understandings of the messianic role. Of course there is no single Judaism: it is not a credal religion. But insofar as Lévinas and the rabbis he cites can be understood to represent one of a number of authentic ways of being Jewish, the Jew is more likely than the Christian to acknowledge and embrace what Blanchot calls failure, as the beginning of a movement toward comforting the other and shouldering her burdens. This is what Blanchot has seen inchoate in Melville's story. It is what

Derrida has seen in Blanchot, and, via Blanchot, in Melville. It is what is driving Derrida's secularization of Kierkegaard. And it is also I believe, what drives Derrida to compare Bartleby to Abraham. He all but ignores the obvious comparison between Bartleby and Jesus—though he retains its messianic overtones. He does not compare Bartleby and Isaac—though this might seem an obvious move (Deleuze, for instance, hints at such a comparison, 1997, 80). Instead he compares Bartleby with the one whose redemptive act is uncompleted, the one who fails to complete the sacrifice, the one who does not, in the end, give the gift of death. If Isaac represents a proto-Christian-messiah, perhaps Abraham, understood in a certain way, represents a proto-Blanchotian-Jewish messiah: a Bartleby who is at the same time moving, beyond Bartleby, into comfort.

This is, to be sure, not Kierkegaard's Abraham. But maybe it is one of Derrida's Abrahams. That, in any case, is my argument, and the upshot of this paper's experiment. Kierkegaard understands Abraham to be the knight of faith, the one who prefers. Derrida compares this Abraham to Bartleby. But Bartleby does not prefer. So maybe, just maybe, we are being led to look at Abraham from a different perspective, to look for an Abraham who is less preferential, and more torn. The extended quotation from *Fear and Trembling* with which Derrida concludes his chapter ends as follows: "Thus, either there is a paradox, that the single individual stands in an absolute relation to the absolute, or Abraham is lost." Maybe when one Abraham is lost, another is found.

There is, part way through Derrida's chapter, tucked away in a footnote, a hint of another Abraham. The note consists of a long quotation from Lévinas expressing, Derrida tells us, "an objection. . . . to Kierkegaard." The gist of the objection is that while for Kierkegaard the greatest moment in the *akedah* is when Abraham raises the knife, for Lévinas it is when God tells him to lower it, returning him to the impure world of competing loves. Lévinas writes that "one can posit the contrary [to what Kierkegaard posits]: the attention Abraham pays to the voice that brings him back to the ethical order by forbidding him to carry out the human sacrifice is the most intense moment of the drama . . . It is there, in the ethical, that . . . sense is given to life in defiance of death" (Lévinas 1996, 77 cited in Derrida 1995, 78 n. 6). Derrida does not highlight the fact that Lévinas speaks of a *gift of life*. Nor does he state overtly that the passage forbids a mediation between Lévinas and Kierkegaard. But these things are there.[7]

At several points in the chapter, Derrida describes the *akedah* as a battleground between the three Western religious traditions. They fight over how it is to be understood, and also over the site where it is said to have taken place:

> a holy place, but also a place that is in dispute, radically and rabidly, fought over by all the monotheisms, by all the religions of the unique and transcendent God of the absolute other. . . . [I]t is useless to deny this in terms of wide-eyed ecumenicism; they make war with fire and blood, have always done so and all the more fiercely today, each claiming its particular perspective on this place and claiming an original historical and political interpretation of Messianism and of the sacrifice of Isaac. (1995, 70)

For all that Derrida has tried—via Melville, Lévinas, and Blanchot—to stretch Kierkegaard's interpretation into an existential description of the dilemma of morality, it remains part of this battle. "As a Christian thinker, Kierkegaard ends by reinscribing the secret of Abraham within a space that seems, in its literality at least, to be evangelical. That doesn't necessarily exclude a Judaic or Islamic reading, but it is a certain evangelical text that seems to orient or dominate Kierkegaard's interpretation" (1995, 80–81). The evangelical text is, as we have seen, *he sees in secret*. In other words, the phrase, and the concepts it supports, are, according to Derrida, part of the Christian-ness of Kierkegaard's reading.[8]

What, finally, about Abraham's secrecy; what about his silence? In Blanchot's messianism each of us is called to recognize distress, count the tears, and offer comfort. But, of course, none of us sees in secret, and so Blanchot's messianism requires communication. We might be able to wiggle out of this conundrum by importing a Blanchotian paradox to the effect that good writing is "not writing," that good speaking is not-to-speak. But let us be as clear as we can. To think the messianic potential of Abraham is to think of his silence as a revelation rather than a secret. Emerging through the text, in the event of lowering the knife, Abraham's silence becomes a speaking, and a comforting.

After all, there are silences and silences. Abraham, Derrida tells us, speaks in order not to speak. When Kierkegaard does not cite Matthew by name, he is doing the opposite: he is not speaking, and is doing so, according to Derrida, in order to speak. What is more, the person to whom Abraham speaks so as not to speak is Isaac; it is surely also the case that his formula is intended, through the medium of the book, to speak out loud to the rest of us—that is, to everybody, *tout autre*. In distinction, Kierkegaard's not-speaking, while also intended as a speaking out loud, only speaks to some. Derrida says that the name of Matthew is "clearly brought to the attention of those who know their texts and have been brought up on the reading of the Gospels" (1995, 81). What about those who are not part of this elect? And for that matter what about those—surely for the most part a different group—who do not have the resources to see the Lévinas under the Derrida?

In Lévinas's lecture, "The Pact," there occurs an interesting aside. Describing an example of the long lists of attributions typical of the Talmud, Lévinas says:

> What a lot of references! Those of you who are perhaps attending a Talmudic lesson for the first time should not be surprised at this piling up. There is always a lot of care taken in the Talmud to specify who said what: a true lesson is that in which the universal nature of the proclaimed truth allows neither the name nor the person of him who said it to disappear. The scholars of the Talmud even think that the Messiah will come at the moment when everybody quotes what they learn in the name of the very person from whom they learnt it. (1994, 84)[9]

Here is an example of Lévinasian particularity, Lévinasian preference. The name is to be there for everyone to see: the messianism referred to is thus for everybody rather than for those who know. But the fact that it is for everybody does not make it a realm of generality in which particularity disappears. The key to the coming of the messiah—that is to say, the existence of messianic responsibility—is that neither name nor person disappear.

Notes

1. Dennis Keenan finds Lévinas running all the way through *The Gift of Death*: he suggests, in fact, that the book can be read "as a supplement to Derrida's other readings of the work of Lévinas," despite the fact that it overtly deals with other thinkers (1998, 6). He also points out that some of the book's most prominent Lévinasian ideas have been filtered through Blanchot, and particularly through *The Writing of the Disaster* (1986).

2. John Caputo offers what is in many ways the most insightful analysis of Derrida's chapter (Caputo 1997, 188–222). He partly anticipates my argument when he writes that "Lévinas leads us to believe that the transition from substitution (singularity) to justice (universality) can be made without sacrifice, that it is possible to formulate a wisdom of love (ethics) without a loss of wisdom (about individuals). Kierkegaard and Derrida, on the other hand, are willing to make the sacrifice of ethics; they think that obligation is an abyss" (1997, 207). I more or less agree with Caputo here, but must add a qualification, and a reflection. First, there *is* sacrifice in the transition between Lévinas's substitution and his social justice; they do not form an either/or, but neither are they in perfect alliance. Second, and more important, Caputo's statement surely acts to clarify what he means when he speaks elsewhere of *a mediation between Lévinas and Kierkegaard* (2000, 295): a mediation between these two thinkers is evidently a choice, since it is made quite clear here that they are not compatible at all. What is more, while Caputo is in a sense correct about the choice Derrida makes—since what emerges in Chapter three of *The Gift of Death* looks nothing like Lévinas, and everything like a secularized, or "deconstructed" (Caputo 1997, 189) Kierkegaard—I am not as sure as Caputo that this represents Derrida's personal position, or his deepest thought.

3. That he does not mention the dead-letter office is all the odder given that he has touched, in Chapter two, on Poe's purloined letter; in fact, he explicitly raises the comparison between the letter hidden in plain sight and the gift of death, and connects the question to the concealment of names (Derrida 1995, 39).

4. Other scholars who have looked at Derrida's relationship to Kierkegaard in *The Gift of Death* have described it as slightly uneasy or incomplete. David Wood, for example, is "disturbed" by aspects of Derrida's argument—mainly the universalization of the *akedah* (Wood 1997, 136). He hints at a deliberate distortion flagged by the fact that Derrida treats the sacrifice as accomplished; moreover he unearths an occulted name in *The Gift of Death*, that of Sartre. David Goicoechea argues that Derrida has been deeply influenced by Kierkegaard, and indeed, that his thinking life has been something of an ascent through Kierkegaard's stages, performed in full knowledge. He also maintains, however, that Derrida is unwilling to take the last step, "the free leap into the unknown" (1999, 224). See also Ralph Shain (2000) and Edward Findlay (2002) on the relationship.

5. R. Nahman in *Tractate Sanhedrin,* 97b. Blanchot has, however, changed the wording of the talmudic passage, following Lévinas (1990, 88).

6. And indeed, almost all of what Blanchot says about messianism in *The Writing of the Disaster* is to be found in Lévinas (1990), which is a transcription of lectures delivered in 1960 and 1961.

7. See also Derrida (1978, 110–111), where he briefly discusses Lévinas's objections to Kierkegaard. The discussion is, however, not as helpful as it might be in defining where Derrida stands. Derrida's main intent is to show that Lévinas cannot do without the structures he criticizes. I believe that this conundrum, while of great insight and interest, is as much a self-critique as a critique of Lévinas. When Derrida writes of "the necessity of

lodging oneself within traditional conceptuality in order to destroy it" (1978, 111), he is speaking of himself, via Lévinas.

8. Later he is even more explicit, stating that Kierkegaard's interpretation of the *akedah* is a "Christianizing or pre-Christianizing . . . as if he were preparing the way for Christianity" (1995, 95): the suggestion here is that *he sees in secret* is a fundamentally Christian way of understanding. Caputo asks, with reference to various passages in Chapter three of *The Gift of Death,* whether Derrida does "not risk widening the war between Christian and Jewish readings of the *akedah?*" He answers in the negative: Derrida's intention is "finally to displace the opposition between Christian and Jew, between the determinate, identifiable messianisms, in the name of a messianic structure to which they all subscribe." Perhaps this is true. Or perhaps it bespeaks a wide-eyed ecumenicism not entirely shared by Derrida. And perhaps, like many ecumenicisms, it hides something else, albeit unseen and unintended. On the same page, Caputo explains that part of the movement from determinate to nondeterminate messianism is "reversing the most dangerous stereotype of all, the Jew as the pharisee, as the money changer, the ruthless creditor, Shylock." Now certainly Caputo holds no such stereotype. But his list may remind us that when we move to nondeterminate messianism we give certain things up: not just the pharisee but also, surely, the Pharisee; not just the ruthless creditor but also Shylock. Are we not back on Shakespeare's turf, with Caputo in the role of Portia? Caputo is appalled by Christian attempts to convert Jews to the "Religion of Love," but has no problem with the deconstruction of everything "Shylockian"—or with its dissolution into the nondeterminate (1997, 218).

9. See *Avot* 6:6; *Hullin* 104b; and *Megillah* 15b. The statement seems most obviously attributable to R. Elazar, and always bears reference to Esther's citing Mordechai as a source for salvific information. Thanks for these references to the members of H-Judaic from whom I learned of them: Jim Diamond, Herb Basser, Marsha Cohen, Aryeh Cohen, Avram Kogen, and Menachem Kellner.

Works Consulted

Blanchot, Maurice. 1986. *The Writing of the Disaster.* Trans. Ann Smock. Lincoln: University of Nebraska Press.

Caputo, John D. 1997. *The Prayers and Tears of Jacques Derrida: Religion Without Religion.* Bloomington: Indiana University Press.

———. 2000. "Adieu–sans Dieu: Derrida and Lévinas." In *The Face of the Other and the Trace of God: Essays on the Philosophy of Emmanuel Lévinas,* ed. Jeffrey Bloechl, 276–311. New York: Fordham University Press.

Deleuze, Gilles. 1997. "Bartleby; or, The Formula." Trans. Daniel W. Smith and Michael A. Greco. In *Essays Critical and Clinical,* 68–90, 192–93. Minneapolis: University of Minnesota Press.

Derrida, Jacques. 1978. "Violence and Metaphysics: An Essay on the Thought of Emmanuel Lévinas." In *Writing and Difference,* trans. A. Bass., 79–153. Chicago: University of Chicago Press.

———. 1993. *Raising the Tone of Philosophy: Late Essays by Immanuel Kant, Transformative Critiques by Jacques Derrida.* Ed. Peter Fenves. Baltimore: The Johns Hopkins University Press.

———. 1995. *The Gift of Death.* Trans. David Wills. Chicago: University of Chicago Press.

Findlay, Edward F. 2002. "Secrets of European Responsibility: Jacques Derrida on Responsibility in the Philosophy of Jan Patocka." *Philosophy Today* 46:16–30.

Goicoechea, David. 1999. "The Moment of Responsibility (Derrida and Kierkegaard)."
    Philosophy Today 43:211–25.
Keenan, Dennis King. 1998. "Responsibility and Death." *Philosophy Today* 42:6–15.
Kierkegaard, Søren. 1983. *Fear and Trembling and Repetition.* Trans. Howard Hong and Edna
    Hong. Princeton: Princeton University Press.
Lévinas, Emmanuel. 1969. *Totality and Infinity*. Trans. A. Lingis. Pittsburgh: Duquesne
    University Press.
———. 1990. "Messianic Texts." In *Difficult Freedom: Essays on Judaism*, trans. S. Hand,
    59–96, 296–97. London: The Athlone Press.
———, 1994. *Beyond the Verse*. Trans. G. D. Mole. Bloomington: Indiana University Press.
———, 1996. *Proper Names*. Trans. M. B. Smith. Stanford: Stanford University Press.
Melville, Herman. 1995. *"Bartleby"* and *"The Lightning-Rod Man."* New York: Penguin.
Shain, Ralph. 2000. "Situating Derrida Between Kierkegaard and Hegel," *Philosophy Today*
    44:388–403.
Wood, David. 1997. "Much Obliged." *Philosophy Today* 41:135–40.

Chapter 11

Justice as Gift: Thinking Grace with the Help of Derrida

Theodore W. Jennings, Jr.

. . . I am interested in Christianity and in the gift in the Christian sense . . .

(Derrida, "On the Gift")

. . . present your members to God as instruments of justice . . . since you are not under the law but under grace

(Paul, Romans)

The question of justice, the one that always carries beyond the law, is no longer separated, in its necessity or its aporias, from that of the gift.

(Derrida, Specters of Marx)

who receive the abundance of grace and the free gift of justice.

(Paul, Romans)

Only when grace is recognized to be incomprehensible is it grace.

(Barth, Commentary on Romans)

Well, now, how is that grace which is not gratuitously conferred? How can it be grace, if it is given in payment of a debt?

(Augustine, On the Grace of Christ)

In the larger project of which this essay represents a part, I am attempting to show how a reading of Derrida may be of help in thinking what Paul is arguing, especially in Romans, concerning justice. The starting point of this discussion is the supposition that it is important to separate the reading of Paul from the ecclesial and confessional presuppositions that continue, even in academic discussions, to set the terms of interpretation. It is thus an attempt at a nonreligious or at least non-confessional reading of Paul;[1] what I have termed in another context, in a description of the project of Hendrikus Boer's work, a "humanistic" interpretation of Paul (Jennings 1990, ix–xvi). In this case it means reading Paul in relation to a powerful contemporary discussion of the theme of justice, namely that of Derrida. Of course in much contemporary and traditional reading of Paul it is not even noticed that Paul is concerned with justice as a political or philosophical problem. That this is Paul's concern has been emphasized above all in Latin American Liberation Theology and is especially present in the work of Jose Porfirio Miranda and Elsa Tamez. Agreeing with these readers of Paul that this is the issue and with Boers that it is important to read Paul not simply as the private possession of a confessional stance but as one whose thought must be understood within a wider and more public and indeed philosophical discourse are the enabling conditions of the project upon which I am embarked.

Derrida has famously maintained that justice is "indeconstructible" and that it may and must be thought outside the law and the laws, which it nevertheless necessarily provokes or incites. It is precisely with such a justice, I contend, that Paul is concerned: a justice of God that is outside the law. Moreover, however much Paul is clear that the law cannot simply be identified with divine (or indeconstructible) justice and that justice must therefore be actualized or actualizable outside or apart from the law, it is still with justice, and with the justice that enables us not simply to be called but to become just, that Paul is concerned.

For Paul and for Derrida it seems that justice is somehow outside the law, exterior in a certain way to law. This apparent contradiction of law and justice becomes clear when we see the connection between law and violence. It is the violence of law that disassociates it from justice. The disjuncture between justice and law is related to what Derrida calls the force of the law or the violence of the law that always destabilizes it relative to justice. Similarly, Paul's disjunction between law and justice depends upon the manifestation of the violence of the law most particularly as the law, both of Israel and of Rome, which rejects, condemns, and executes the messiah who is the coming of divine justice. Now these are complex arguments, both in Derrida and in Paul, and all the more so in their interrelation, and so cannot even be summarized here but only named. But naming them helps to set the stage for the discussion that follows. For it shows that there is a certain commonality of interest and procedure in Paul and Derrida in that both seem to think of the tension between justice and law. And neither wants, it would appear, simply to dismiss law. Yet both find a certain violence to be at the heart of law, a violence that means that justice, if it is to be thought, must be thought apart from the law. If this is so, how then is justice to be thought?

For Paul, as we know, the justice that is outside the law is to be somehow expected on the basis of a certain gift or grace. But how is this to be thought, and especially how is this to be thought without relinquishing our interest precisely in justice and thus in accomplishing that which justice promises and calls for? In order to rethink Paul's reflections on grace and the difficulties this thought entails, I will seek help from the reading of Derrida on gift. It is this which, I will contend, sheds light both on the significance of what Paul is up to and on the difficulties that he runs into as he tries to think justice as, or on the basis of, gift.

Gift and Debt in the Thought of Derrida

Before turning to Paul it is important to clarify the main contours of Derrida's reflections on the gift and its relation to economy. We will first show that Derrida's thinking of gift is related to his thinking of justice. It will then be necessary to indicate how the impossibility of the gift relative to economy does not mean the end of thinking about gift but is the basis for thinking more clearly about gift. This will provide us with basic tools for attempting to clarify Paul's thought about grace in relation to justice.

Relation to Justice

Derrida has already linked gift and justice in his earliest explicit reflections on justice. Thus in *The Force of Law* he had suggested that deconstruction had already obliquely touched upon justice in so far as it had touched upon the question of gift. He had said: "It goes without saying that discourses on . . . the gift beyond exchange and distribution . . . are also, through and through, at least oblique discourses on justice" (2002, 235).

But is the relation between justice and gift even more stringent than the impression given through a listing of a discourse on gift as one of the kinds of discourses that are obliquely related to the question of justice? In a later reflection Derrida will make this connection rather more explicit. "The question of justice, the one that always carries beyond the law, is no longer separated, in its necessity or in its aporias, from that of the gift" (1994, 26). Here at least we are pointed to what seems an even more stringent relation, in that justice and the gift are said to be somehow inseparable; and, moreover, that to think justice means to think gift. But how can this be so? It would seem that something more is at stake here than a similarity of structure, if we may provisionally put it like that, or a similarity of method: we think of gift in the same way that we think of justice: namely in such a way as to expose or bring to light the aporia, the non-self-evidence of these familiar notions. More than this seems to be claimed, namely that if justice is the question, we can no longer engage in this question without reference to the question of gift.

Derrida does in fact go further in specifying this inseparability: "Once one has recognized the force and the necessity of thinking justice on the basis of the gift . . ." he says in *Specters of Marx* (1994, 27). If we are to think justice we will have to do so "on the basis" of thinking gift. This seems a startling claim and that for several reasons. It is startling first because it seems to propose a certain hierarchy[2] in thinking in which the thinking of gift serves as the basis, a sort of ground (groundless itself as we shall see), for thinking justice. It is startling as well because of the way we are immediately put in mind of something Paul says that he is concerned with: "being made just as God's gift by grace" (3:24). We seem, then, to be at least on the right track in supposing that the help we need for thinking with Paul about gift as the basis for justice may be forthcoming from reading Derrida.

In "The Deconstruction of Actuality" Derrida again speaks of the heterogeneity of justice relative not only to law but also to rights and even "respect" for the other: "Justice is not the same as rights; it exceeds and founds the rights of man; nor is it distributive justice. It is not even, in the traditional sense, respect for the other as a human subject" (2002b, 105). But this in turn leads him directly to a consideration of gift: "it is the experience of the other as other, the fact that I let the other be other, which presupposes a gift without restitution, without reappropriation and without jurisdiction" (2002b, 105). Once again we see that there is to be some fundamental connection between justice and gift.

Before we leap too hastily into this last question (gift or grace as the basis of justice) we should retrace our steps to discover more precisely how the question of gift and that of justice bear at least a necessary relation to one another.

Toward the beginning of his reflections on the gift in *Given Time* Derrida points to the relation (in part, one of opposition) between gift and economy, and suggests "a sort of tautology [which] already implies the economic within the nomic as such" (1992b, 6). This is related to the way in which "*Nomos* does not only signify the law in general, but also the law of distribution (*nemein*), the law of sharing or partition" (1992b, 6). We are thus already put on the track or trace of at least a curious parallel between gift and justice: both stand in a similar relation to law. And we have already seen as well that Derrida supposes a disjuncture between justice and distribution (or retribution); that is, to what we may now call an economic view of justice, which is still to be understood as on the side of law in the disjunction of law and justice. Here this is anchored in the relation between *nomos* and *nemein*, between law and distribution as well as that between *nomos* and economy.

That the relation between gift and economy has a certain parallel to the thinking of the relation between justice and law is also indicated in terms of the way in which the opposing terms also seem in a certain way to require one another. For this is what he says about gift in relation to economy:

> Now the gift, *if there is any*, would no doubt be related to economy. One cannot treat the gift, this goes without saying, without treating this relation to economy, even to the money economy. But is not the gift, if there is any, also that which interrupts economy? That which, in suspending economic calculation, no longer gives rise to exchange? (1992b, 7)

Certainly this will remind us of what we have read in connection with justice, that it is necessarily related to the law, but that it also is beyond or outside law; or, as here, that it interrupts law. But what is interrupted is law precisely as the law of exchange, the law or "nomy" of economy. Moreover, as that which interrupts economy, "the gift must remain aneconomic" (1992b, 77) in much the same way that justice remains outside or beyond the law. And here we may recall that in *On Hospitality* Derrida has said a similar thing about law in so far as it is like justice: that it is a "*nomos anomos*" (2000, 80).

Thus far we have established that gift and justice have a remarkable relationship such that both are outside but in necessary relation to law. We have not yet got to the point where we can see clearly how gift will come to serve as the basis of a thinking of justice. We will therefore return to this question.

The Impossibility of the Gift

Before we do so we must address another issue: that of the impossibility of the gift. This is a much misunderstood view of Derrida. There are those who suppose that Derrida's reflections on gift and the impossibility of gift entail the abolition of the thought of gift. This is a mistake. Thus, I will first try to indicate briefly how the gift is impossible, and in what sense this is so, and then indicate how this means precisely that the gift gives itself to be thought or, put another way, that the gift is important precisely because it is impossible.

Having just noted that the gift is aneconomic Derrida says ". . . it is perhaps in this sense that the gift is the impossible," and clarifies "Not impossible but *the* impossible" (1992b, 7). In order to make this clear Derrida begins with what would seem to be the structure of the idea of gift: A gives B to C—there is a subject (giver), a recipient, and that which is given. Now this common sense structure of gift and giving begins to crumble if any sort of intellectual pressure is brought to bear upon it. This becomes clear as soon as we admit that reciprocity destroys gift by making it an item in an economy of exchange. "It is annulled each time there is restitution or countergift. Each time, according to the same circular ring that leads to 'giving back' (*render*), there is payment and discharge of a debt" (1992b, 12).

The reciprocity of gift giving makes it a trade, or subject to a "market." If I give you $50 for that pot, there has been no gift, rather an exchange.

> For there to be a gift, there must be no reciprocity, return, exchange, countergift, or debt. If the other *gives* me *back* or *owes* me or has to give me back what I give him or her, there will not have been a gift, whether this restitution is immediate or whether it is programmed by a complex calculation of a long term deferral or difference. (1992b, 12)

Let us apply this to the situation of the giver. I give you $50 but I don't want a pot in return. Nor is it a loan that you will someday repay (with or without interest), for then repayment or compensation is merely deferred. So I give you $50 without asking anything in return, I say. The problem is that I already may reward myself. My awareness of my own generosity is itself repayment. Derrida explains:

> . . . the gift must not even appear or signify, consciously or unconsciously, *as* gift for the donors, whether individual or collective subjects. From the moment the gift would appear as gift, as such, as what it is, in its phenomenon, its sense and essence, it would be engaged in a symbolic, sacrificial, or economic structure that would annul the gift in the ritual circle of the debt. The simple intention to give, insofar as it carries the intentional meaning of the gift, suffices to make a return payment to oneself. The simple consciousness of the gift right away sends itself back the gratifying image of goodness or generosity, of the giving-being, who, knowing itself to be such, recognizes itself in a circular, specular fashion in a sort of auto-recognition, self-approval, and narcissistic gratitude. (1992b, 23)

And what of the recipient? Someone gave me $50. I know this and that they have done it. Perhaps they have said that it is a gift. But I am or sense myself to be indebted or obliged. "Much obliged" we say in the South. I may even simply offer my gratitude; it would seem churlish not to. But in that case have I not returned something for the gift, and so made the an-economic, economic after all?

And finally the gift itself, the "present." (Derrida makes a good deal of this relation between gift as present, presence, the present and so on—capitalizes on it, we might say.) In so far as I take possession of the gift (and if I cannot, has it really been given?), then it has already become not gift but possession; if and as it becomes mine it is no longer gift. As soon as it is "present," it disappears as gift.

These reflections have as their goal to make clear that what we take to be the conditions of a gift (that there be a donor, a donee, and a donated or don) are at the same time the conditions of the impossibility of the gift as gift. At each point the gift falls back into exchange, into economy, into the law of exchange, distribution and so on. Thus it would seem that the gift is impossible.

In another text Derrida reflects somewhat more on this idea of the impossible: In *Sauf le nom*, he writes: " . . . deconstruction has often been defined as the very experience of the (impossible) possibility of the impossible, of the most impossible, a condition that deconstruction shares with the gift . . ." (1995b, 43). This is important first because we have deconstruction associated here with "the gift," something we also have encountered with respect to justice. But it is not only that deconstruction is related to gift and justice, related in such a way that they may actually seem to be much the same thing; but also because the impossibility of gift is here related to the idea of impossible possibility, and the possibility of the impossible.[3] The theologian at least will recognize this language. It is the very language in which Barth and Bultmann have spoken of grace and faith. Now whatever may have been said about their use of this vocabulary of impossibility I do not think that anyone has imagined that because they use this language they simply dismiss faith or grace. That would be absurd, as any reader of their work would know. But Derrida has been accused of rendering the gift, because impossible, also unthinkable. And not only by those who for professional reasons may be supposed to be ignorant of theologians like Barth and Bultmann (for philosophers do not often read theologians, certainly not as often as theologians read philosophers).

Thus in yet another text Derrida clarifies: "The gift as such cannot be known, but it can be thought of. We can think what we cannot know" (Caputo 1999, 60). Not only can we think what we do not know, it seems to be the case that thinking is decisively connected to what we do not know. Thinking requires a certain impossibility even to get underway precisely as thinking. Especially if thinking means something that aims to stay with, rather than liquidate, the question.

The relation between thinking as opposed to knowledge in relation to the gift is amplified, indeed was already amplified, in *Given Time*: "This gap between, on the one hand, thought, language, and desire and, on the other hand, knowledge, philosophy, science, and the order of presence is also a gap between gift and economy" (1992b, 29). The thinking of the gift, then, is in a certain way exterior to "knowledge, philosophy and science" and for that reason is like or associated with "thought, language and desire."

It is important to note that the impossibility is again decidedly linked with thinking even if not with knowing: "if the gift is another name for the impossible, we still think it, we name it, we desire it. We intend it" (1992b, 29).

Accordingly Derrida has sought to explain, even against his "friends," that the idea of impossibility is not meant to stop but rather to start thought. Thus he maintains in his essay in *God, the Gift and Postmodernism*:

> I tried to precisely displace the problematic of the gift, to take it out of the circle of economy, of exchange, but *not* to conclude, from the impossibility for the gift to appear as such and to be determined as such, to its absolute impossibility. [. . .] . . . it is impossible for the gift to exist and appear as such. But I never concluded that there is no gift. I went on to say that if there is a gift, through this impossibility, it must be the experience of this impossibility, and it should appear as impossible. (Caputo 1999, 59)

In an expression that takes us somewhat further than Derrida seemed prepared to go in *Given Time* he can even say: "The gift is totally foreign to the horizon of economy, ontology, knowledge, constantive statements, and theoretical determination and judgment" (Caputo 1999, 59). It is here that we seem to get a formulation of the exteriority of gift and economy to one another that corresponds to similar statements concerning the heterogeneity of justice and the law.

The Gift "in the Christian Sense"

In *God, the Gift and Postmodernism*, Derrida goes on to say that his attempt to account for or to think the gift has led him precisely to try to think the gift " . . . not only in economy but even in Christian discourse" (Caputo 1999, 59). In discussion with Jean Luc Marion, Derrida can even affirm that what interests him in thinking the gift is precisely the gift in the sense of a certain Christianity "I am interested in Christianity and in the gift in the Christian sense . . ." (1999, 57). The gift in the Christian sense means here, it seems to me, the understanding of grace that Paul seeks to clarify, especially in Romans. That is, Derrida's reflections on gift are meant to be, intended to be, a reflection also on what Christians, and perhaps especially Paul, call grace.

Just as we have seen that justice is divine as the justice of God so also, in another text, Derrida takes note of a way in which giving (or gracing) can also be thought of as divine. Reflecting on Angelus Silesius, Derrida writes that he " . . . interprets the divinity of God as gift or desire of giving" (1995b, 56). While it is not my intention in this essay to reflect on the meaning of God under the conditions of deconstruction, a theme that is already being treated by theologians to the exclusion of too much else, this does at least suggest the pertinence of what we have been reading for an attempt to think with Paul about the grace or gift that is divine.

Paul and Grace

In attending to Paul's thought of gift/grace we will have to notice several things that will connect it to what we have read in Derrida. Among these are: the connection of gift and grace; the priority of grace as related to justice; the exteriority of grace and law; the exteriority of grace to debt or work; the instability of grace relative to debt/work; and the grace that surpasses knowledge (but not thought).

Grace and Gift

It is first necessary to indicate the way in which for Paul gift and grace, although semantically different, are nevertheless identified in his thought. The terms *charis* (grace/favor) and *dōrēma* (gift) are consistently brought into intimate connection in Paul's thought in Romans. Thus already in a text to which we will have had occasion to refer in a discussion of justice: "they are now made just by divine grace (*chariti*) as a gift (*dōrean*) . . ." (3:24). We will return to the question of the relation to justice in a moment. But for now we simply underline the association of gift and grace. A similar, perhaps even more emphatic association we discover when Paul again returns to speak of what may be called the Christ event or, perhaps better the "messiah event."[4]

> But the free gift (*charisma*) is not like the trespass. For if the many died through one man's trespass, much more surely have the grace (*charis*) of God and the free gift (*dōrea*) in the grace (*chariti*) of the one man, Jesus Christ, abounded for many. And the free gift (*dōrēma*) is not like the effect of one man's sin. For the judgment following one trespass brought condemnation, but the free gift (*charisma*) following many trespasses brings justification. If because of the one man's trespass, death exercised dominion through that one, much more surely will those who receive the abundance of grace (*charitos*) and the free gift (*dōreas*) of justice exercise dominion in life . . . . (5:15–17)

This passage, so rich in provocations to thought, serves at this point to establish the equivalence that Paul articulates between gift and grace, an equivalence so intricate that the translator is unable to maintain a distinction at all between these terms or the terms developed from these roots.

This should serve to indicate the pertinence of a reflection on the problem of gift (as we have it in Derrida) for an attempt to think what Paul is up to in attempting to think grace.

Grace and Justice

We have already seen that for Paul, as for Derrida, there is a recognition that justice cannot be thought simply as a compliance with the law; that law and justice are disjoined and that this comes to expression through the violence of the law. But if law cannot serve as the basis of justice then perhaps gift can. This at least is what Paul affirms. And he does so first of all in the very passages where he has associated gift and grace. Thus in a kind of thesis statement that announces what is to be explicated Paul has said: "they are now made just by divine grace (*charis*) as a gift (*dōrean*) . . ." (3:24). The coming (to be) of justice is precisely what the gift has in view. It is the gift that serves as the "ground" of justice. And this is also affirmed in the other passage we have cited where gift and grace are brought into connection: "but the free gift (*charisma*) . . . brings justification." And subsequently: " . . . who receive the abundance of grace (*charitos*) and the free gift (*dōreas*) of justice" (5:16, 17). Again we are trying to proceed step by step. And the step taken here is that justice and the becoming or being made just (justification) are established precisely as gift.[5] Unfortunately, this connection between justice and grace has not often been seen by the theological "friends" of Paul. For they have more generally concluded that because grace is distinct from law it must also abrogate or suspend the claim of justice. But at least so far Paul is maintaining the opposite: namely, that grace, so far from suspending the claim of justice, actually renders that claim effective; actually "grounds" that claim in a way that law could not do. In order for this to be clear we turn then to how grace suspends law (but not justice).

Grace Versus Law

That grace serves as the basis of justice would lead us to suspect that grace, like justice, stands in a certain tension with, even exteriority, and perhaps opposition to, law. And this is precisely what we find in certain formulations of Paul. "You are not under law but grace" (6:14). This assertion not only disassociates grace and law but serves as the basis for Paul's exhortation to his readers to be tools or instruments of justice rather than injustice. That is, they are exhorted to serve justice rather than injustice, precisely because they are not under the law (which cannot produce justice as we have seen) but under grace which does and must produce justice rather than injustice. The rather odd language in which Paul asserts this claim should not distract us from the fact that it is precisely this claim that is made: "No longer present your members to sin as instruments of injustice . . . [but] present your members to God as instruments of justice . . . since you are not under the law but under grace" (6:13–14).[6] The effect of this passage is regularly mitigated in English by the habit of translating injustice (*adikias*) as "wickedness;" as well as that of translating justice (*dikaiosunēs*) as "righteousness." The effect is to abrogate the connection between grace and justice so that the critique or suspension of the law comes to be thought as the suspension of the claim of justice. Nothing could be further from Paul's language and thought. In an even more startling formula, Paul can even speak of being "slaves of justice" as a consequence of being set free from sin (or injustice, as I am now inclined to say; 6:18). So little is the claim of justice set aside by grace that it is possible even to describe those who are not under law but under gift as "slaves of justice" (6:18, 19) that is, as those who are even more than before answerable to justice, captive (we might even say hostage) to its claims and demands. In this way Paul can even say that the ones he is addressing are not only (called to be) slaves of justice but also "slaves of God" (6:22)—an alarming formulation that at least serves to make clear the equivalence we earlier posited between justice and God, justice as divine justice. Or as John Caputo asks: Is justice another name for God or is God another name for justice? (Caputo 1997, 68, 116).

Grace as Exterior to Debt/Works

In order to clarify this it may be helpful to see how the reflections of Paul are related to what we have seen in Derrida's reflections on gift and economy or exchange. In that connection we noted that economy is to be understood as operating within the domain of law, the "nomy" of economy. And the law of economy is precisely that of exchange, of debt, of payment, and so on.

Paul also wishes to establish a certain exteriority of grace or gift to the economy of payment and debt. This he does by associating the idea of "works" with that of law. In this case what seems to be in view is an acting in compliance with the law or in accordance with a certain legality. This compliance or legality is in turn linked with the idea of "boasting" which here seems to function in much the same way as what Derrida has termed a good conscience. That is, boasting is the self-congratulation that satisfies itself that it has complied with the law and therefore is owed some payment or reward. It is not only self-congratulatory in this way but is able to display itself before others as deserving of praise as a reward or payment that is due.

This is perhaps what Paul is struggling to say when he characterizes those who in his view have sought justice on the basis of law.

> . . . but Israel, who did strive for the justice that is based on the law, did not succeed in fulfilling that law. Why not? Because they did not strive for it on the basis of faith, but as if it were based on works. (9:31)

In the terms that we have been developing this would mean not that they in fact did not succeed in fulfilling the law as written, but that in doing so they do not fulfill the intent of the law, that is justice. For this can only be put into effect through that which corresponds to gift (here called faith) and not by an economy or ergonomy of works. Of course what Paul says here concerning his own people is by no means his last word on this subject. Nor can it be supposed that it does not accurately characterize many who are called, not without reason, Christians. He further says: "being ignorant of the justice that comes from God, and seeking to establish their own, they have not submitted to God's justice" (10:3), and goes on to speak again of the end of the law through the messiah which aims at making justice effective for all (10:4) who not only hear and heed the call or claim of justice but who respond or correspond to the gift that is the very basis of justice.

I am all too aware of the ways these texts have been used to drive a wedge between Christians and Jews and thus are implicated in the atrocities of Euro-Christianity. But I take it as axiomatic that any interpretation of these texts today must understand this opposition, if it is one, to run through all religious traditions, and especially to subvert the claims of any who seek to establish their own place in relation to "God" or "justice" (Boers 1994) at the expense of others or to satisfy themselves of a good conscience, often enough by perpetrating the most terrible deeds in the name of their own "righteousness" or the "evil" that is attributed to others.

In this concern for a good conscience[7] we encounter an economy, perhaps we might say a symbolic economy, that renders gift impossible. For what one receives in the way of praise or what have you is no more than is already deserved.[8] It is precisely this symbolic economy that Paul wants to overcome by way of his talk about gift or grace. He thus is able to make use of a rather commonsense appeal to what is knowable about economy: "Now to one who works, wages are not reckoned as a gift but as something due . . ." (4:4). Here, works are linked to wages, to what is due or owed, indeed to debt, for that is the word used here. The wage for work is not and cannot be a gift. But gift is the basis, he is arguing, for justice. Here another term is deployed which functions to identify that which corresponds to gift (as work corresponds to the economy of law). That term is "faith." Whatever this term is used to mean, here it is enough to see it as that which corresponds to gift (and so to justice), and as such opposed to work, wages, debt, and so on. Thus boasting, Paul will say, is excluded not by the law of works (economy, or perhaps we should say, ergonomics = *ergon* + *nomos*) but by the "law of faith"; that is, by that which corresponds to gift (3:27). It is this that counts as or for or toward justice (4:5). Thus it is that which is, or establishes, or founds, justice, precisely the justice of faith (4:13).

Again the point here is not to give content to the idea of faith but only to notice how it functions. Positively it is that which corresponds to justice and to gift; or to justice as, or on the basis of, gift. Negatively it is that which is opposed to a certain economy or ergonomy of works, wages, and debt. Hence he can say in connection with a later development of his argument "If it is by grace, it is no longer on the basis of works, otherwise grace would no longer be grace" (11:6). To this some manuscripts add: "But if it is by works, it is no longer by grace, otherwise work would no longer be work." What is at stake here in the shorter or the longer formulation is the exteriority of works (economy) to grace or gift. A gift is not a gift if one is thereby rewarded for doing. And if one is rewarded for doing then the gift has disappeared into the economy of payment, of exchange, of debt.

Instability of Distinction

And yet. We have already seen in our discussion of Derrida that gift, however it may and must be thought as exterior to economy, nevertheless, is always implicated in and by economy. "Now the gift, *if there is any*, would no doubt be related to economy. One cannot treat the gift, this goes without saying, without treating this relation to economy, even to the money economy" (1992b, 7). As we have seen it is precisely this relation to economy that makes the gift impossible or rather *the* impossible.

If on this basis we were to suppose that the distinction between gift and economy tends to be rather unstable in Paul's thought, we would not be disappointed. Indeed the very metaphor of slave (slave of Christ, slave of justice, slave of God), is nothing if not an economic metaphor making use of the very basis of economics in the slave empire; much like "worker" in the case of what is sometimes called "democratic capitalism."

Paul struggles against the tendency of this distinction to collapse. He writes for example: "For the wages of sin is death, but the free gift of God is eternal life . . ." (6:23). Here Paul places gift and wage in opposition. But to what extent is this "eternal life" really free? really unconditional? At what point does it come to seem almost as a payment? This is not simply a theoretical question. For Paul can use the vocabulary of economy to speak of that which is presumably beyond economy. He can describe himself as a "debtor" on the basis of the gospel (1:14). Yet he pulls himself up short when his rhetoric almost leads him to say that those who receive the gift or grace of God are debtors to this gift or the one who gives it. This is noteworthy since he has not shrunk from speaking of these as slaves of justice or of God. The passage is Romans 8:12 where he begins: "we are debtors, not to the flesh . . ." here one might expect "but to the Spirit." Instead what we get is "But if by the Spirit you put to death the deeds of the body, you will live" (8:13). Paul seems to pull back from the brink here but not without making the work of putting "to death the deeds of the body" seem to have a reward or payment: "you will live."

In order to clarify this problem we will have to turn later to the discussion of duty beyond debt (Derrida) and of the obedience of faith (Paul).

How Much More

Before we do that however we may pause to ask just how it is that the disjuncture between gift and economy comes to expression in Paul. This is like the question that must be addressed concerning the disjuncture between justice and law. There we would see that this disjuncture appears in the recognition of the violence of law. This is not the case, I believe, with the appearance of the disjuncture of gift and economy. That is, what comes into play here is not the violence of economy, although one could certainly make a case for that in so far as what is in question is the "nomy" of economy, the deployment of law to protect the order of the economy.

Instead there is another kind of disjuncture here, one that will help us to think how it is that gift is not only like justice in relation to law but also (the question we had earlier suspended) how gift is the basis of justice, and as the basis, is also, to a certain degree, unlike that which it makes possible.

Briefly, if it is violence that makes clear the heterogeneity of law relative to the claim of justice, what is it that makes clear the heterogeneity of gift relative to economy? The answer it seems to me is something like excess, or abundance.

This thought of excess or of superabundance is first "anchored" in the story of Abraham and Sarah for it is their God (the one associated with gift), who "gives life to the dead and calls into existence the things that do not exist" (4:17). It is this "logic of excess" that then comes into play precisely where what is at stake is the clarification of the gift character of grace. The key phrase here is "much more" (*pollō mallon*). Thus the death of Christ (as that which separates us from the law) is compared to that which is to come (salvation, let us say). The difference is "*how much more*" (5:9). Similarly if our resentment toward God is overcome, again by the violence that separates God (justice) from the law, then *how much more* will "we be saved by his life" (5:10). This logic, if it is that, is then applied to the thought of gift as exceeding the need indicated by sin "*how much more* the grace of God and the free gift . . . abounded to the many" (5:15). And if the "wages of sin is death" then we are also told of the "*much more* the abundance of the grace and the gift" (5:17) will redound to our benefit, beyond debt. Now without going into a detailed reading of these passages, it is enough simply to indicate that the reference to excess and abundance is what seems to separate the thought of gift from that of economy.[9]

It may be the case that Bataille may give us more help here than Derrida, for exuberance, excess, and abundance is not a prominent theme when Derrida thinks of justice, politics, and ethics and so on. This is not to say it is alien to his thought or to his work. How could that be so for the author of *Glas* or *Ulysses Gramophone*? But there is, it seems, a certain reticence with respect to this vocabulary in connection with the thought of justice.[10] Even so it is unquestionable that for Derrida it is also the case that it is precisely abundance that separates the thought of gift from economy.

This is already clear in his discussion of Mauss in *Given Time* when he notes that it is precisely at the point of having to give an account of potlatch that the economistic conceptuality within which Mauss tries to think the gift goes into a kind of paroxysm. "His language goes mad at the point where, in the potlatch, the process of the gift gets carried away with itself" (1992b, 46). But before the "madness of economic reason" (the name of this chapter of *Given Time*) is thus exposed, Derrida will have already noted in his reading of Mauss:

> The problem of the gift has to do with its nature that *is excessive in advance, a priori exaggerated*. A donating experience that would not be delivered over, *a priori*, to some immoderation . . . would not be a gift. . . . the most modest gift must pass beyond measure. (1992b, 38)

Gift to be gift must be characterized by the "how much more," the excessive. Otherwise it is merely exchange.

Later we encounter other texts of Derrida that are even more explicit in relation to this excess. In *The Gift of Death* he speaks of "two economies," "one of retribution, equal exchange, within a circular economy; the other of absolute surplus value, heterogeneous to outlay or investment" (1995a, 105). Then in speaking of what he calls authentic filiation he says that this occurs on condition that there is a gift, a love *without reserve* (1995a, 106). This notion of excess or surplus is indeed made the basis of any talk of responsibility in *Points* "responsibility is excessive or it is not responsibility. A limited, measured, calculated, rationally responsibility is already the becoming-right of morality" (1995c, 286). In these and other texts Derrida points to the way in which the gift is heterogeneous to the law of economy precisely as excess, as surplus, as a "without reserve." In these ways his reflections on gift seem to be in concord with Paul's emphasis on the "how much more" of gift or grace that separates it from the economy of debt and death.

Beyond Knowledge

We have noticed that for Derrida the thinking of gift takes us beyond knowledge even if not beyond thought. It is important to notice that there is something similar going on in Paul although it might be rash to conclude that it is precisely the same thing. Paul's ways of speaking of what we have termed the messiah event entails, he insists, a certain rupture with the domain of knowledge. He makes much of the distinction between wisdom and folly in order to subvert these categories in speaking about his own message concerning the messiah event. Thus he speaks of his message (one that he has sought to make intelligible) as "folly" in contrast to Greek wisdom (1 Cor. 1:18) while maintaining that "divine foolishness is wiser than human wisdom" (1 Cor. 1:25).

This comes to expression in Romans precisely as he has been reflecting again on the effect of the messiah event. Here again he will be thinking of divine wisdom that exceeds the order of knowledge even though it is what he has been attempting to make intelligible. And in speaking of this wisdom that exceeds knowledge he will also speak of gift beyond exchange or debt; of the gift of the divine grace that is not contained within the economy of debt and exchange. "O the depths of the riches and wisdom and knowledge of God! . . . who has given a gift to him, to receive a gift in return?" (Rom. 11:33, 35). In the last reference to gift Paul is citing while turning almost on its head a passage from Job 35:7 where Elihu, Job's friend, is, in effect, accusing him and counseling him to refrain from interrogating God for Job's misfortune. In the case of Paul, however, the aneconomic relation points not to a situation of deprivation (Job's misfortunes) but to one of astonishing abundance whereby the divine promise reaches out to include even those who seem to have rejected it. Thus it is a gift that is not motivated by any prior condition but which over-rides all such conditions. It is this of which, according to Paul, we may and must speak, even if our thinking must exceed what can be ordinarily circumscribed within the order of knowing or of human (as opposed to divine) wisdom.

Event

Now it is not the case that Paul can simply say, as does Derrida, that the gift is impossible or even as Bultmann would say, an impossible possibility. For the difference between Paul and Derrida at this point is precisely that Paul is not restricted by a quasi-phenomenological bracket, with a reflection on the possibility, but rather is obligated to speak of an event, rather than the possibility of this event.

For the messianic event for Paul has, in some sense, already come, even if the mode of this already remains still in the register of that which in a certain way is yet to come. But it is the former modality, that it has arrived, that sets apart the mode of Paul's reflections from those of Derrida. I do not say this in order then to seek to adjudicate which is right. For both are constrained by the genre of discourse within which they operate. It is not that Paul is overly confident of an event that has occurred or that Derrida falls short of a recognition of some sort of evangelical truth. Both are struggling within and against a certain language game, but different language games too. Thus it is the homology that we notice; not the identity of content.

In his contribution to *God, the Gift and Postmodernism* Derrida explicitly links the thinking of gift and the thinking of event: "An event as such, as well as the gift, cannot be known as an event . . ." (Caputo 1999, 60). The unknowability of event opens up onto the question of revelation, the appearing of gift and so the question of the revelation of event or as event. Derrida places this in relation to Heidegger in order to open the question of revelation and revealability:

> Translated into Heidegger's discourse, which is addressing the same difficulty, this is the distinction between *Offenbarung* and *Offenbarkeit*, revelation and revealability. Heidegger said, this is his position, that there would be no revelation or *Offenbarung* without a prior structure of *Offenbarkeit* without the possibility of revelation and the possibility of manifestation. That is Heidegger's position. I am not so sure. Perhaps it is through *Offenbarung* that *Offenbarkeit* becomes thinkable, historically. That is why I am constantly really hesitating. That is part of—what can I call this here?—let us say, my cross. (Caputo 1999, 73)[11]

Although Derrida will go on to question this alternative in terms of what a reflection on *khora* may offer, it is already much that he gives us to think at this point. For first we may recognize here in the possible inversion of Heidegger's priorities the position that has been emphasized by Karl Barth, namely that for theology at least the possibility of revelation must be thought from the event of revelation, that is from revelation as something that has happened. It would seem that there is not as much of a disjuncture here between Paul and Derrida as we had thought. But of course here Derrida is going beyond phenomenology, as he has said he must, if he is also to think gift (Caputo 1999, 66).

Even more startling here is the linking of this indecision relative to the actuality or possibility of revelation to what, hesitantly, he calls his cross. A cross that is not unrelated to the cross that is also, if Paul is to be believed, the event in which we are given what he calls grace.

Derrida also goes on to say that this is what he is trying to get at with *khora* and that this aims at a new basis for politics. But he also says: "Perhaps, and this is my hypothesis, if not a hope, what I am saying here could be translated after the fact into Jewish discourse or Christian discourse or Muslim discourse, if they can integrate the terrible things I am suggesting now" (Caputo 1999, 77). The "terrible things" have to do with *khora*. And I must, for now, leave that aside. But what Derrida hypothesizes here—or even hopes—is that what he is saying can be translated "after the fact" into, for example, Christian discourse. This is precisely what we are trying to do here with respect to at least that part of Christian discourse that derives from Paul. But, and this is what must be emphasized, this translation can by no means be an exclusive one such that it would disqualify a Jewish or Muslim translation (and other translations besides).

Thus far we have seen that the justice that exceeds, goes beyond or is outside the law is a justice that is given its decisive impetus through a gift that is outside economy and which has the character of a certain excess or gratuity. But precisely how does this result in or give justice? In order to suggest how this may happen it would be necessary first to have recourse to Derrida's reflections on a duty beyond debt. This would enable us to think more clearly about some of the ways in which Paul maintains that, for example, love, as that which goes beyond what is owed, is a fulfilling of the law.

A further part of the argument entails attending to what Derrida suggests about hospitality and welcome as an opening to what may be termed cosmopolitanism as a concrete instantiation of a certain justice beyond the law. In this connection it would be important to show how Paul's own reflections on welcome of the other, the other who has a different practice/opinion and thus in a certain way a different religion, bears precisely on the question of justice and on that question as one of particular urgency also today.

In his discussions of welcome and hospitality Derrida connects this to the question of forgiveness, or rather, of pardon. I have been arguing throughout that the reduction of talk of justification to a certain (forensic) forgiveness has obliterated Paul's concern for justice. Accordingly it will be important to show that forgiveness may also be understood as a crucial political notion and that it has a place as such in Paul's thought even if not the place conventionally assigned to it. In this project I will again argue that the reading of Derrida will be of considerable help in enabling us to think what Paul is driving at.

In this project, the scope of which I can really only hint at here, it is not my contention that reading Derrida will illuminate all that Paul is concerned with, even in Romans. Nor is it that everything Derrida says, for example about Paul, is equally helpful. I certainly do not suppose that either body of text, whether that signed by a certain Derrida, or that signed by a certain Paul, is reducible to one another, that they are simply saying the same thing even after making allowances for differences in culture and context. Rather, what I suppose is that both are wrestling with crucially important questions, questions that were and are important not only for a certain select circle, whether that circle be called philosophy or theology, but for a humanity yearning to become human (and just).

Notes

1. The terminology of a "non-religious" interpretation is one that derives from Bonhoeffer's appropriation of a Barthian distinction between faith and religion. Since Derrida begins from a different context in which he seeks—from within the enlightenment itself—to question the enlightenment marginalization of religion, the term "non-confessional" or nondogmatic would be more congenial than "non-religious." I retain that term in order to signal a concern for a certain theological tradition.
2. In "Negotiations," the lead interview in *Negotiations*, Derrida has said: "I do not believe in the erasure of hierarchy. What I am opposed to is always a certain stabilizing or stabilized coding of hierarchy" (2002, 21).
3. Richard Beardsworth in his fine analysis of the relation between Derrida's thinking on law and justice and that of the philosophical tradition from Kant to Hegel and Marx, and continuing to Heidegger and Lévinas, has rightly maintained: "Impossibility is not the *opposite* of the possible: impossibility *releases* the possible" (Beardsworth 1996, 26).
4. Throughout I will be using Messiah for Christ and messiah-event for Christ event. This is both to insist on the basic "Jewishness" of Paul's thought and to prevent the language from automatically slipping into the familiar presuppositions of Christology. At the end of the larger project of which this essay is a part, I will indicate some of the issues that may be dealt with in order to clarify Paul's messianic perspective with the aid of Derrida's own reflections on the messianic and related themes.
5. We noted above that Derrida claims that justice must be thought on the basis of gift. The question of how this is so for him was left suspended. But we are able to see that at least for Paul the affirmation that grace is the basis of justice is important.
6. Already in 2 Corinthians Paul had used this metaphor to speak of his own comportment: "*with the weapons of justice for the right hand and for the left*" (2 Cor. 6:7). The members here, the hands, are the way in which one deals with other people and the world and it is this interaction that is "armed" for justice. It is this which seems to be the sense of "*the power of God*" to which he refers just prior to this metaphor, and the previous qualities (genuine love, truthful speech, and so on) are what give content to that justice with which one is armed by the "power of God." In Romans it becomes clear that this divine power is precisely the gift of justice.
7. In the Roundtable discussion "On Forgiveness" in *Questioning God* (Caputo 2001), Derrida says: "So you cannot prevent me from having a bad conscience, and that is the main motivation of my ethics and my politics" (2001, 69). While this might seem to be a "hyperbolic" statement, Derrida is quite consistent in his writings that a "good conscience"

is, shall we say, unconscionable. Lévinas had often cited the statement of Dostoevsky "We are all guilty of all and for all men before all. And I more than the others" (cited, for example in Emmanuel Lévinas, *Ethics and Infinity* (1985, 98). While the importance of a bad conscience for a certain personal ethic may be attributable to a certain religious attitude what is most important is that this is said to be the basis of politics; that is, what is at stake here is, quite simply yet comprehensively, the question of justice—that justice which comes as or on the basis of gift.

8. In this respect the Jesus of Matthew's Gospel can say of one who has a good conscience that he "already has his reward" (6:2).

9. The logic of "how much more" as the distinction between law and gift is already present in 2 Corinthians where Paul writes: "if there was splendor in the service (*diakonia*) of condemnation [referring to the law of death, verse 7 above] the service of justice must far exceed (*pollō mallon*) it in splendor" (2 Cor. 3:9). The idea that the service of law is accompanied by splendor or glory (*doxa*) is developed by Paul in relation to the glory shown in Moses' face and which necessitated his wearing a veil, which in turn leads to Paul saying that we (that is those who serve justice) don't need a veil. This last comes in for some comment, perhaps irritable, from Derrida in *A Silkworm of One's Own* (2002a, 346–47) but Derrida does not comment on the antecedent distinction between law and justice and the glory attributed (though distributed differently) to each.

10. The exuberance of Caputo's reading of Derrida provides an illustration of the relation between excess and the thought of justice. See, for example, 1997, 168–69. While an exploration of the trace of this excess in Derrida's emphasis on affirmation as prior to the questioning would take us far afield from our immediate concerns, consideration of the "affirmation that motivates deconstruction" is found in "Eating Well" (1995c, 286).

11. See also Derrida 1996, 80.

Works Consulted

Beardsworth, Richard. 1996. *Derrida and the Political*. New York: Routledge.

Boers, Hendrikus. 1994. *The Justification of the Gentiles*. Peabody, MA: Hendrikson.

Caputo, John. 1997. *Prayers and Tears of Jacques Derrida: Religion Without Religion*. Bloomington: Indiana University Press.

Caputo, John, M. Dooley, and M. J. Scanlon, eds. *Questioning God*. Bloomington: Indiana University Press.

Caputo, John and M. J. Scanlon, eds. 1999. *God, The Gift and Postmodernism*. Bloomington: Indiana University Press.

Derrida, Jacques. 1992a. *Acts of Literature*. Ed. Derek Attridge. Chicago: University of Chicago Press.

———. 1992b. *Given Time: 1. Counterfeit Money*. Trans. Peggy Kamuf. Chicago: University of Chicago Press.

———. 1994. *Specters of Marx: The State of the Debt, The Work of Mourning, and the New International*. New York: Routledge.

———. 1995a. *The Gift of Death*. Chicago: University of Chicago Press.

———. 1995b. *On the Name*. Stanford CA: Stanford University Press.

———. 1995c. *Points . . . : Interviews 1974–1994*. Stanford CA: Stanford University Press.

———. 1996. *Archive Fever*. Chicago: University of Chicago Press.

———. 1999. "On the Gift: A Discussion between Jacques Derrida and Jean-Luc Marion. In Caputo and Scanlon (ed.) 1999. 54–78.

———. 2000. *Of Hospitality*. Stanford CA: Stanford University Press.

Derrida, Jacques 2001a. *Acts of Religion*. Ed. Gil Anidjar. New York: Routledge.
————. 2001b. *Negotiations*. Stanford CA: Stanford University Press.
————. 2002a. "Force of Law: The Mystical Foundation of Authority." In Derrida, *Acts of Religion*. Ed. Gil Anidjar. 228–298.
————. 2002b. "The Deconstruction of Actuality." In *Negotiations: Interventions and Interviews 1971–2001*, ed. and trans. Elizabeth Rottenberg, 85–116. Stanford: Stanford University Press.
Jennings, Theodore W., ed. 1990. *Text and Logos: the Humanistic Interpretation of the New Testament*. Atlanta: Scholars Press.
Lévinas, Emmanuel. 1985. *Ethics and Infinity*. Pittsburgh: Duquesne University Press.
Miranda, Jose Porfirio. 1974. *Marx and the Bible: A Critique of the Philosophy of Oppression*. Maryknoll, NY: Orbis.
Tamez, Elsa. 1993. *The Amnesty of Grace*. Nashville: Abingdon.

Chapter 12

Trembling in the Dark: Derrida's *Mysterium Tremendum* and the Gospel of Mark

Andrew P. Wilson

The Transfiguration (Mark 9:2–8) and the scene at the Empty Tomb (16:1–8) are two fear-filled moments that stand in stark contrast to each other in the context of Mark's Gospel. One is typically characterised by the overflowing hope and brilliance of God's radiant glory; the other crushes expectations with a stark and scandalous absence. Despite these differences, the distance between these scenes is bridged by a primal fear that marks them as encounters with something wondrous and at the same time terrifying: a dread-filled mystery before which one can but tremble. Words fail, faces blanch and limbs quake before the *mysterium tremendum*.

Traditional scholarship reads the Markan Transfiguration as brimming with presences: light, clarity, vision, voice, etc. The Empty Tomb in contrast is marked by a conspicuous absence and a puzzling abruptness: Jesus' body is missing and the Gospel ends mid-sentence. Despite these differences, however, by the end of the Gospel both scenes are read in ways that bring reassurance that God's overarching plan has been received and fulfilled: fractures are repaired, ruptures are filled, and any absences are converted into presences. Could it be, however, that when read through a lens of fearfulness, fearfulness that pervades both these texts, it is possible to reread them as moments when traditional formulations are radically subverted? The task of this essay is to pursue this possibility by applying a Derridean perspective to these texts, particularly with respect to his reading of the *mysterium tremendum*. In this, Derrida's longstanding challenge to the privileging of presence will be particularly helpful. The goal here is to develop a reading that engages with the various themes and motifs in such a way that they are not celebrated solely for their synonymity with the hallmarks of a metaphysics of presence.

At first glance, the *mysterium tremendum* serves to unite two equally powerful but thematically polarised scenes. In the Transfiguration scene we are presented with the fullest, clearest and most intimate picture of glory the Gospels have to offer (see Garland 1996, 343; Hughes 1989, 15). God's presence is blindingly evident, as all the dazzling elements of this passage converge in a thoroughly familiar conception of glory. Yet, despite this, there is another side to the Markan Transfiguration that is far more enigmatic. For instance, although there is classic vocabulary and imagery of glory in abundance, traditions drawn from the templates of the Hebrew Bible,[1] it is curious that amidst such a spectacular vision of the divine, the word for glory, δόξα, is not actually used.

In accommodating this absence, some commentators suggest that the promise of the δόξα of Jesus, vividly yet incompletely sketched in the Transfiguration, is to be found in its fullness after Jesus' death.[2] But at Mark's Empty Tomb, one is offered little comfort. Mark's Gospel does not end the way one might have hoped: there are no dazzling scenes of bright sparkling brilliance and Jesus does not return clothed in power from on high offering promises of enduring presence. Instead, Mark's Gospel ends with a sense of something still lacking (still mourned?) amidst the darkness of an empty tomb.[3] Mark ends/suspends his story on a note of fear: "So they went out and fled from the tomb, for the terror and amazement had seized them and they said nothing to anyone, for they were afraid" (Mark 16:8). While accepting 16:8 as a possible ending, recent interpretation seems less willing to come to terms with this moment of gaping absence.[4] In fact, in many cases absence is quickly substituted with a fresh set of "presences," often in the most resourceful of ways. Thus John Dominic Crossan argues for a "message of non-message" and an abiding absence, and nonetheless conjures an absence that becomes more present than presence: "Indeed, [absence] may well be the deepest and most permanent form of presence" (1978, 53).[5]

Regardless of scholarly frustrations, it seems the impulse to trace a notion of glory from the fullness of the Transfiguration to the seemingly contradictory emptiness of the Tomb endures. But in anticipating a certain well-established notion of glory, have commentators unwittingly set themselves up for disappointment? Is there more to this notion of glory than can be accommodated by a fully present vision marked by light and voice and understanding? Can frustrations be allayed, and new interpretative possibilities opened up if one asks how conceptions of glory are affected when read alongside the encounter with the *mysterium tremendum,* that moment of sheer terror that accompanies both of these Markan episodes?

In *The Gift of Death* (1995), Jacques Derrida reformulates the experience of the *mysterium tremendum* so as to invest a well-established phenomenon with a number of alternate resonances. Derrida's insights are particularly welcome in this inquiry because they offer a vision of glory that is not tied to the standard dichotomies of either presence or absence. Derrida's *mysterium tremendum* avoids, to some extent, a number of these "logocentrisms" by evoking a powerful paradox whereby identity is intimately embraced while at the same time radically subverted.

Although a certain amount of reliance on established metaphysical language, imagery and structures is unavoidable, the effort in this paper will not be to invent a new language, but merely to extend the boundaries of interpretation so as to allow for the possibility of going beyond the parameters that have traditionally encircled scholarship on these passages. A certain slippage back into the traditional structures and language of metaphysics is unavoidable, and not so problematic so long as there is some challenge offered to these enduring boundaries that continue to shape the course of interpretation.

I will begin by briefly explicating Derrida's reading of the *mysterium tremendum* from *The Gift of Death* (1995). From here I will turn to the texts themselves, investigating the episode involving Peter's so called "error" in the Transfiguration passage, a traditionally problematic episode that is permeated with the most acute fear. Peter's enigmatic response to the vision of Jesus transfigured can be put into dialogue with Derrida's reading of the *mysterium tremendum*. Moving to the Empty Tomb, the implications of Derrida's *mysterium tremendum* for this scene are further developed by turning to Derrida's postal metaphor from *The Post Card* (1987). From the perspective of the postal metaphor and the *mysterium tremendum*, the fear that abruptly ends Mark's Gospel can be reread in such a way that the emptiness of the tomb is preserved as a scandalous ambiguity.

Keeping the *Tremendum* Mysterious

Rudolf Otto investigates the tradition of the "fearful mystery" in *The Idea of the Holy* (1926). Here he looks to the nonrational experience of the "numinous"—of essential "mystery." He recognises that *rational* accounts of religious experience tend to dominate, often to the exclusion of all else (Otto 1926, 2). And yet, religious experience appears to go beyond what can be elucidated by rationalistic means: "Religion is not exclusively contained and exhaustively comprised in any series of 'rational' assertions . . ." (1926, 4). Otto sets out to examine these "outer" areas of religious experience that take one away from the rational. He focuses particularly on experiences of the "holy" or "sacred" (1926, 4). In these particular, nonrational "moments," one is afforded a primary and pure experience of the "numinous"—an experience not yet rationalised and prior to any schematisation. This initial, raw experience is marked by a sense of the eerie, the uncanny and the dreadful, and in this, its most primitive form, Otto uncovers what he describes as a kind of "daemonic dread": "This crudely naïve and primordial emotional disturbance, and the fantastic images to which it gives rise, are later overborne and ousted by more highly-developed forms of the numinous emotion, with all its mysteriously impelling power" (1926, 16).

For Otto, the history of Christianity charts the development of this raw and pure experience of the numinous as it becomes increasingly rationalised and is subjected to ever more complex and expansive systemisation (1926, 80). But that daemonic, primitive encounter remains, even in the highest forms of the "holy," and is marked by: "Spasms and convulsions . . . the strangest excitements . . . intoxicated frenzy . . . It may be the hushed, trembling, and speechless humility of the creature in the presence of . . . that which is a mystery inexpressible and above all creatures" (Otto 1926, 13).

In focussing on a specific feature of religious experience, which escapes the dominant discourse of rationalism, Otto could be seen to be effecting, in his own way, a form of deconstructive reading. He is engaged in an investigation that uncovers repressed features, swept aside by an overlying rationalistic religious discourse. It is not surprising, therefore, to see Derrida taking an interest in Otto's ideas regarding the encounter with the *mysterium tremendum*.

In *The Gift of Death* (1995) Derrida writes in a way reminiscent of Otto, while at the same time nuancing this encounter with the *mysterium tremendum* to suit his own purposes.[6] Like Otto, Derrida sees a daemonic seed at the heart of the *mysterium tremendum*, a mystery that he charts as having evolved from the daemonic or orgiastic through the Platonic to find itself now understood in terms of a thoroughly Christian mystery.[7] At the same time, however, Derrida notes (as does Otto), that the most primitive mystery remains hidden within the structure of this sublime Christian encounter with the "wholly other." As deeply buried as it may be, this kernel of the primordial continues to prevent the structure of ordered Christian responsibility from encompassing and owning the entire experience of "mystery." Just as Otto observes that there is something that eludes a rationalistic understanding of religious experience, so too, Derrida sees something about this encounter with mystery that succeeds in eluding not merely rationalism, but language, thought and indeed any "economy" that makes shared meaning possible.

Derrida refers to Heidegger's notion of a "being" standing face-to-face with the singularity of his or her own death: that un-substitutable moment which radically individuates and isolates on the most fundamental level. This confrontation with our own death is a moment that cannot be shared, and yet takes us beyond ourselves. It is also a moment when we do not encounter the "Other" so much as the "otherness" that is our own death—that which is simultaneously the most intimate and individuating of all experiences. As "otherness" to what we are, death represents our annihilation and dispersal as beings. However, death represents more than just the destruction of the flesh, it is also the chaos of disorder, of engulfing meaninglessness and of absolute opacity. Derrida speaks about this confrontation with the pure "mystery" of our own death as an encounter that is radically individuating and which insists upon an authentic response. It is also a moment when one becomes aware of the gaze of the "other" which stares from behind its impenetrable secrecy. As such, it is a radical "otherness," the contours of which cannot be known. It is this alarming confrontation with our own death, an encounter of intimate self-knowledge and simultaneously impenetrable mystery, that is identified by Derrida as "the frightening, terrifying mystery, the *mysterium tremendum*" (1995, 28). He observes: "I tremble at what exceeds my seeing and my knowing although it concerns the innermost parts of me, right down to my soul, down to the bone, as we say" (Derrida 1995, 54).

When confronted with the mystery of our absolute singularity, our first reaction is to respond with fear and trembling. To attempt to communicate this moment would necessarily be to change it because "[a]s soon as one speaks, as soon as one enters the medium of language, one loses that very singularity. Speaking relieves us, Kierkegaard notes, for it 'translates' into the general" (Derrida 1995, 60).

Just as this experience eludes the grasp of language, it also resists containment within any other shared system of thought, collective agreement or ethical consensus about what is "right." Such attempts only serve to abandon the individual in favour of the collective and thus abandon the "truth" of the experience: "Far from ensuring responsibility, the generality of ethics incites to irresponsibility. It impels me to speak, to reply, to account for something, and thus to dissolve my singularity in the medium of the concept" (Derrida 1995, 61). Derrida demonstrates in his discussion of Abraham's near sacrifice of Isaac in Genesis 22 that the only authentic way to respond in the face of such mystery is to respond as an individual in a way that maintains individuality. This is to respond from outside of these systems and collective structures—in effect, not to respond at all, or to respond *irresponsibly*.

In essence God says to Abraham: I can see right away [*à l'instant*] that you have understood what absolute duty towards the unique means, that it means responding where there is no reason to be asked for or to be given. Abraham is thus at the same time the most moral and the most immoral, the most responsible and the most irresponsible of men, absolutely irresponsible because he is absolutely responsible, absolutely irresponsible in the face of men and his family, and in the face of the ethical, because he responds absolutely to absolute duty, disinterestedly and without hoping for reward, without knowing why yet keeping it secret; answering to God and before God—a relationship which is without relation because God is absolutely transcendent, hidden, and secret. (Derrida 1995, 72–73)

Derrida goes on to say that if the God of Abraham is completely "other"—"God" being " . . . the figure or name of the wholly other . . ." (Derrida 1995, 77)—then this God is to be found in all experiences of the wholly other. It is from this point that Derrida introduces the phrase: *tout autre est tout autre* (1995, 78). There are two important senses to this tautologous phrase: "In one case God is defined as infinitely other, as wholly other, every bit other. In the other case it is declared that every other one, each of the others, is God inasmuch as he or she is, *like* God, wholly other" (Derrida 1995, 87).

In other words, "otherness" is "otherness," and does not differ in quality from one instance to another. Consequently, Derrida explains, because individuals are wholly other to each other—"each of us, everyone else, each other is infinitely other in its absolute singularity, inaccessible, solitary, transcendent, nonmanifest, originarily nonpresent to my *ego*" (1995, 78)—then this encounter with what is "wholly other" is also an everyday encounter occurring in the midst of every human interaction. This encounter with the wholly other lies not just in the space between two people, however. The "wholly other" is encountered in what is essentially the *mystery* of our own impending death. In this case, one engages with an "otherness" located not on an "outside," but rather in the interiority of one's own death—a moment which is incapable of being shared.

By locating a disruptive and subversive heart within all structures of communal interaction, within every "ethical generality" (1995, 78), Derrida is describing a fundamental aporia: an incommunicable and unknowable "other" that demands the irresponsible response and inhabits every encounter between every person—interactions which are at the same time governed by structures of generality. In more specific terms, the experience of confronting one's own death, when understood as a secret interiority, cannot be translated using the tools of a system which would allow its meaning to be shared. The process whereby such a secret is translated into a general economy can do nothing but change forever this sense of radical individualism. At the same time, this encounter with the secret mystery that is one's death could be seen, in itself, to be the condition which makes possible one's own sense of individuality or self, and thus facilitate participation in the general economy of meaning. So, in a tremendous paradox, the mystery becomes the condition that fundamentally threatens the cohesion of the self, while at the same time making this *experience* of selfhood possible.

The actual term, *mysterium tremendum*, indeed, the very words themselves are thoroughly informed by this aporia. There are two distinct levels of experience involved here. On one level, as a concept and as language, the term is used to allow this experience to be known and shared collectively. On another, however, the experience itself, as never anything but individual, always eludes the attempts to transcribe it within a shared economy of meaning. In other words, to "name" the encounter with the impenetrable "mystery" of death is like sharing a secret: "We share with Abraham what cannot be shared, a secret we know nothing about, neither him nor us. To share a secret is not to know or to reveal the secret, it is to share we know not what: nothing that can be determined" (Derrida 1995, 80). To share this secret entails trying to provide a structure to, or include within a structure, that which undermines the very possibility of structure itself.

By means of this paradox, Derrida is suggesting that a subversive kernel remains within the *mysterium tremendum*. The most vivid sign of this daemonic kernel is the initial reaction of fear and terror: "For it is a terror that brings us close to the absolute secret, a secret that we share without sharing it" (Derrida 1995, 79). And fear and trembling are the most appropriate of responses because they are preverbal; they are responses that emerge prior to language as a system of meaning.

Peter's "Error"[8]

Although commentators attempt to account for the fear mentioned in Mark 9:6 in a variety of ways, it seems that it cannot be easily separated from the response Peter gives in the previous verse.[9] Thus, in order to explore further the significance of the fear of the disciples in this passage, a reevaluation of Peter's response is called for. Traditional readings of the response are remarkably uniform in that they quickly dismiss his reaction as erroneous (hence what has become known as Peter's "error").[10] It is as though commentators are saying that Peter, in his obtuseness, has missed the point—it seems that *that* much can be taken for granted—and we ought to concentrate on the real task here which is to reflect on the reason (theological, rhetorical, or otherwise) for this erroneous statement (Gundry 1993, 72).

Peter's comments immediately follow the vision of Jesus transfigured and the appearance of Elijah and Moses. His response here can be seen to be three-fold. First, Peter comments on the situation: "Then Peter answered Jesus 'Rabbi, it is good (καλόν) for us to be here' " (9:5). Second, Peter suggests the building of three tabernacles: "Let us make three dwellings (σκηνάς), one for you, one for Moses and one for Elijah" (9:5). Finally, Peter and the other disciples are revealed to have been dumbfounded and terrified throughout this scene: "He did not know what to answer, for they were terrified (ἔκφοβοι)" (9:6). This *extreme* terror is mentioned in such a way that it informs and infuses the entire encounter.[11] Understood in this way, Peter's prior suggestion, as well as his statement about it being "good" that they are there, are both informed by and infused with this terror. Despite this, commentators seem more inclined to minimize the impact of the fear, seeing it, for instance, as a standard rhetorical technique used here, as in other places in Mark's Gospel, to signify a direct response to divine manifestations with little other narrative significance.[12] Consequently, apart from noting a certain incongruity, commentators tend to downplay the disparity between Peter's almost cheerful comment and his enigmatic suggestion on the one side, and the pervasive feeling of extreme terror that informs this encounter on the other.[13]

By contrast, the explanation for Peter's second comment to build three tents, has provoked a considerable amount of scholarly debate.[14] In many ways, concern over the reason for Peter's suggestion has overshadowed or repressed the other details of this small section, and scholars tend to diagnose the suggestion as a simple symptom of Peter's misunderstanding. The drive behind the numerous interpretations seems to be to reach some sort of fullness in Peter's response: to say that Peter attempts to "sum up" the situation, even if this attempt on Peter's part at full understanding then has to be labelled erroneous or incomplete. Peter's response can then be understood to contribute, rather than detract from, the glorious abundance that purportedly dominates this scene.

The various reasons given by commentators for Peter's suggestion are not unimportant, but maybe there is a different point to be made here: What if Peter's suggestion is necessarily deficient, and if the lack it intimates evokes something of what he and the other disciples have just experienced? Moreover, what if one were to reevaluate the apparent disparity between Peter's suggestion and his subsequent expression of fear alongside Derrida's reworking of the *mysterium tremendum* encounter?

In his suggestion, Peter posits the building of tabernacles or tents, genuine "dwelling places" for the more abstract "presences" that are before him. Perhaps if he constructs these tabernacles he will succeed in encapsulating these presences in such a way that it will be possible to communicate the significance of this encounter to others. The suggestion to build tents can be read as a way of "making a place" for these figures—and also, in a sense, making a place for Peter's interpretation (in verse 5 Peter has already given his own shape to the event by putting Moses before Elijah and rearranging the order in which these figures are introduced in verse 4). By building a tent for each of these figures, it is irrelevant whether or not what the disciples are encountering actually dwells within these places, as these presences would in effect be *replaced* by the tents themselves. The tabernacles would come to represent and in this way assure the "presence" of these heavenly figures and this encounter, long after the event the disciples are experiencing has ended. In this way, the heavenly figures would be able to become part of and participate in a history and a faith where their ongoing signification would proliferate. Indeed in current scholarship, this is exactly what can be seen to be the case, when commentators attempt to account for the presence of Elijah and Moses. These two figures invite a richness of meaning and the search for their significance alone has resulted in a plethora of interpretations—both in relation to this text and well beyond.

Peter and the other disciples are witnesses to the appearance of Elijah and Moses and to Jesus' dazzling metamorphosis, but they are also encountering something quite "other" in the midst of this vision. Their fearful reaction gives us a clue as to the quality of "otherness" they encounter. By wanting to build tents, Peter is in effect suggesting that the meaning of this event be tied to a ground, inscribed onto the mountaintop. In time, the vision itself may vanish, but it nonetheless is able to endure by being translated, transformed into, and substituted by elements that are meaningful within a traditional, historical, and religious economy. These translated elements maintain their meaning, not because they refer back to the vision, but because they are given significance by their new context. In this way, it is possible to share and maintain certain meanings, even if these meanings can no longer capture this encounter with "otherness" on the mountaintop.

One can't help wondering, however, how reliable a tent really is as a structure for preserving meaning? The term σκηνή, may refer to the tabernacle, the dwelling place of the divine *shekinah*, but it simultaneously refers to a nomadic tent that, although not a temporary structure, is pitched only temporarily before being moved on (see Louw-Nida 1988, 7.9).[15] In this way, even though the tent itself endures through time, it is constantly being shifted and moved from "ground" to "ground." In other words, even if the tabernacles were set up for Moses, Elijah and Jesus, as Peter suggests, their meaning and significance would not necessarily be fixed to the particularity of this foundation of meaning for very long. The warp and woof of these "houses made of cloth" (Louw-Nida 1988, 7.9) bring together a network of interconnected references, and in so doing become part of the infinite fabric of meaning. This network of meaning functions regardless of the ground upon which it is pitched, and as such these tents are not necessarily pegged down to any one particular foundational referent and will not necessarily remain within any one particular interpretative framework. There are no guarantees here for the preservation of a fixed set of meanings. The only guarantee is that these tents, if ever erected, will have the potential for meaning.

Peter's translation of the experience into an economy of shared meaning coincides with a demonstration that this event is simultaneously incommunicable. The difficulty in cleanly separating Peter's suggestions from a pervasive fearfulness, the sense that these elements are coalescing while remaining contradictory, is reminiscent of Derrida's conception of the *mysterium tremendum*, and his identification of a certain paradox therein. In the encounter with *mysterium tremendum*, one finds an experience that, while shared, and in some sense "known" by a common humanity, is simultaneously an experience of which it is impossible to speak. It is an experience of impenetrable mystery that is radically individuating but which in turn makes possible an individual's participation in an economy of meaning. Each term of this contradictory relation, the shared and the incommunicable, depends upon and makes possible the other but without the possibility of resolution.

The aporetic relation, which forms the very heart of the *mysterium tremendum*, is mirrored in Peter's response to the Transfiguration encounter. The symptoms Derrida describes as arising from that incommunicable encounter with one's own death compares well with the quality of fear that runs through the Transfiguration. At the same time, the extent to which the experience of such an incommunicable interior mystery is shared, is indicated by Peter's suggestion to build tabernacles. With the inclusion of Peter's enigmatic reaction, incompatibilities are brought together and form an impasse that resists resolution as the terms are linked tighter still. Moreover, in accordance with this Derridean reading and with specific reference to the Empty Tomb, Peter's fearful trembling can be read as a demonstration of a certain responsibility (precisely in his unresponsiveness) to the "truth" of this encounter, because in his speechlessness, he stops short of attempting to articulate the inexpressible: the secret remains a secret. In Peter's enigmatic response and fear-filled reaction, these incompatibilities are brought together. They tell different stories: first, of an impenetrable opacity that shares the heart of a scene that seems to brim so vividly with presences; and second, of the impossibility of a desire to share what cannot be shared.

In accounting for Peter's "error," commentators pardon his obtuseness, claiming it is "right" for him to misunderstand the significance of this encounter. His true "error" lies in his failure to acknowledge that only after the path of suffering and death have been trod can one truly appreciate the fullest vision of God's saving glory.[16] And so turning from here to the end of Mark's drama, one feels justified in cultivating a certain expectation that this most complete vision of glory will have arrived to be witnessed with fullest understanding. However, what one finds instead, much to the consternation of commentators, is that expectations are dashed and one is left to deal with the darkness, absence, fear, and failure of an empty tomb.

Tomb Without End

On the basis of commentators' readings of the Empty Tomb, one would be forgiven for thinking that, despite the premature ending, the messages and meanings of Mark's Gospel nonetheless arrive and are present to the reader. In deftly finding these "presences" in a moment of gaping absence, the meaning of the Gospel is finally able to be drawn to a close. Just as the Transfiguration is a scene that exceeds the parameters of presence and fullness, could it be that the Empty Tomb can be read for more than closure and resolution? Rather than finding closure of one sort or another in the Empty Tomb, is it possible to preserve a scandalous sense of incompleteness? What if this abrupt ending is read not in terms of a yearned-for fullness, but as a moment when previous expectations and possibilities are lost or abandoned? By ending the story mid-sentence and fleeing before the fullest vision of glory arrives, is it possible to read in Mark's Gospel a radical openness that subverts not only the closure of the story, but the coherence of the self?

The women's reaction at the Empty Tomb, a reaction of fear and terror that causes them to flee, provides a clue that they, like the disciples in the Transfiguration (9:6), are reacting to an encounter with the *mysterium tremendum*. They, too, tremble in the face of an annihilating death. In this encounter, they are confronted by a vision of absence that dwells at the heart of presence: the singularity of their own death that pervades their sense of life. On one level, the failure of both the male and female disciples to *communicate* "the meaning" of the death and resurrection of Jesus by either "getting it wrong" (as in the Transfiguration, 9:5) or simply fleeing the scene (16:8) is indeed a failure and a scandal. Once at the Empty Tomb, there is no longer any possibility of communicating this goal to which the Gospel ostensibly moves. At the moment of this abrupt ending, the goal of seeing God's glory fulfilled in and through Jesus is possible only by locating new endings that lie beyond the scope of the Gospel story.

If we resist the urge to go "beyond" the Empty Tomb to less scandalous endings, resist moving from absence to presence, is tragedy our only alternative? In *The Post Card* (1987), Derrida challenges these criteria for success or failure as they relate to the transmission and destination of meanings. Derrida does this by taking a closer look at the structure of the postal service. Rather than marking the efficiency of a system where meaning reaches its intended destination, for Derrida, the flag flying above the mailbox marks instead a point of closure. The arrival of the letter at its intended destination marks its end, its journey finished and its purpose fulfilled. But at the same time, the possibility of the letter not reaching its intended destination has also had to be considered in the development of the postal service, and indeed has been dealt with formally through the establishment of the "dead letter office." What the existence of the "dead letter office" signifies for Derrida is formal acknowledgement that

> a letter can always not arrive at its destination . . . Not that the letter never arrives at its destination, but it belongs to the structure of the letter to be capable, always, of not arriving. And without this threat . . . the circuit of the letter would not even have begun. But with this threat, the circuit can always not finish. (Derrida 1987, 444)

The letter, which is no longer tied to a singular destination, maintains a "life" of unlimited potential destinations, a potentiality that is otherwise lost in the death of arrival. What Derrida shows is that, because the possibility of a "letter" not arriving is part of its structure, a "letter" is always from the beginning divided, torn into pieces, and never truly arrives in its entirety.[17] There is always some element of the "letter"—and writing[18]—that fails to complete the journey, an element that essentially remains in the "dead letter office." This remainder always exceeds the frames of reference used to guide meaning to a destination. And so, the "dead letter office" at once signals the disconnection of the letter from teleological determination—the comfort of a meaningful beginning and end—and opens up a plurality of possible meanings.

At the Empty Tomb the address has been given, and the reader expects the arrival of this particularly glorious "letter" at the site of the tomb, but what one finds instead is that the letter has gone astray and the tomb is empty. The "letter" is either lost, or at the very least the expected destination has been changed: "He is going ahead of you to Galilee" (16:7). The letter remains on its journey, still in the process of being sent, and at the end of the text the letter has not arrived, even though the promise of its arrival is maintained. In this way, the message of Mark, like the structure of the "letter," will always be partially located in the "dead letter office." The message, like the "letter," is fractured and will never fully arrive at any one destination.

The reaction of fear at the end of Mark's Gospel signals an awareness, not just of the *mysterium tremendum*, but at the same time, of the effect of the dead letter office. In the same way that the disciples see that which undermines their coherence in their confrontation with death and annihilation, the reaction of the women demonstrates their sudden awareness of the dead letter office. The expression of fear holds within it the awareness of that which undermines meaning without going beyond meaning, and in this sense avoids mapping out an "exteriority." For, by delineating a "beyond," one would effectively be sketching the parameters of a "transcendental signifier." This fear, however, avoids this by being read as an affirmation of the power and catalyzing effect of that which exceeds a metaphysics of presence—while not actually going "beyond" metaphysics at all.

This suggests ways of reading the disciples, the women, and their collective fear as more than symptoms of misunderstanding or foils to aid the arrival of the "letter." By *not* grasping the theological message as traditionally charted through the Gospel, but by displaying a profound terror instead, the disciples maintain their authenticity before that blank potentiality which remains undefined by a conclusion, by closure and end. By fleeing in fear and by not delivering their message, the women respond out of respect for the "life" of the dead "letter." In these terms, the women appreciate the absence of Jesus' body and the significance of his and their own "deaths." This deathly catalyst, the obscure impetus for potentiality, an unformed, undifferentiated splice, is both a fundamental threat to coherence and, at the same time, the condition which makes possible not only gospel theology in general, but the structures of language and thought and identity.

In what seems a curious exchange, when the women enter the Tomb, Jesus is gone, but in his place they find a "young man" (νεανίσκος). The white robes worn by a "young man" in the Empty Tomb have often been connected to those of Jesus at the Transfiguration.[19] As on the mountain, the robes are described as brilliantly white (λευκός) (16:7). Paralleling the disciples, it is as though, upon entering the Empty Tomb, the women enter the cloud that descends at the Transfiguration scene (9:7). It is as if they have found, in this cloud that blocks out the sun, the shining white robes, more splendid than ever. However, the body of Jesus is absent and the young man explains that Jesus' presence is not to be found here; the time when they will see him is yet to come (16:7). But it is not at this future time in Galilee that Mark ends his story, it is with "ἐφοβοῦντο γάρ" (16:8).

Mark ends his Gospel with fear, and with "for" (γάρ). As a conjunction, the Greek word γάρ is an intermediary word, a link, however remote or tenuous, between two ideas or events (Louw-Nida 1988, 89.23). As such, the Gospel "ends" with an intermediary term, with a sending, an "envoi." By all accounts a curious ending, and yet if the dead letter office reveals the postal service to be "a relay to mark there is never anything but relays" (Derrida 1987, 192), then the fear of ending with γάρ is as much about avoiding an end, about resisting arrival as it is about ending with a nonending. Jesus' absent body will not "arrive," in the sense of being present at a destination. But, by the light of the Transfiguration, the Empty Tomb is revealed to be an eternal *différance,* a resistance to meaning whereby the body of Jesus becomes but a trace. It emerges at various points (as robes worn by the young man in the tomb; in Galilee) but is never yet truly, fully present.

It is the interruption of this subverting potentiality that evokes the fear of the women, and they flee rather than take the risk that they, themselves, will provide a destination for the body of Jesus. In their scandalous flight from the Tomb, the women affirm the "truth" of their fear, whereby the realisation takes one essentially beyond the voice, beyond meaning and toward the disruption of the coherent self. To speak, to attempt to give voice to this "divine insight" which has accompanied both these encounters, would be to limit and reduce it. The fear shared by the disciples and the women is a fear of an unspeakable, ungraspable subversion, an infinite lack in both subject and spectacle. The fear is a response to that which both enables the emergence of any system of meaning, while at the same time posing a fundamental threat to it. This is the impassable paradox that inhabits the *mysterium tremendum*, the rupturing vision of Jesus transfigured and the horror of a tomb without end.

Notes

1. Take for instance the references to the Sinai archetype which are particularly rich: "The echoes of Exodus 24 and 34 suggest that a Moses typology under girds Mark's shaping of the Transfiguration" (Garland 1996, 343). Garland also compares the vision of Jesus's robes with "a man dressed in linen" in Daniel 10:4–11:1 and the Ancient of Days, whose clothing was "white as snow" (Dan. 7:9; Garland 1996, 343).

2. In Matthew's gospel this is certainly the case (cf. Matt. 28:9, 16–20).

3. One commentator laments the "narrative gap" at the Empty Tomb: "[T]he narrator could easily have filled the gap. He did not, after all, hesitate to represent Jesus as conversing with Elijah and Moses on the mountain (9:2–4), and Jesus, dressed in dazzling white clothes and having a dialogue with these two heavenly figures, would not have been out of place here" (Iersel 1998, 484).

4. Commentators seem to feel cheated by the absence of a glorious vision at the end of the gospel: "Thus we have a right to expect one final revelatory moment at the end of the Gospel where Jesus' true identity would be made known to the disciples. In short, we would expect the recounting of at least one or two appearances of the risen Jesus to the disciples" (Witherington 2001, 47).

5. Interpretations have ranged widely some see in this scene a final irony in a Gospel brimming with ironies (the ongoing obtuseness of the disciples with regards to Jesus' identity, in the face of many very obvious signs, for instance), while others find here a reassuring parallel for an oppressed readership (the Markan community suffering under persecution). Not finding satisfactory closure within the narrative, another common interpretative move resolves the abruptness by placing responsibility for closure with the contemporary reader (Williamson 1983, 286; Danove 1993, 221; Rhoads, Dewey, and Michie 1999, 143; Hooker 1991, 392; Brooks 1991, 275). The fear of the women fleeing the Tomb is tied into these explanations, either as a sign that what they have just experienced within the Empty Tomb is "beyond" words, or in association with the promise of 16:7 ("he is going ahead of you to Galilee").

6. In his investigation of the *mysterium tremendum* in *The Gift of Death* (1995) Derrida looks particularly at the heretical writings of Jan Patocka and the question of responsibility, specifically with reference to Abraham's call to sacrifice Isaac in Genesis 22. Curiously, Derrida does not refer to Otto at all, although it seems likely that Otto has had an influence. However Derrida takes a different trajectory to Otto, and does not end by repositing a metaphysical system. For instance, Otto may challenge rationalism, but his recourse to images of the sublime, to the "void", or to silence and awe to depict the "exterior" or "outside" of rationalism inevitably reposition him within the larger metaphysical system within which he is working. In some ways, Otto substitutes the "being" of God for a sense of absence which can be just as effective a transcendental signifier. Consequently, Otto unconsciously represses that which is not only outside rationalism, but any economy or system of meaning. For examples of Otto's use of these negatively expressed metaphysical images to posit the "outside" of rationalism (see Otto 1926, 62–73). Derrida attempts to get around this problem of substituting terms by, among other strategies, positing an "outside" which simultaneously remains on the inside of the system—the confrontation with the "otherness" of one's own death (see below for further discussion).

7. Derrida takes up this insight of Patocka's: "Patocka speaks of 'incorporation' or 'repression': incorporation in the case of Platonism which retains within itself the orgiastic mystery it subordinates, subjects, and disciplines, but repression in the case of Christianity which retains the Platonic mystery" (1995, 8–9).

8. This is a reduced version of a more in-depth study. This study includes discussions of the image of Jesus Transfigured and the accompanying metaphor of the bleacher, the figures of Elijah and Moses, the descending cloud and the voice issuing from it. Moreover, in exploring the broader implications of the *mysterium tremendum* for Mark's gospel, links are drawn to the Baptismal Scene and the Crucifixion in addition to the Empty Tomb.

9. Examples of ways scholars account for the fear include: attributing the show of fear to a literary device that prevents the reader from overlooking Peter's "error" (Gundry 1993, 460; Heil 2000, 159); seeing in this reaction a sign of the ignorance of the disciples, perfectly in keeping with the Markan theme of puzzled discipleship (Best 1983, 206–226; Witherington 2001, 263–264; Schweizer 1970, 182; Nineham 1963, 236); linking this show of fear to the spectacle of God's glory just revealed, a reaction in keeping with Otto's more traditional formulation of the *mysterium tremendum* (Dwyer 1996, 143; Hooker 1987, 66; see note 6 above).

10. It is interesting to note that the critical attention Peter's suggestion has received, and the scholarly response it has provoked, is prolific, far outweighing that given to the "central" image of Jesus transformed in verses 2–3 (possibly because the meaning of the latter appears to be quite self-evident by comparison).

11. Verse 6 is a complex verse syntactically because of the two incidences of the word γὰρ. Each instance of this word is seen to qualify what has come before, γὰρ functioning as "a mark of cause or reason between events" (Louw-Nida 1988, 89.23). In the first case, the reason Peter said what he did was "because he really did not know what to say," and following on from this, the reason he did not know what to say was "because they were afraid."

12. Other points in the gospel where fear is expressed in this way are in 4:41; 5:15, 33; 9:32; 10:32; and 16:8. It is interesting to note however that the use of the word εκφοβοι is only used once in Mark, the slightly less fearful φοβέομαι being the word used in the other instances, even in the case of 16:8 where the women flee the empty tomb.

13. Gundry describes Peter's first comment as "happy" and thus strangely incongruent with the expression of terror that follows (Gundry 1993, 460).

14. For differing interpretations compare Riesenfeld 1947, 146–205; Taylor 1952, 391; Kee 1972, 147; Ernst 1981, 257–58; Hurtado 1983, 146; Hooker 1987, 64–65; Juel 1990, 128; Gundry 1993, 460, 479–80; Heil 2000, 161.

15. Hooker notes that the term σκηνάς can evoke a whole range of ideas, from the Feast of Tabernacles to a reference to the wilderness experience (1987, 64–65).

16. cf. Mark 8:31. For examples of this interpretation, see: Taylor 1952, 391; Hurtado 1983, 146; Juel 1990, 128.

17. And the opposite is exactly what Lacan's Seminar sought to do with their analysis of Poe's *The Purloined Letter*. According to Derrida, it sought to suppress the fragmented quality of the letter, replacing it with an idealised solid and singular letter which would arrive in one piece: "If it were divisible, it could always be lost en route. To protect against this possible loss the statement about the 'materiality of the signifier,' that is, about the signifier's indivisible singularity, is constructed. *This 'materiality,' deduced from an indivisibility found nowhere, in fact corresponds to an idealization.* Only the identity of a letter resists destructive division" (Derrida 1987, 464).

18. In a translator's footnote, Allan Bass explains this connection between the letter and writing: " '*La structure restante de la lettre . . .*' For Derrida, writing is always that which is an excess remainder, *un reste*. Further, in French, mail delivered to a post office box is

called *poste restante*, making the dead letter office the ultimate *poste restante*, literally "remaining mail." Thus, Derrida is saying that Lacan's notion that the nondelivered letter, *la lettre en souffrance*, always arrives at its destination overlooks the structural possibility that a letter can always *remain* in the dead letter office, and that without this possibility of deviation and remaining—the entire postal system—there would be no delivery of letters to any address at all" (Derrida 1987, 443 n. 17).

19. See Taylor 1952, 606; Gundry 1993, 991; Hooker 1991, 384; and Lane 1974, 587 all who make a link here with Jesus's robes at the Transfiguration and, along with Anderson (1976, 355), comment on the presence of robes here as a general indication of the splendour of God's glory.

Works Consulted

Anderson, Hugh. 1976. *The Gospel of Mark*. Met Century Bible Commentary. Grand Rapids: Eerdmans; London: Marshal, Morgan & Scott.

Best, Ernest. 1983. *Mark: The Gospel as Story*. Edinburgh: T. & T. Clark.

Brooks, James A. 1991. *Mark*. The New American Commentary 23. Nashville: Broadman Press.

Crossan, John Dominic 1978. "A Form for Absence: The Markan Creation of Gospel." *Semeia* 12:41–53.

Danove, Paul L. 1993. *The End of Mark's Story: A Methodological Study*. Leiden: E. J. Brill.

Derrida, Jacques. 1987. *The Postcard: From Socrates to Freud and Beyond*. Trans. Alan Bass. Chicago: University of Chicago Press.

———. 1995. *The Gift of Death*. Trans. David Wills. Chicago: University of Chicago Press.

Dwyer, Timothy. 1996. *The Motif of Wonder in the Gospel of Mark*. Sheffield: Sheffield Academic Press.

Ernst, Josef. 1981. *Das Evangelium nach Markus*. Regensburg: Verlag Friedrich Pustet.

Garland, David E. 1996. *Mark*. NIV Application Commentary. Grand Rapids: Zondervan.

Gundry, Robert H. 1993. *Mark: A Commentary on His Apology for the Cross*. Grand Rapids: Eerdmans.

Heil, John Paul. 2000. *The Transfiguration of Jesus: Narrative Meaning and Function of Mark 9:2–8, Matt 17:1–8 and Luke 9:28–36*. Analecta Biblica 144. Rome: Editrice Pontificio Istituto Biblico.

Hooker Morna, D. 1987. " 'What Doest Thou Here, Elijah': A Look at St. Mark's Account of the Transfiguration." In *The Glory of Christ in the New Testament. Studies in Christology in Memory of George Bradford Caird*, ed. L. D. Hurst and N. T. Wright, 59–70. Oxford: Clarendon Press:

———. 1991. *The Gospel According to Saint Mark*. London: A. & C. Black.

Hurtado, Larry W. 1983. *Mark*. New International Bible Commentary. Peabody, MA: Hendrikson Publishers.

Hughes, Kent R. 1989. *Mark: Jesus, Servant and Saviour*. Vol. 2. Westchester, IL: Crossway Books.

Iersel, Bas M. F. van. 1998. *Mark: A Reader-Response Commentary*. Sheffield: Sheffield Academic Press.

Juel, Donald H. 1990. *Mark*. Augsburg Commentary on the New Testament. Minneapolis: Augsburg Fortress Press.

Kee, Howard Clark. 1972. "The Transfiguration in Mark: Epiphany or Apocalyptic vision?" In *Understanding the Sacred Text: Essays in Honor of Morton S. Enslin on the Hebrew and Christian Beginnings*, ed. J. Reumann, 135–52. Valley Forge, PA: Judson Press.

Lane, William L. 1974. *The Gospel According to Mark*. Grand Rapids: Eerdmans.

Louw, J. P. and E. A. Nida. 1988. *Louw-Nida Greek-English Lexicon of the New Testament Based on Semantic Domains*. 2nd ed. New York: United Bible Societies. In BibleWindows 2001.

McGuckin, John Anthony. 1987. *The Transfiguration of Christ in Scripture and Tradition*. Studies in the Bible and Early Christianity 9. Lewiston, NY: Edwin Mellen Press.

Nineham, D. E. 1963. *Saint Mark*. Pelican New Testament Commentaries. Harmondsworth: Penguin Books.

Otto, Rudolf. 1926. *The Idea of the Holy : An Inquiry into the Non-Rational Factor in the Idea of the Divine and its Relation to the Rational*. Trans. John W. Harvey. London: Oxford University Press.

Ramsey, Michael. 1949. *The Glory of God and the Transfiguration of Christ*. London: Longman.

Rhoads, David, Joanna Dewey, and Donald Michie. 1999. *Mark As Story: An Introduction to the Narrative of a Gospel*. Second edition. Minneapolis: Fortress Press.

Riesenfeld, Harald. 1947. *Jésus Transfiguré: L'arriére-plan du récit évangélique de la transfiguration de Notre-Seigneur*. København: Ejnar Munksgaard.

Schweizer, Eduard. 1970. *The Good News According to Mark*. Trans. Donald H. Madvig. Richmond: John Knox Press.

Taylor, Vincent. 1952. *The Gospel According to St. Mark*. London: Macmillan.

Williamson, Lamar Jr. 1983. *Mark*. Interpretation: A Biblical Commentary for Teaching and Preaching. Atlanta: John Knox Press.

Witherington, Ben, III. *The Gospel of Mark: A Socio-Rhetorical Commentary*. Grand Rapids: Eerdmans.

Chapter 13

Death At The Gate: Who Let Him In?

Responsibility for Death in the Wisdom of Solomon and Derrida

Marie Turner

In the Wisdom of Solomon the sage, through the voice of the narrator, claims that the creator God did not "make death":

> God did not make death,
> and does not delight in the death of the living,
> for God created all things that they might exist;
> the generative forces of the world are wholesome,
> and there is no destructive poison in them;
> and the dominion of Hades is not on earth. (Wisd. of Sol. 1:13–16)

Instead, the narrator places the blame for death's entry to earth at the feet of ungodly people and an envious devil (*diabolos*), thus:

> ungodly people by their words and deeds summoned death;
> considering him a friend, they pined away,
> and they made a covenant with him,
> because they are fit to belong to his party. (Wisd. of Sol. 1:16)

and, in Wisdom of Solomon 2:23–24,

> God created humankind for incorruption,
> and made them in the image of God's own eternity,
> but through the devil's envy death entered the world,
> and those who belong to his party experience it. (Wisd. of Sol. 2:23–24)

This "theology of exoneration" of God needs to be challenged on two fronts. First, the text does not consistently support the narrator's argument that God is not responsible for death.

Second, this theology re-inscribes the dualism inherent in the claim that death is an alien presence in the world. Any creation theology that does not envisage a place for death and decay will not have a convincing voice in the contemporary world. When death is seen in dualistic opposition to creation, a "scapegoat" must be found to bear responsibility for its existence. In the Wisdom of Solomon the scapegoats are ungodly humans and the devil. Derrida reflects on Freud's observation that we do not like to be reminded of the existence of evil and that it seems to contradict the sovereign goodness of God. Consequently, if the devil is seen to be irreconcilable with God, then it can also exculpate God by being made responsible for radical evil (see Derrida 1996, 12–13). Thus in the creation theology of the Wisdom of Solomon, the devil and the devil's human face, the ungodly, serve as an excuse for God when death is seen to be an evil, something alien and inimical to creation. The sage praises God for the gifts of life and the glories of creation, but cannot conceive of death and decay as anything but destructive poison (Wisd. of Sol. 1:14). Death is the gift of Hades rather than the gift of a loving creator God.

My reading of chapters 1–2 of the Wisdom of Solomon, a canonical book in the Roman Catholic and Orthodox traditions, focuses on the death of nonhuman creation as well as the death that humankind experiences. I do not differentiate here between spiritual death and physical death, because "spiritual death" can refer only to the experience of humankind, whereas the text quite clearly includes the death of nonhuman creation in its frame of reference. The text claims that God created all things, *ta panta* in Greek, to exist and that the realm of Hades is not on earth. The death of nonhuman creation must refer to physical death, since there is no indication in the text that nonhuman creation is to be rescued from death, a claim the text makes for the righteous. A theology of the immortality of the souls of the righteous is a comforting approach to the death of humankind, but what of nonhuman creation? In any theology of creation that deals with matters of life and death, an honest investigation of the meaning of death or decay for nonhuman as well as human creation is required. Does the narrator mean what he says when he claims that God created everything to exist? Does God's delight in living things (Wis. 1:13) extend to nonhuman matter? Has death, the most radical other, been spoken deliberately by God into creation, or has the devil, opponent of God in dualistic theology, had the last word? J. L. Crenshaw goes to the point, thus:

> The human compulsion to deny death is exceeded only by a desire to absolve the deity of responsibility for injustice. In truth, the two motivating forces are integrally related to one another, for death stands as the ultimate question mark attached to any defense of God. (1983, 1)

Death, the common fate of all creation, human and nonhuman, is the subject of investigation of this study. Is it the gift of God or poison/ *das Gift* from Hades? The theme will be explored in the Wisdom of Solomon 1–2 by exposing aporias in the text concerning the responsibility for death. In the Wisdom of Solomon the righteous are rescued from death, but nonhuman creation is left to face a fate brought on by the ungodly, if we are to accept the narrator's argument. Derrida's *Work of Mourning, A Taste for the Secret* and *The Gift of Death* provide fertile ground for comparing the attitudes to death of Derrida and the ungodly. Neither Derrida nor the ungodly are explicit believers in immortality, but they present very different attitudes to issues of life and death. Derrida's writings on death inspire a celebration of life and a sanctuary for the memory of the dead. The nihilism of the ungodly, on the other hand, would encourage the exploitation of creation. While I present Derrida as a representative of the contemporary "ungodly," this is not intended as a value judgment. It is used in the context of a challenge to the barriers between religion and atheism. In his own person, Derrida challenges these barriers. He prefers to say of himself that he "rightly passes for an atheist" rather than claim the label of atheist for himself.

Matter and Spirit: God's Presence in Nonhuman Creation

In a dualistic approach to creation, matter is regarded as the inferior member of the matter-spirit pair. Yet in the Wisdom of Solomon a consistent dualism is not sustained. A reading of the texts dealing with nonhuman creation reveals that God's presence is in all creation, human and nonhuman. The sage claims that the realm of Hades is not on earth and that the actions of the ungodly are responsible for death's presence. It is clear from the text that death has spread to all creation and not just to the ungodly. This suggests that the ungodly are responsible for the presence of death and decay among nonhuman as well as human creation. A dualistic approach to matter on the part of the sage is suggested by Wisdom of Solomon 9:15:

For a perishable body weighs down the soul
And this earthly tent burdens the thoughtful mind.

This verse expresses a negative attitude towards the material. Yet a close reading of the text of Wisdom of Solomon 1–2 shows that the material and nonmaterial are not presented unequivocally as hierarchical, dualistic opposites. While the God of the sage clearly transcends creation, and is "other" than a world subject to corruption, mortality and finitude, the opening chapters of the book reveal a positive attitude toward the body. Wisdom of Solomon 1:4–6 says this:

. . . wisdom will not enter a deceitful soul
or dwell in a body enslaved to sin.
For a holy and disciplined spirit will flee from deceit,
And will leave foolish thoughts behind,
And will be ashamed at the approach of unrighteousness.
For wisdom is a kindly spirit,
But will not free blasphemers from the guilt of their words;
Because God is witness of their inmost feelings,
And a true observer of their hearts,
and a hearer of their tongues.

In Wisdom of Solomon 1:4 the narrator claims that wisdom will have no part in a deceitful soul or a body enslaved to sin. The paired set, "deceitful soul" and "a body enslaved to sin" are not opposites. Implied in the statement is "the other side of the coin," namely, that wisdom would remain in the soul if it were not deceitful, and would dwell in a body that is not enslaved to sin. There is no dualistic opposition between body and soul. Rather, the dualistic opposition is between deceit/sin and righteousness. The body as well as the soul is the locus of moral righteousness or unrighteousness. Wickedness is essentially false reasoning externalized in speech (see Kolarcik 1991, 65). The author refers to ears that hear, slandering tongues, and a lying mouth. God is a witness of inmost feelings, a true observer of hearts and a hearer of tongues. Inquiry will be made into the counsels of the ungodly and a report of their words will come to the Lord to convict them of lawless deeds. The narrator exhorts the readers against bringing destruction by the work of their hands.

> Because the spirit of the Lord has filled the world,
> And that which holds all things together knows what is said,
> Therefore those who utter unrighteous things will not escape notice,
> And justice, when it punishes, will not pass them by.
> For inquiry will be made into the counsels of the ungodly,
> And a report of their words will come to the Lord,
> To convict them of their lawless deeds;
> Because a jealous ear hears all things,
> And the sound of grumbling does not go unheard.
> Beware then of useless grumbling,
> And keep your tongue from slander;
> Because no secret word is without result, [or: will go unpunished]
> And a lying mouth destroys the soul.
> Do not invite death by the error of your life,
> Or bring on destruction by the works of your hands. (Wisd. of Sol. 1:7–12)

Unrighteousness is perpetrated through the body, and a lying mouth destroys the soul, while righteousness comes about through correct reasoning, correct speech and lawful deeds. The body is thus an instrument of destruction for the soul and potentially an instrument of righteousness. Thus the dualism breaks down. Michael Kolarcik describes the use of metonymy whereby a part of the body is used to represent a human activity thus:

> The accusatory attacks of the wicked are presented through metonymy, wherein a particular bodily aspect of speech is employed to represent the verbal function. With such images as blasphemous lips (v. 6), God being a hearer of tongues (v. 6), the utterances of the wicked (v. 8), and a lying mouth (v. 11), emphasis is placed on the damaging effect of slander perpetrated through the false speech of the wicked. (1995, 65)

Kolarcik is accurate when he speaks of juxtaposition rather than opposition. He speaks of the "positive terms," justice, the Lord, Wisdom, and the Holy Spirit as being placed in juxtaposition to the "negative terms," injustice, crooked thoughts, and a deceitful mind. The effect of the juxtaposition is a "heightening of tension and conflict" with the locus of conflict residing in the human person. Love of justice and union with God requires the renunciation of wickedness (1995, 65). It is the whole human person, active in and through the body, which is the responsible moral agent.

This emphasis on the whole human person as the moral agent is maintained in Wisdom 2 in the speech of the ungodly. The language is dualistic, but it is not a hierarchical dualism. According to the narrator, the unrighteousness of the wicked results in their unsound reasoning:

> Thus they reasoned unsoundly but they were led astray,
> For their wickedness blinded them.

In the narrator's argument the hierarchical opposition between the material and the nonmaterial presumed in Wisdom of Solomon 9:15 is not sustained.

According to Wisdom of Solomon 1:13–14, God's creative act does not include death, neither for human or nonhuman creation:

> because God did not make death,
> and does not delight in the death of the living.
> For God created all things that they might exist,
> and the generative forces of the world are wholesome,
> and there is no destructive poison in them;
> and the dominion of Hades is not on earth.

According to these lines, Hades, metonym for death, is an alien presence on earth. Those responsible for death are the ungodly who invite death on to the earth, and the devil, whose envy provides the border-crossing for death. As the ultimate other in regards to creation, death has no place in the sage's theology of the creator. In the theology of the sage, the righteous who die young are rescued by the action of God in whose hand are the souls of the righteous (Wisd. of Sol. 3:1). While this rescue from death applies explicitly only to righteous human creation, the sage, nevertheless, has much to say about God's presence in nonhuman creation. A positive approach to it is contained in several verses scattered throughout the book, thus:

> . . . the spirit of the Lord has filled the world,
> And that which holds all things (*ta panta*) together knows what is said. (1:7)
> . . . wisdom, the fashioner of all things (*panta*), taught me. (7:22)
>
> Because of (wisdom's) pureness she pervades and penetrates all things (*panta*)
> . . . and while remaining in herself, she renews all things (*panta*). (7:24, 27)
>
> She reaches mightily from one end of the earth to the other,
> And she orders all things (*ta panta*) well . . .
> For she is an associate in God's works . . .
> what is richer than wisdom, the active cause of all things (*ta panta*)? (8:1, 4–5)
>
> O God of my ancestors and Lord of mercy,
> Who have made all things (*ta panta*) by your word,
> And by your wisdom have formed humankind
> To have dominion over the things that you have made,
> And rule the world in holiness and righteousness. (9:1–3)

When the earth (*gēs*) was flooded because of him, wisdom again saved it. (10:4)

You spare all things (*panta*), for they are yours, O Lord, you who love the living.
For your immortal spirit is in all things (*en pasin*). (11:24–12:1)

For all people who were ignorant of God were foolish by nature;
and they were unable from the good things that are seen to know the one who exists. (13.1)

According to these texts, nonhuman creation was created not for death, but for existence. *Ta panta*, all things, come from the creative action of Sophia and all created things carry the presence of the divine. Is Hades a demonic distortion of God's plan of life for all of creation? Is it reasonable to lay at the feet of an alien presence in the *kosmos* responsibility for death? If the sage is to retain his monotheism, and at the same time excuse God of responsibility for death, it seems a demonic entity must be introduced. In the verses quoted above, Sophia is shown to be the agent of creation, the fashioner and active cause of all things, the one who penetrates and renews all things. She is an associate in God's works and has formed humankind. She is savior of the world from the flood. God's spirit, most probably to be identified with Sophia in this book, holds all things together and is in all things. She is creator, sustainer and savior. Is she also the bringer of death?

Responsibility for Life and Death in the Wisdom of Solomon

A close reading of the appropriate verses leads to the conclusion that Sophia must bear the responsibility for creation and life and therefore death. In Wisdom of Solomon 9:1–2 Solomon addresses God thus:

O God of my ancestors and Lord of mercy,
Who have made all things by your word,
And by your wisdom have formed humankind.

According to this text God makes things through the word (*logos*) and has formed (*kataskeuasas*) humankind through wisdom. Both word and wisdom are instruments of God's creative action. The association of wisdom and creation is consistent throughout the book. In other places we are told that wisdom is the active cause of all things (8:5), she is fashioner (*technitis*) of what exists (8:6), humankind is formed by wisdom (9:2), and wisdom was present at creation (9:9). Sophia thus has responsibility for creation. In several verses she is connected with eternity, immortality and incorruption. In three places the word "eternal" or a related term is used. Wisdom of Solomon 2:23 states that God created humankind for incorruption, and made humankind in the image of God's own eternity (2:23); 7:26 states that Sophia is a reflection of eternal light, a spotless mirror of the working of God, and an image of God's goodness (7:26); 17:2 states that when lawless people supposed that they held the holy nation in their power, they themselves lay as captives of darkness and prisoners of long night, shut in under their roofs, exiles from eternal providence. The word "eternal/eternity" is connected with God in each of these texts, but in 7:26 the words "wisdom" and "eternal" are linked through the notion of Wisdom as image of the eternal light of God. Wisdom is reflection, mirror, and image. In Wisdom of Solomon 2:23 the narrator tells us that humankind is made in the image of God's own eternity. This statement suggests that humankind is made, not in the image of God as in Genesis, but in the image of Sophia, who is herself the reflection of eternal light. (Gilbert [1973, 87] points out that humankind is not created in the image of God, but in the image of God's own nature. Note that Gilbert is here accepting the textual variant *idiotetos*.) According to Wisdom of Solomon 17:2, however, lawless people are captives of darkness, excluded from eternity. They are thus diametrically opposed to wisdom, the reflection of eternal light.

In four places wisdom is connected with immortality. Wisdom of Solomon 6:18–19 states that love of wisdom is the keeping of her laws, and giving heed to her laws is the assurance of immortality, and immortality brings one near to God. Wisdom of Solomon 8:13 states that, because of wisdom, Solomon will have immortality, and leave an everlasting remembrance to those who come after him. Wisdom of Solomon 8:17 states that Solomon pondered in his heart that in kinship with wisdom there is immortality. Wisdom of Solomon 12:1 declares that wisdom's immortal spirit is in all things. In 12:1, immortality is used in connection with *ta panta*, all things. In 2:23 the word "incorruption" is used. This term may not be simply an interchangeable term for immortality, but a clue as to the nature of immortality for human beings. Reese gives an enlightening account of the Hellenistic background behind the use of the words for "immortality" and "incorruption." He argues that the term "incorruption," as used in 2:23, is not merely a stylistic synonym for "immortality" (1970, 66). The sage may be informed by its use in Epicureanism. Epicureans did not believe in personal immortality for human beings but they thought that the gods, while being material beings, lived forever. Although they were corporeal and, as such, subject to corruption, they possessed the quality of incorruption, which enabled them to enjoy endless existence. This quality prevented them from losing the atoms that make up their being. Thus their bodies, although material, never disintegrated and they were perfectly happy (1970, 65). Reese argues that according to 2:23, humankind's original condition was to be "in" incorruption (rather than "for" incorruption). Reese argues that this incorruption is thus not a goal toward which humankind moves but a positive quality granted from the beginning to humankind to enable them to enter into a special relationship with the creator (1970, 66). This gift given to humans is lost through the actions of the ungodly in inviting death into the world. Thus, when 2:23 states that God created humankind for incorruption and made us in the image of God's own eternity, the presumption is that this is the original condition of humankind, a condition that has been distorted by death's entry. It is this incorruption that enables righteous humankind to be in relationship with the creator even after death. Like the Epicurean gods, because of this gift righteous human beings would be enabled to escape death, and would only seem to have died (Wisd. of Sol. 3:2). This incorruption is the secret purpose of God for humankind (Wisd. of Sol. 2:22).

Death's Entry

Through the devil's envy death spreads to everything. There are cracks here in the text. If humankind alone is made for incorruption, how is God's immortal spirit in all things? Does this spirit not bestow the gift of incorruption to nonhuman creation? The sage may have broken new ground in his vision of incorruption, proper to the gods, being extended to godly human beings, but his vision does not explicitly extend to nonhuman creation. At the same time a close reading of the text has shown that immortality and incorruption are in the hands of Sophia, and God's immortal spirit is in all things. How can this be taken away by an enemy unless that enemy is more powerful than God and God's image, Sophia? Is Sophia, the active cause of all things, rendered powerless by sinful humankind?

The sage sees death not as the absence of life, but as something that is made, something concrete, yet something not made by God. The sage also tells us that the ungodly invited death into the world. According to the sage, then, death is an alien presence, the "other" of life. Yet a close reading of the speech of the ungodly in Wisdom of Solomon 2:1–20 reveals a crack in the sage's argument. The narrator condemns them for their belief that humankind is born by mere chance and that the spirit will dissolve like empty air at the time of death. But there is no denial of the impact that the decay of the rosebud makes upon the ungodly: "Let us crown ourselves with rosebuds before they wither" (2:8). The sage has tried to present an argument that there was a time before a Fall when there was no place for death in the world; it was not in God's purpose. Yet in the speech of the ungodly we have clear indication that death in the world is the cause rather than the result of their lack of trust in God. Death is therefore not the "other," not an alien presence on earth, but something that is always "keeping watch" (Jacques Derrida's farewell to "Jean-Marie Benoist," in 2001a, 110). The withering of the rosebud alerts the ungodly to a vulnerability that is already present. It is because of this vulnerability of the other that the ungodly ally themselves on the side of the *diabolos*, the adversary, and turn to unrighteousness:

> But let our might be our law of right,
> For what is weak proves itself to be useless. (Wisd. of Sol. 2:11)

Derrida on Immortality

It is appropriate that Jacques Derrida, who certainly does not believe in immortality in any conventional sense, should offer some light on a text dealing with immortality. Appropriate, because the idea of immortality is always challenged by its other, mortality; appropriate, because of the celebration of life that we find in Derrida's writings on death. In his work of mourning for Sarah Kofman, Derrida gives one of his most powerful affirmations of life even while he mourns the death that she has taken to herself. In his reflections upon Kofman's *Conjuring Death*, he refers to the doctors in the Rembrandt painting, "The Anatomy Lesson of Doctor Nicolaes Tulp." The doctors gaze away from the corpse and towards a book and Derrida explains:

> Instead of seeing here a simple negativity of *distraction* (negation, denegation, lie, occultation, dissimulation), Sarah Kofman seems to sense in this repression, in a no doubt very Nietzschean fashion, a cunning affirmation of life, its irrepressible movement to *survive*, to *live on* [*survivre*], to get the better of itself in itself, to lie by telling its truth of life, to affirm this truth of life through the symptom of repression, to express the irrepressible as it is put to the test of repression, to get, in a word, the better of life, that is to say, of death, giving an account of life: to defeat death by affirming a "hold on the truth of life," a "science of life and its mastery."
>
> There would thus be a secret of life. Life would hold the secret of the secret, and all secrets would keep life alive. For the claim over such a secret, even if it is not justified, even if it is merely an allegation of anguished scholars, could still be read as a redoubled affirmation of life. (2001, 176)

The denial of death suggested in the averted gaze of the doctors is in the end truly laughable, concludes Derrida ("and Sarah laughed"). It is an affirmation of life by "anguished scholars". The sage of the Wisdom of Solomon seems to be one such "anguished scholar," but without the laughter. Into the mouth of the ungodly the sage places the words:

> Come, therefore, let us enjoy the good things that exist,
> And make use of the creation to the full as in youth.
> Let us take our fill of costly wine and perfumes,
> And let no flower of spring pass by us.
> Let us crown ourselves with rosebuds before they wither.
> Let none of us fail to share in our revelry;
> Everywhere let us leave signs of enjoyment,
> Because this is our portion and this is our lot. (Wisd. of Sol. 2:6–9)

This is not the defiant yet affirming laughter of Sarah, but the enjoyment of creation at the expense of that creation, a creation seen as expendable. In the words of the ungodly lies the mourning for life that speaks so eloquently of the fragility and the beauty of life. The difference between Derrida and the ungodly in their denial of immortality lies in their response. The ungodly see their limit of days as an excuse to exploit creation. Derrida sees this limit as a reason to affirm life. While the ungodly share Derrida's rejection of immortality, they display a nihilism that does not resonate with Derrida's writings. The challenge of Derrida's writings is to read them with regard to all the nuances of his thought, a care that is often lacking in the polemic of some of his critics.

In the nihilism of the ungodly, not even memory remains. The argument of the ungodly is that life is transient and comes about by chance, that the body will turn to ashes and the spirit will dissolve like empty air (Wisd. of Sol. 2:1–3). From this sense of nihilism and purposelessness stem their wicked deeds as they exploit the creation that will shortly be lost to them. Evil does not stem from a perishable body weighing down the soul, but from human moral agents despairing of a fleeting created world and exploiting that same creation. For the ungodly, breath and reason, body and spirit, name and deeds will cease to exist. Derrida refers to the separation of name and body in the corpse: "it is as if death cut the name off in the midst of life, severed the name from the living one who bore it, and this would be precisely its work as death, the operation proper to it" (2001, 178–179). It is this severing that Derrida elsewhere refers to as the "secret," from the Latin *secretum*, meaning separated or distinct (1995, 12). In a passage that echoes Derrida's concept of the signature as carrying within it the separation of the person from the name, and thus the constant reference to the person's death, he says "and this happens to us all the time, especially when we speak, write and publish" (2001, 179). Yet the very *Work of Mourning* ensures that the name(s) live(s) on.

Derrida, too, dreams of immortality although he claims no explicit belief in it. In his farewell to Paul de Man he refers to a conversation in which de Man spoke to Derrida's son of the small wooden piece called the *âme* (soul) of a violin:

> I didn't know why that at that moment I was so strangely moved and unsettled in some dim recess by the conversation I was listening to: no doubt it was due to the word "soul," which always speaks to us at the same time of life and of death and makes us dream of immortality, like the argument of the lyre in the *Phaedo*. (2001, 75)

For Derrida, memory does not die out. In his work of mourning for Louis Althusser he refers to the loss of a world in which two human beings live a unique shared story. In death, this story becomes irreplaceable. He refers to this world as sinking into the abyss "from which no memory—even if we keep the memory, and we will keep it—can save it" (2001, 115). The ungodly reject even the memory:

> Our name will be forgotten in time
> and no one will remember our works. (Wisd. of Sol. 2.4a)

The ungodly mourn obliquely the withering of the rosebud, symbol of the death of nonhuman creation. In their work of mourning, however, they seek to possess the other: "Let us crown ourselves with rosebuds before they wither." The reader of this line might recall Derrida's caution, via the words of Benoist, that we must not seek to reannex the other:

> [Benoist] does not teach us that we must not cry; he reminds us that we must not *taste* a tear: "The act of tasting a tear is a desire to reannex the other;" one must not "drink the tear and wonder about the strangeness of its taste compared to one's own."
> Therefore: not to cry over oneself. (But does one ever do this? Does one ever do anything but this? That is the question that quivers in every tear, deploration or imploration itself.)
> One should not develop a taste for mourning, and yet mourn we *must*.
> We *must*, but we must not like it—mourning, that is, mourning *itself*, if such a thing exists: not to like or to love through one's own tear but only through the other, and every tear is from the other, the friend, the living, as long as we ourselves are living, reminding us, in holding life, to hold on to it. (2001, 110)

Derrida is speaking of the death of a friend who was once able to respond. His words are pertinent also to nonhuman creation. The ungodly in their own tears seek to hold on to life by annexing the rosebuds. Derrida allows the dead to remind him to hold on to life without reannexing the other.

The hope of some power over death is expressed by the author of the Wisdom of Solomon's claim of incorruption for the righteous. Derrida reaches for hope—opens his texts out toward hope for what is yet to come, without ever defining it as, say, immortality, resurrection, the coming of the specific Messiah, or eschaton. In *A Taste for the Secret* he writes:

> That is why the eschatological or messianic, even if they have the form of expectation, hope, promise—motifs that are apparently so striking—is also the experience of death. When I say this I know I am also speaking of my death—where to be sure, I can reappropriate nothing, where I will no longer be able to reappropriate the future. Only a mortal can speak of the future in this sense, a god could never do so. So I know very well that all this is a discourse—an experience, rather—that is made possible as a future by a certain imminence of death. The imminence here is the fact that death may arrive in any moment. (2001a, 23)

This eschatological future is only possible when it is not determinable, when it defies reappropriation:

> If there is a future as such, it cannot even announce itself, it cannot be pre-announced or over-announced [*se sur-annoncer*] except in the eschatological and messianic—but in a messianic and an eschatological that would be the kenosis of the eschatological and messianic. (Derrida and Ferraris 2001, 21)

Derrida comes closest to pure hope at the very moment he most deeply questions its existence. If there is indeed some hope of immortality, then it can only be pure hope if there is none of the certainty that the sage seeks to give the righteous. For all creation, death is what meets them on the eschatological horizon. This is determinable. The sage seeks to reveal the mystery of God, the secret purposes for which humankind was created. Derrida's thoughts on the eschatological and the messianic challenge us with the idea that a future whose horizon is clear loses its purity. Thus, once the sage claims to know the mystery of God in relation to our future, the future is no longer entitled to be called eschatological or a messianic hope. The value of a deconstructive reading of the text of Wisdom lies precisely in its resistance to a metanarrative of all things moving ever upwards away from death and towards immortality with God. The reality of God's creation is that all things move towards death and decay. The final outcome of that movement must remain secret if it is genuinely eschatological.

Who is Responsible for Death?

In the monotheistic faith of the sage, God is not responsible for death. I have argued that a deconstructive reading of the book shows that death is indeed the responsibility of God and Sophia. The sage has introduced other characters to resolve the issue of death's presence. Are death and the devil radically other, or are they expressions of the "shadow side" of God? My reading of the text of Wisdom of Solomon 1–2 has laid the blame for the responsibility for death at the feet of the creator and Sophia. Cracks appear in the text because the sage is a monotheist and at the same time convinced that a creator God does not "make death." Thus the sage blames the ungodly and the devil. Death is presented as waiting for the invitation to enter the earth and thus is connected with the devil of 2:24 where death is shown to have already entered the world by virtue of envy. This text follows immediately on "for God created human beings for incorruption and made them in the image of God's own eternity." But what is it that the devil is envious of? It must be the incorruption given to humankind and the fact of humankind's creation in the image of God's eternity, that is, of Sophia. In Genesis 3 it is the gods who are zealous to protect their right to immortality and they take steps to bar humankind from this property. The sage has shifted this responsibility on to an envious devil, aided by the ungodly. The ungodly thus subvert life, and are effectively, the human equivalent of the devil.

Derrida does not absolve the deity of responsibility for death. In *The Gift of Death* he speaks of the *mysterium tremendum*, caused by that "frightful mystery" or secret that leaves us in fear and trembling before a God who "decides for us although we remain responsible, that is, free to decide, to work, to assume our life and death" (1995, 56). This "frightful mystery" echoes in a converse way the claim of the narrator of Wisdom that the ungodly did not know the "mystery" of God that humankind was created for incorruption. In the sage's desire to exonerate God of blame for death's presence, he introduces the "mystery." In Wisdom of Solomon 2:22 he refers to "the secret purposes of God" (*mysteria theou*). He implies that this mystery is the incorruption that God wills for humankind. There is no mention of the fate of nonhuman creation in this mystery. Yet in an inverse way, Derrida would remind us that this process of assigning to God what we cannot comprehend and calling it mystery or secret is in fact our only option in the face of the totally other. When he deals with Kierkegaard's reading of Paul's admonition to the Philippians to work out their salvation in fear and trembling, Derrida says this:

> If Paul says "adieu" and absents himself as he asks them to obey . . . it is because God is himself absent, hidden and silent, separate, secret, at the moment he has to be obeyed. God doesn't give his reasons, he acts as he intends, he doesn't have to give his reasons or share anything with us: neither his motivations, if he has any, nor his deliberations, nor his decisions. Otherwise he wouldn't be God, we wouldn't be dealing with the Other as God or with God as *wholly other* [*tout autre*]. If the other were to share his reasons with us by explaining them to us, if he were to speak to us all the time without any secrets, he wouldn't be the other, we would share a type of homogeneity. (1995, 57)

Derrida argues that religion only properly exists when "the secret of the sacred, orgiastic or demonic mystery has been, if not destroyed, at least integrated, and finally subjected to the sphere of responsibility" (1995, 2). In a different way, my study has sought to integrate "the secret of the sacred" and the secret of death and the devilish/demonic to the sphere of responsibility. If God is responsible for creation, then God is responsible for death. While we refuse to exonerate God and are unconvinced by the sage's resort to demonic forces responding to the invitation of the ungodly, this is not to say that there is reason to indict God for the presence of death. A theology of creation must include a theology of death and decay. Derrida speaks eloquently of "the gift of death" that is "accomplished without any hope of exchange, reward, circulation, or communication." Communication would entail some sort of exchange, and this would mean that the gift is not truly gift. The ungodly seek a one-sided exchange with the rosebud: "let us crown ourselves with rosebuds before they wither" (2:8). Yet Derrida's work is powerful evidence that "ungodliness" can lead to responsibility toward the other rather than the exploitation of the other. In its brief moment of life, and in the absence of any hope of incorruption, the rosebud speaks as powerfully of life as it does of death. If God has not offered it the gift of incorruption, neither does its brief existence speak of the failure of God's purpose for creation.

Derrida refers to the "secret" that lies below the surface of a text:

> There is in literature, in the *exemplary* secret of literature, a chance of saying everything without touching upon the secret. When all hypotheses are permitted, groundless and *ad infinitum*, about the meaning of a text, or the final intentions of an author whose person is no more represented than non-represented by a character or by a narrator, by a poetic or fictional sentence, when these are detached from their presumed source and thus remain *locked away* [*au secret*], when there is no longer even any sense in making decisions about some secret beneath the surface of a textual manifestation, when it is the call of this secret, which points back to the other or to something else, when it is this itself which keeps our passion aroused, and holds us to the other, then the secret impassions us. (1992, 23–24)

The search for a satisfying theology of the death of human and nonhuman creation impassions me even while it escapes me. Sophia's role in the life and death of the righteous lies neatly on the surface of the text. She judges them to be righteous and thus worthy of rescue from a final mortality. This may be a theology that is too comforting, consigned too facilely to the secret purposes of God. But what of those who are left to mourn the nonresponse (1999, 5), those who have tasted death too young or too cruelly, those who wonder if our fate is no more than the fossil that once also clung to life. Sophia slips through the cracks of the sage's treatment of life and death, but, with her immortal presence in *ta panta*, in all things, she keeps my passions aroused and impels me to keep searching for the secret that lies somewhere below the surface of the text.

Works Consulted

Crenshaw, James L., ed. 1983. *Theodicy in the Old Testament*. London: SPCK.
Derrida, Jacques. 1992. "Passions: 'An Oblique Offering'." In *Derrida: A Critical Reader*, ed. David Wood, 5–35. Oxford & Cambridge, MA: Blackwell.
———. 1995. *The Gift of Death*. Trans. David Wills. Chicago: University of Chicago Press.
———. 1996. *Archive Fever: A Freudian Impression*. Trans. Eric Prenowitz. Chicago and London: University of Chicago Press.

Derrida, Jacques 1999. *Adieu to Emmanuel Levinas*. Trans. Pascale-Anne Brault and Michael Naas. Stanford, CA: Stanford University Press.

———. 2001. *The Work of Mourning*. Ed. Pascale-Anne Brault and Michael Naas. Chicago: University of Chicago Press.

Derrida, Jacques and Maurizio Ferraris. 2001. *A Taste for the Secret*. Ed. Giacomo Donis and David Webb. Trans. Giacomo Donis. Cambridge: Polity Press.

Gilbert, Maurice. 1973. *La Critique des Dieux dans le Livre de la Sagesse*. Rome: Biblical Institute Press.

Kolarcik, Michael. 1991. *The Ambiguity of Death in the Book of Wisdom 1–6. A Study of Literary Structure and Interpretation*. Analecta Biblica Series 127. Rome: Editrice Pontifico Istituto Biblico.

Reese, James M. 1970. *Hellenistic Influence on the Book of Wisdom and its Consequences*. Rome: Biblical Institute Press.

endings

Chapter 14

The End of the World: *Archive Fever*, Qohelet 12:1–7, and *Lamentations Rabbah*

Francis Landy

A spectral messianicity is at work in the concept of the archive and ties it, like religion, like history, like science itself, to a very singular experience of the promise.

(Derrida, Archive Fever, 1996, 36).

The Bible, at least the Tanakh, is a book without an ending, and with multiple beginnings, a beginning which is beginningless, which sinks in the grammatical aporia between בראשית and ברא.[1] It is haunted by its ending, by the consummate conclusion, by a festination infinitely protracted, a new world and a new language on the other side of catastrophe, and of a text that remains resolutely embedded in discommoding history. But it is also a text which internalizes its conclusion; at the centre of its life, at least one of its lives, is the Temple, in which eternity is realized.[2] There is a similar moment in Qohelet.[3] The officiant in the Temple is the anointed priest, a messianic figure. The Messiah of Aaron and the Messiah of David, the priestly and the political, are in tension as well as interdependent throughout the Tanakh.[4]

My companion on this enterprise will be *Archive Fever* (1996), a book that accompanies me always, always in the accompaniment of a mourning, the lost steps of Gradiva whose trace will haunt us always (*Archive Fever*, 98–101). And I come across this passage from Annie Dillard:

On the dry Laetoli plain of northern Tanzania, Mary Leakey found a trail of hominid footprints. The three barefoot people—likely a short man and woman and a child *Autstralopithecus*—walked closely together. They walked on moist volcanic turf and ash. We have a record of those few second from a day 3.6 million years ago—before hominids even chipped stone tools. More ash covered the footprints and hardened like plaster. Ash also preserved the pockmarks of the raindrops that fell beside the three who walked; it was a rainy day. We have almost ninety feet of the three's steady footprints intact. We do not know where they were going or why. We do not know why the woman paused and turned left, briefly, before continuing. "A remote ancestor," Leakey said, "experienced a moment of doubt." Possibly they watched the Sadiman volcano erupting, or they took a last look back before they left. We do know we cannot make anything so lasting as these three barefoot ones did. (Dillard 1999, 157–158)

And this brings me to the supreme poem of forgetfulness, and the inexorability of remembrance.

Archive Fever begins with the split derivation of the word "archive," from *arche*, "commencement" and "commandment" (*Archive Fever*, 1). The archive is the repository of events and of laws, emanating from a beginning and from an authority which institutes, compiles and classifies it. The desire to establish archives, the *Archive Fever*, is both to preserve memories, not to lose anything of human experience, and to bring those memories into a certain locale, and under a certain control. But the drive to preserve memories attests to their fragility, to what Derrida calls the "anarchivic drive" to destroy them (*Archive Fever*, 10). Death-drive, preceding all beginning and order, is the true *mal d'archive*, the inherent malady, the root of evil (*Archive Fever*, 20), infecting every archive, against which they feverishly seek to defend themselves. We seek to remember because we forget, and because we die. Violence is at work too in the archival institution, as it uses its control of memories to assert its hegemony. Forgetfulness, however, is complicit in every memory. Every item in the archive is the mark of a death, of a past that can never be recovered. It will never be "spontaneous, alive, and internal experience" (*Archive Fever*, 11). Each is a trace, ash, a footprint of the past, preserving, in their absence, the lost lives of their owners. The work of Freud is, in part—and this is the first of the theses with which *Archive Fever* comes to a penultimate conclusion—a reversal of the archive, an attempt to recover live memory, like Proust's *A la récherche* (*Archive Fever*, 92–93).

The core of the book, disingenuously entitled "Foreword," is a critical dialogue with Yosef Hayim Yerushalmi's *Freud's Moses: Judaism Terminable and Interminable*, itself a discussion of Freud's Jewishness and that of psychoanalysis. *Freud's Moses* culminates in an open letter to Freud, a dialogue with the spectral master, whose climax is the "futile" question "whether psychoanalysis is really a Jewish science" (FM: 100). As Derrida acknowledges, he himself is implicated in this question—his own relation to Judaism, to his ancestors and his children, and that of deconstruction. It is a question of the future, the future of science, psychoanalysis, and Judaism, but also of the archive, for the archive always opens up to the future, is preserved for the sake of the future, and it is only then that it will be understood (*Archive Fever*, 37). It is here that Derrida introduces the idea of messianicity, in the sentence which I have used as an epigraph. Yerushalmi suggests that Freud may be at his most un-Jewish on the question of the future (FM: 95), and that Judaism is characterised uniquely "by its specific hope for the future," for the resolution of the Oedipal conflict (FM: 95). It is here that Derrida fundamentally disagrees with Yerushalmi. For Derrida, the messianic cannot be predicted, and it cannot be exclusive. Once Judaism, or Jewishness, claims an exclusive prerogative over the messianic future, once it claims knowledge of the One, a particular relationship to monotheism, then it does violence to the Other, and to all others. What Derrida has learned from Levinas was Judaism as a religion of ethical responsibility. A Judaism that denies its ethical responsibility is not Judaism. For

Judaism to be truly Jewish, and to fulfil its messianic promise, it must be unJewish, or at least not exclusively Jewish. In this sense, Derrida declares himself to have a secret affinity with the Marranos (*Archive Fever*, 70),[5] or, shall we say, Shabbateans?

The future depends on the past, on memory, the memory which Yerushalmi contends is a primary commandment to the Jews (*Archive Fever*, 76, citing Yerushalmi 1982, 9), and hence on the archive, which, as we have seen, is both vulnerable to anarchic violence, to forgetfulness, and the work of death-drive, the preservation of the dead as dead. The messianic age will restore justice to the dead, and hence undo the archive, and history, at the same time that it fulfils it. The Messiah never comes and is always here.

The two texts to which I now turn concern catastrophe. The question in both is whether death is ultimate. I do not know, and I am not sure that they know, the answer. Both can be and have been considered deconstructive.[6] Whether they are depends, I think, on the spectral messianicity that is, or is not, present in both.

I will begin with Qohelet 12:1–7:

1. And remember your creator in the days of your youth, before the days of darkness come, and the years arrive of which you will say, "I have no delight in them." 2. Before the sun darkens, and the light, and the moon, and the stars, and the clouds return after the rain. 3. On the day when the guardians of the house tremble, and the men of valour are crooked, and the grinders cease, for they are few, and the watchers in the windows are darkened. 4. And the doors are closed in the marketplace, and the sound of grinding is diminished; and one rises up to the sound of a bird, and all the daughters of song are laid low. 5. Also they are fearful of that which is above, and there are terrors in the way, and the almond blossoms/putrefies, and the grasshopper is overladen, and caperberry fails, for man goes to his eternal home[7], and the mourners circle the marketplace. 6. Before the silver cord is snapped, and the golden bowl is shattered, and the pitcher is broken over the well, and the wheel is fractured in the pit. 7. And the dust returns to the earth as it was, and the spirit returns to God who gave it.

Qohelet 12:1–7 is an apocalypse, as Fox (1988, 63–67; 1989, 290–293) and Seow (1997, 353) have argued, but a strange one, an anti-apocalypse. The end of the world, communicated through such traditional imagery as the sun darkening, is not the sudden transformative vindication beloved of prophetic writers, but literally a grinding to a halt. The passage has long been read as an allegory for old age.[8] This interpretation is reductive, as Fox (1988, 69–70; 1989, 282) has shown, because it insists on a single interpretive key for the passage, and it cannot account for the strange hybrid images, the multiple ambiguities, through which it acquires supplementarity, an excess of indeterminable meaning. In v.5, for instance, the almond, grasshopper, and caperberry perhaps represent the irony of spring in the decayed city,[9] senility, or sexual impotence,[10] but they are also distractions and enigmas. Why these images in particular? May שָׁקֵד, "almond," mean "watcher," as in Jeremiah 1:12, and carry implications of fear, elaborating on the "terrors of the way" that immediately precede it, or of indifferent spectatorship? What is the life of the overburdened grasshopper? The cosmos, as throughout the book, is contained in, reflected by, the moribund human person, and also in the polis, that emblem of human and Hellenistic accomplishment,[11] whose economy has become spectral, a circulation of lament. The cosmos, the individual and the polis are subject to an entropy which is neither salvific, nor an affirmation of divine power, nor a recreation on the apocalyptic model, but an uncreation. Hence the irony of the initial phrase, "Remember your creator," זכור את בוראיך in which the verb ברא used here for the only time in the book, recalls the unbreached confidence of the creation narrative. But why? Why remember one's origins in the face of the disaster, the absolute disaster? It is perhaps a warning note; "remember your creator" is synonymous with "remember God," and in particular with the reminder two verses previously that God calls all the pleasures of youth into judgement. The God who judges everything, whose memory is implacable, the archive itself, is the origin of the light, sun, moon and stars, which in this passage are metonymous with youth and sexual pleasure. The killjoy reminder, typical of the sage in wisdom literature, will make "following in the ways of your heart and the visions of your eyes" a gloomy enterprise. The question concerns the relationship, the equivalence perhaps, of remembering and forgetting, creation and uncreation: remember that you forget, or because you forget; remember creation because it is, or will be, uncreated. The dissolution of the luminaries results in a reversion to primordial darkness, undoing the order of time and the delimitation of percepts. God presides over, judges, and is responsible for the order—the archive, according to Derrida—of a vanished cosmos. The antithesis and mutual implication of creation and uncreation is most evident from the conflation, at the extreme ends of the passage, of בוראיך and בור the "pit" in v.6,[12] creation, and the creator itself, debouches into, is negated by, or is, the pit. This is typical of the destructive rhetoric of Qohelet, whereby antinomies not only contradict themselves interminably but are indistinguishable. Even clearer, or finally clear, is the last phrase of the passage "and the spirit (רוח), shall return to the God who gave it." This is, to all appearances, the end of the book, before its absurd or pious epilogue. We can breathe a sigh, the last sigh, of relief. We have reached the culmination of the many circles in the book. The wind (רוח), goes round and round, we learn at the beginning (1:6–7), and it finally ends up with God. Except that in the previous verse the "wheel," גלגל, is shattered in the pit.[13] The breaking of the circle is the completion of the circle.

The wind/spirit (רוח), changes gender; in 1:6–7 it is a masculine noun, while here it is feminine. Correspondingly, the sun is feminized; its darkening (ותחשך) concludes its wearisome diurnal cycle, transmitted through masculine verbs in 1:5. ותחשך governs all the celestial bodies in 12:2, and characterizes the universe, and light, as feminine. Feminization here decomposes the exclusive masculine perspective in the book, the overt misogyny of 7:26–28, and even the affirmation of heterosexual love in 9:9, in which woman is a silent partner. We live in a feminine universe, and even our spirit (רוח), assuming it to be a human essence, is feminine. God gives us, and the world, a feminine animating principle. It is, nonetheless, a dying world. The return of the spirit is death, as well as reclamation by and in God, as its origin, its arche. The shattering of the wheel as a figure for death in 12:6 results in the disintegration of the body and the release of the spirit. The doubling of the syllable גל in the word גלגל is elaborated in the dualisms of body and spirit, earth and God, masculine and feminine. Between them there is a space, a transposition of the "pit," the בור, of v.6 into the gap where everything, הכל, is הכל, meaningless or empty (12:8). The fissure in the wheel, between גל and גל, is the opening, the rupture, of the pit.

The wheel revolves around the void, the emptiness at the centre of the book.[14] The wheel is the pit, becomes the pit, or, if one adopts the metaphor of a potter's wheel, shapes it. The arche is anarchic, it contains, harbours and is dislocated by death-drive, which, Derrida says, is above all "archiviolithic" (*Archive Fever*, 10). The spirit returns to God who gave it, but God, without cosmos, is utterly inscrutable. Home, nostalgia, is then to that which is acosmic, which precedes beginning, or, more literally, to death itself.

גלגל reflects, and doubles, the "golden bowl," גלת הזהב, in the first half of the verse, a correspondence underlined by conspicuous parallelism. The ruined golden bowl is the relic of an ancient feast and a past civilization; it is also a memento mori, a sign of our future desolation. The bowl and the wheel are a composite image, each surrounding or shaping an absence, and each elaborating on the circumambulation of mourners in the market place in the previous verse. The wheel differs from the bowl, in its ever repeated dynamic, and the addition of a syllable.

For the first time in the book we have female subjects, the grinders and watchers through the windows of 12:3, the daughters of song of 12:4. Their subjectivity is evoked and diminished at the same time: the grinders cease for they are few; those who look are darkened; the daughters of song are bowed low. The city is full of female sounds, from a secluded or invisible domestic space, and is infused with the female gaze. The woman at the window motif appears, perhaps for the last time in the Hebrew Bible, as everywhere associated with death; it is, however, fading out. The darkening of the onlookers recollects that of the feminized sun in 12:2, and the optic imperative throughout the book. Qohelet insistently looks, in the relentless illumination of a sun under which everything is illusory, emphasized by the refrain, "under the sun." The climax of these visual references is to the sun itself, in 11:7; in defiance of ophthalmology, and perhaps with a direct reference to Plato, Qohelet claims that "it is good for the eyes to look upon the sun." Now the sun is darkened; and with it the gaze of the seers. The women, half hidden, peer out at a man's world, the public realm of political action and philosophical speculation, from which they are excluded. But the man's world is literally on its last legs; there is nothing to see. The women's eyes reflect the growing darkness, but they too can hardly be discerned in the gloom. What the seer, the critical and all-seeing eye of Qohelet, sees and imagines is a failure of sight, specifically of women's sight. Similarly, the daughters of song in 12:4 may be associated with the erotic or with lament; in either case, they recollect a world that is passing.[15] Their prostration, whether out of grief or simply as a lowering of the voice, contrasts or is aligned with the startling voice of the bird that immediately precedes them, which in turn parallels the diminished sound of the grinding stone. The sounds of the city merge with those of the country, and are vanishing into silence. Women's voices, expressive of their personality, seduction, and feeling, are attenuated; they replace and draw attention to the absence of the man's world, but also to their own extinction. The transfer from male to female, from the dominant closed phallocentric social and symbolic world of the book to women's discourse and society, is ironic; as everywhere in the book, opposites cancel themselves out. If the cosmos with its celestial luminaries is maternal, it is also deadly.

Except, and this is where Derrida's concept of messianicity may enter, there is always excess, supplementarity, painful indeed, but exorbitant. The excess of the vegetation and insect life, of the extra syllable in גלגל, of the persistent voices of women, of the imagination over its demise. And, amidst all these, there is the voice of Qohelet, which for all its weariness, its rejection of any possible messianism, any answer to its questions, does not and cannot stop.

There is an extended commentary on Qohelet 12:1–7 in petihta 23 of *Lamentations Rabbah*, the exemplary midrash of catastrophe. A petihta is a midrashic genre whereby a remote text is related to the base text, in this case the first word of Lamentations, *eikhah*; thereby the unity of scripture is affirmed, if only ingenuously. *Lamentations Rabbah* begins with 34 (probably originally 36)[16] petihtas, of which petihtas 23 and 24 are the longest and most celebrated.

Petihta 23 consists of five sections, which may be summarized as follows:

A. Jerusalem
B. Account of Nebuchadnezzar's expedition against Jerusalem.
C. Central anecdote of the Temple
D. Nebuchadnezzar's image. The arrival of the exiles in Babylon
E. Babylon

As one might expect, the catastrophe here is the destruction of the Temple. If Qohelet is notably indifferent to history, the apocalypse of our passage is transposed into historical terms. The cosmos is the Temple, the sun the Davidic dynasty, and so on. On one level, the exposition is fractured and consumed by the base text and the catastrophe to which it refers; Qohelet is the parable or *mashal* to Lamentation's *nimshal*, or message. The real meaning of Qohelet is the destruction of the Temple. Insofar as the network of quotations and exegeses implicates at least the entire Bible, the Torah is swallowed up by the destruction. On the other hand, the interpreted text of Lamentations is disrupted by the text which interprets it; midrash is notoriously fissile and episodic. The only unifying element in the petihta is the interpretative text, whose connection to the base text, *eikhah*, is indeed rather perfunctory. Especially when the point of the exegesis is recherché, obscure, or nonexistent, the distance between the interpretative text and the base text increases. The interpretative text retains its autonomy. Its resistance to being absorbed into the base text and the narratives that substantiate it and comprise the body of the midrash repeats the resistance of the images of the poem to interpretation. The supplementarity of these images is emphasized by their disconnection from their midrashic context. The metanarrative that fills the space between interpretative text and base text and constitutes their dialogue is challenged by metonymic details, like the overburdened grasshopper,[17] that signify poetic excess and entropy, and whose interpretation in the midrash is entirely arbitrary. The interpretative text is used, fractured, and denied its overt meaning as a poem about death; it retains, however, its difference and its imaginative distinctiveness. More important, the negations, and negativity, of both texts affect each other. The anti-apocalypse refers to the central catastrophe of the Hebrew Bible, and turns it into an anti-apocalypse.

At the centre of the petihta, as of the poetic world of *Lamentations Rabbah*, is the Temple. The Temple, founded by Solomon, the alleged author of Qohelet and the discourse of the petihta,[18] is the centre of Israel's life and sacrality. The petihta is concentric: two anecdotes concerning Nebuchadnezzar (B, D) surround the central passage (C), and these in turn are framed by the contrast between Jerusalem and Babylon, the point of departure and the destination (A, E). As ever, the structure is subject to disturbance and displacement; the artistry of composition, with its intimation of poetic order, is repeatedly subverted. In the centre of the concentric circles is an effervescent pool of blood, which insists on the claim for reparation of the murder of Zechariah, the archetypal crime for which the Temple was destroyed. I will quote the passage in full:

> But he brings iniquity to mind, to catch" (Ezek. 21:28). This is the sin of Zechariah, of whom it is said, "And the spirit of God clothed Zechariah son of Yehoiada the priest, and he stood above the people" (2 Chron. 24:20). Now was he really over the heads of the people, that you should say "above the people"? No, but he considered himself higher than all the people, as king's son-in-law, High Priest, prophet, and judge. He began to speak grandiosely, as it says, "And he said to them, 'Thus says God, "Why do you transgress the commandments of YHWH? You shall not prosper, for you have forsaken YHWH, and he has forsaken you."'" And they banded against him and stoned him with stones" (2 Chron. 24:20–21). They did not treat his blood like the blood of the deer or the gazelle, of which it is written, "And he shall pour out its blood and cover it with dust" (Lev. 17:13), for here it says, "her blood is in the midst of her" (Ezek. 24:7). And why was all this? "To stir up wrath, to exact vengeance" (Ezek. 24:8).
>
> R. Yudan asked R. Aha, "Where did Israel slay Zechariah, in the Court of Women, or in the Court of Israel?" He replied to him, "Neither in the Court of Women nor in the Court of Israel, but in the Court of the Priests. Nor did they treat his blood like the blood of the deer or the gazelle, of which it is written, "And you shall pour out its blood and cover it with dust," for here it says, "upon the glaring rock" (Ezek. 24:7). And why all this? "To stir up wrath, to exact vengeance, I set her blood on the bare/glittering rock, that it should not be covered."
>
> Seven sins Israel committed on that day: They killed a priest, a prophet, and a judge; they shed innocent blood; they desecrated God's name; they defiled the Court; and it was the Sabbath and the Day of Atonement.
>
> Now when Nebuzaradan arrived, the blood began to boil. He said to them, "What is the nature of this blood?" They replied, "It is the blood of bulls, rams, and lambs which we were slaughtering." He sent and brought the blood of sacrifices, but it did not behave likewise. He said to them, "If you tell me, good; but if not, I will comb the flesh of these men with iron combs." They answered, "What can we tell you? There was a prophet who reproved us, and we rose against him and killed him. For several years now his blood has not rested." He said, "I will placate it."
>
> He brought before him the Greater and Lesser Sanhedrins, and killed them, until their blood reached the blood of Zechariah, to fulfil that which is written, "They burst forth, and blood touches blood" (Hos. 4:2). But still the blood boiled. He brought youths and maidens, and killed them by it; but still it did not rest. He brought schoolchildren and killed them by it, but still it did not rest. He brought 80,000 novice priests and killed them until their blood reached the blood of Zechariah, and still the blood was boiling. He said, "Zechariah, Zechariah, all the best of them I have destroyed. Is it your pleasure that I should exterminate them all?" Immediately the blood rested.
>
> At that moment he contemplated repentance, and said, "If for one of these, it is thus, how much worse will it be for that man who has killed so many!" He fled, sent a gift to his house, and converted.

The blood of Zechariah reverses all the connotations of the Temple; it is an anti-sacrifice, as is indicated by the failed attempt to pass it off as sacrificial blood and the denial to it of the respect due to the blood of even non-sacrificial animals, the deer and the gazelle. Sacrificial blood is the agent of purification and communion with God; in this blood is concentrated every possible desecration, as the list of seven (in fact, eight) sins perpetrated through it shows. It is absolutely exigent, representing a demand for justice that can never be met. The greater and lesser Sanhedrins, youths and maidens, schoolchildren, and 80,000 novice priests—conventional figures for innocence, vitality, and holiness—fail to propitiate it. The Temple is deadly, annihilating Israel's social and sacred order. At the beginning of the petihta, the destruction of the Temple intervenes between memory and forgetfulness, creation and uncreation. At its centre, the Temple contains—Galit Hasan-Rokem (2000, 170–171) speculates that an actual place may be memorialized—a place that opens up and consumes it. It is its own destruction, the pit (בור) which in Qohelet paronomastically converges with creation (בוראיך). Creation is uncreation, cosmos anti-cosmos.

The aporia, however, is also an interpretative one. The exposition of Qohelet 12:1–7 lapses and is supplanted by excurses on Ezekiel 21:26–28 and 24:7–8. The interruption suggests a breach in the dialogue between the two texts, especially since on either side of the gap interpretations mirror each other.[19] The core of the midrash, in other words, is inserted from a different interpretative and emotional discourse, and is both alien and integral to the main sequence. It exposes the discontinuity in the poem from Qohelet, its inability to speak for its constitutive trauma. In the space between "the terrors of the way," whatever they might be, and the putrefying or blossoming almond,[20] whatever that signifies, like the boiling blood, the real concerns, fears, dream work and drives of the passage come to the surface. The lapse, slippage from one intertext to another, imparts unease, a dislocation or absence of the centre, and the violence that threatens the metaphorical equivalences that comprise the main body of the petihta. The dislocation of the centre is suggested too by prooftexts such as על צחיח הסלע, "on the glaring rock,"[21] which turn the Temple into a desert.

Zechariah, and his blood, acquire a personality. Already the midrash presents him as suffering from a sense of superiority, which after his death turns into an unappeasable grievance. Nebuzaradan's question, "Zechariah, Zechariah, is it your pleasure to exterminate them all?" exposes him as absurdly vindictive, even to himself; the blood stops seething. But Zechariah is an agent, a prophet, of God. His exhortation and consequent murder have been ordained by God "to stir up wrath, to exact vengeance," a refrain repeated twice. It is God's vengeance that is excessive. Nebuzaradan then turns into a critic of God, or one who recalls God to himself. Even if Zechariah's blood is autonomous—an interesting variant attributes the change of heart to God[22]—God has still instigated events, just as he overcomes the resistance of Nebuchadnezzar and fixes the omens.[23]

Nebuzaradan, the other protagonist, is typecast as the cruel persecutor who masks his bloodthirstiness in a façade of strict retribution for an ancestral crime, like the Emperor Hadrian in the story of the Ten Martyrs , down to the detail of the iron combs whose prospect extorts the truth.[24] But with a difference—that he converts! His conversion is anticipated by his cry to Zechariah: he evidently has wearied of slaughter, or perhaps feels remorse; at any rate, his ruthlessness, and his confidence that he can staunch the flow, is no match for Zechariah's (or God's?) implacability. He initiates the conciliation of prophet and God. His conversion is apparently impelled by fear of divine justice, but one may supplement it with wonder at the marvel, and bafflement before a power greater than his own. Whatever the cause, the enemy has become one of us. And our representatives, the prophet and God who personify intractable Judaism, are our enemy. The reversal, which one may compare to the role of the centurion or even Pilate in the story of the Crucifixion, makes exile and alienation intrinsically Jewish, and vice versa. Judaism henceforth survives in masquerade, as in the pathetic story that follows in section D of the deportees of Jeconiah who celebrate the Babylonian triumph to inquire after the fate of their relatives.[25]

If the blood in the Temple is the ultimate pollutant, antithetical to sacrificial blood, the slaughter of Zechariah in the priestly court on the Day of Atonement makes him into a perverse counterpart of the sin offerings of that day, as the reference to its being placed on the glaring rock suggests: these may correspond to the horns of the altar or the desert crag on which the goat sent to Azazel was shattered, according to the Mishnah. Zechariah is also a sacrifice, a martyr, for God, whose death occasions, and has been prescribed by, God's vengefulness against his people. God desecrates himself; the sacrifice is an anti-sacrifice.

The flow of blood, however, evokes the other principal source of impurity: menstruation. The Temple is frequently feminized in biblical and rabbinic sources; in particular, the bottomless pit beneath the altar has vaginal connotations.[26] Menstruation excludes and contaminates the sacred; the sight of menstrual blood, the lurid blood of the prophet, is a prime abomination, turning inside out, according to the Levitical code. Which means, of course, a prime site of repression, the impression of secret traces, a secret language. God is turned off, or on, by the efflux in the Temple, which represents not only his destructive wish, but a perverse pleasure— according to Leviticus 18:19—and the body as violent and anarchic. The Temple as matrix, as open wound and womb, threatens to consume the people and all the significations, the language, with which it, and the midrash, are constructed, and for the neglect of whose 49 ways of midrashic interpretation it is vulnerable to Nebuchadnezzar's 49 enchantments, whose association with dangerous femininity is inescapable.[27] The language of Torah is subsumed by the language of magic.

The interpretation of the Temple as menstruant is confirmed a little later in the midrash, when the precious metal of the Temple is used to shore up the top-heavy statue of Nebuchadnezzar, in fulfilment of the verse that their gold should be as an unclean thing, literally a menstruant woman. The Temple is displaced outside itself, and becomes the foundation for imperial ideology and idolatry. The transformation of blood into gold and silver, the centre into the abject, the sacred into idolatry, suggests both a nexus linking the imperial cult, magic, menstruation, idolatry and the sacred, and an inversion of the idealization of the Temple as cosmos at the beginning of the petihta. At the base of the Empire is the polluted Temple. Nebuchadnezzar is a comic figure, a well-established satiric type, whose reluctance to attack Jerusalem is only matched by his self-glorification afterwards. Comedy is the weapon of the impotent, and exposes the pretensions of their masters. It is, however, infectious. Perhaps the story of Zechariah's blood could be seen as comic, at the very least as grotesque. A hint of the comic could also be found in God's commission to Nebuchadnezzar, (in fact, it is never very far from midrash), through the motifs of repetition (for 18 years), its strange prooftext, its exorbitance.

> "And one will rise up to the sound of a bird" (Qoh. 12:4). This is Nebuchadnezzar the Wicked. Rabbi said, "For 18 years a heavenly voice would resound in Nebuchadnezzar's palace, saying, 'Oh wicked servant, go and destroy the house of your master, whose children do not listen to him.'"

God is the *alazon*, the excessively angry father who cuts off his nose to spite his face. The comic potential conceals, and disavows, the grief that becomes overt in the next petihta, in which God weeps, and begins to tell a parable, which he cannot complete, about a king whose own son dies under the wedding canopy.

The Temple destroys itself; however, there are intimations that this is not the true catastrophe. In the opening sequence (A), the mills that cease are identified as the Mishnaic collections of Rabbi Akiba, R. Oshaia, and Bar Kappara, all post-destruction teachers. When Israel went to into exile, they forgot their Torah. In the recapitulation towards the end of the petihta, the shattered golden bowl is the Torah. The catastrophe then, as in Qohelet, is amnesia: the midrash supplants, preserves and mourns the Temple; it is the site of forgetting, or remembering that we have forgotten. "Said Rabbi Aha to Rabbi Yudan: where did Israel kill Zechariah?" Why did he need to know? Why mark the spot?

Yet the Torah is never forgotten, as in Rabbi Samuel bar Nahman's comparison of Israel to grinding stones in section A (is it the murmur of recitation, or their capacity for close reading?) The catastrophe has already been, and it will never come.

Petihta 24 is the longest and most complex of the petihtas of *Lamentations Rabbah*, and has been the subject of extensive readings by David Stern, Galit Hasan-Rokem, and Tod Linafelt. The petihta consists of two antithetical parts. In the first, God laments the destruction of the Temple, his impotence and his folly. In the second, he is unmoved by the pleas of the angels, the Patriarchs and Moses, and even the letters of the alphabet with which the world was created refuse to endorse his condemnation of Israel. I wish to turn to the climax. Moses has just chided God for his silence and his disregard of the Torah, in which it is written, "An ox or a sheep: it and its offspring you shall slaughter on one day" (Lev. 22:28), when indeed many mothers and children have been slain. I will quote the following passage in its entirety:

> Then our mother Rachel leapt in before God and said: "Master of the Universe! It is revealed before you that your servant Jacob loved me with a surpassing love, and worked for my father for my sake for seven years. At the completion of those seven years, when the time of my marriage to my husband came, my father planned to substitute my sister for me. It was very hard for me, for the plot was known to me, and I informed my husband and gave him a sign whereby he should distinguish between myself and my sister, so that my father should not replace me. But subsequently I reconsidered, thwarted my desire, and felt compassion for my sister, that she should not be ashamed. In the evening, when they substituted my sister for me, I passed on to her all the signs I had given to my husband, so that he should be convinced that she was Rachel. Not only that, but I went under the bed on which he lay with my sister. When he spoke to her, she was silent, and I would answer every word, so that he should not recognize the voice

of my sister. Thus I showed devotion (*hesed*) to her, I was not jealous, and I did not let her go forth to shame. If I, flesh and blood, dust and ashes, was not jealous despite my distress and did not let her go forth to shame, how can you, the living and compassionate king, be jealous of insubstantial idols and exile my children, that they are slain by the sword and the enemy does with them as it wills."

Immediately God's compassion came to the fore, and he said: "For your sake, Rachel, I will restore Israel to their place, as it is written 'Thus says the Lord: A voice heard in Ramah, lamentation and bitter weeping, Rachel weeping for her children . . .' (Jer. 31:15) . . . and it says further, 'Hush your voice from weeping and your eyes from tears, for there is a reward for your labour . . . and the children will return to their borders.'"

(Jer. 31:16)

God experiences, imagines, intercourse, at one remove, just as we readers do, but from a woman's perspective. He imagines, he is compelled to imagine, what Rachel feels, under the bed. God imagines himself into, or as, the body of a woman experiencing orgasm—at one remove. Rachel pretends to be, fantasizes herself as the body of, Leah, while retaining her own voice;[28] Leah knows what it is to be Rachel, allows herself to be loved as Rachel. Both figures experience displacement; Leah learns how unloved she is, suppresses her own voice, just as Rachel suppresses her desire. Jacob has intercourse, unknowingly, with a composite figure, both Rachel and Leah, which comprise the impossible, ever thwarted, unity of Israel. One recalls the competition and mutual envy of Rachel and Leah, and its reverberations in Israel's history. Rachel, as the mother of Israel, becomes a figure for irretrievable loss, for an alienation, apostasy, preceding and prefiguring the destruction of the Temple. In reminding God of this loss, and the renunciation from which it originated, Rachel reminds him of her own displacement as Jacob's loved one. The injustice done to Rachel reflects on God's own injustice, and the injustice of history.

Rachel accuses God, explicitly, of a lack of self control. "If I, flesh and blood, dust and ashes, was not jealous . . . how can you . . . ?" She may have added, "If I, a mere woman . . . " Self-control, in ancient Judaism and antiquity in general, is the essential masculine virtue, which distinguishes rational men from passionate women.[29] God is the exemplar of heroic self-restraint in his refusal to punish Israel's enemies. Here the motif is turned upside down; God's desire, as in petihta 23, is to destroy Israel. That a woman, mother of the apostate northern kingdom, should claim greater potency than God is an evident weapon of shame.[30]

The affective centre of the story, however, is Rachel's solidarity with Leah. It is a narrative about a bond between women that overrides heterosexual need and love. There is no obvious reason why God should be moved by Rachel when he does not respond to the memory of the Akedah, or to Jacob's and Moses' quasi-maternal upbringing of God's children. Except that it is unexpected. This is indicated by the detail that Rachel "leapt in" (קפצה).[31] God imaginatively crosses gender,[32] and is shown an example of human commitment (*hesed*) unrelated to himself. He has to enter into another world.

But Rachel is also the *mater dolorosa*, a figure of inconsolable maternity. God implicitly acknowledges this through his citation of Jer. 31:15. If Rachel calls to mind her erotic self-sacrifice, God responds to maternal bereavement. Rachel's weeping reawakens God's memory of his grief earlier in the petihta, but it is also a female specialization. As Galit Hasan-Rokem (2000, 108–129) has brilliantly argued, *Lamentations Rabbah* represents a female tradition, that of lament, and may actually express female voices, if only in disguise and at one remove. Rachel's voice under the bed then is infused both with male fantasies of ideal women's self-denial, since Rachel conforms to a type of "good" women, and with the trace of real women's pain, longings and frustrations, and the demand to be heard. It is a voice, moreover, that God needs. In the first part of the petihta, as I have mentioned, God weeps and begins to tell Jeremiah a parable about a king whose son died under the wedding canopy. He breaks off, unable to complete it, and accuses Jeremiah, of all people, of an incapacity for weeping. He instructs him to resurrect the Patriarchs and Moses, since "they know how to weep"! God's weeping is perhaps inadequate; at any rate, he requires human solace and amplification. The episodes repeats one earlier in the midrash. In petihta 2, there is a parable about a king who killed his two sons;[33] he wept for the first, but for the second he found himself beyond weeping. For that reason it says, in Jeremiah 9:16, "Call to the wailing women . . ." The mourners whom God requires are women, whose role in our petihta is transferred to the Patriarchs and Moses, and finally to the initial, archaic, mourning mother Rachel, who is "our" mother, who dies giving birth to us, for whom our beginning is the threshold she cannot cross, liminal, sublime, tragic, who will only be consoled when the children return to their borders, when the arche, or the archiviolithic, is no longer at the cost of that which it represses—the dead and the mother, and that which precedes creation. God needs her voice, and that of the mourning women, the Patriarchs and Moses, because otherwise he would be silent. God's silence in the second half of the petihta corresponds to the impotent God who cannot weep in petihta 2. As Hasan-Rokem (2000, 134) points out, there the mourning women lament for himself as well as for his children; his identification with the children makes their murder self-destruction, suicide. God's silence in our petihta, beyond language, Torah and creation, is perhaps related to his weeping; it is that which is unspoken, helpless, in his weeping, in his sense, as he wanders, surrounded by angels, Patriarchs and prophets, through the smoking ruins of his Temple, that he has failed, is senile and demented. "Woe to the king who in his youth succeeded, and in his senility did not succeed!"

Petihta 24 is the mirror image of petihta 23, in ways I cannot explore. Petihta 23 also ends with an image of maternity. The converse of the Temple, as cosmos and matrix, is Babylon. Babylon is the original home of Israel; its history ends where it began, beyond patriarchy or at least the patriarchs. But Babylon is a mother who kills her children: "Why is it called Shinar? Because there they die young" (*ne'arim*). Other exegeses associate the name Shinar with suffocation and with the Flood, since it is the nadir of the world, where the waters of the Flood drained away. The final comment contrasts Babylon, as the earth to which the "dust" returns, with the departed spirit. Babylon, the lethal mother, is the antithesis of Rachel, the bereaved mother, who brings about an ultimate restoration of the dead to the living, of a voice to God.

The midrash does not end there, however, and the figure of Rachel recurs in many guises. As Linafelt (2000, 115–116) says, she is a displacement of Mother Zion, who reaches out through her to her lost sister. It really is Rachel who sleeps in Leah's bed, and is the mother of her children, or so her acknowledgement as "our" mother suggests. But we live in a real world, after the Shoah and the destruction. Petihta 24 is recollected in the story of Miriam Bat Tanhum (*Lamentations Rabbah* 1:16), itself a wry retelling of the legend of Hannah and her seven sons. Here, however, after the seventh son is martyred, the mother goes mad, falls off the roof, and dies. Whether this is suicide is unclear—in the next midrash the Shekhinah laments Israel's madness in *not* committing suicide—but in either event, it is an affective suicide.

We could pursue this trail indefinitely, but get no further. For there is one voice in *Lamentations Rabbah*, at least, that refuses any consolation, will not accept any messianicity. I would like just to cite, without comment, the midrash's version of the Nativity story:[34]

It happened that a man was ploughing. One of his oxen lowed. An Arab passed by and asked him "What are you?" He replied, "I am a Jew." He said, "Untie your ox, loosen the plough." He said, "Why?" "Because the Temple of the Jews has been destroyed." While they were talking the ox lowed a second time. He said, "Bind up your ox, bind up the plough, for the Redeemer of the Jews is born." He said to him, "What is his name?" He replied, "Menahem is his name." "And his father's name?" "Hezekiah." "Where does he live" "In Biryath Arba by Bethlehem of Judah." The man sold his oxen and his plough, and bought swaddling clothes. He went from city to city, country to country, until he reached that place. All the villagers came to buy, but the mother of the child did not buy. He asked her, "Why did you not buy swaddling clothes?" She said, "Because I fear troubles on account of my child." He said, "Why?" "Because when he was born the Temple was destroyed." He replied, "Let us trust in the Master of the World, that on his heels it was destroyed, and on his heels it will be rebuilt." He said to her "Let me leave you with some of these swaddling clothes." She said, "I have no money."[35] He said, "You take some of these swaddling clothes, and after some days I will come to your house and collect payment." He left her the clothes and departed. After some time, he said, "I will go and see what has become of the child." He went and asked, "What has happened to the child?" She said, "Did I not tell you that I feared troubles on his account? Ever since that time there have been winds and whirlwinds, and they have carried him away . . ." (*Lamentations Rabbah* 1:16)

Notes

1. Perhaps the best literary reading of this aporia, comparing it to the beginning of Proust's *A la recherche*, is Josipovici (1989, 53–64).
2. Idel (1998, 13, 38–39), under the influence of the Myth and Ritual school, identifies this aspect of biblical messianism with the ideology of sacred kingship. He does not recognize, however, that there may be a tension between priestly and royal ideologies, though he does note, in passing, that priests were anointed (1998, 13).
3. Qoh. 3.11: "he put eternity into their hearts."
4. This tension and complementarity is most evident in the coupling of the two Messiahs in the Dead Sea Scrolls.
5. One may note, in passing, the extraordinary role of conversos and ex-conversos in crossing the boundaries between religions and cultures in the sixteenth to eighteenth centuries, and hence preparing the way for the Enlightenment. On this, see Kaplan (2002).

6. Sneed (2002) provides a full bibliography of contributions to the deconstructive criticism of Qohelet (2000, 115–116 nn. 3–8). His article is an excellent study of the ambivalence, aporiae, and alternation between radicalism and conservatism in the book. The relationship between midrash and deconstruction has been a lively subject of scholarly discussion since Handelman's provocative contribution (1982). A good discussion of the relevant issues is to be found in Stern (1996, esp.15–38). The focus of debate has, however, been the alleged polysemy and indeterminacy of midrash and its limits. My interest in this essay is in the thematic conflicts and tensions of the texts. Stern (1996, 91) makes an interesting comparison with the role and interpretation of ancient Greco-Roman myth in antiquity.

7. I cannot find inclusive language equivalents that would preserve the very familiar language of the passage and the interesting androcentricity of the text, of which more later.

8. Fox (1989, 280–285) and Seow (1997, 372–374) provide convenient summaries and critiques of the allegorical interpretation.

9. Fox (1988, 62) writes: "Then: the budding, growing, blooming of plants. But this rebirth is without cheer, because it mocks the finality of our end."

10. חגב, "grasshopper, locust," may refer either to the insect or to a plant e.g. the pods of the carob tree. Some derive אביונה from אבה, "desire," (e.g., NRSV). Interpretations of both images as referring to sexual incapacity go back to the Talmud (*Sanhedrin* 152a). Fox (1989, 305) remarks "it is easy to see sexual implications in the most diverse images."

11. My student, Benjamin Berger (2001, 146 n.9), notes that the city is first evoked, as a symbol for order and reason, at the moment of dissolution.

12. Seow (1997, 351–352, 375) notes the wordplay, which he traces to *Avot* 3.1.

13. Most commentators deny that גלגל can refer to "wheel" in this context (Fox 1989, 307–308; Seow 1997, 367) and postulate that it means some kind of vessel, on the grounds that waterwheels were not common in ancient Palestine. This is to overlook the broader symbolic resonance of גלגל, "wheel," as a metaphor in and for the book.

14. Berger (2001, 162) says that instead of creating a poetic world, Qohelet creates a poetic "black hole" and argues that it is characterized by a "stylistics of emptiness" (2001, 163).

15. Seow (1997, 359) identifies the "daughters of song" with birds, because of the parallel with "one will rise up to the sound of the bird," and suggests that they swoop down on prey. Fox (1989, 304–305) holds that they are mourning women, bowed down in grief. The possibilities are not exclusive.

16. 36 is the gematria of 'eikha, "How", the first word of Lamentations, on which each petihta comments.

17. The grasshopper is interpreted as Nebuchadnezzar's statue. There is, however, no obvious exegetical connection between the two.

18. The text is framed as a speech by Solomon to Israel.

19. For instance, there are references to Jeremiah's prophecy and to the loss of Torah on both sides of the central passage.

20. וינאץ may refer to "blossom" or "decay," depending on whether one adopts the Qere (וינץ "blossom") or the Ketib.

21. This is Greenberg's felicitous translation of the rare and obscure צחיח (Greenberg 1997, 500).

22. *Lamentations Rabbah* 2:2, and 4:13. In each case, God points to the blood and it disappears.

23. In section B of the petihta, Nebuchadnezzar is a very reluctant conqueror who tries his best to avoid attacking Jerusalem. God arranges the omens so that they fall on Jerusalem, and not on Rome or Alexandria.

24. In that narrative, recited liturgically on the Day of Atonement, R. Akiba's flesh was curried with iron combs (*TB Berakhot* 61b). The crime for which the martyrs were executed was the sale of Joseph.

25. "They were clothed in black on the inside, and white on the outside. They greeted him with 'Hail, conqueror of the barbarians!' and they would ask 'What happened to father? What happened to mother? What happened to my son? What happened to my daughter?'"
26. In *TB Sukkah* 49b, the "pits" under the altar are associated with the exegesis of the description of the woman's body, and in particular with the phrase, חמוקי ירכיך, "the inturning of your thighs," in Song of Songs 7.2.
27. In the exegesis immediately preceding the central passage, the very obscure phrase שבוי שבעות (Ezek. 21.28) is interpreted as referring to the 49 modes of midrashic interpretation whose neglect is recompensed by Nebuchadnezzar's 49 ways of magic. The association of magic with women is pervasive in Talmudic writings, for instance in the statement that most women are witches (*TB Sanhedrin* 67a). On this and comparable statements, see Leeses (2001).
28. Hasan-Rokem (2000, 129) quotes the Rabbinic saying that "a woman's voice is her sexual organ."
29. The classic statement is that of Ben Zoma in *Aboth* 4:1: "Who is strong? He who controls his desire!" God's silence as a proof of his strength is exemplifed by *Mekhilta Shirata* 8: 19–22 (Lauterbach, ed.)
30. As Stern (1996, 85) puts it, "God's masculine hardness submit(s) to the compassionate softness of the matriarch's plea." Daniel Boyarin has argued in various works that the rabbis saw themselves as feminized (1997, 1999).
31. Hasan-Rokem (2000, 127) contrasts Rachel's initiative with the more sober account of how the Patriarchs and Moses are summoned before God.
32. Stern (1996, 85) argues against the possibility that Rachel's plea evokes a feminine side in God, on the grounds that such did not exist in Rabbinic Judaism. However, what happens here, in my view, is that God is forced to imagine what it is like to be human, and a woman. Stern appropriately calls this *imitatio hominis* (1996, 86).
33. The text says, rather more dramatically, that he beat them to death.
34. Hasan-Rokem discusses this strange story and its relationship to the Gospel narratives at length (2000, 152–160).
35. In my version of the text, this phrase is missing. I have borrowed it from Hasan-Rokem's translation.

Bibliography

Berger, Benjamin. 2001. "Qohelet and the Exigencies of the Absurd." *Biblical Interpretation* 9:141–79.
Boyarin, Daniel. 1997. *Unheroic Conduct: The Rise of Heterosexuality and the Invention of the Jewish Man*. Berkeley: University of California Press.
———. 1999. *Dying for God: Martyrdom and the Making of Christianity and Judaism*. Stanford, CA: Stanford University Press.
Derrida, Jacques. 1996. *Archive Fever: A Freudian Impression*. Trans. Eric Prenowitz. Chicago and London: Chicago University Press.
Dillard, Annie. 1999. *For the Time Being*. London: Penguin.
Fox, Michael. 1988. "Ageing and Death in Qohelet 12." Journal for the Study of the Old Testament 42:55–77.
———. 1989. *Qohelet and his Contradictions*. (Journal for the Study of the Old Testament Supplement Series 71; Bible and Literature Series 18. Sheffield: Almond Press.

Greenberg, Moshea. 1997. *Ezekiel 21–37: A New Translation with Introduction and Commentary*. Anchor Bible 22A. New York: Doubleday.

Handelman, Susan A. 1982. *The Slayers of Moses: The Emergence of Rabbinic Interpretation in Modern Literary Theory*. Albany: State University of New York Press.

Hasan-Rokem, Galit. 2000. *Web of Life: Folklore and Midrash in Rabbinic Literature*. Trans. Batya Stein. Stanford, CA: Stanford University Press.

Idel, Moshe. 1998. *Messianic Mystics*. New Haven and London: Yale University Press.

Josipovici, Gabriel. 1989. *The Book of God*. New Haven and London: Yale University Press.

Kaplan, Yosef. 2002. "Bom Judesmo: The Western Sephardic Diaspora." In *Cultures of the Jews: A New History*, ed. David Biale, 639–69. New York: Schocken Books.

Leeses, Rebecca. 2001. "Exe(o)rcising Power: Women as Sorceresses, Exorcists and Demonesses in Babylonian Jewish Society in Late Antiquity." Journal of the American Academy of Religion 69:343–75.

Linafelt, Tod. 2000. *Surviving Lamentations: Catastrophe, Lament, and Protest in the Afterlife of a Biblical Book*. Chicago and London: Chicago University Press.

Sneed, Mark. 2002. "(Dis)closure in Qohelet: Qohelet Deconstructed." *Journal for the Study of the Old Testament* 27:115–26.

Seow, C.L. 1997. *Ecclesiastes: A New Translation with Introduction and Commentary*. Anchor Bible 18C. New York: Doubleday.

Stern, David. 1996. *Midrash and Theory: Ancient Jewish Exegesis and Contemporary Literary Studies*. Evanston, IL: Northwestern University Press.

Yerushalmi, Yosef Hayim. 1982. *Zakhor: Jewish History and Jewish Memory*. New York: Schocken Books.

———. 1991. *Freud's Moses: Judaism Terminable and Interminable*. New Haven and London: Yale University Press.

Chapter 15

Decomposing Qohelet[1]

Jennifer L. Koosed

This essay presents the book of Qohelet as an exploration of the limits of signification, limits imposed on meaning through the gift of death. Death in Qohelet entails two themes: (1) the loss of memory, and (2) and leveling of differences. At the level of the physical body, no one is remembered after death and there is no differentiation made in death between the wise and the foolish, or even between the human and the animal. Death comes for all. Qohelet then enacts this inevitable decay of the body through a decay of the text. The physical body and the body of the book are intertwined. At the level of the textual body, meaning requires both repeatability and differentiation (Jacques Derrida's concept of "iterability"), two things extinguished by death. Qohelet enacts this through an incoherent structure, the positioning of "a time to die" in Qoh. 3:2–8, and the puzzling final poem in Qohelet 12:1–8. Finally, what is left after the disruption of death in life and in the text? Using Derrida's analysis of the gift of death, this article argues that what is left is responsibility.

Death permeates the book of Qohelet to such an extent that H. Wheeler Robinson voiced a visceral reaction: Qohelet has "the smell of the tomb about it" (1946, 258). As signaled by this almost physical recoil, death is encoded in the body of the book in a variety of overlapping ways. The first part of this article will briefly review the ways in which Qohelet speaks of death. Second, I will demonstrate how death is manifest not only in the content of the book, but also in its very form. In other words, the structure of the book, often called a "riddle," is in a state of decay. But perhaps the most significant inscription of death, for it is the one that constitutes the very (im)possibility of the others, is God's gift of death. God "gives" (נתן, ***nātan***) in Qohelet more than God is involved in any other activity. Employing Jacques Derrida's analysis of the gift, the third part of this paper will illuminate God's giving in and giving to Qohelet.

Qohelet's Vigil

It is almost a truism that Qohelet is the most philosophical book of the biblical corpus. Despite the frequency of Qohelet's references to God (40 times), it is the philosophical as opposed to the theological dimensions of this book which persist in the minds of readers. Perhaps part of the reason is because the mournful tolls of the death knell drown out any other note sounded, and death is the intimate partner of philosophy. As Derrida writes, "Philosophy isn't something that comes to the soul by accident, for it is nothing other than this vigil over death that watches out for death and watches over death, as if over the very life of the soul" (1996, 15). In Qohelet's confrontation with death, we see him as a philosopher, a philosopher watching and waiting and writing.

In the opening poem, the cycle of birth and death is part of the workings of nature: "A generation goes, and a generation comes, but the earth remains forever" (1:4; all quotations unless otherwise noted are from the NRSV). Intertwined here with the concern about death is the concern about memory: "The people of long ago are not remembered, nor will there be any remembrance of people yet to come by those who come after them" (1:11). For Qohelet as for Derrida, the name may survive death, but once detached and remaindered—left on its own—the memories it evokes cannot be controlled or guaranteed. Meditating on Sarah Kofman after her death, reading her work, Derrida writes "But there is no longer any doubt: such testimonies survive us, incalculable in their number and meaning" (2001, 170). The name after death continues on, proliferating endlessly, mutating in each new context, multiplying meaning, "keeping the last word—and keeping silent." (2001, 170)

In the second chapter where Qohelet makes a test of pleasure, death is also in attendance: "I searched with my mind how to cheer my body with wine . . . until I might see what was good for mortals to do under heaven during the few days of their life" (2:3). The concern with memory, and its connection to writing is present implicitly in this section. Here, Qohelet is imitating royal inscriptions of the Ancient Near East, particularly West Semitic and Akkadian royal inscriptions. These texts were written in stone and intended to preserve the memory of the king and his deeds. The similarities include the lauding of the wisdom of the king, the boast of surpassing all predecessors, and a series of first person singular perfect verbs. There are also similarities in content. For example, the Assyrian rulers Sargon II and Sennacherib boast of great building projects, the creation of a garden, orchards, and irrigation canals (Seow 1995). Yet, as Qohelet points out, it is all הבל, *hebel* (vanity, nothing, ephemeral, absurd, vapor).[2] Stones change so slowly that they appear to us permanent and stable. We attach our hopes of memory to them—piles of stones as a memorial, writing names on stones, placing stones on graves, pictures of stones on works of mourning . . . Despite human hopes and efforts, there is no permanent monument in memory to one's name, not even those written in stone by conquering kings.

After this garden of delights, Qohelet has his first extended meditation on death:

So I turned to consider wisdom and madness and folly; for what can the one do who comes after the king? Only what has already been done. Then I saw that wisdom excels folly as light excels darkness. The wise have eyes in their head, but fools walk in darkness. Yet I perceived that the same fate befalls all of them. Then I said to myself, "What happens to the fool will happen to me also; why then have I been so very wise?" And I said to myself that this also is *hebel*. For there is no enduring remembrance of the wise or of fools, seeing that in the days to come all will have been long forgotten. How can the wise die just like fools? So I hated life, because what is done under the sun was grievous to me; for all is *hebel* and a chasing after wind. (2:12–17)

Besides the theme of memory, another important aspect of Qohelet's obsession with death is introduced here. Death is the great leveler. It comes for all, indiscriminately and without warning. And one has no control over who or what comes after one's death (cf. Qoh. 6:12).

Death levels all of the deeds of the living, and this includes leveling human and animal:

> For the fate of humans and the fate of animals is the same; as one dies, so dies the other. They all have the same breath, and humans have no advantage over the animals; for all is *hebel*. All go to one place; all are from the dust and all turn to dust again. Who knows whether the human spirit goes upward and the spirit of animals goes downward to the earth? (3:19–22)

And despite the advice Qohelet gives about right relationship to the divine (see especially Qoh. 5:1–7), in the end there is no distinction:

> Since the same fate comes to all, to the righteous and the wicked, to the good and the evil, to the clean and the unclean, to those who sacrifice and those who do not sacrifice. As are the good, so are the sinners; those who swear are like those who shun an oath. This is an evil in all that happens under the sun, that the same fate comes to everyone. (9:2–3)

There is no living on (sur-vivre; over-living), either in the sense of survival, or resurrection. There is only, minimally, Sheol (9:10), a shadowy underworld or place of shades, where all go together.

Death, then for Qohelet, entails these two themes: (1) the extinguishing of memory, and (2) the leveling of differences. Ostensibly, writing should preserve memory, should stabilize the sign. But the book is a body as well. "This book stands up to, and stands in for, the body: a *corpse* replaced by a corpus, a *corpse* yielding its place to the bookish thing . . ." (Derrida, 2001, 176). As the body grows old and its memory becomes confused, the book is unstable—it enacts in syntax, diction, and structure Qohelet's concerns with the decaying body and its fading memory.

In order to signify, the sign must be repeatable and thus engaged in memory, yet it also must be distinguished from others, to stand out, to be significant. Without these two features, a sign is meaningless. Derrida (1988) refers to this phenomenon as "iterability." In order to be meaningful, the name or word must be as unique (singular) as the person who or object that bears it; and yet, in order to function, it must be repeatable (conform to a general law). It must be able to be used in a variety of contexts, repeated and understood, and function in the absence of its bearer. As Qohelet meditates on the corrosive power of the death of the body to extinguish memory ("For there is no enduring remembrance of the wise or of fools, seeing that in the days to come all will have been long forgotten") and level differences ("How can the wise die just like fools?"), death in effect also renders signification impossible by erasing both repeatability and differentiation. Qohelet's book becomes a meditation on the dearth/death of meaning both at the level of the physical body, and in the body of the book. We are all together caught in the natural processes of flesh. Qohelet's vigil is over death as the limit of signification, the open wound of meaninglessness. "No one has power over the wind to restrain the wind, or power over the day of death" (8:8a). *Hebel* blows all around.

"The Riddle of the Sphinx"

The search for the structure of this strange little book has dominated past scholarship. In his recent commentary, Choon-Leong Seow sums up the history of this scholarship by noting that the "[s]cholarly opinion regarding the structure of the book falls between two poles. There are those who find no order whatsoever, and those who discern a carefully constructed structure" (1997, 43). As with almost every other aspect of the book of Qohelet, the debate is between two mutually exclusive hypotheses.

Two of the major proponents of theories that discern an elaborate structure are J. A. Loader, and Addison Wright. For Wright, until the structure of the book of Qohelet is discerned, the other "essential riddles" of message, genre, and unity cannot be solved (1968, 313). Using a truncated version of New Criticism[3] in which he investigates such structural indicators as repetitions, inclusions, chiasm, symmetry, and refrains, Wright concludes that there are "three successive patterns of verbal repetition" in Qohelet 1:12–11:16 (1968, 313). The first section (1:12–6:9) is marked by the refrains "vanity of vanities" and "chasing after wind." Here, Qohelet is reporting on his investigations and observations about life; thus there is a "continuity of thought" as well as a repetition of phrase. The second section (chapters 7–8) is distinguished from the first by the cessation of "chasing after wind" and the introduction of the words "not find" and "who can find." The third section (9:1–11:6) is related to the second (both form the second half of the book) but the repeated words shift to "do not know" and "no knowledge." These final two sections make up Qohelet's conclusions about the investigations that he undertook in the first section. The title (1:1) and the introductory poem on toil (1:2–11) as well as the final poem on youth and old age (11:7–12:8) and the epilogue (12:9–14) are outside of this schema.

Wright (1980) later expands upon this initial proposal through a calculation of the numerical values which, he claims, underlie the structure. Wright begins with the fact that there are 222 verses in Qohelet, with the halfway point being at the break between 6:9 and 6:10. He argues that this is not an arbitrary result of later versification, but part of the deliberate intention of the author. The key to this proposal is verse 1:2. The recurrent phrase and theme *hăbēl hăbālîm, hakōl hebel* has the numerical value of 216 (using Hebrew numerology, or Gematria). In addition to this, the numerical value of *hebel* is 37 and it is used 3 times in this verse for the total value of 111. There are two groups of 111 verses (6:9 being the middle), disregarding the epilogue which Wright assumes is added by an editor. In the first line, דברי (*dîvrê*, "words of") has the value of 216. The first verse of the epilogue contains the word ויתר (*vĕyōter*, "and more"), the ו having the value of six. The ו signals to the reader that the author is adding six additional verses. The value of *dîvrê* (216) plus the value of ‎1 (6) equals 222, the total number of verses in the book. Wright continues on in this matter, spinning a web of interrelated words and numbers throughout Qohelet. For Wright, these are not coincidences. Instead, the mathematically orientated and adept author Qohelet deliberately structured his book using this numerical template.

In the end, Wright must manipulate the data to fit the theory. For example, sometimes the refrain that Wright is using to mark the end of a section actually occurs in the middle of a unit (see Qoh. 11:2). Sometimes Wright ignores one of the formulaic phrases all together because it does not appear where he needs it to appear (for example, 4:4). And there are many repeated phrases that are integral parts of Qohelet's distinctive vocabulary which Wright completely brackets out ("under the sun," "I turned to see") (Crenshaw 1987, 42). Problems multiply in his numerical analysis. He even goes so far as to suggest that one of the verses containing the word *hebel* is a later addition (either 5:6 or 9:9) since its removal would decrease the total *hebel* count from 38 to 37, thereby making the number of times *hebel* appears in the book equal to the numerical value of the word. This is one of the moments in his argument where the numbers control the interpretation rather than visa versa; consequently, the reasoning becomes hopelessly circular.

After the "making many books" (12:12) on the subject of Qohelet's structure, we are no closer to discerning it than we were before the modern era of scholarship. Rather than siding with one proposal or another, with one pole of the debate or the other, I believe that the contours of the question must be changed.

Michael Fox has moved in this direction. He wryly observes that proposals of structure rarely persuade anyone but their authors (1999, 148). Instead of following the typical paradigm, Fox looks to Ludwig Wittgenstein's tome *Philosophical Investigations*. Excerpting here what Fox quotes in full, Wittgenstein describes his own structure thus:

> I have written down all these thoughts as *remarks*, short paragraphs, of which there is sometimes a fairly long chain about the same subject, while I sometimes make a sudden change, jumping from one topic to another . . . After several unsuccessful attempts to weld my results together into such a whole, I realized that I should never succeed. The best that I could write would never be more than philosophical remarks; my thoughts were soon crippled if I tried to force them on in any single direction against their natural inclination. And this was, of course, connected with the very nature of the investigation. (Fox 1999, 149–150)

Comparing his remarks to landscapes through which he has long journeyed, Wittgenstein warns the reader that she or he will not find a structure more coherent than this. The reader too is about to enter sketches of scenery through which she will journey. Fox believes that this describes Qohelet exactly. Thus for Fox, while there are no clear division of segments, or progression of content, there is a "conceptual organization . . . reinforced by uniformity in tone, ideas, and style" (1999, 150) and it is in this that the book coheres.

What Fox gives with one hand—a proposal that resists imposing a structure—he takes away with the other by offering his own cushion of coherence. I would rather "take hold of the one without letting go of the other" (7:18). While it is true that there is a certain uniformity of tone, this does not overshadow the incoherence of structure—both are present in Qohelet existing in an uneasy tension, and the book cannot be tamed by hierarchically subordinating one to the other. As will be demonstrated through an investigation of Qohelet. 3:2–8 and 12:1–7, it is death that intervenes to subvert any coherence in the body and in the book alike. "[A]s a book always comes to take the place of the body . . ." (Derrida 2001, 169), corpse into corpus, the book of Qohelet reflects the death and decay of the body.

Death is enacted in the overall structure of the book, a structure that decays and disintegrates like the dying body. Wright's inability to embalm Qohelet in his theory is emblematic. Verses encroach out of place, while others are lacking where they are wanted. Wright ignores whole phrases and they clamor for attention, repeating themselves throughout the text. And finally, an extra *hebel* intrudes to break—or elude—his net of numbers. It is telling that one of the words that Wright needs to delete in order to make his theory perfectly fit the text is *hebel*. This should be a warning to us. *Hebel* is a word that means nothing, a word that signals absence and ephemerality like vapor, like death itself, the name of that which, by definition, eludes all tightly woven theoretical nets. It is the very principle by which all desire for stable meaning must unravel.

The text approaches coherency only to pull away again, the structural theory almost fits but in the end the text slips away in a dance between disintegration and integration. The body grows and lives, but from the moment we are born, we are growing toward nothing but death. The grave pulls us inexorably toward its dark embrace—it is our fundamental seducer. Living is a dance between integration and disintegration, because life is predicated on death, the most permanent and pervasive absence of them all. All proposals of structure are motivated by a search for meaning that Qohelet, in principle, can never satisfy. These analyses of structure necessarily fail because Qohelet is an attempt to speak to the absence at the heart of meaning. Body and text alike decompose.

The Emperor Worm

Qohelet 3:2–8 is arguably he most rigidly structured passage in the entire book. It contains seven stanzas of seven pairs of binary oppositions. Seven is a perfect number in Hebrew numerology. The number is built into the very structures of the universe for it took seven days to create the world (Genesis 1:1–2:4a). This passage is rhythmic like the steady beat of the heart, or the inhale/exhale of breath through the nose, lips, mouth, chest rising and falling. As our heart and lungs form the core of our fleshy being, Qohelet 3:2–8 is the core of the book's structure. But, upon closer examination, there are moments when the beat skips, and the breathing falters.

The majority of the verses move at a fast clip, being composed of four words only for each couplet, following this pattern: עת ל--- ועת ל---. However, the ל (*lamed*) that introduces the infinitive is missing in two of the fourteen pairs: Qohelet. 3:4c–d, and Qoh. 3:8c–d. In addition to this, the verses in 2d and 5a–b and 5d are longer than the other verses. Additional words are added after the infinitive thus weighing down the sentence and slowing down the reader. In the most rigidly constructed poem in the book, there are slippages in its strict style.

It is a common method to elaborate further on the structure of this passage by dividing the couplets into negative and positive poles, like the opposite ends of a battery, that then drive the text and make it work. Commentators then look for some sort of pattern. For example, Loader discerns a chiastic pattern based upon his positive and negative division. Wright (1981) also has a structural proposal which divides the couplets into two sections (3:2–4, and 3:5–7) each of which ends with a remark about mourning. The obvious difficulty with proposals of this ilk is in determining if a particular act or event is "positive" or "negative." While it may be clear that peace is better than war, verse 3:5a has been particularly vexing: is it better to cast stones or to gather them up? In the end, these structural systems can only be maintained by assigning value (somewhat arbitrarily), and then supressing textual elements that do not fit.

But these are not the only disruption in the smooth surface of structure. The poem twists out of our control at the first verb: ללדת (lāledet). A prominent interpretation of this poem as a whole is that the 28 acts or events enumerated in its verses instruct the reader in the importance of knowing the right way to act and the right time to do so. The first actions—"a time to be born, and a time to die" (as generally translated, see for example the NRSV, NIV, JPS)—are not actions that one can choose to perform. The person is the passive recipient of the events in this verse only, but it makes sense that a pair that encompasses the outer limits of human experience and existence would introduce the poem (Blenkinsopp 1995, 56).

However, this is where the problems begin, for lāledet simply does not mean, "to be born." It is not in a passive construction; rather it is an infinitive construct which should then be translated as "to bear a child" or "to beget," depending on the sex of the subject. Commentators and translators twist the literal meaning of the word in order for it to be a perfect counterpart for למות (lāmût) "to die." Commentators desire this parallelism because if lāledet is translated accurately as "a time to bear" or "beget" then lāmût becomes the only event in the 28 that is outside of human control. Therefore, interpreters mistranslate lāledet in order to pull lāmût (death) into the structural system. By making birth a complement to death, death is given a role and thus becomes a "manageable" alterity. But death cannot be tamed and managed. In the Hebrew lāmût stands alone in alterity that interrupts life just as it disrupts stable and enduring meaning. Death cannot be contained by any system, for it is always in excess of our systems, or the lack at their heart. In Qohelet 3:2–8, death quite literally upsets the structure of the text thereby disrupting meaning and interpretation. The text decomposes.

My second example, chapter 12:1–8, is in the words of D. C. Fredericks (1991, 519) "the most obscure passage in Ecclesiastes." This passage is difficult for several reasons. First of all, there are many textual and grammatical problems in the passage, as well as words of uncertain meaning. Second, and more significantly, the referent(s) of the words on the page are indeterminate, and no one knows what Qohelet means. Why are the heavenly luminaries darkening (12:2)? Who are the guards, the strong men, the women who grind (12:3)? What are the birds doing exactly, and why (12:4)?

The dominant interpretation has been to read the passage as an allegory for the aging and dying body (Dulim 2001, 268–269). It is, in fact, the only passage in Qohelet that is consistently read in terms of the body, yet this body appears only symbolically, and its presence in the passage is far from certain. The connections between the signifying words and the signified body are tenuous and rely on a reader's hard work. The body here persists in the commentaries, but, paradoxically, in the text it is a veiled body, obscure, elusive, slippery, perhaps not even there at all.

The list of geriatric maladies that are diagnosed from these textual symptoms are extensive: blindness, deafness, impotence, constipation, ischuria, acrophobia, agoraphobia, anorexia, white hair, osteoporosis, isolation, tooth decay and loss . . . (Power 1952, 123–126). But in order to sustain the allegory or extended metaphor, the interpreter must sweat and strain. How else can one explain the equation of the locust in 12:5 with an aging penis? The failure to make the text fit this hermeneutical framework is usually laid at the feet of the author himself, instead of being seen as a problem with the interpretive device itself. George Barton, for example, blames Qohelet's "[o]riental richness of imagination and carelessness in exact use of metaphor" (1908, 187) for the difficulties he has keeping his allegory up.

There have been a few alternatives proposed. Some reject the allegorical meaning and present some sort of literal reading instead. These include the actual experience of the old (M. Gilbert, 1981), descriptions of winter and the coming of spring (O. Loretz, 1964), a gathering thunderstorm (Ginsburg, 1861; and Leahy, 1952), a ruined house (Sawyer, 1976; and Witzenrath, 1979), and a description of a community in mourning (C. Taylor, 1874). As this short list demonstrates, "literal" has a very different meaning for each interpreter (Fox 1988). Apocalyptic readings have also been proposed. For example, Timothy K. Beal reads these last words of Qohelet as "envisioning cosmopolitical disjuncture and breakdown" as well as "a longing for and a beckoning of what is beyond it" (Beal 1998, 292–293). Similarly, Yvonne Sherwood writes that Qohelet is "hollowing out the genre of eschatology" by contracting it "to the end of the world that all of us know—the 'end of my world, creeping up on me'" (2002, 113–114).[4]

The difficulties in interpreting the poem as a whole are a reflection of the difficulties in interpreting each word and phrase. For example, the passage begins with the command to "Remember your creator (בּוֹרְאֶיךָ *bôr'êkā*) in the days of your youth . . ." Qohelet uses an unusual word for the divine here, unique in the text and in the Bible as a whole. The uniqueness of the word in conjunction with doubts about how well any reference to God fits the context of the passage has caused many to propose dropping the clause altogether, or at least emending the word (for a list of those who hold these positions see Fox, 1988, 72; Seow 1999, 351–353). Dropping the א (*aleph*) yields "your pit" which can also be a reference to "your grave." However, there is no textual witness to support such an alteration of the word. And, although this designation for God is unusual, the idea of creation both human and divine is seen throughout the text. Qohelet is full of unusual constructions and unique words. Its phrases are plurivocal, equivocal, evocative, and unsubsumable—no overarching interpretation can suffice to bind all the diverse elements together. Could it be that Qohelet uses this unusual word for God precisely because it also conjures up images of the grave? In this case, nothing stands between "your creator" and "your grave" but an *aleph*, and since the *aleph* is nothing more than a hard breath of air, nothing stands between "your creator" and "your grave," birth and death, but a gasp.

In Qohelet 12:1–8, the stars blink out (v. 1), the grinders disappear (v. 3), the body returns to the earth (v. 7). Creation is undone. Qohelet describes and enacts the uncreating of the world experienced at one level as decay in the body, at another level as the dissolution of the social world and the cosmos, at another level in the decomposing of the book. In the text there are gaps, fragments, uncertain words, convoluted grammar, corrupted syntax. In this context, the pervasiveness of the allegorical interpretation is ironic. The body, or rather "the body," is a superimposition upon the text to resolve the resistances in the text to interpretation. The text is resisting interpretation because meaning itself is subject to death.

As a result, the meanings imposed on the text by interpreters multiply as if the text in its own death throes spews forth an excess of signification. At one moment the text is perhaps speaking about the body, the next a storm, house, scene of mourning, then the universe, social world, cosmos . . . the interpreter moves back and forth between allegory, symbol, literal meaning, metaphor, never able to secure the text to any one interpretation. Reenacting in a radical manner the condition of all language and the fate of all bodies, Qohelet decomposes.

The Gift of Death

God is the subject of the verb "to give" (*nātan*) more than God is the subject of any other verb in the book—in fact, God gives no less than twelve times in the book of Qohelet. God gives that which makes up human life: eating, drinking, and enjoyment; wisdom and knowledge; gathering and heaping; wealth, possessions and honor; all of the business with which we are busy. In sum, God gives life itself and, by implication, the death that makes life possible: "The affirmation of life is nothing other than a certain thought of death; it is neither opposition nor indifference to death—indeed one would almost say the opposite if this were not giving in to opposition" (Derrida 2001, 175). They are the same giving, the same gift: "a gift of life, or, what amounts to the same thing, a gift of death" (Derrida 1996, 97).

God's giving begins early in the book, and continues through the final chapter:

> There is nothing better for humans than to eat and drink, and find enjoyment in their toil. This also, I saw, is from the hand of God; for apart from him who can eat or who can have enjoyment? For to the one who pleases him God gives wisdom and knowledge and joy; but to the sinner he gives the work of gathering and heaping, only to give to one who pleases God. This also is *hebel* and chasing after wind. (2:24–26, cf. 6:2)

> I have seen the business that God gives to humanity to be busy with; he has made everything beautiful in its time; moreover he gives eternity into their hearts. (3:10–11)

> Also, it is God's gift that all humanity should eat and drink and take pleasure in all their toil. (3:13)

> Behold, this is what I have seen to be good: it is beautiful to eat and drink and find enjoyment in all the toil with which one toils under the sun the few days of the life God gives us; for this is our portion. (5:17 [Hebrew], 5.18 [English], cf. 8.15, 12:7)

> Also all humanity t whom God gives wealth and possessions and whom he enables to enjoy them, and to accept their portion and find enjoyment in their toil—this is the gift of God. (5.18 [Hebrew], 5.19 [English])
>
> And the dust returns to the earth as it was, and the breath returns to the God who gave it. (12:7)

What is a gift? This question is not as simple as it may at first appear. A gift, according to Derrida, must be freely given and freely received. It must not be a part of any system of return, barter, or debt. If it is, it ceases to be a gift and enters into an economy of exchange: "If the other *gives* me *back* or *owes* me or has to give me back what I give him or her, there will not have been a gift, whether this restitution is immediate or whether it is programmed by a complex calculation of a long-term deferral or différance" (1992, 12).

So in order for the gift to escape the economy of exchange, there must be a radical forgetting on the part of the giver as well as on the part of the one who gives: "If he recognizes it *as* gift, if the gift *appears to him as such*, if the present is present to him *as present*, this simple recognition suffices to annul the gift" (1992, 13). This involves a complete act of forgetting, both on the part of the giver and on the part of the recipient:

> For there to be gift, not only must the donor or donee not perceive or receive the gift as such, have no consciousness of it, no memory, no recognition; he or she must also forget it right away and moreover this forgetting must be so radical that it exceeds even the psychoanalytic categoriality of forgetting. (1992, 16)

But is this ever possible? Derrida points out that the conditions of the possibility of the gift are the conditions of its impossibility as well.

In this way, the gift is an aporia, and it signals alterity—it must be outside of the economy of human purpose. It must not be known, it must not be acknowledged, and it must not be remembered. It exceeds any categoriality or systematicity. In Qohelet, death is the eraser of memory and the extinguisher of differences. It comes from outside of us without warning, without expectation. All categories—animal and human, pious and impious, rich and poor, wise and foolish—are overcome by death. "There is gift, if there is any, only in what interrupts the system as well as the symbol, in a partition without return and without division . . ." (1992, 13). Perhaps the only gift possible is the gift of death.

The giving of death (dis)orients Qohelet's worldview—it (mis)shapes his theodicy, and his ethic. It is around "that" around which the other systems in the book gather and constitute themselves, but cannot be included or contained in any system "itself." The question of theodicy arises in the first statement of God's giving (2:24–26). In this passage, God is responsible for both the pleasures and pains of living. What any one individual receives is dependent upon their ability to please the deity. Or so it seems at first. But the summary statement ("This also is *hebel* and chasing after wind") introduces the undecidable—*hebel*—that undercuts Qohelet's traditional piety in a manner typical of the book as a whole. *Hebel* is the undecidable because it is a word that means nothing, a word that is empty and thus always signals the absence of meaning. This continues in the book with a fundamental questioning of a just system of reward and punishment (or at least any just system that humans could know and predict). For example, Qohelet states, "All that I have seen in the days of my *hebel*, there are the righteous who perish in their righteousness, and there are the wicked who prolong their lives in their wickedness" (7:15; cf. 8:14).

For Qohelet, death levels differences and this undermines any system of divine reward and punishment. How then should one act in the world? Does death render ethical action meaningless as well? Not quite, for Qohelet holds *hebel* in tension with a poignant concern for the well being of others: "Again I saw all the oppressions that are practiced under the sun. Look, the tears of the oppressed—with no one to comfort them! On the side of their oppressors there was power—with no one to comfort them" (Qoh. 4:1). For Derrida too, the gift of death does not annul ethical action but rather arouses an even more deeply felt impulse toward responsibility; it is in fact that which incites responsibility:

> The gift made to me by God as he holds me in his gaze and in his hand while remaining inaccessible to me, the terribly dissymmetrical gift of the *mysterium tremendum* only allows me to respond and only rouses me to the responsibility it gives me by making a gift of death, giving the secret of death, a new experience of death. (1996, 33)

The gift of death is made "to me." My death only happens to me. It cannot be taken away (if someone sacrifices himself for another, his death only postpones the other's death, it does not in fact replace it), nor can it be given in an act of murder (if someone kills another, that death is sill irreducibly the other's own—even though it is not something that s/he can possess) (1996, 41). It is in this sense that the gift is dissymmetrical and absolutely singular. It is out of this space of dissymmetrical goodness (the infinite given to the finite, see Qoh. 3:11) and "irreplaceable singularity" that responsibility arises. When locked in God's gaze, before God's face, we can only respond, be responsive, be responsible.

In Qohelet, death renders the desire for determinacy, memory, presence, and coherence—in short, the desire for meaning—*hebel*. The gift of death is an experience beyond our control, transgressing our boundaries, breaking our limits. Death literally breaks our bodies and this is enacted by Qohelet in the fracturing of the book's structure, the intrusion of death that resists systematicity (Qoh. 3:1–8) and coherent interpretation (Qoh. 12:1–8). The breaking open of the body and the book thereby opens us up to responsibility. The open wound of meaninglessness in Qohelet opens us up to the *mysterium tremendum,* the wholly other, and to the responsibility that the face of the other demands.

Notes

1. I would like to thank Joel Beaupré for his philosophical guidance and insightful editing of this essay.
2. No translation of this enigmatic and multivalent word suffices, for each attempt forecloses on too many other meanings and resonances. Therefore, I will retain the Hebrew throughout this chapter.

3. He employs a "careful verbal and structural analysis" but dispenses with the theory of the intentional fallacy. Though at the heart of New Criticism, Wright sees this dictum as a "weakness."
4. Neither Sherwood nor Beal argues for an exclusively eschatological meaning.

Works Consulted

Barton, George. A. 1908. *A Critical and Exegetical Commentary on the Book of Ecclesiastes.* International Critical Commentary. Edinburgh: T. & T. Clark.

Beal, Timothy K. 1998. "C(ha)osmopolis: Qohelet's Last Words." In *God in the Fray: A Tribute to Walter Brueggemann*, ed. Tod Linafelt and Timothy K. Beal, 290–304. Minneapolis: Fortress.

Blenkinsopp, Joseph. 1995. "Ecclesiastes 3:1–15: Another Interpretation." *Journal for the Study of the Old Testament* 66: 55–64.

Crenshaw, James. *Ecclesiastes.* Old Testament Library. Philadelphia: Westminster.

Derrida, Jacques. 1988. *Limited Inc.* Evanston, IL: Northwestern University Press.

———. 1992. *Given Time I: Counterfeit Money.* Trans. Peggy Kamuf. Chicago: University of Chicago Press.

———. 1996. *The Gift of Death.* Trans. David Wills. Chicago: University of Chicago Press.

———. 2001. *The Work of Mourning.* Ed. Pascale-Anne Brault and Michael Naas. Chicago: University of Chicago Press.

Dulim, Rachel Z. 2001. "'How Sweet is the Light': Qohelet's Age-Centered Teachings." *Interpretation* 55: 260–270.

Fox, Michael. 1988. "Aging and Death in Qohelet 12." *Journal for the Study of the Old Testament* 42: 55–77.

———. 1999. *A Time To Tear Down and A Time To Build Up: A Rereading of Ecclesiastes.* Grand Rapids: Eerdmans.

Fredericks, Daniel C. 1991. "Life Storms and Structural Unity in Qohelet 11:1–12:8." *Journal for the Study of the Old Testament* 52: 95–114.

Gilbert, M. 1981. "La description de la vieillesse en Qohelet XII 1–7, est-elle allégorique?" *Supplements to Vetus Testamentum* 32: 96–109.

Ginsburg, Christian David. 1861. *Coheleth.* London: Longman. [Reprint. New York: KTAV. 1970].

Leahy, Michael. 1952. "The Meaning of Ecclesiastes (12:2–5)." *Irish Theological Quarterly* 19: 297–300.

Loader, J. A. 1969. "Qohelet 3:2–8—A 'Sonnet' in the Old Testament." *Zeitschrift für die alttestamentliche Wissenschaft* 81: 240–242.

Loretz, Oswald. 1964. *Qohelet und der alte Orient: Untersuchungen zu Stil und theologischer.* Freiburg: Herder.

Power, A. D. 1952. *Ecclesiastes or The Preacher.* New York: Longmans, Green, and Co.

Robinson, H. Wheeler. 1946. *Inspiration and Revelation in the Old Testament.* Oxford: Clarendon.

Sawyer, J. F. A. 1976. "The Ruined House in Ecclesiastes 12: A Reconstruction of the Original Parable." *Journal of Biblical Literature* 94: 519–531.

Seow, Choon-Leong. 1995. "Qohelet's Autobiography." In *Fortunate the Eyes that See*, ed. A. Beck *et al.*, 257–282. Grand Rapids: Eerdmans.

———. 1997. *Ecclesiastes.* Anchor Bible. New York: Doubleday.

Sherwood, Yvonne. 2002. "'Not with a bang but a whimper': Shrunken Eschatologies of the Twentieth Century—and the Bible." In *Apocalyptic in History and Tradition*, ed. Christopher Rowland and John Barton, 94–116. Sheffield: Sheffield Academic Press.

Taylor, C. 1874. *The Dirge of Coheleth in Ecclesiastes XII*. London: Williams and Norgate.

Witzenrath, H. H. 1979. Süss ist das Licht . . . Eine literaturwissenschaftliche Untersuchung zu Koh 11,7–12,7. St. Ottilien: EOS.

Wright, Addison G. 1968. "The Riddle of the Sphinx: The Structure of the Book of Qohelet." *Catholic Biblical Quarterly* 30: 313–334.

———. 1980. "The Riddle of the Sphinx Revisited: Numerical Patterns in the Book of Qohelet." *Catholic Biblical Quarterly* 42: 38–51.

———. 1981. "For Everything There is a Season: The Structure and Meaning of the Fourteen Opposites (Ecclesiastes 3:2–8)." In *De la Torah au Messie: Mélanges Henri Cazelles*, ed. J. Dore et al., 321–328. Paris: Gabalda.

Chapter 16

And Sarah Died

Yvonne Sherwood

But is what we call deconstruction not above all a taking into account of forces of dissociation, dislocation, unbinding, forces, in a word, of difference and heterogeneity, such that a certain "and" itself can translate them?

(Derrida 2000, 291)

Would the logic of sacrificial responsibility within the implacable universality of the law, of its law, be altered, inflected, attenuated or displaced, if a woman were to intervene in some consequential manner? Does the system of this sacrificial responsibility and of the double "gift of death" imply at its very basis an exclusion or sacrifice of woman, according to one sense of the genitive or the other?

(Derrida 1993b, 76)

. . . I feel that I am also an heir: faithful as far as possible, loving, avid to reread . . . I love repetition, as if the future were entrusted to us, as if it were waiting in the cipher of a very ancient speech—one which has not yet been allowed to speak. All this, I realise, makes for a bizarre mixture of responsibility and disrespect. My attention to the present scene is at once intense, desperate, and a little distracted, as if anachronistic . . . We have gotten more than we think we know from "tradition," but the scene of the gift also obligates us to a kind of filial lack of piety, at once serious and not so serious, as regards the thinking to which we have the greatest debt.

(Derrida 1995b, 130)

Grammar Lesson

An "and" is a curious little thing. At its most minimal, it's merely a mark of spacing, punctuation, respiration—something negligible like a German filler-word such as *mal, doch, aber, halt, denn,* or *schon,* or a mere comma or a pause for breath. At its most good-natured or "tender" it functions as a "grammatical magnet," (Derrida 2000, 291), a mark of communitarian gathering. And/*But* an "and" can also have more of a "but" about it: it can mark objection, opposition, qualification, incompatibility, privation, a "to the exclusion of," "against," or "for want of," a sense that one needs the extra "and" (and maybe more than one) to supplement an inadequacy, lack, or un- or partial truth in what has preceded it. Logically the conjunction is always haunted by disjunction and vice versa: whether one is talking about something seemingly straightforwardly copulative (Abraham and Sarah, for example)[1] or about a conjunction strained to the point of seeming dissolution (Derrida and the Bible, perhaps), formal logic and the rules of grammar insist that the "and" always borders on the "but."[2] And (or "what's more," or "finally") should this overworked, over-stretched little "and" need some respite, it can be relieved, depending on the circumstances, by conjunctions ("but," "then," "for," et cetera) or adverbs ("therefore," "finally," "what's more") or link-words that double as adverb or conjunction, such as "also" or "thus."

The "and" (or "*waw*") is even more plastic in biblical Hebrew, as Derrida knows, even though he complains that Hebrew is all Hebrew to him and says that (though one can hardly make a monolingual "mother-tongue" amidst all those hyphens) he is more at home in philosophical Graeco-German and Christian-Anglo-Latin-French. Laying out his Hebrew homework in "Et Cetera," Derrida notes that in biblical Hebrew the *waw*, as (qualified, sort of) "and," marks the beginning of many sentences and modifies the *aspect* of the verb—meaning that it converts a completed (perfect) action into an uncompleted (imperfect) action (an effective "past" to an effective "future") *and* vice versa. He also talks about the particularly (?) tender, hospitable Arabic *wa*, "which can mean 'also' also, along with 'with,' or at the same time 'at the same time'," and wonders "whether the function thus marked [overtly] in *Hebrew or Arabic* is not at work, silently or otherwise, or differently, in all languages, in all texts?" (Derrida 2000, 291; my italics). But his sources seem to be mainly Arabic and he doesn't say explicitly how this might apply to Hebrew. This particular page of his Hebrew homework seems to be missing.

If (bearing with me) we turn to our Hebrew primers, we do indeed find the *waw* described by Derrida: the so-called "*waw consecutive*," "*waw conservative*," or "*waw conversive*," that little line (ו) that frustrates all students with its seemingly perverse back-flips between past and future, complete and incomplete. The fact that even the very un-Derridean Weingreen's *Grammar for Classical Hebrew* maintains that (Western) logic "fails"[3] to explain this simple line that works, effectively, as a grammatical hinge, axis of rotation or fold in time, suggests that the *waw* could potentially serve (in ways that no one, including Derrida, has yet explored) as an unexpected ancient ally for deconstruction. For isn't deconstruction constantly working at the tense/tension between the "archive" and the "to come," so that another appropriate description of deconstruction might be "the opening up of passageways between the complete and the incomplete"? However, as well as the "waw consecutive" there is *also* (and this is what Derrida's account of the Hebrew *waw* elides), the charmingly titled "*waw copulative*": the *waw* that very tenderly, very eagerly couples with amazing agility in a variety of positions. *The Dictionary of Classical Hebrew* informs us that the *waw copulative* runs the whole gamut of conjunction-disjunction from "together with, in the company of," "likewise, just as, just like," "and especially, in particular," "as for," "both and," "and another, and a different," "but, on the contrary," "when, even though," "so," "so, in that case," "or," "but," "thus," "for, because," "therefore," "upon, after," "when," "then" (conditional *and* causal), "since," "seeing that," "and yet," "now then," to "together with," and/but that it can also signify a mere pause for breath (like the one required at the end of this list); *while* (another modulation of the "and") that well-thumbed classroom resource known as "Brown Driver Briggs" romanticises the infinitely pliable *waw* as preserving the economy and "lightness and grace of movement" loved by the Hebrew "ear" (Clines, *The Dictionary of Classical Hebrew* Vol. II 1995; cf. Brown et al., *A Hebrew and English Lexicon of the Old Testament* 1939 [1906], 252). And though grammars tend to keep the "copulating" and "converting" *waw* apart from one another in different chapters, the so-called *waw conversive* leads to similar problems of translation. When you read what would otherwise be "he went" with a *waw*, as Derrida puts it, "agglutinated" (Derrida 2000, 290) on the front, you not only have to "convert" the aspect to "he will go" (complete to incomplete) but you also have to think about the relationship between adjacent phrases and sentences. As well as "modifying" or converting the tense, the *waw* introduces what Derrida calls a "principle of discernment" (Derrida 2000, 290) raising the question "Is this 'But he will go,' or 'So he will go,' 'Then he will go'?" *et cetera*, and so on.

Luckily, the grammar-weary reader need only take two points away from this high-speed, crash-course version of *Biblical Hebrew 101*:

1. Unlike Modern Hebrew, Biblical Hebrew has no regularly used "but" (or even "or") and so no resources for at least attempting to *draw a line* between conjunction and disjunction. It only has a line, a ו which functions, often undecideably, like the Derridean fold or the tender/divisive device that we call the stroke/slash.[4]
2. Because the *waw* is structurally necessary to any Hebrew narrative but also ambiguous in the nature of its "copulation," it compels us to *decide*: between a grammatical no-thing and some-thing; between a purely incidental pause and a necessary pause *for thought*; and between sentences and clauses that merely *happen* to have been gathered together and those that must be brought to bear on one another because they *caused* one another to happen, in time. By consistently translating the "*waw*" as "and," the *Authorised Version* replicates the problem and defers the decision to the English reader. For example, obsessing on that crucial biblical moment where "She took the fruit thereof and did eat, *and gave also to her husband with her; and he did eat.* And the eyes of them both were opened, and they knew that they were naked" (Genesis 3:6–7), English Literature critic John Mullan recently observed how the action that we gloss, starkly and unidirectionally, as "the fall" is in fact enmeshed in parataxis reminiscent of Don DeLillo. There could not be a starker illustration of the importance of the minutiae of grammar, for whole worlds of cultural histories and gender disjunctions/conjunctions are balanced on that little "and" (Mullan 2003).

The subject of this essay is not the woman called Eve/*Havvah*/"Life" (Genesis 3:20) who, according to a certain pointed inflection of the *waw*, brings death to the world, but Sarah, a woman who, in a much less familiar way, interrupts the world of the beginning with death. Whereas the clause "and [she] gave also to her husband and he ate" brings about a necessary rupture *required* by the Christian theological narrative, the phrase "And Sarah died" (Genesis 23:2) brings about a series of disruptions that fundamentally unsettle the peaceful tranquillity of the Abrahamic family, and it does so specifically through the ambiguation of the *waw* . . .

And Sarah Died

Genesis 23, following hard on the heels of the "sacrifice" of Isaac by Abraham in Genesis 22, begins:

[1] And the life of Sarah was one hundred and twenty seven years; this was the span of Sarah's life [or lives].[5] [2] And Sarah died (ותמת שרה) at Kiriath-arba (that is Hebron) [this is the biblical author's own parenthesis] in the land of Canaan; and Abraham went in to mourn for Sarah and to weep for her there. [3] Abraham rose up from beside his dead and said to the Hittites, [4] "I am a stranger and an alien residing among you; give me property among you for a burying place, so that I may bury my dead out of my sight."

[Derrida's commentary, and my analysis that follows, is based on the whole chapter, and so those who want to participate in this little Bible study are advised, at this point, to consult the biblical text.]

The extinguishing of the life (or two lives?)[6] of Sarah and the ensuing scene in which Abraham reverse-negotiates so as to pay Ephron the Hittite a full, even excessive, price for the cave of Machpelah as a burial place for her is a scene that Derrida returns to, appropriately enough, twice. The ghost of the biblical Sarah finds her way into a work of mourning entitled simply "Sarah Kofman":

At what moment does Abraham reawaken the memory of his being in a foreign land? For Abraham does indeed recall that he is destined by God to be a guest (*gêr*), an immigrant, a foreign body in a foreign land ("Go from your country and your kindred and your father's house," "your offspring shall be guests in a land that is not theirs" [Genesis 12:1; 15:13]). Presenting himself as a foreigner who has no home, keeping watch over the body of the dead, his dead, Sarah (the woman who laughs when told she is to have a child, and then pretends not to have laughed),[7] Abraham requests a place for her. A final dwelling, a final resting place. He wants to be able to give her a place worthy of her, but also a place that would separate her from him, like death from life, a place "in front of me" says one translation, "out of my sight" says another (Genesis 23:4). And for this— you know the scene—he wants to pay, this husband of Sarah, the woman who laughs; he insists on it, he wants at all costs that this not be given to him. In fact, Abraham had himself also laughed on hearing the same news, the news of the belated birth of Isaac. (*Yiskhak*; he laughs: Isaac, the coming of Isaac, makes them both shake with laughter, one after the other; Isaac is the name of the one who comes to make them laugh, to laugh about his coming, at his very coming, as if laughter should greet a birth, the coming of a happy event, a coming of laughter, a coming to laugh: come-laugh-with-me.) The moment having come to laugh was also the moment when Elohim named Sarah. He gave her a new name, deciding that Abraham, who had himself received a new name, would no longer call her Sarai, my princess, but Sarah, princess [Genesis 17:15, 17] (Derrida 2001c, 187).[8]

And Derrida returns to the grave of Sarah, located in foreign-promised land, in the "Hostipitality" seminar:

> . . . In the scene of Genesis 23, Sarah's burial, as a scene of hospitality—since Abraham opens by saying, "I myself am an alien among you" when he asks for a burial ground—this scene which follows the so-called interrupted sacrifice of Isaac, that is the substitution of the ram for the son ["Abraham went and took the ram and offered it up as a burnt offering instead of his son" (22.13)—"in place of (à la place)" says Dhormes, "at the site (au lieu de)" says Chouraqui, his "unique son," "your only one" as God said: it is a matter of substituting an animal for the unique beloved, the preferred unique one—J.D.], the scene of Sarah's burial, Sarah whom Yahweh had, you recall, "visited" (Dhormes), "sanctioned" (Chouraqui), in order to give her Isaac in her old age—the scene of Sarah's burial can also be read as a scene of sacrifice and of substitution. Indeed, Abraham absolutely insists on paying for the field and the cave, the site of burial that the Hittites absolutely insist on giving him. In this extraordinary scene (that I will read in part) in which one insists on paying, the others on giving without being paid, one has the feeling that Abraham insists on sacrificing what he calls "the full price" or "four hundred shekels of silver" in order to mourn Sarah and to owe nothing. Both parties want to cancel the debt with a gift, but a sacrificial gift, a gift that presupposes some sacrifice. And it is Hebron, the site of Sarah's burial but also of Abraham's, upon which the scene of sacrificial appropriation has not ceased perpetuating itself until now, just yesterday, through so many *substitueries*. (Derrida 2002b, 415)

Derrida invokes the scene with a Lacanian wave of the hand ("You know the scene"), as if we were all still, these days, avid Bible readers, as if this story of Sarah's death were not permanently in the shadows of the more sensational scene of near-death that precedes it; and/*but* then goes on to read this allegedly "familiar" text as one that introduces strange[r]ness at the heart of the "Abrahamic" home. The first densely packed commentary is woven together with the personal memories and the written archive that are, for Derrida, "Sarah Kofman." The biblical death of Sarah seems to insert itself here because it refracts Derrida and Kofman's own intermingling themes: of the separation of the name and the body that comes with writing and dying (and so the question of memory/memorial and the labour of mourning); of laughter that is *not* the opposite of anxiety and suffering; and of the bondedness between the "thought of death" and "the affirmation of life" (Derrida 2001c, 175). Although this is to venture much further than Derrida does, at least explicitly, into wider biblical terrain, it seems to me that this resonant evocation of the biblical Sarah who *laughs* and *dies* and, together with her husband, "*shakes* with laughter," evokes something of the relentless absurdity, fragility, laughter *and* (yet/but) convulsion and terror that characterises the life of Israel: a convulsiveness embodied in the figure of Sarah's son, "Isaac/He Laughs" (father of Jacob/Israel/"He struggles"), squeezed from a ninety-year old belly as absurdly-miraculously as a divinely-inspired belly laugh, only then to be balanced precariously on a knife-edge moment between the intervening angel and the fire. The liminal state of the dangling *fils*[9] as son and cord (evoking that strange male umbilical cord that strings together the genealogical chains of life that pass from father to son to grandson) highlights the miraculous sur-viving, over-living that characterizes, from the beginning, the convulsive, fragile life of Israel. The laugh-death child is deeply suggestive of ways in which the existential figure of "Israel" becomes an extreme icon of the precariousness of human living, that makes one want to laugh till one cries and cry till one laughs.

And—thus—Isaac evokes the peculiar characteristics of the promise: that which seeks out the most unpromising of contexts in order to draw attention to itself. (For it is no accident that the promise becomes precariously material/incarnate as a son given because/despite the barrenness of a mother and as a land given because/despite its possession by others: for from the moment of that first giving, Yhwh makes it clear that the land is already teeming with Kenites, Kenizzites, Kadmonites, Hittites, Perizites, Rephaim, Amorites, Canaanites, Girgashites, and Jebusites, and that Abraham is to be a foreigner, foreign-body, *hôte*, late-come "host" and (*but*) firstly "guest").[10] It is this second dimension of the promise, this aspect of dwelling, that Derrida dwells on, most explicitly in the "Hostipitality" seminar, where the death of Sarah is put in its scriptural home among *unheimlich* Genesis texts that foreground the counterintuitive figure of Abraham the stranger. By way of contrast to the familiar, welcoming, figure of the Abrahamic as emblem of hospitality, ecumenism and inter-faith negotiations; by way of counterpart to the widely known scene at Mamre where Abraham welcomes the three angels (Genesis 18:1–15), Derrida tracks an itinerant Abrahamic whose meandering path wanders from God's command in 12:1, "Go from your country and your kindred and your father's house" (and, in Derrida's gloss, "*be a stranger*"), through 15:13 "Know for certain that your offspring [*ceux de ta race*] shall be aliens [*des hôte* or *des métèques*—"aliens" in the pejorative sense] in a land that is not theirs," to his confession to the Hittites that he is "a stranger and an alien" (23:4), and not (yet?) one of the *am ha-aretz* (23:12).[11] What Derrida does not say is that this protracted narrative resulting in the purchase of a cave- or grave-sized piece of promised land (a six by four piece of Canaan, with surrounding field and trees thrown in) is typical of the soap-opera-like biblical saga of beginning as it moves, falteringly, towards the attainment of son and land on the principle of one-step-forward and four-steps-back. As, after many false starts, Abraham has had, and almost killed, a son, so he who has *already* gone down into Canaan, only to be expelled from it by famine and driven out to be an "alien" in Egypt (12:10) (and one has to ask why the gravitational pull of Genesis seems to be constantly tugging Abraham Egyptwards, towards four hundred years slavery in a land not his or his descendants' own [Genesis 15:13]) is now, as the NRSV translation puts it, "going in"[12] again. The patriarch, as if in *passing*, puts down minor roots in Canaan and (but) does so, Derrida says, not through birth but through death (Derrida 2002b, 414). If it is to be taken field-by-field and death-by-death, the possession of Canaan is sure to be a slow and unsure one. And what does it suggest when those who go ahead into the land are the corpses, as if the front line of occupation is a cemetery? Is this then to be a land occupied by the dead?[13]

Taking their stand on the firm, if dangerously pedestrian, ground of empiricism and solid historicity, and strangely eschewing what could (loosely) be called existential questions, professional biblical commentators tend to focus, exclusively, on questions of dating and authorship. The main concerns of the professional workers who mine these texts seem to be: the historical feasibility of "Hittites" (who seem to be rather geographically and chronologically lost in this chapter); the fit, or otherwise, between the biblical narrative and ancient codes of negotiation (this story appears as something of a delightful "miniature" of "adroit Oriental conversation" according to Gerhard von Rad); the question of whether, and how far, this story can be seen as an aetiology of an Israelite stake in the ancient sacred site of the "tombs of the patriarchs"[14] (with the associated question of whether the biblical narrative is "unspiritual" if it simply describes how Abraham erected an "Abraham, the Ur-Israelite was here" marker in a piece of promised land); and the question of the authorship of this minor addendum to the "sacrifice" story (since it reflects an obsession with genealogy, minutiae and material possession, this minor vignette is read as belonging to the lesser [?] Pentateuchal source [formerly?] known as "P").[15] For Derrida, the text is less, well, "buried," in the hermetically sealed zone of the past, and becomes far more than a minor priestly detour from the really important business of beginning, as the burial of Sarah is made to resonate with existentially and universally resonant questions of gift, negotiation, mourning, and above all *sacrifice* as the *longed-for absolution of debt*. Crucially—and here he departs from all the biblical commentators who seem to be preoccupied with the Patriarch-Hittite axis of negotiation—Derrida's Abraham is involved in *bilateral* negotiations with the Hittites *and with Sarah*, whose strangely nonpassive body is envisaged as some kind of accusing agent or *existential creditor*. His focus is on the reverse barter situation between Ephron and Abraham—a curious scene of competition for outgiving and out-losing played out at the level of shekels and property and, one could add, (though Derrida does not) strangely amplified by the competition in word- and status-loss that takes place between Abraham's abasing description/confession[16] of himself as a mere "stranger and alien," and the Hittites' elevation of him as a "prince of God/mighty prince/elect of God among us" (23:6). (This exchange seems in turn to suggest ongoing *negotiation* of the status of the ever-travelling, unsettled Abrahamic, as it moves between "an Abraham below the Hittites" and "an Abraham well above them, like an Abraham-god.")[17]

Derrida's Abraham "*insists*" on paying the full price of four hundred shekels (that is, forty six kilos!) of silver—seemingly the perfect antithesis of a "good price," given that David was able to buy the temple site and the materials of sacrifice for just fifty silver shekels (2 Sam. 24:24; Vawter 1977, 265)[18]—and he does so in order, through a substitutionary sacrifice of money, to "owe nothing." The exact phrase that Derrida uses to describe Abraham's purpose in purchasing what must be the most overinflated piece of real estate in Old Testament/Tanakh is "*to mourn Sarah and to owe nothing*"—a phrase in which mourning and owing and Sarah and debt are provocatively connected by "ands," and in which those "ands" can even be read as saying that the ultimate debt is *not* to the Hittites *but* to Sarah. Crucially the strangely active corpse of Sarah is regarded as seeing Abraham and demanding something of Abraham, so that undergirding his surface negotiations with the Hittites are the "mighty prince's" more pressing posthumous negotiations with his "princess" (Genesis 17:15). (This move, unique as far as I know, in the last two hundred years of professional labour on Genesis 23[19]—feminist, womanist and otherwise—would then make Sarah's corpse so much more than a limp object of negotiation in these [reverse] exchanges between men.) For Derrida, it seems, this passage is not so much about the authenticated passage of land into Abraham's hands and so substantive *possession*, but about Abraham's struggle to *dispossess* himself of his dead wife. The major struggle is not that of a "foreign body" for legitimate and rightful possession of a little bit of Canaan, but that foreign body's struggle with his own "foreign body."

Like the ancient annotators and "pointers" of the text who note in the margin that this is the only occurrence of the term "*maiti*; מתי" "*my* dead,"[20] as if that might (one day) mean something, and become a *point*,[21] Derrida seizes on the distinctive wording of Abraham's request—that I might bury "*my dead* [*maiti*]" "out of my sight," or literally "from *before me*" or "from before my face" (23:4)—and suggests that perhaps that little dot or hiriq and yod, that little first person suffix on מתי, is making a point of Abraham's need to separate "death from life," and "her from him." If so, then Abraham's debt to "my dead" would point to the universal sense of guilt, of obligation of those who sur-vive, or "overlive," and to the labour of mourning that is connected to the [over]remuneration of the dead—poignantly expressing itself in the lavish sacrificial "waste" of Taj Mahals or polished mahogany coffins. And the itinerant, wandering Abraham would become a universally recognisable itinerant worker/labourer in mourning. Sarah's body would also represent (and here we allow a little bit of Derrida to mingle with a little bit of Kristeva) the human waste which we must thrust aside, scarcely and with difficulty, to go on living (Abraham's need to bury Sarah out of sight in the land of milk and honey is reminiscent of nothing so much as the instinctive recoil from those repugnant precursors of death and human waste such as blood, body fluids, shit, the "skin of milk"; Kristeva 1982, 2–3).[22] But universals aside, might there also be something very singular about the magnitude of this *particular* debt? The fact that the overpayment is so excessively large—that it amounts to sacks of silver piled up on such a tiny piece of land, as if attempting to be a very hyperbole of disproportion—and the fact that this is the only biblical narrative where the death and burial of anyone, let alone a woman, is so belaboured (the only remote analogy being the burial of Jacob in the very same field of Ephron the Hittite [Genesis 49:29–50:14]) suggests that there might be some particular freight to this work of mourning that runs to a pile of shekels and a pile of words (twenty verses to be precise). And (moreover) the way in which the narrative heaps, as it were, on top of all these words and shekels Abraham's "weeping" over Sarah, and Isaac's need for comfort over the lack of her (Genesis 24:67), suggests that this particular woman's body leaves a very *pointed* narrative absence.[23]

Abraham "Sacrificed" *and* ("in the same way") Sarah Died (Complementary Relations Between Genesis 23 *and* Genesis 22)

Even as it takes its cue from them, the preceding discussion goes beyond Derrida's two self-confessedly "partial" readings of the death of Sarah, which are clearly written in the shadows of the mightier text that haunts him: the virtual "sacrifice" of Isaac in Genesis 22. By reading Genesis 23 as a relatively minor appendix to the more fundamental test that precedes it, Derrida comes close to the professional biblical commentators (who tend to cast Sarah's burial as a minor "P" epilogue to a major "E" text that has already climaxed on Mount Moriah)[24] although, without recourse to the editorial scissors that cut the text up into discrete sources (thus absolving the critic of responsibility to think in terms of relationship), Derrida does attempt to conjugate the conjunction and probe the relationship/rationale between the two. And yet (my "and yet" here having a sense of qualification, disagreement) the "principle of discernment" (Derrida 2000, 290) between the two texts is conjugated by Derrida in one direction only, as the "and" in "And Sarah died" becomes a reflective, comparative "and," an "as . . . so," or "likewise" along the lines of "In the same manner, Sarah died, and (again), Abraham sacrificed, Abraham substituted, Abraham *paid*." For Derrida, the death of Sarah, *like* the near-death of Isaac, becomes a scene of *sacrifice* and *substitution*: as the Abraham of Genesis 22 offers a ram instead of (literally "in the place of") Isaac and so discharges, at some remove, his obligation to the voice of God, so the Abraham of Genesis 23 attempts to discharge his debt to Sarah's body and to the foreigner through the "sacrifice" of silver shekels.

Thus Derrida's reflections on the death of Sarah are *modest* and *moderate*: insofar as he conceives of the relationship between the two texts as basically peaceable (coexisting in mimetic togetherness); insofar as he sees Genesis 22 as coming before and setting the paradigm for Genesis 23 (thus reading chronologically, that is, *straightforwardly*); and insofar as he uses the man Abraham and the substitutionary acts of Abraham as the axis of reflection (his reading of these scenes of sacrifice is Kierkegaardian in this respect).[25] Though Derrida sees Abraham as in some (as yet unspecified) sense in debt to his wife, he does not explore what might happen if he were to be substituted by her, as the central source of action in the text. In his reading, the two texts join hands across the shared, conventional figure of patriarch-as-agent, just as surely as they join hands across the essentially comparative *waw*. In Derrida's implied typology, Genesis 23 seems to reflect Genesis 22 back to itself as in a mirror darkly: this second, secondary text is to Genesis 22, effectively, what the "ram" is to Isaac and the "shekels" are to Sarah (thus Genesis 23 supplements Genesis 22 and does it no harm). For all the strange and foreign ways in which he declines the Abrahamic grammars (Abraham as foreign body, foreign worker, itinerant worker in mourning, guest, and host, Abraham in default, sacrificing to acquit himself of debt to God, the Hittites, and Sarah, and so on, *et cetera*), Derrida ultimately declines—or rather seems unaware of the possibility of—the most radical declension of the Abrahamic grammar: the one that would bring it into contact with the accusing, active, deconstructive force of Sarah's death. For Derrida, for now, the two chapters exist peaceably side by side and merely chart the two parallel tracks through which human sacrifice is metaphorized and metamorphosized. The first text maps the displacement of human blood into the blood of an animal, or scape-ram (compare the substitution of the human firstborn by the paschal lamb in Exodus, or the scapegoat on Yom Kippur [Leviticus 16]), and the second the substitution of flesh by money (compare the monetary redemption of the son in the ancient Jewish tradition of *pidyon ha-ben*[26]).

In Derrida's configuration of Genesis 22 and 23 the two narratives cross around figures of gifts of, and to, death; around the metaphorisation and substitution of obligation and sacrifice; and around a certain shaking and trembling with laughter and (but?) fear. The coming of Isaac that, in Derrida's gloss makes his parents "*shake* with laughter" reminds me of all that trembling, and all that delicate analysis of what might be meant by trembling, that spreads out from the metaphorical epicentre that is Kierkegaard's *Fear and Trembling* in the first few pages of the third chapter of *Donner La Mort/The Gift of Death*. (For these remarkable paragraphs on trembling and the *mysterium tremendum* see Derrida 1999, 79–82; 1993b, 53–56. All the quotations sprinkled across this paragraph are taken from this passage.) Here, in a way that resonates with Kristeva's work on abjection and all that we have said so far about the fragility and precariousness of nascent Israel, dangling on a *fils*, Derrida outlines that which precisely cannot be outlined or diagnosed (that is, trembling) as the body's response to what we cannot see, or foresee, and to what exceeds and *undoes* "my seeing and my knowing [*mon voir et mon savoir*]" although "it concerns the inner parts of me, right down to my soul, down to the bone." Trembling has to do with the future and with the eye of the other who sees and thinks me in secret (without me ever knowing who/where I am in their regard); it has to do with unknowing, with the disproportion of knowing and a default of the I that finds its ultimate expression in the theological figure of the eye of God who sees me, thoroughly, and sees the future, thoroughly, without that exhaustive gaze being reciprocated or under my control. And this has everything to do with responsibility for "It is on the basis of this gaze that singles me out [*ce regarde qui me regarde*] that my responsibility comes into being." Derrida, in a certain sense, "reads" trembling, like laughter, like tears (and remember that Abraham *weeps* for Sarah) as an enigmatic symptomatology of the body, as a symptom of all that lies outwith the domain of the active and controlling "I." For trembling, like laughing, happens to us as if from way beyond or deep within us: one does not make oneself tremble any more than one makes oneself laugh. Trembling, like crying, like mourning, like laughing, intimates something insufficient, un-able,[27] insolvent about the self—something that has to do with responsibility as culpability, the unfulfilled obligation of the self to others and to God, that finds its expression in delicate/poignant theological discourses of religious soteriology and its ritual expression in sacrificial gifts. Trembling also has to do with time: with the unknown relations between what is completed (and so known) and what is incomplete, unknown, and yet to come. It has to do with the inability to predict, in advance, the logics, ties, binds, and tangles through which "an irrefutable past (a shock that has been felt, a traumatism that has already affected us)" will repeat, displace, substitute itself again.

Crossing, as they do, around laughter, trembling and sacrifice, Derrida's analyses of Genesis 22 and 23 share the hallmark closeness of that very *close*, very intimate, "Derridean" reading that takes the biblical texts *down* into the Lilliputian minutiae of disarming, child-like questions (asking, with a Kierkegaardian or Augustinian faux(?)-naivety, why we tremble, why we mourn, why we laugh), and at the same time *out* into the Brobdignagian realms of what we loosely call global politics, and questions of what is going on (often, but not always, "so badly") in the name of religion today. As, unlike any existing professional biblical commentary, *The Gift of Death* locates Abraham's foundational sacrificial altar as the deep foundation of the contemporary flash-(fire/knife)-point that is the Jewish Temple Mount and also the site of Dome of the Rock and the Al Aqsa Mosque, not far from the way of the cross (for Moriah is also intimately bound to the Golgotha of the Christian passion), so

Derrida reads Genesis 23 as bound to another particular "trench war" in the ongoing wars of the Abrahamic.[28] Derrida interrupts his 1997 "Hostipitality" seminar to observe how "just yesterday" (as close, in fact, to 1997 as 1994) this site that hosted ancient sacrificial and substitutionary negotiations became a site of more *substitueries* (and, like Gil Anidjar, I can think of no English translation that would even begin to do justice to the combination of *substituer* and *tuer*, "to kill," in French). Resisting the traditional historical reification of the biblical as a museum piece or artefact preserved in the temperature-controlled, cool zones of scholarship (a professional insulation every bit as stifling as the "fundamentalist" wrapping of the "biblical" in the swaddling of the "sacred" in the sense of perfect-literal-holy-free-from-question-free-from-taint), Derrida folds the text—as if on the hinge of a *waw*—to explore how this text of completed, past action opens up, converts, twists, flips into the uncompleted actions of our todays and our too-near yesterdays. He sets up "Genesis 23 *and/but* March 1994" as a provocative, tangled conjunction/disjunction in which the "and/but" can be taken neither as simple linear arrow of scriptural cause and contemporary effect (as if the Bible makes Baruch Goldsteins, or as if Abraham coming to mourn from Kiriath Arba leads directly to Goldstein coming down from Kiriath Arba to wreak carnage at the *el-Haram el-Ibrahimi el-Khalil* mosque), nor as an arbitrary, negligible juxtaposition (as if the Bible is in no way related to such aberrant interpretations of the "Abrahamic"); for there can be no escape here into pure conjunction or pure disjunction, as too-credulous defenders of a pure secularism and of a pure religiosity want, respectively, to say. By pressing the question of relation between the first "Abrahamic" corpse and the corpses of twenty-nine Arab Muslims piled, as it were, on top of her, Derrida is responding to the always imperfectly fulfilled obligation to negotiate between what we loosely call "the present" and "the past"; he is effectively setting up negotiations between Abraham's negotiations (with his foreigners and with his dead) and con-temporary negotiations between the living and their dead (for how can this outbreak of violence be severed from the desire to do perfect justice to the Abrahamic dead, preserved in sacred scriptures and buried in a special corner of promised land?). Derrida's reading of Genesis 23 can be read as a piece of interventionist exegesis structured around an Abraham who, as if in contestation of the spectre of the Fundamentalist Absolute Patriarch or simplistic Ur-Father, is *always already* in negotiation and is conglomerate *hostandstranger* (and, one could add, *princeandalien*) from the very beginning. It can be seen as a strategic attempt to probe the shortfall in responsibility of the biblical to the contemporary and vice versa (to raise the question of the falling short of one in the eyes of the other), and an attempt to rewrite the biblical in such a way that it bears the scars and pressures of what is loosely called "the times."[29] And thus inevitably, (and unconsciously) it begs the question of the shortfall of responsibility in professional biblical scholarship.

Derrida's analyses of Genesis 22 and 23 share another hallmark of typically "Derridean" biblical exegesis: a certain universalisation, humanisation and translation of the text into existential questions that will mean something to all poor existing individuals (be they "Abrahamic," atheist, agnostic, or one of the many inhabitants of the globe to whom the name and scriptures of Abraham have never meant anything),[30] and at the same time an acute respect for the idiosyncrasy and untranslatability of this particular text. Thus, as he is dramatically compelled to *choose* between his competing obligations to God and to Isaac, the Abraham of *The Gift of Death* becomes a figure for all of us who, tangled in a thicket of competing obligations, must choose between greater and lesser loves, responsibilities, others and make those decisions/calculations silently, in secret; and (but) at the same time, he remains uniquely Abraham, resistant to all extrapolations and comparisons because "the absolute uniqueness of Yhwh does not tolerate analogy" and "we are not all Abrahams, Isaacs or Sarahs either" (1993b, 79). Similarly, the briefer, slighter, Derridean Abraham extracted from Genesis 23 seems to become a figure for the universal obligation to works of mourning, but at the same time, according to the same logic that he applies to Genesis 22, Abraham must also be something *more and less than Everymourner* just as Sarah must be *more and less than EveryCorpse*. However, the particularity of Abraham's obligation to *his* dead and the *particular* significations of the lives and deaths of Sarah are not questions addressed by Derrida, even though he *begs* them, as he draws attention to Abraham's insistence on paying so-much-more-than-the-full-price, and to his textually *marked* desire to remove (bury) his guilt/his dead/ responsibility from before his eyes.

The idiom of a question *begged*, but not pursued, implies the shortfall of faithfulness and fullness that defines and provokes all acts of reading and writing, and suggests that, like Abraham, Derrida has not yet done enough for/with the figure of Sarah's corpse. And—yet—the question is *begged* precisely as a consequence of the question that Derrida raises, for the first time, of the *debt to Sarah*: that is, the debt of his own slim text becomes more overt because of the potential fecundity of its questions (conversely the seemingly self-sufficient self-adequation of a piece of writing increases in inverse proportion to the safeness and smallness of the questions that it ponders, which perhaps explains, by way of contrast, the seeming exhaustiveness, even saturation, of the commentary genre).[31] And (moreover) slim and slender hints as to how we might, in our writing, render the debt to Sarah, and parse the *precise* meanings of Sarah, can be gleaned by scavenging in corners of "Sarah Kofman" and *The Gift of Death*. The first hint comes in "Sarah Kofman" where the two lives and deaths of Sarah (those of Sarah Kofman and Sarah-wife-of-Abraham) cross around figures of laughter-as-suffering and also (at least in the subterranean levels of the essay and in footnotes) laughter as that which causes suffering/trembling within the cultural monuments and edifices that are (relatedly?) idealising and man-made. Derrida imagines the ghost of Sarah Kofman stalking his prose, "making fun of [him]," "taking [him] to task," preventing him from "denying, transfiguring, sublimating, or idealising" the story of their "impossible friendship": he wants to amplify her dissenting, protesting laughter and explore the ways in which, in him and in this piece of writing, the "she in me . . . take[s] me to task" (2001c, 173). And (then, similarly) in a footnote, he imagines her biblical namesake's laughter as deflating divine omnipotence and provoking divine anger: "When told about the coming of Isaac (*yiskhak*: he laughs), Sarah laughs and then pretends not to have done so. But God becomes indignant that she might be doubting his omnipotence and contradicts her denial: 'Oh yes, you did laugh' (Genesis 18:15)" (from Derrida's own footnote, reproduced here in footnote 7). The second, slightly larger, paragraph-long hint in *The Gift of Death* parses the declensions and meanings of Sarah around the figure of the "sacrifice of Sarah," as, in a provocative twist on Kierkegaard, Derrida suggests that Hyper-Secret-Abraham is out-silenced and out-secreted by the woman, Sarah:

It is difficult not to be struck by the absence of women in [this] monstrous yet banal stor[y], it is the story of father and son, of masculine figures, of hierarchies among men (God the father, Abraham, Isaac; the woman Sarah is *she to whom nothing is said*). *Would the logic of sacrificial responsibility within the implacable universality of the law, of its law, be altered, inflected, attenuated or displaced, if a woman were to intervene in some consequential manner? Does the system of this sacrificial responsibility and of the double gift of death imply at its very basis an exclusion or sacrifice of woman, according to one sense of the genitive or the other? Let us leave the question in suspense.* (Derrida 1993b, 76–77; my italics).[32]

Like Grace Jantzen (see her frustrated "Why? Why not pursue it" in Jantzen 1998, 136), I confess that I am disappointed with the suspension of the question of "the sacrifice of Sarah"—a suspension in danger of leaving women feeling like an Isaac eternally poised (stuck) between their "redeeming angel" and their "knife;" between a sense that the figure of the sacrificed-sacrificing mother might lie at the very heart of all that *The Gift of Death* wants to say about secrets, substitution, and sacrifice, and (*but*) that "she" is also just a footnote, a mere paragraph/addendum to essentially gender-neutral questions of life and death. And (but) yet, at the same time, Derrida is alone in beginning to speak of a Sarah who must, necessarily, be sacrificed (as object) or be presumed to sacrifice (as absent complicit subject); of a Sarah whom the text excludes because it fears that if she enters, its logic of altars will be radically altered; and of a Sarah whose absence is both the evidence of a displaced metaphorical murder (a scene of Freudian crime) and a symptom of the text's defence against its own precariousness.[33]

The haunting figure of the "sacrifice of Sarah" that Derrida both declines and begins to decline, can be gently nudged a little further in the direction of a Sarah who is the necessary blind spot in the text all about "seeing,"[34] and a Sarah whose speech/presence threatens to "inflect" the Abrahamic grammar in such a way that it revolts against its own structures and paradigms—perhaps turning it into a completely other (foreign) language, perhaps making it incoherent, or even dissolving it into chaotic, pre-verbal, inarticulate noises like a scream, a cry, a laugh. With just a little push beyond this paragraph, Derrida's "Sarah" becomes the figure, or name, for the crux of the text's deconstruction, precisely because her exclusion/silence is aporetically necessary *and/but* also unbelievable; because it is as impossible to believe in the complicity of the mother as it is to believe in her total and effective exclusion from the private, Abraham–God *tête-à-tête*. This Sarah would then become the ultimate sign of the crisis, or suspension, also represented in the son—the son who is also, in a different way, stranded between "one sense of the genitive and the other" in the phrase *the sacrifice of Isaac* which, like the text that never consults him, leaves us uncomfortably uncertain as to whether he is the subject or object of sacrifice, a willing martyr or a passive-victim-lamb.[35] This Sarah would raise the thorny ethical question of what we nowadays call, euphemistically, "collateral damage"—just like the son, but in an arguably *more* disturbing way, because she is the *other* sacrifice necessitated by Genesis 22. As the woman-outside-the-text, necessarily "sacrificed" as a consequence of the text, this Sarah would raise the disquieting prospect of a chain of (at least?) metaphorical *substitueries* set in process by the Akedah. She would point to the trembling and the trauma and the tangled skein of repercussion in which the complete opens into the incomplete and the past into an uncertain future.

What would happen if we took these admittedly pale and thin Derridean spectres of Sarah and attempted what might be called, in today's jargon, some "joined up thinking" of Genesis 23 and Genesis 22? What would happen if we pursued Derrida's hint that the lives and deaths and figures and corpses of Sarah would, in all probability, have a laughing, doubting, accusing, interrupting relation to the Abrahamic, or if we allowed "the silence of Sarah," "the sacrifice of Sarah" and the "debt to Sarah" to become active, textually demanding protagonists in themselves? Then, just as in Derrida's interpretation, surface negotiations with Hittites are seen to cover over a deeper Abrahamic negotiation with Sarah's corpse, so Derrida's own discussion of these texts around the theme of substitution and sacrifice (the substitution of Sarah by shekels, of Isaac by a ram, and of Genesis 22 by Genesis 23) might be seen as covering over (burying?) a more potentially catastrophic series of displacements and sacrifices all hinging on Sarah, through whom, as he warns, *the very logic of substitution and sacrifice* is in danger of being "altered, inflected, attenuated or displaced" (1993b, 76). Then, perhaps, Abraham's and the narrator's curiously marked desire to pay (off) Sarah's corpse and remove her from his (their?) eyes might be read as a symptom of the need to bury the Sarah in him (them?) who would subvert their idealising high "sacrifices" with doubting, subverting laughter or, worse, intrude with accusing evidence of those additional *substitueries* required to preserve the integrity and internal peace (strained though it is) of that fundamental text. Then Genesis 23's curious emphasis on the *physical* necessity of Sarah's burial might be seen as uncomfortably *repeating* the *metaphorical* necessity of her removal from Abraham's (and God's) face or eyes a chapter earlier, and Sarah's accusing eternal silence in Genesis 23 might be heard (by Abraham, God, the narrator, the reader?) as accusingly echoing, and amplifying, her enforced silence in Genesis 22. Then we could even begin to suspect that Sarah dies because she *has* to (because everyone knows that if her voice or being were allowed to continue beyond the end of Genesis 22 she would spoil things with her disbelieving laughter or recrimination), and we could begin to venture sentences such as "having been forced to give up her voice, Sarah is now forced to give up the ghost" or "(in a vicarious dying, designed to protect the health of the most precious, and precarious, sacrifice narrative) she who was just expelled from before the eyes alive, is now being terminally expelled." The curiously anomalous chapter-long devotion to a burial and its meticulous, belaboured attention to the chain of *negotiations* set in process by that burial might find its rationale in the *particularly* impossible work of this *particularly* incomplete work of mourning. And the extensive attention to the pure mechanics of buying a burial plot might be seen as a deflection away from the comparatively impossible mental work involved in forgetting Sarah, or interring a restful, peaceful figure of Sarah in the biblical archive and in the labyrinthine echo-chambers of Abraham's (and the Abrahamic's) memory.

Pressing Derrida's own substitutionary readings a little further, in directions that the biblical texts, at least, seem to be begging to go, we could even say that, as the sources of Abraham's perceived obligation to whom life, blood or money are owed, as Abraham's *existential creditors*, the dead body of Sarah and the biblical God seem curiously, metonymically, related. (Note that Sarah and God are the only creditors so superlatively overpaid in the whole of the Old Testament/Tanakh; note too the relationship begged between David's desire not to "offer burnt offerings to the Lord that *cost me nothing*" [2 Samuel 24:24], Abraham's hyperbolic willingness to give God a whole son, and his willingness to overpay the corpse of Sarah; and note that little God-like something about Sarah's corpse-eye, as the eye that seems to see Abraham's secret, and to whom Abraham is in default or debt.) To the eye of Sarah, as well as the eye of God, one could perhaps apply the maxim that "It is on the basis of this gaze that singles me out [*ce regarde qui me regarde*] that my responsibility comes into being" (Derrida 1993b, 91) and we might imagine Abraham seeing himself reflected in the accusing eye of Sarah, like Cain in Passaroti's etching "Cain and the Eye of Abel" in *Memoirs of the Blind* (figure 16.1; see Derrida 1993c, 38). Is Abraham

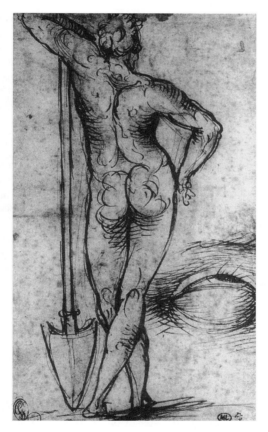

Figure 16.1   Bartolomeo Passaroti, "Cain and the Eye of Abel" or "Abraham and the eye of Sarah"(?), Louvre, Paris. (I imagine Abraham-Cain, as almost-murderer, seeing himself reflected as 'naked' and vulnerable in the giant eye of Sarah-Abel, looking up at him from the ground. However at that point the analogy stops, for the homoerotic connotations of this etching are not easily transposed to Abraham-Sarah . . .)

perhaps confessing/ intimating in that phrase "my dead" that "his" dead is *not* securely in his possession, that she so dispossesses and unnerves him that he must possess a piece of ground to bury her and so repossess himself? Is this very strangely posthumously *active* (demanding) corpse there not just to represent the normal remuneration that the dead demand from those who remain (a decent burial; a sense of debt for the not-done and not-said and for living on) but to beg a chain of questions that cannot be answered, or even asked, because asking them threatens (or promises?) to be fatal for the text?

If any of this were so then Sarah—laughing-suffering Sarah—would become something of a figure for what is meant by "deconstruction," by which I emphatically do not mean "play" or joking subversion (as if the spectre of Sarah were just a little poltergeist conjured up by tricksy "deconstructors" with a penchant for making incidental, but ultimately trivial, mischief), but rather a phenomenon that rises up, as it were, from *inside* as a result of a vision/dream of perfect-impossible responsibility, justice, ethics to which all selves (readers, writers, texts, patriarchs, and even Gods) are always in a relation of fall or debt. Laughing-suffering-dying-Sarah seems to intimate something of what I have described elsewhere as the "mortality and fragility" of deconstruction: a "deconstruction" that, a long way from the popular trope of a Highly-Complex-Master-Machine, has to do with an experience of powerlessness and "not being able" (which has to do, in turn, with trembling, laughing, mourning); with a radical disappropriation of the self through heteronomy, the law of the other; and with the need to be fully responsible to the other, indeed to every other, to which we can never be faithful/true enough.[36]

Derrida has already written of these two adjacent texts in terms of the Abraham who lacks, who owes (God, foreigners, corpses) and so sacrifices to become solvent, to be *saved*, and has also indicated something incomplete about this chain of sacrifices in the report of one *substitution* by a lamb followed by another substitution by shekels, as if sacrifices inevitably entailed knock-on effects. I am going further and saying that the corpse of Sarah is the figure for the fundamental wound of conscience, the default of responsibility which Genesis must thrust aside in order to live. As a figure of "fragile and fallacious chance" (Kristeva 1982, 2–3), she is the point at which the delicately poised story of Israel threatens to tip from life-on-the-verge-of-death to simply, starkly, death.

But Sarah Died (Oppositional Relations Between Genesis 22 and Genesis 23)

But in fact I'm not "going further" because all this has been said, in so many words, by ancient commentators (although for reasons of economy I am only discussing a few sample Jewish midrashim here, related texts can also be excavated from the archives of Christianity and Islam).[37] This, for example, is how *Genesis Rabbah* (ca. 400–450 C.E.) binds Genesis 22 and 23 together in a dense thicket of "becauses" and "therefores":

> From where did Abraham come [to mourn Sarah]? From Mount Moriah, *because Sarah died because of that very anguish* . . . "And Abraham came to mourn Sarah." From where

did he come? . . . R. Yosi said that he came from Mount Moriah and Sarah died from that pain. *Therefore* [the story of the Akedah] is next to "And Sarah's lifespan was." (*Genesis Rab.* 58.5 based on the translation in Freedman and Simon 1939)

And this is how the French Jewish exegete Rashi (1040–1105) binds the two texts together in a logic of causation:

The death of Sarah follows the binding *of* Isaac because *by that binding*, when her son seemed destined to be slaughtered, her soul floated up from her, and she died.

(Note how for Rashi the binding seems to escape beyond the borders of Genesis 22 to become something of a noose around Sarah's neck.) And, this is how the consequential overlaying of the Akedah and Sarah's death is glossed and expanded, firstly by the *Pirke de Rabbi Eliezer* (closed in the early ninth century though, like all the midrashim, incorporating layers of much earlier material) and secondly by *Leviticus Rabbah* (closed in the mid-fifth):

When Abraham returned from Mount Moriah in peace, the anger of Sammael was kindled, for he saw that the desire of his heart to frustrate the offering of our father Abraham had not been realized. What did he do? He went and said to Sarah "Have you not heard what has happened in the world?" She said to him "No." He said to her "The old man took the lad, Isaac, and slew him and offered him up as a burnt offering upon the altar. And the lad wept and cried aloud because he could not be saved." She began to weep and cry aloud, three times, corresponding to the three sustained notes [of the shofar],[38] and three howlings, corresponding to the three disconnected short notes [of the shofar], and her soul fled, and she died. (*Pirke de Rabbi Eliezer* 72b)

When Isaac returned to be with his mother, she said to him "Where have you been, *my son*?" He replied, "My father took me up mountains and down valleys, and took me up one of the mountains, built an altar, arranged the wood, prepared the offering-place, and took the knife to slaughter me, and an angel called out to him [to stop]." And she said "Woe unto *my son*! Were it not for the angel you would already have been slaughtered?" To which he answered "Yes." At that moment she screamed six times corresponding to six blasts [on the shofar]. They say that she died before finishing the six screams. (*Leviticus Rabbah* 20:2)

And this is how certain midrashim remove the seeming gag that "binds" Isaac in his narrative: when the Abraham of *Genesis Rabbah* tells Isaac "You are the lamb," Isaac tears his hair and replies: "*Is this what you have told my mother?*" (56:4); while *Midrash Bereshit Rabbati* and *Midrash Tanhuma* imagine him either instructing his knife-wielding father to present a casket of ashes to his mother so that she can "weep" over the burnt body of her son, or as warning Abraham "[not to] tell my mother when she is standing by a pit or when she is on the roof because she will fall and die" (*Midrash Bereshit Rabbati*, 55, 90; *Midrash Tanhuma Vayera* 81).

These ancient meditations go much further than Derrida in probing the potentially deconstructive effects of the "sacrifice of Sarah" (in one sense of the genitive or the other)—a claim hardly likely to elicit shock or resistance from someone who, ever faithful to Kierkegaard, has always nurtured suspicion of those who cast themselves as ever "going further" (bravely, boldly onwards into, say, the *post*-modern); one who does more than most contemporary thinkers to refute facile retrojections of the "pre-critical" religious (as passive, submissive, unquestioning); and who describes his own "attention to the present scene" as "at once intense, desperate, as if a little anachronistic," as if waiting for a future written in the "cipher of a very ancient speech" (Derrida 1995b, 130).[39] They go much further than the contemporary commentators who, absolved by their own devout historicism, do not have to raise the question of *relation* between these two adjacent texts of "death" and death, and also further than Derrida, who, for all his work on the "hostipitality" of Abraham (as host and guest), underestimates the "hostipitality" of the *waw* and its hostile-hospitable predilection to bind and unbind Genesis 22 to/from 23. Whereas Derrida reads the *waw* in "And Sarah died" as a mildly comparative "as . . . so" or "likewise," these readings subject the existential text (or test) that Jewish tradition knows as the *Akedah*, the Binding, to what Derrida calls the deconstructive "forces of dissociation, dislocation, *unbinding*" (2000, 291), and they do so across the *waw*, putting it through every possible angle of rotation, conjugating the strangely active death of Sarah as:

> "*So* Sarah died"
> and/but "*Thus/therefore* Sarah died"
> and/but "*But, on the contrary*, Sarah died"
> and/but "*And yet*, Sarah died"
> and, what's more, "*What's more*, Sarah died."

They deflect Derrida's patriarch-centred substitutionary chain along the line(s) of "Abraham sacrificed and Abraham sacrificed again" into the stranger terrain of "Abraham sacrificed and *Sarah [was?] sacrificed*," and move beyond metaphorical *substitueries* (human body to ram to shekels), towards the catastrophic movement from "death" (the suspended, redeemed, metaphorised, metaphamorphosised death of Isaac) to literalised, actual physical death (and hence accusation and recrimination). More Derridean, in a sense, than Derrida, they imagine the two "deaths" as taking place in a tangled thicket of time and consequence, where Abraham sacrifices and Sarah screams and dies *at the same time*—an "at the same time" in which "the same disagrees with itself all the time, a time that is [particularly] 'out of joint,' disturbed, dislocated, deranged" (Derrida 2002a, 93). They take two complete actions, "Sarah died" and "Abraham 'sacrificed'," and make them incomplete in relation to one another across the *waw*; they take the big hinge *waw* between 22 and 23 as an excuse to make lots of other disruptive little *waws* that pointedly draw complicating lines between discrete moments from the two chapters. Thus Isaac's "Where is the sheep?" is embellished precisely in relation to the "And Sarah died" so that from the midst of the first story, Isaac can already invoke the inevitable death/shock/trauma of the mother, as if by way of protective charm, and accusation, against the violence of the fathers. Similarly God's "Take your son, your only son," is interrupted and contested by Sarah's corrective "*my* son" to Isaac in *Leviticus Rabbah* making the point that Isaac is in truth *only* her only, for Abraham has another son—Ishmael. Thus the increasingly plastic *waw* mutates from single line—lying on its side as connecting hyphen, or standing upright like the axis of a mirror—into a tangled thicket of opposition, qualification, incompatibility, heterogeneity, and negotiated conse-quence. Questions proliferate for *causation* leads (inexorably) to *accusation*. Surely something must be amiss from the beginning if the form of the beginning results in such a catastrophic ending; surely it begs that we begin again, begin otherwise. Surely Genesis 22 is unsettled by being performed in the shadow of Sarah's preexistent grave-stone—a gravestone inscribed with the words "*Sarah. Mother of Isaac. Excessively [Revealingly?] Mourned Wife of Abraham. D. Kiriath-arba from Terminal Akedah-Pain.*"

By way of summary, here are the five most radical declensions of the death of Sarah potentially or actually provoked by midrash. (Note how they echo and amplify the Derrida-provoked declensions of Sarah above, precisely along the lines of Sarah-as-acute-discomfort, Sarah-as-necessary/inevitable-sacrifice, and Sarah-as-site-of-dissent-or-incredulity/disbelief).

The Death of Sarah as Effective Suicide

Like Derrida, the midrashim suggest we read "the death of Sarah" simultaneously, in one sense of the genitive and the other. They suspend her, delicately and undecideably, between the *victim* of the mountain-sacrifice and/or the one who responds to the almost-gift of death in Genesis 22 with a more literal (suicidal) interpretation of *se don-ner le mort* (giving oneself death). The traumatic effects of a Sarah who dies accidentally, as it were, are discussed below; but the figure of Sarah-wife-of-Abraham who actively dies, wants to die, and so by implication kills herself (so coming closer than Derrida knows to Sarah Kofman), radically amplifies to the very limit of testimony all her dis-senting, disrupting, accusing, protesting effects. The midrashim allow us to read Sarah's death as a way of "saying," in a silent act as counter-eloquent as Abraham's, that texts or tests like this should take place *over her dead body*,[40] while the way in which her very active, intentional soul "flees" in *Leviticus Rabbah*, encourages thoughts of a kind of *Yiddishe Mama* Sarah, who shakes her head, mutters "*vey, vey*" and walks away. Note how "sacrifice" *only* in the subjunctive, or *only* in inverted commas, is still enough to traumatise *Leviticus Rabbah*'s Sarah to the point of vacating her own life. Her soul still "flees" even though she knows that Isaac was saved (cf. Gellman 2003, 97).

The Death of Sarah as Fatal Accident ("Collateral Damage"?)

A Sarah whose life is taken, rather than who takes her own life, is no less of a wound to the self-assurance of Genesis, for her dead body warns us that texts/acts of "sacrifice" can so easily become texts/acts of sacrifice (so metaphors and inverted commas are not enough to protect us), and makes it ominously clear that the gift of death required by God is never retracted, but only displaced. Death is not only passed on down the line onto the ram, as divinely-sent surrogate, but is also passed on (acciden-tally) to the mother. Think of the famous Rembrandt painting (figure 16.2) where the knife seems to be falling from Abraham's hand right into the exposed torso of

Figure 16.2 Rembrandt van Rijn, "The Angel Preventing Abraham from Sacrificing Isaac" (1635), Hermitage, St. Petersburg.

Isaac, and then imagine the knife, miraculously, missing him and falling downward, straight into the next chapter, where it skewers Sarah instead.[41] The Sarah who dies accidentally personifies what we today call "collateral damage", a phrase that euphemistically tries to cover over "disaster"—that is, pain that cannot be incorporated into a redemptive sacrificial system (where suffering is always, as they say, "worth it") and where death remains so much irredeemable, unresurrectable *waste*.[42] Sarah's damaged corpse is so damaging precisely because she is just like Everycorpse (no signs of new life sprout from her wounds; no starry-visions twinkle in her eyes); because she personifies the danger (or even inevitability) of radical misfire in this text of knife and fire; and because she exemplifies the pain/loss that is *necessary* to sacrifice and yet always in danger of spoiling sacrifice by overrunning the circle of economy that contains it.[43]

The Death of Sarah as Necessary Accident (An Accident that the Rabbis Want or Need to Happen)

And—thus—far from being an arbitrary interpretative consequence of an accidental "and," the "And (*But*) Sarah died" is strategically used as a lever to *press* crucial questions of "religion and (*but*) ethics," and "sacrifice and (*but*) pain." It is necessary that she brings death into the world of Genesis—not in the same way that it is necessary to the Christian theological narrative that Eve bring death into the world—but precisely because her death as a minor (unpredicted) accident, rather than a massive choreographed event, is small and accidental and so unassimilatable. Because they are reading from a tradition in which the protection of life is the paramount value, because they are traumatized by the aw(e)ful specter of an Abraham who is an outlaw (an out-Torah), the Rabbis need Sarah to be something like a brute lump, a stone over which the text stumbles, a little piece of grit in the system, a corpse-accident that one cannot quite remove from before one's face. They seem to want her dead body to signal a certain overdetermination, problematisation, and imperfection of origins that is there from the beginning—a sense of a text that is not-yet-full-enough, not yet-safe-enough, that spawns a very Derridean mode of writing-reading as inheriting, mourning, mending, and ongoing negotiation of a mutually outstanding debt.

Sarah as More-Than- or Anti-Abraham

Because Sarah really *dies* whereas Isaac only "dies," the relationship between the two adjacent narratives threatens to develop along the lines of the Rabbinic *qal ve homer* (literally, "the little and the large"), so that Sarah's actual death, as *homer* ("large") eclipses Abraham and Isaac's virtual "sacrifice" (in both senses of the word) as relative *qal* ("small"). This Sarah could conceivably turn round to Abraham and Isaac and say, with another famous sacrificing mother from Jewish tradition (and one to whom she is explicitly compared by the midrashim), "Yours was a trial, mine was an accomplished fact."[44] Whereas the other mother, the mother of the seven Maccabean martyrs, is apostrophised as having a steely, "unwavering" soul just like Abraham's (4 Macc. 17:17–22); whereas she is something of a feminine factorial who supplements and multiplies the Abrahamic by the power of actuality and the power of seven (she offers seven sons, all of whom actually die), midrashic Sarah threatens to become a "dangerous supplement" who, instead of increasing the Abrahamic by increments, subjects it to guilt, accusation, *lack*. It is hard to imagine how the "and" in "And Sarah died" could simply *add* to what has gone before and not, in some sense, accuse, detract, subtract.

Sarah as Language-Dissolving Laugh or Scream

It seems to be no accident that midrashic Sarahs are associated with howls of pain and laughter. *Leviticus Rabbah* and the *Pirke de Rabbi Eliezer* hear the voice of Sarah as scream, howl, and lament: by having her howls stop short of the full six blasts,

Leviticus Rabbah seems to cast her as something of an incarnation of the Hebrew lament (*qinah*) genre which evokes lack by dropping the last note or syllable, while Isaac's "Is this what you have told my mother?" seems deliberately designed to raise a laugh. Sarah thus becomes the point at which the sacrificial grammar and the Abrahamic languages are radically "altered," "attenuated" or "displaced," and descend into pre-articulate babble (laughing, crying, trembling). She becomes the missing note that suggests a certain debt, lack or guilt in the Genesis script—the scream now forever bound (by way of under- or overtone) to the shofar's sonorous affirmation of faith. She becomes a figure of irretrievable loss, a less famous echo of that famous rabbinic figure of Rachel crying for her children, analyzed by Francis Landy in this volume.[45] And as with *mater dolorosa* Rachel, her suffering constitutes an accusation of God. Thus she embodies a note that is absolutely crucial in the complex, composite performances of Rabbinic and Derridean writing: a note of suffering-and-laughing and suffering-as-laughing, a sense of the fundamental cries of vulnerable life to which all justifying words and systems must be held accountable (to borrow the words of Elaine Scarry, laughing-suffering Sarah becomes the incarnation of the point of inarticulate pain at which "all the created world of thought and feeling, all the psychological and mental content that constitutes both one's self and one's world, and that gives rise to and is in turn made possible by language, ceases to exist"; Scarry 1985, 30).[46] To put it another way, Sarah is the "negative incredulous," as opposed to Abraham as the positive incredulous; for whereas Abraham encourages the reader to say "That's incredible" in an admiring, aspiring tone, Sarah encourages us to say "That's incredible" in a tone of dissent or disbelief, even laughter, and to ask how it could be possible to pass through the fire and knife of such a test without some-body suffering some aneconomic leftovers of pain?[47] As a deconstructive figure she embodies crucial things such as doubt as the partner of belief; pain and disaster as the shadow side of sacrifice; the struggle between religion and ethics, and between mountaintop vision and the grounded protests of flesh. She is the seism that *happens* to the truth, the source of a nonnegligible chain of questions taken even to the point of inarticulacy and even to the point of death.

And/*But* Hagar (Awkward Appendix)

It is impossible to discuss the tangled sequences and consequences of sacrifice and substitution that congregate around Mount Moriah without at least mentioning the woman who substitutes for—and is sacrificed by(?)—the house of Israel, and whose expulsion and (almost) death and removal from before our eyes lies just on the other side of the mountain to the death of Sarah (compare her removal in Genesis 21 and the related text of Genesis 16 with Sarah's removal in Genesis 23). And yet it is somehow fitting to have her buried here as a minor footnote, a little appendix, an awkward remainder that, if allowed to grow, would undermine the economy of this essay, as if by way of mimesis of the priorities of the story of nascent Israel. Like, and beyond, the "And Sarah died," this "And Hagar" threatens to *subtract* (no simple addenda "she") and to subject the Abrahamic to further bonds and counterbonds, debits, responsibilities. This brief fleeting meditation (as this article walks off into the distance, into the desert, foregrounding its own sense of partiality and partialness and lack) takes its cue from Derrida's only mention of Hagar as, provocatively, a "*mère porteuse*" or "surrogate mother," and from the article to which that brief meditation is a response: Fethi Benslama's brilliant "*La répudiation originaire.*"[48]

Hagar's complicating surrogacy roles extend way beyond literal physical services rendered. At the most fundamental level she is "surrogate" because she performs the simple literal physical service of substituting for the barren body of Sarah (well-to-do matriarchs have options in the biblical worlds) and yet, unlike those biblical "concubines" or "handmaids" who meld with their mistress's body and "bear upon her knees" (Genesis 30:3), Hagar splits off and becomes a rival line or rival body. She becomes, in complex ways, a surrogate Sarah and (but) an anti/*ante*-Sarah, the first mother who is always there before her, thus strangely mirroring Sarah's own division into an anti-Abraham and an ante-Abraham, laying down her oppositional body in the sacrificial path of Abraham and, at least in the chronological tangle of the midrashim, *preceding* his act of sacrifice with her demanding already-death. As Abraham needs to remove Sarah's corpse or eye from before his face, so Sarah is cast as expelling the picture of herself imaged in that other eye: Hagar is expelled to get rid of that other eye through which Sarah sees herself accused for *lack* of child (Genesis 16:5). Like the mutinying "OfFred" in Margaret Atwood's *The Handmaid's Tale* (1987), Hagar functions as OfAbraham, OfSarah, OfGod and/*but* also as a dangerous supplement; the one who supplies a foundational boy brick to build up the house of Abraham (cf. Sarah's desire to be "built up [בנה]" by her, Genesis 16:2) but who also builds foreign territory, the annex of other houses, into the very foundations of the house (the Hagar-Ishmael-Egyptian extension, there before the foundations of the house, mirrors the aporia of Abraham-as-host-and-guest). Hagar is a narrative surrogate in the sense of *false* start, the weaker, bastard beginning: as *Midrash Rabbah* puts it, she is there as the "thorn" that conceives easily, as opposed to the "grain" that must be divinely "made to grow" (and, we could add, nurtured with sacrificial toil and pain), and her solid "wild-ass", animal-like son, conceived by physical intercourse is there as foil to the supernaturally-, miraculously-elicited fragile-promise-laugh-child (*Midrash Rabbah* 45.4).[49] But yet this false start comes by way of supplement to a lack of giving in God and Abraham: Sarah gives Hagar to Abraham saying "You see that the Lord has prevented me from bearing children" (16:2), and, in a way that reminds me of the curious metonymy between God and Sarah discussed earlier, Sarah gives her "the gift of filling up the lack in God, in her place" (Benslama 1998, 123). The giving/conceiving of a woman, and the giving/conceiving of God (which also means the imagining of "woman" and of "God"), are placed in a tangled, supplementary relationship that is antithetical and also more than antithetical.

Surrogate Hagar, in other words, is the physical embodiment and effect of that subversive, sceptical, unbelieving, protesting laughter, the laughter that takes place behind God's back, behind a tent flap, with one's face to the ground, and that makes God indignant at the challenge to his omnipotence (see Derrida's footnote cited in note 7 above). She is the negative incredulous, like the laugh and death of Sarah, that is both expelled by, and the necessary and inevitable companion to, the positive incredulous that is the Abrahamic sacrifice and the Abrahamic dream. Hagar is *like* laughing-suffering Sarah in that her story elicits complicating empathy for the

expelled or buried one *at the same time* that it enforces the necessity of her repudiation (thus she is narrative and physical surrogate for her mistress). And the related
stories of her expulsion/flight into the desert with Ishmael (physically and *in utero*) in
Genesis 16 and 21, provocatively take the form of a curious, inverted narrative surrogate for the Exodus. *Why* tell the story of Hagar as an anti/*ante*-Exodus in which the
Egyptian slave finds, in the desert, water, angels, and sanctuary from the Israelite
oppressors who wanted her to "build" their houses with boy or straw-bricks?; why
tangle time, make the flight of Hagar and the flight from Egypt incomplete in relation to one another, and use all those implied *waws*, and complicated attachments
such as ברח ("to flee"), גרש ("to expel") and ענה ("to oppress")? [50] And, worse (or
better), why allow Hagar to function as an ante/anti-Abraham and allow Genesis 21
and 16 to take the form of a premature version of Genesis 22, of woman born? Why
have Hagar see her son almost die, see him retrieved from the brink of death by an
angel and receive a pseudo- "Abrahamic" (Hagaramic?) [51] promise that God will
greatly multiply her offspring so that they cannot be counted for multitude (16.10),
and then connect Genesis 21 and 22 with an "After these things," by way of a kind of
emphatic *waw,* if not to suggest that the story of Israel is in some sense preempted by
her (just as God's giving is preceded by her supplementary giving). Just as Sarah
receives an unparalleled chapter-long devotion to her burial, so Hagar receives unparalleled attention and status from God and the narrator: her epiphany of God makes
her like a "prophet," Spinoza says (Benslama 1998, 125 citing Spinoza 1965, 49); her
naming of a well as "The well of the Living One who sees me" makes her that
completely anomalous thing, a female-patriarch (only patriarchs stick name-
signposts in plots of land in Genesis; compare Abraham's naming of Moriah, the
place of vision as, undecideably, *Jehovah Yireh* [יהוה יראה], "He shall be seen" or "He
shall see to it [or, provide]" in Genesis 22:14). But the specific name of the well suggests
a Hagar who is seen and sees, who reciprocates the divine gaze in a God-human eye-
to-eye, and exposes God (and the narrative and the house of Israel) to the disruptive
effects of what Benslama calls "l'oeil d'Agar" (1998, 131). Imagining themselves seen
through this eye, God, the Abrahamic, and the archive of the Abrahamic must see
themselves as guilty of necessary-but-culpable oversight—the repudiation of Hagar is
necessitated by the greater story of Abraham, in the same way that the Abrahamic gift
to God of Isaac *necessitates* the overlooking of Sarah. The lavish gift to Hagar of a
multitude of sons and precious words borrowed from men and from the narrative of
Israel is symptomatic of a sense of remaining debt and guilt, and is reminiscent of the
overpayment of words and shekels that characterises the burial of Sarah.

But too much payment over the full (sensible) price leads to an inflation of
questions. It leaves us with an *Akedah* tangled in a complicating thicket of words and
obligations: flanked and besieged, on the one side, by the story of how Abraham was
obligated to discharge debt to Sarah's corpse and to foreigners, and, on the other, with
the story of the expulsion of the ur-foreigner, whose curiously surrogate story suggests
guilt in us (she is the slave on whom we who were/will be slaves had no pity), mimesis of us (she is uncannily like Abraham our father), lack in us (she intimates a certain
lack in Sarah, and so in Abraham and God), and decision between her and us (her
presence seems to beg a certain "May the Lord [and the reader] choose between
you and me" [cf. Genesis 16:5]). It leaves us with a marked sense of other *existential*

creditors: the foreigners, the women, the mothers and the accidentally dead ones who are our existential creditors as much as God (and who are, in some sense, curiously like God). The fact that too much is said, too much is given away (both to us by others and to others from us), leaves us with a story of revelation-seeing-vision complicated by an Argos-Panoptes of other eyes (Hagar's eyes, Sarah's eyes, all those other eyes that make our perception of the revelation unfocussed and stigmatic), and a story of Genesis as complex and convoluted as a DNA spiral, coiling around itself and its others in a complex chain of substitution, sacrifice, gift, debt, retention, lack.[52] It leaves us with the story of a birth of a nation beset by "complications" from the very moment of conception: this is no straightforward delivery for it passes through the *womb* of a figure who opens out into a conflicted *matrix* of connotations (anti-Abraham, surrogate Abraham, anti- and ante-Sarah, first mother, necessary supplement, foreigner-with-us-from-the-beginning, through whom the beginning gets started and finds its definition). Even as it comes down its very complicated birth canal, this birth of the nation is overshadowed by (unnecessary?) death, pain, trauma: the fundamental moment of the making, or execution, of Israel by God is the virtual "execution" of the promise child that always threatens to tip over into the wasteful, guiltful, actual execution of Sarah. Given that every writer/author/god *chooses*, why choose to tell it thus? Is it, as Benslama suggests, that "God doesn't give without giving account, without archiving" (1998, 125), that as meticulous Book-keeper he keeps accounts of all transactions, even when those transactions are counter*productive* to the literary production of himself and Israel (is this, then, deliberate self-risk or self-sacrifice?). Or is it that, given that all writing and self-telling is shortfall, fall, confession, then somehow Scripture (capital letter Writing) makes this falling short overt? Is it that there is at least an aspect of the biblical that plunges us into insolvent life lived within a thicket of obligations, where actions have unpredictable (unwanted) consequences, and where imperfectly discharged obligations await their redemption in a fully solvent interpretation always yet-to-come—that Scripture is, in this sense, the perfect opposite of a popularly received image of scripture, an Other Word, in other words?

Notes

1. In fact the relationship between Abraham and Sarah is anything but straightforwardly copulative. As this essay will show, far from merging as a complementary couple, "Sarah" and "Abraham" seem to symbolically pull apart. Moreover Genesis 21:1 says "And the Lord visited [פָּקַד] Sarah . . . and she conceived," suggesting that Isaac is born of something more—and less—than straightforward copulation between the patriarch and his wife.
2. "This is a general law of formal logic: a conjunction slips and insinuates itself into every disjunction, and vice versa" (Derrida 2000, 291).
3. For G. R. Driver's description of the logical "failure" and the "strangeness" of the *waw* (quoted without reference) see Weingreen 1959 [1939], 252–253.
4. For a related point about the divisive "slash" versus the tender "stroke" see Stephen Moore 1998, 377.
5. By adding slightly different vowels to the consonantal Hebrew שרה חיי שני an alternative reading turns "the years of the life of Sarah" into "the two lives of Sarah."

6. See the note above.
7. This is Derrida's own footnote, reproduced here verbatim: "When told about the coming of Isaac (*yiskhak*: he laughs), Sarah laughs and then pretends not to have done so. But God becomes indignant that she might be doubting his omnipotence and contradicts her denial: 'Oh yes, you did laugh' (Genesis 18:15). Later (21:3, 6) at Isaac's birth, 'Abraham gave the name Isaac to his son whom Sarah bore him: *Is'hac*—he will laugh!' Sarah says 'God brought laughter for me; everyone who hears will laugh with me' ".
8. Whereas all the other works of mourning in the same volume have a title, this one is simply listed on the contents page as " . . . . . ." (Derrida 2001c).
9. I am transplanting the far-more-than-punning connection between *fils* (son) and *fils* (thread) to Genesis from Derrida 1993c, 16.
10. In French *hôte* means the giver *and* receiver of hospitality, the equivalent of English "host" and "guest."
11. This Abrahamic itinerary is a summary of that given in Derrida 2002b, 414.
12. This translation of ויבא אברהם as "he *went in* to mourn for Sarah," locates the narrator outside, rather than inside, Canaan and so emphasises the theme of incursion into foreign land.
13. "Death and the Promise" or, more specifically, "Death and the Promised Land," is a theme that would merit a paper in itself. Suffice to remember here that the spies who go down ahead into the land return with reports of giant grapes, pomegranates, figs, surfeits of milk and honey, but also a land that "*devours its inhabitants*" (Num. 13:32), and that is filled with sword-wielding giants. Remember too that Moses dies on the borders of the promised land (Deut. 34:6) and is buried, unlike Sarah, in an unmarked non-Canaan site.
14. The site does indeed seem to have been an ancient one. The *el-Haram el-Ibrahimi el-Khalil* mosque in Hebron dates from the seventh century C.E., but was preceded by a Byzantine church and an enclosure by Herod the Great (37–34 B.C.E.), indicating that the site was venerated during, and perhaps well before the time of, Herod. See Vawter 1977, 261.
15. For a flavour of commentary, see Vawter 1977, 260–65 (this is the most questioning and rich of the commentaries listed here, though still dominantly historical); Claus Westermann 1985 [1981], 369–376; von Rad 1972 [1949], 246–250 (for von Rad's comment on the text as "delightful miniature" of "adroit Oriental conversation" see p. 247). Tugging the commentary genre more toward the kinds of questions posed by Derrida, Vawter makes the point that the meaning of the story is not dependent on an "exotic milieu" that can only be "conjectured," and argues against regarding the Abraham-Hittite negotiations as "inscrutably oriental" and "exclusively ancient" (1977: 264). He also ventures that "The Bible . . . is not really interested in antiquarian authenticity so much as it is in validating the patriarch's stake in the Land of Promise" (1977: 263). Compare Westermann's more typical exclusively historical analysis of the narrative and his bold statement that "J. Wellhausen proposed . . . by acquiring the plot Abraham acquired a legal claim to the land; there are echoes of this also in O. Procksch. This is rightly rejected by H. Gunkel, G. von Rad, B. Jacob and others" (1985 [1981], 376; note the inventory approach, lining up "right" and "wrong" scholars, with no discussion as to why "rejection" is "right"). Note also the separation of the "material" and the "spiritual" that leads von Rad to conclude that, because this narrative is clearly concerned with possession of land, it shows "how little ancient Israel's faith was satisfied with the blessings of a spiritual relationship with God" (1972 [1949], 249). The traditional association of the text with "P," the Priestly, most "Jewish" author of the Pentateuch, is uncomfortably related to this material–spiritual division, for "P" texts generally tend to be demoted in the grand scheme of things. (For the nonspecialist reader, it may be helpful to know that the composite

nature of Pentateuchal literature led to the postulation of four different strands, J, E, D, and P representing different contexts and ideologies).

16. Compare Derrida's related observation that, since it is driven by the impossibility of being perfectly faithful or full enough, all self-writing or self-telling (even the self-telling of an Abraham or a God), is *confession*. Read this way, Abraham's presentation of himself as "stranger and alien" may be an exaggerated performance of the necessary default of self-presentation writ large, rather than a simple formality of extreme *politesse*. For the most famous Derridean meditation on the relation between Western cultures of selfhood and sin, confession, fall, see Derrida 1993a, but see also 2001a (esp. 385–386, 390). On the self-confession of the God of the Hebrew Bible, see Derrida 2004 and 1999 (esp. 185–202).

17. The ancient midrashim focus (with Derrida) on the strange reverse bartering but also (beyond Derrida) on the curious mutual verbal self-emptying of Abraham and the Hittites. Fascinatingly, in a way that would resonate with Derrida's own exegesis of the death of Sarah in terms of sacrifice and substitution (see below) the conflict between what seems to be two scales of Abraham (Abraham as "alien and stranger" and Abraham as "Mighty Prince") is resolved by the midrashim through the logic of sacrifice: Abraham *becomes* a mighty prince because he empties himself as alien and stranger, and possesses the land *because* he humbly seeks to purchase it. (See *Midrash HaGadol* 1:347; *Jubilees* 18:3–4; but cf. the more belligerent Abraham of *Bereshit Rabbah* 58:6, who says to the Hittites "If I wish, I shall claim the rights of the owner, since God promised me this land.)"

18. The Chronicler, who rewrites to elevate the value of the religious in the preexisting text of Samuel–Kings, literally elevates when it comes to the costs of the temple. The fifty silver shekels of 2 Samuel 24:24 undergo extreme inflation in 1 Chronicles 21:25 to six hundred gold shekels. The excessive cost of the temple seems to be pegged to the sense of the vast, insolvent debt to the God of the temple: compare 2 Samuel's David's desire not to "offer burnt offerings to the Lord that *cost me nothing*" (24:24). Existential debt and compensatory overpayment are markedly absent from commentary: cf. Westermann's (1985 [1981], 369–376) prosaic and hugely overreaching "deduction," based on Genesis 23:8–9 and 1 Chron. 21:22–24, that בכסף מלא is an idiom meaning "the current price" or "going rate"(!) thus eradicating any sense of a *full* to overflowing price. (Westermann's deduction also raises the question of how far two texts can constitute a sufficient basis for an alleged idiom.)

19. With the exception of the ancient midrashim, discussed below.

20. Please note that this is not a perfect phonetic transliteration; merely an attempt to convey the sound of the Hebrew to the non-Hebrew reader.

21. For readers of Hebrew, I am referring to the Masoretic notes known as the Masora Parva, where the phrase "my dead" מתי is marked with a ל meaning "the only time that this construction occurs."

22. For a further attempt to explore biblical abjection see Beal (1994), Tarlin (1997), and Sherwood (2000).

23. I deliberately use the phrase "absence in the text" to thwart a naïve, anachronistic, Romantic view that would see this account of weeping and needing to be comforted as indicating the real feelings of a real Abraham and Isaac about a real Sarah. My question is, rather, what point the narrative may be trying to make (or may unwittingly be making) by making Sarah such a lamented, marked, and buried absence.

24. See note 16 above. (To an extent, "redaction criticism," the exploration of the work of biblical editors, does point out linking passages strung between separate strands of narrative, but it is beyond its historical remit to explore the effect of the conjunctions/ disjunctions.)

25. Derrida's reading is also Kierkegaardian in that he reads Genesis 22 through *Fear and Trembling* (and so through Luther, and lurking just behind Luther's shoulder, Paul).

26. In the ritual of *pidyon ha-ben*, the firstborn son is "redeemed" at thirty days, by giving a token amount of silver to the *kohen* as a representative of the priestly family. In this very ancient tradition, the son is redeemed through monetary "sacrifice".

27. Note that when Derrida risks some least bad definitions of deconstruction, he ventures "the movements of . . . ex-appropriation," a questioning of *pouvoir* as power/being able, and the experience of *suffering* as "not being able." See, for example, Derrida 1998a, 141; 1995a, 385; 2001a, 396.

28. For the connection between the ancient site of sacrifice and contemporary wars waged in the name of fidelity to the Abrahamic, which only a "wide-eyed ecumenism" can deny, see Derrida 1993b, 69–70. For the Tomb of the Patriarchs as "a common and symbolic trench" of the Abrahamic religions, see Derrida 1998b, 5.

29. For Derrida's meditations on "the times" and the mediation of the times and "actuality" by the media ("*les actualités*"), see Derrida 2002a.

30. I use the term "existential" very loosely, rather as Theodore Jennings, in his contribution to this volume, uses the term "humanist" in an attempt to describe the same effects. ("Humanist," like "existential," like "material" all attempt to suggest something of Derrida's engagement with questions of existence, though he is by no means "existential-ist" or "humanist" in any simple, generic sense, and would certainly depart from all con-notations of active and authenticating [atomised?] selves). The phrase "poor existing individuals" is borrowed from Kierkegaard, the philosopher to whom Derrida says he has been "most faithful" (see his confession that " . . . it is Kierkegaard to whom I have been most faithful and who interests me most: absolute existence, the meaning he gives to the word subjectivity, the resistance of existence to the concept of the system—this is some-thing I attach great importance to and feel very deeply . . ." [2001b, 40]).

31. This is not an idle aside: one of the most frequently asked questions within the discipline of biblical studies is "Is there a future for biblical commentaries" which implies "Has it not all, already, been said and done?" A situation in which biblical commentary, as a genre, is dying at the hands of its own (presumably) rhetorical question, highlights the self-sufficiency, to exhaustion, of the microcosm.

32. The other story elided from this quotation is Melville's *Bartleby the Scrivener*, dealt with so effectively in the essay by Oona Eisenstadt in this collection.

33. Cf. Sigmund Freud: "The distortion of a text is not unlike a murder . . . The difficulty lies not in the execution of a deed but in doing away with the traces" (1985, 283–284).

34. The way in which Genesis 22 orbits around the eye and figures of looking, seeing and rev-elation is evident even from the English translation. Thus Genesis 22 relates to Genesis as a whole, tangled as it is around metaphorical optic nerves of revelation and deception, see-ing and not seeing.

35. For a (literally) *related* analysis of the deconstructive effects of the son, see my "Isaac to Abraham," Sherwood (2004c).

36. For Derrida's "least bad" definitions of deconstruction as an interrogation of *pouvoir* as ability and power see note 27 above. For further thoughts on the "mortality and fragility of deconstruction," see Sherwood and Hart (2004). For an analysis of the popular reception of the machine of deconstruction, see also Herman Rappaport's excellent *The Theory Mess: Deconstruction in Eclipse* (2001).

37. For a broader discussion of texts from the three "Abrahamic" religions, see Sherwood (2004a).

38. The *shofar* referred to is the ram's horn, sounded on *Rosh Hashanah* when the story of the binding of Isaac is read and (largely) affirmed as a foundational story in which Abraham's obedience, and God's memory of that obedience, pulls taut the ties of the covenant and seals God and the children of Abraham's mutual fidelity and mutual love. While it would

go beyond the bounds of this paper to detail the importance of the binding of Isaac in Judaism, it should not be supposed that the movement of recoil, qualification and critique that I am documenting here simply dominates "the" Jewish response. For a broader discussion of the range of uses that traditional Judaism makes of this text, see Sherwood (2004b).

39. For Kierkegaard's scathing denunciations of dreams of always "going further," see *Fear and Trembling, Dialectical Lyric by Johannes de Silentio* (1985, 41–42, 145–146); see especially his "Suppose someone wanting to dance said: 'For hundreds of years now one generation after another has been learning dance steps, it's high time I took advantage of this and began straight off with a set of quadrilles' " (1985, 75). Cf. Derrida (1995b, 130) cited as an epigraph to this essay. In his parasitic obsession with old, unfashionable texts, and old–new languages, a very Kierkegaardian Derrida shows his aversion to concepts of originality, ever "new-" or "post-" ness.

40. I discuss this effect in more detail in Sherwood (2003).

41. Compare the Scottish writer Frank Kuppner's extrapolation of the next moment in the painting: "The knife, plunging (generally speaking) towards earth, had instead fallen deep into the child's body somewhere about the midriff, and the life's blood had already substantially poured out over him and dripped down onto the grass . . ." (1999, 13).

42. For this definition of disaster and of "flesh," of which Sarah's dead body is a clear instance, see Caputo (1993, 28–29, 209).

43. One could add that pain is in a sense rather like the wonderful, impossible, inexpressible, inspiring "things" that Derrida calls "justice" or the "gift" in that it ruptures the solvent economy or law of sacrificial exchange. But pain is the negative incredulous whereas justice and gift are the positive incredulous, and whereas "justice" or the "gift" positively-impossibly break out of the circle, pain negatively ruptures the circle by "clogging the wheels" of the system or the machine (cf. Caputo 1993, 211). Another way of saying this is to say "How to believe in something like the perfect gift or perfect justice?" but "How *not* to believe that the circle of sacrifice would involve an anecomonic remainder of pain?"

44. For the Maccabean mother Hannah's imagined speech to Abraham, see for example *Yalkut Deuteronomy* 26 and *b. Git.* 57b. For the link between Sarah and Hannah, see the passage from *Midrash Tanhuma*, cited above. Isaac's fear that Sarah will fall off a roof and die should she hear of this seems explicitly to link her fate to "Hannah" who, according to some traditions, hurled herself from a roof to her death.

45. Not only does the less well-known figure of dying Sarah seem to echo the roles of rabbinic Rachel, but Sarah and Rachel are explicitly linked in the *Rosh Hashanah* liturgy (see further Sherwood 2004b).

46. Also relevant here is Scarry's description of pain as that which "plunges the sufferer into a state anterior to language, where they can only utter pre-articulate sounds and cries" (1985, 4).

47. For a rather different reading of Abraham and Sarah as *disjunctive* principles, see Gellman (1998, 57–67). Using Kabbalistic and Hasidic principles, Gellman reads Abraham as *hesed* and Sarah as *din*, but comes to strikingly similar conclusions to the ones arrived at here. The essay, which I excitedly discovered towards the end of writing this piece, concludes: "The *shofar* thus incorporates a twin spiritual consciousness, one of *hesed* and one of *din*, two religious ideals, one embodied in the sacrificial life of Father Abraham, Sacrificial Man, and the other embodied in the life of Mother Sarah, who died from her pain over the binding of Isaac" (1998, 66).

48. As Gil Anidjar observes, the revised French edition of *Donner la Mort* inserts a few more Ibrahims and Ishmaels than the earlier edition (see Anidjar 2002, 10 n. 29), but still seems to follow the Qur'anic tradition of not (yet?) mentioning Hagar. For this and other crucial observations about Hagar see Fethi Benslama's very rich "*La répudiation originaire*" (1998),

pp. 111–153; for Derrida's response, see his "Fidélité à plus d'un" in the same volume (1998, 237). An important question, and one related to questions of the monolingualisms of the Academy, is "How does one bring Fethi Benslama's very important article in French into the orbit of the largely Anglo-American-German world of Biblical Studies?"

49. Benslama goes a little too far in naming Isaac as "l'enfant de la communauté du rire entre Dieu et les hommes, autrement dit l'esprit" (1998, 132), and generally seems to assume too much closeness between OT and NT, Christianity and Judaism, as opposed to Islam. Compare Jon Levenson's more careful statement that, while though there is clearly something of the counter/super-natural about Isaac, it would be going too far to translate this scene into Christian idioms of the replacement of "birth" with "faith," and the "natural" with "spirit" (1993, 70, 126).

50. For a discussion of the relationship between the expulsion of Hagar and the Exodus see, for example, Phyllis Trible (1984, 9–35). Though other elements of the narrative have been compared, no one to my knowledge has yet noted the comparison between Hagar as the one who builds up the house of brael boy-bricks and the Israelites as builders with straw bricks (implied in the use of the verb בנה).

51. This may sound bizarre, but bear in mind that the Bible talks in terms of the "Hagarites" (1 Chron. 5:10, 19, 20) and the "Hagarenes" (Psalm 83:6).

52. Compare Benslama's detailed analysis of Hagar's place in a chain of "gifts," "counter-gifts" and "holding-backs" throughout "*La répudiation originaire*" (1998).

Works Consulted

Anidjar, Gil. 2002. "Introduction: 'Once More, Once More'." In Jacques Derrida, *Acts of Religion*, ed. Gil Anijar, 1–39. New York and London: Routledge.

Atwood, Margaret. 1987. *The Handmaid's Tale*. London: Virago.

Beal, Timothy. 1994. "The System and the Speaking Subject in the Hebrew Bible: Reading for Divine Abjection". *Biblical Interpretation* 2: 171–89.

Benslama, Fethi. 1998. "La répudiation originaire." In *Idiomes, nationalités, déconstructions: rencontre de Rabat avec Jacques Derrida*, ed. Fethi Benslama, 111–53. Les éditions Toukbal: Casablanca.

Brown, Francis, Driver, S. R., and Briggs, Charles A. 1939 [1906]. *A Hebrew and English Lexicon of the Old Testament*. Oxford: Oxford University Press.

Caputo, John D. 1993. *Against Ethics: Contributions to a Poetics of Obligation with Constant Reference to Deconstruction*. Bloomington and Indianapolis: Indiana University Press.

Clines, David J. A. (ed.). 1995. *The Dictionary of Classical Hebrew*. Volume II: *Bet-Waw*. Executive ed. John Elwolde. Sheffield: Sheffield Academic Press.

Derrida, Jacques. 1993a. "Circumfession." In Geoffrey Bennington and Jacques Derrida, *Jacques Derrida*. Chicago: University of Chicago Press.

———. 1993b. *The Gift of Death*. Trans. David Wills. Chicago and London: University of Chicago Press.

———. 1993c. *Memoirs of the Blind: The Self-Portrait and Other Ruins*. Trans. Pascale Anne Brault and Michael Naas. Chicago and London: University of Chicago Press.

———. 1995a. "Passages—from Traumatism to Promise." In *Points . . . Interviews, 1974–1994*, ed. Elizabeth Weber, 372–95. Trans. Peggy Kamuf et al. Stanford: Stanford University Press.

———. 1995b. "Unsealing ('the old new language')." In *Points . . . Interviews, 1974–1994*, ed. Elizabeth Weber, 115–31. Trans. Peggy Kamuf et al. Stanford: Stanford University Press.

———. 1998a. "Afterword: Toward an Ethic of Discussion." In *Limited Inc.* Trans. Samuel Weber. Evanston, IL: Northwestern University Press.

———. 1998b. "Faith and Knowledge: The Two Sources of 'Religion' at the Limits of Reason Alone." In Jacques Derrida and Gianni Vattimo, *Religion*, 1–78. Cambridge: Polity.

———. 1998c. "Fidélité à plus d'un: Mériter d'hèriter où la généalogie fait défaut." In Fethi Benslama, *Idiomes, nationalités, déconstructions: rencontre de Rabat avec Jacques Derrida*, 221–65. Les éditions Toukbal: Casablanca.

———. 1999 (second edn). *Donner la Mort*. Paris: Editions Galilée.

———. 2000. "Et Cetera." In *Deconstructions: A User's Guide*, ed. Nicholas Royle, 282–305. New York and Basingstoke: Palgrave.

———. 2001a. "The Animal That Therefore I Am (More to Follow)." Trans. David Wills. *Critical Inquiry* 28, 2:385–86.

———. 2001b. "I Have a Taste for the Secret." In Jacques Derrida and Maurizio Ferraris, *A Taste for the Secret*, 1–92. Trans. Giacomo Donis. Oxford: Polity.

———. 2001c. "Sarah Kofman (1934–94)." In *The Work of Mourning*, ed. Pascale Anne Brault and Michael Naas, 165–88. Chicago and London: University of Chicago Press.

———. 2002a. "The Deconstruction of Actuality." In *Negotiations: Interventions and Interviews 1971–2001*, ed. and trans. Elizabeth Rottenberg, 85–116. Stanford: Stanford University Press.

———. 2002b. "Hostipitality." In *Acts of Religion*, ed. Gil Anidjar, 356–420. New York and London: Routledge.

———. 2004. "Epoché and Faith." In *Derrida and Religion: Other Testaments*, ed. Yvonne Sherwood and Kevin Hart. New York and London: Routledge.

Freedman, H. and Simon, Maurice eds. 1939. *Midrash Rabbah*. London: Soncino Press.

Freud, Sigmund. 1985. *Moses and Monotheism*. Harmondsworth: Penguin.

Gellman, Jerome. 2003. *Abraham! Abraham!: Kierkegaard and the Hasidim on the Binding of Isaac*. Aldershot: Ashgate.

Gellman, Yehuda. 1998. "And Sarah Died." *Tradition*: 57–67.

Jantzen, Grace. 1998. *Becoming Divine: Towards a Feminist Philosophy of Religion*. Manchester: Manchester University Press.

Kierkegaard, Søren. 1985. *Fear and Trembling, Dialectical Lyric by Johannes de Silentio*. Trans. Alastair Hannay. Harmondsworth: Penguin.

Kristeva. Julia. 1982. *Powers of Horror: An Essay in Abjection*. New York: Columbia University Press.

Kuppner, Frank. 1999. "A Lesson for Us All." In *In the Beginning There was Physics*. Edinburgh: Polygon.

Levenson, Jon D. 1993. *The Death and Resurrection of the Beloved Son: The Transformation of Child Sacrifice in Judaism and Christianity*. New Haven and London: Yale University Press.

Moore, Stephen D. 1998. "Ugly Thoughts on the Face and Physique of the Historical Jesus." In *Biblical Studies/Cultural Studies: The Third Sheffield Colloquium*, ed. J. Cheryl Exum and Stephen D. Moore, 376–99. Journal for the Study of the Old Testament Supplement Series 266; Gender Culture Theory 7. Sheffield: Sheffield Academic Press.

Mullan, John. 2003. "And then he ate the apple . . . ," *The Guardian Review* August 2, 2003.

Rad, Gerhard von. 1972 [1949]. *Genesis*. Trans. John H. Marks. London: SCM.

Rapaport, Herman. 2001. *The Theory Mess: Deconstruction in Eclipse*. New York: Columbia University Press.

Scarry, Elaine. 1985. *The Body in Pain: The Making and Unmaking of the World.* Oxford: Oxford University Press.

Sherwood, Yvonne. 2000. "Prophetic Scatology: Prophecy and the Art of Sensation." In *In Search of the Present: The Bible Through Cultural Studies*, ed. Stephen D. Moore, 183–224. *Semeia* 82. Atlanta: Scholars Press.

———. 2003. "Over Sarah's Dead Body." Unpublished paper presented at the Gender, Sexuality and the Bible section of the *Society of Biblical Literature* annual meeting, Atlanta, November, 2003.

———. 2004a. "Binding-Unbinding: Divided Responses of Judaism, Christianity and Islam to the 'Sacrifice' of the Beloved Son." *Journal of the American Academy of Religion* 72 (4).

———. 2004b. "Textual Carcasses and Isaac's Scar, or What Jewish Interpretation Makes of the Violence that Almost Takes Place on Mount Moriah." In *Sanctified Aggression: Violent Legacies of Biblical and Post-Biblical Vocabularies*, ed. Jonneke Bekkenkamp and Yvonne Sherwood. London and New York: T&T Clawk.

———. 2004c. "Isaac to Abraham." In *Yours Faithfully: Virtual Letters from the Bible*, ed. Philip Davies. London: Equinox.

Sherwood, Yvonne and Hart, Kevin. 2004. "Other Testaments." In *Derrida and Religion: Other Testaments*, ed. Sherwood and Hart. New York: Routledge.

Spinoza, Benedict de. 1965. *Traité Théologico-politique.* Trans. Charles Appuhn. Paris: G.F. Flammarion.

Tarlin, Jan. 1997. "Utopia and Pornography in Ezekiel: Violence, Hope and the Shattered Male Subject". In *Reading Bibles, Writing Bodies*, ed. Timothy K. Beal and David M. Gunn, 175–183.

Trible, Phyllis. 1984. "Hagar: The Desolation of Rejection." In *Texts of Terror: Literary-Feminist Readings of Biblical Narratives*, 9–35. Overtures to Biblical Theology. Philadelphia: Fortress.

Vawter, Bruce. 1977. *On Genesis: A New Reading.* New York: Doubleday.

Weingreen, Julius. 1959 [1939]. *A Practical Grammar for Classical Hebrew.* Oxford and New York: Oxford University Press.

Westermann, Claus. 1985 [1981]. *Genesis 12–36.* Minneapolis: Augsburg.

postscripts

Chapter 17

Pardon Me . . .

Mary-Jane Rubenstein

But is there not still something unassimilable about the term "Derridean Bible Study"? Does it not still provoke a wince, a smirk, a shrug, a sharp nasal exhalation—some visceral interjection that marks, but leaves unresolved, a certain uncanniness stirred by the unexpected, almost embarrassing, emergence of something that perhaps ought to have remained hidden? And could this discomfort lie behind this volume's fascination with the secret?

There is, one could say, something monstrous about Derridean Bible Study (especially when released from its imprisonment within quotation marks), something stitched together and at times ungainly that manages, as only a hopeless misfit can, to point to (*monstrare*) that which the normal order of things occludes, precludes, excludes. Reading the Bible "alongside" Derrida has something—perhaps everything—to do with interrupting all safe and self-assured textual practices on both sides of this alongside. It is a matter of mobilizing the monstrous to disrupt at each turn the carefully guarded interiors of the ordinary and intelligible, constantly reconfiguring the limits of the thinkable in response to the shock of the unthinkable.

This is most likely the reason for this volume's strategic preference for Derrida's recent "conceptual genealogies": those *danses macabres* through the aporetic inscription of our most common linguistic inheritances. When pushed out to its conceptual limit, Derrida teaches us, even that which we believe we understand easily eludes all efforts to comprehend it. Ultimately, the very concepts upon which our ethics and ontologies rest are only possible as impossible. This noetic impasse is the gift of a double-logic within the philo-theo-literary "heritage," which finds articulation through an "irreconcilable but indissociable" tension between conditional and unconditional imperatives (Derrida, 2001, 37). So while the conditional laws of hospitality, for instance, require that I welcome the stranger as long as she states her name, place of origin, and good intentions, *unconditional* hospitality would require "that I open my home and that I give not only to the foreigner (provided with a family name, with the status of being a foreigner, etc.), but to the absolute, unknown, anonymous other, and that I *give place* to them, that I let them come, let them arrive, and take place in the place I offer them, without asking of them either reciprocity (entering into a pact), or even their names" (Derrida, 2000, 25). "Pure" hospitality, construed in this manner as the suspension of all calculation and reciprocity, would be humanly impossible, not to mention exceedingly dangerous. But Derrida's hope (if one might risk such a scandalous ascription) lies in the relentless oscillation between the conditional and the unconditional—in the possibility that an encounter with the impossible might shatter the narrow confines of the possible, opening out unforeseen practices and alignments.

The pieces collected here appeal to these possible/impossible (anti-)structures, both in order to (dis-)locate their doubly bound inscription within the Hebrew Bible and New Testament, and more importantly, in order to disrupt and re-imagine the range of "possible" readings of Scripture. In addition to their constant concern with the secret, these essays work through the problems of the gift, the promise, messianism, responsibility, friendship, identity, decision, memory and forgetting, and hospitality, all of which, when abstracted from their restrictive, earthly conditions of possibility, are possible only as impossible. Puzzlingly, the only recent Derridean impossibility about which this volume remains silent is that of forgiveness.

Like hospitality, friendship, and the gift, forgiveness comes to us in two different forms. On the one hand, we are called upon to forgive those who confess, repent, and do some sort of penance for the sake of reconciliation. On the other hand, the same tradition that presents us with this "conditional" logic *also* suggests that forgiveness must be extended unconditionally; that is, even to those who cannot, or will not, apologize or promise to reform themselves. Through a series of careful readings of Augustine, Paul, Shakespeare, and Vladimir Jankélévitch, Derrida argues that this latter, unconditional imperative is "true" forgiveness. If forgiveness is possible, understandable, or sensible, he insists, then it is not forgiveness. A forgivable trespass might call for forgetting, restitution, or reconciliation, but only the absolutely unforgivable calls for forgiveness. To this already complicated analysis, Derrida adds the concern raised by Emmanuel Lévinas that forgiveness places the giver in a position of sovereignty with respect to the criminal. Traditionally reserved for the monarch (earthly or divine), the "power" to pardon exalts its possessor as He Who Has the Right to Bestow or Withhold Forgiveness upon the lowly offender. Who, one must therefore ask, has the right to forgive?

Reduced to the Lévinasian *visage-à-visage*, the ethical scene of forgiveness would take place between one victim and one criminal. Yet who has the right to forgive the criminal if his victim is dead? His descendants? His ruler? His community? Even if the victim is alive, is he still a victim if the "power" of forgiveness makes him *magister* over his enemy? Likewise, if the criminal repents and humbly transforms herself, then what has become of the violent criminal whom the former victim is called upon to forgive? And what is one to do when the scene expands to include whole families, nations, and races? Because forgiveness must forgive the unforgivable, and because of the maddening instability of accuser and accused, forgiveness—if there is such a thing—is only possible as impossible.

To be fair, *Derrida's Bible* does mention forgiveness five times in passing—negligible secretions that nevertheless betray some sort of secret—but none of these apparitions is addressed at any length.[1] This is a strange omission indeed, not only because so much of what we know (and cannot know) of forgiveness, we owe to the biblical tradition, but also—and more pressingly—because the Bible confronts us with so many scenes of transgression that might be read as "unforgivable." These very essays present us with an unconscionable thicket of broken covenants, fratricidal nations, claims of divine impregnation, blessings that curse, curses that bless, poisonous gifts, unrecoverable loss, stolen land, perjured oaths, conflicting obligations, expelled sons, nearly-murdered sons, discarded wives, scheming mothers, inconsistent fathers, a mispronunciation that leads to a mass-slaughter, and above (it) all, a divinity who allows death and sin into creation, who persecutes the righteous on a diabolical dare, hardens the hearts of tyrants to increase his own glory, drowns his creation, and demands sacrifices, near-sacrifices, and deadly substitutions. Why, as these studies wrestle anew with these unforgivable passages, do they not also wrestle with forgiveness?

Perhaps—and it could be unforgivable even to suggest such a thing—this resonant silence has to do with the feeling one gets that there is something unpardonable, or at the very least highly transgressive, going on in these thought-experiments themselves. These "risky," "uncommon," "disturbing," even "heterodox" readings know they take place on "dangerous ground," ground that demands fear, trembling, and even the sophisticated dressing-down or un-saying of that which is ventured—through, say, the excessive modesty of a Kierkegaardian disavowal.[2] To be sure, this volume blazes its critical paths by trespassing. Here the biblical slips when it feels so inclined not only into the theological, but also into cultural studies, literary theory, politics, and philosophy. This disciplinary promiscuity, in turn, violates the integrity of the miniature divisions within Biblical studies and offends the sensibilities of those purists on both sides of the great divide it negotiates. More traditional biblical scholars will no doubt fear in this cavorting with the flighty, "Continental" enemy an outlandish and irresponsible ungrounding of stable exegetical practices. And for their part, the Derridean orthodoxy (a heretical coinage I will risk) will fear a contamination of their sacred secularity with the hopelessly pre-post, onto-theological remnant of Biblical studies, which remains not only secretly confessional, but also unregenerately Kantian-Hegelian.

Yet what sort of transgressions are performed here if they find authorization in Derrida's "own," increasingly direct, engagement with biblical texts? As Yvonne Sherwood points out, anyone who missed the biblical ghosts in Derrida's early writings would have to try fairly hard to ignore (or forget) them at this point (Sherwood, "Derrida's Bible," 1). In fact, it is with his recent work on the possible-impossible coding of ethical concepts that Derrida awakens his sleeping biblical daemons, making it very difficult for any of us to tell "Derrida" apart from the "Bible" that possesses and dispossesses him. This volume is, in other words, as much a sketch of the Bible's Derrida as it is of Derrida's Bible.

It is in this sense that Sherwood can call a particular series of violent Biblical substitutions "more Derridean . . . than Derrida," and that Brian Britt can proclaim, "the biblical is Derridean and . . . Derrida is biblical" (Sherwood, "Sarah," 25; Britt, 12). After all, these readings uncover a biblical world of fundamentally split origins, empty tombs, incommunicable terrors, haunted mourners, absent authors, enforced forgetting, misunderstood revelation, a book that effects its own decomposition, the drunken conflation of friends and enemies, and words that start wars. Are these uncannily Derridean moments products of Derridean readings, or have they always been "in" the Bible? Is it Francophile "word play," or the relentless overdetermination of Hebrew and Greek that underwrites these diverse thought-experiments? Is it Derrida or the Bible that enables us to read God as, let us say, a gender-bending mess of relational inscrutability who refuses to function as a decent transcendental signified? Where does the Bible's property give onto Derrida's? And how on earth have we fallen into such a scandalous conflation?

Throughout the pages bound together here, Derrida is not only identified in a persistent "certain sense" with the Bible; he is also compared to Ezekiel, anticipated as Elijah, dubbed "Retro-Rabbinic," aligned with religious fundamentalists, and positioned for the sake of argument among "the ungodly."[3] Derrida is not, in other words, either simply located or swallowed whole. In fact, many of the readings are surprisingly unfaithful to the master—taking a disavowal as an avowal, dwelling "too long" on a parenthesis, reading Lévinas back into (and against) Derrida, contesting Derrida's incontestable reading of "Bartleby," pointing out his own ghosts and silences, charging him (or his disciples) with elitism, or even accusing him of ethical failure.[4] And *in a certain sense*, these readings are similarly unfaithful to the very "Bible" they re-read and therefore rewrite through Derrida: what would the "tradition" do if it knew that Ishmael, Sarah, and Hagar had been reintroduced into the inviolable duo of Abraham and Isaac? Or that the pseudo-Pauline epistles had been likened to postcards? Or that the only structure of *Ecclesiastes* is the vanity of structure?[5] How is one to interpret these multi-vectored infidelities, especially those that announce themselves—either explicitly or implicitly—as "for Derrida"?[6] Who is on whose side here?

In *The Human Condition*, Hannah Arendt locates possibility's own condition of possibility in forgiveness. Forgiveness is—or would be—a surprise "interference" into the self-certain course of history, an eruption of new possibilities from the interruption of the "relentless automism" of violence and revenge. "Forgiving," she suggests, "is the only reaction which does not merely re-act but acts anew and unexpectedly" (Arendt, 241). What does it mean to raise the specter of forgiveness in this "place"; that is, in a postscriptural interruption to a collection of texts that look to interrupt all scholarly smugness, disable all "disengaged" exegetical warfare, and provoke the emergence of the new and unexpected—precisely by reading the unforgivable unforgivably? Who might forgive whom here? And for what?

At its best, this volume stages the sort of treachery, perjury, and enmity that signals the most profound indebtedness and respect. The most effective of these studies read Derrida with the Bible until only the *with* remains. They work through, across, within, and against the rift separating "deconstruction" from "biblical studies," creating a monstrous network of indiscretions, thanks to which it ultimately becomes impossible to tell offender from offended, ally from foe, or transgression from fidelity. Liable to leave its readers within a tangle of unclaimed possibilities, unsure of how or whom to thank, blame, forgive, or forget, "Derridean Bible Study" becomes most promising at its most unpardonable.

Notes

1. These brief appearances can be found in Brian Britt's reference to Deuteronomy 32:33; Mark Brummit's citation of Jeremiah 36:3; Christopher Heard's reference to the Christian

doctrine of substitutionary atonement; Theodore Jennings's reference to Derrida's connection of hospitality and forgiveness; and Andrew Wilson's brief rhetorical flourish on what one could be forgiven for thinking on the basis of commentators readings at the beginning of the section "Tomp Without End".

2. Cf. Jobling, Heard, and Sherwood, "Derrida's Bible."
3. Cf. Sherwood, "Derrida's Bible," and Turner, "Death at the Gate."
4. Cf. Britt; Eisenstadt; Yamada; and Jobling.
5. Cf. Heard; Sherwood, "And Sarah Died"; Seesengood; and Koosed.
6. Cf. David Jobling's implied parody of Derrida's "for Marx".

Works Consulted

Arendt, Hannah. 1998. *The Human Condition*. Chicago: University of Chicago Press.
Derrida, Jacques. 2000. "Foreigner Question/Question of the Stranger." Trans. Rachel Bowlby. In *Of Hospitality: Anne Dufourmantelle Invites Jacques Derrida to Respond*, 3–73, odd pages. Stanford: Stanford University Press.
————. 2001. "On Forgiveness." Trans. Michael Hughes. In *On Cosmopolitanism and Forgiveness*, ed. Simon Critchley and Richard Kearney, 27–60. London and New York: Routledge.

Chapter 18

Beliebigkeit

John Barton

Beliebig, *adj.*, as is agreeable, to your liking, at your pleasure, any (you like), whatever, optional, arbitrary; *in beliebigier Größe*, of any size you choose; *zu jeder beliebigen Zeit*, at any time that will suit.

(*Cassell's German and English Dictionary, seventh edn. 1962*)

Beliebigkeit in meaning is the great demon for "historical" critics. All varieties of postmodern thinking are suspect because they seem to make the meaning of texts *beliebig*. The text means whatever you like, or perhaps it even means whatever you don't like, so that you can attack it—so that you can give the text a bad name and hang it. At any rate it doesn't mean what *it* means. The suspicion that "Derrida's Bible" will be just whatever Derrida chooses to make it, whether that is something Derrida likes or, deliberately, something he doesn't, is what provokes unreconstructed historical critics such as me to write sarcastically and even flippantly about postmodernism. Yvonne Sherwood has been ultra-generous in giving me an opportunity to revisit my sarcasm in *Reading the Old Testament* (Barton 1996) without specifying that I have to recant. I do, at least partially, but I begin by explaining why anyone might think that the deep seriousness of postmodernist interpretation is itself flippant or at least frivolous. The suspected frivolity does not lie in any trivialization of the text, but in what looks like a refusal to accept that it *constrains* the interpreter, a playfulness about what words can mean, an inability to look the text straight in the eye. To us it seems that you can make all the right noises about the profundity of a text and yet be deeply frivolous so long as you think its meaning is, ultimately, *beliebig*. So my sarcastic comments were not made casually or simply from a failure to see that Derrida et al. are serious; they were principled, a reaction to a perceived *betrayal* of the text. Perhaps someone should psychologize historical critics (perhaps someone has) and ask what deep drives make them so insistent on feeling constrained, but whatever the reason that's the fact of it. And of course we all know that the sense of constraint is often an illusion: historical criticism constantly produces perfectly (and dangerously) *beliebig* interpretations itself, as no one has shown more effectively than Sherwood (1996 and 2000). But you need to see where we are coming from if you are to understand why we react as we do.

Here, however, begins the recantation. The trouble (one trouble) with historical criticism is that in its pursuit of interpretative purity it is all too often thin, chopping logic rather than engaging with the *matter* of the text, as Luther called it, the *res scripturae*. A concern for *realia*, historical context, textual stratification, origins and authors, keeps it from seeing the length and breadth and depth and height of the text. It keeps its eye firmly on the ball but somehow fails to watch the game. This need not be so, and is not always so, I would maintain—and thereby hangs a book.[1] But very often it is so. And the same cannot be said of Derridean readings. These may strike the likes of me as wilful or even perverse, but they are not trivial. And they draw attention to features which an honest "historical" critic must acknowledge once pointed out, but which that critic would never have noticed unaided.

Brian Britt's "Erasing Amalek: Remembering to Forget with Derrida and Biblical Tradition" argues "that the biblical is Derridean, and that Derrida is biblical, in a certain sense." He points out that the Bible and Derrida share "the interdependence of canonical text and commentary; an understanding of writing and speech as authorized discourse; an understanding of textual coherence that includes fragmentation." Any reader will understand the "wilful forgetting" enjoined in the curse on Amalek better for having encountered Derrida's work on memory and "the archive". This is not a case of producing a "Derridean reading" of Exodus 17 and Deuteronomy 25, but of noticing an intellectual confluence between the ancient text and the postmodern one which illuminates both. Robert P. Seesengood's "Postcards from the (Canon's) Edge: The Pastoral Epistles and Derrida's *The Post Card*" similarly shows readers things about the Pastorals they would scarcely have observed from reading traditional commentaries, however voluminous. The paradox that these (probably) pseudepigraphical documents "tell" us more about Paul as a person than his authentic letters seems not to have been commented on before; yet arguably they have created the Paul of Pauline reception-history more effectively than Romans or 1 Corinthians. It is "2 Timothy" (3:16), not the "real" Pauline letters, that produced the doctrine of scriptural inspiration held by millions of evangelical Christians—just as postcards, marginal and casual as they are, may tell us more than solemn and carefully phrased letters. Postmodern concern for the marginal and "trivial" reorientates the reader who has grown up with a traditional "historical-critical" map.

Derridean readings seem like *jeux d'esprit* to such a reader, and indeed in a sense that is what they are. But a *jeu d'esprit* can be the bearer of serious ideas. I do not think I was wrong to suspect a 'ludic' intention in much postmodern writing, but I was wrong to forget that play can be a serious business. From that point of view I am not sure I was in error in illustrating postmodern thinking from *Alice in Wonderland*, for Carroll was a postmodernist *avant la lettre*; but I should have made it clear (as I did not) that my intention was not to suggest any infantilism in Derrida et al. Many of the best literary *jeux d' esprit* can be found in a writer I have long loved and often quoted, Borges, and he anticipates many of the types of insight to be found in the present volume: think, for example, of his suggestion that "every writer creates his own precursors", so that it is only through Kafka that we can begin to understand Kierkegaard. The notion that Derrida creates the Bible would not have seemed odd to him, and nor does it to me once I stop to think about it as a serious and *of course* also ludic proposal. But it will take a long time for "historical" critics to see the truth in it and not only the much more obvious falsity.

So I find myself not wishing to deny anything that is said in *Derrida's Bible*, but wanting—perhaps more irritatingly, I don't know—to annexe it to traditional biblical criticism and to declare that it is not so alien to that world as it seems. Derrida and those who follow him alert us to aspects of the biblical text we would otherwise overlook. I want to say that these aspects are "really there", and in this I reveal my ultimately objectivist character; but I want also to thank postmodernism for making them apparent. I am afraid that this is itself another example of *Beliebigkeit*, taking a postmodern chart on board a "modern" ship, making of it what I choose and reading it "as it suits". But my hope is that there could at least be conversations during the journey to replace the present mutual deafness.

Note

1. See J. Barton, *The Nature of Biblical Criticism*, Louisville, Kentucky: Westminster John Knox Press, forthcoming (with any luck).

Works Consulted

Barton, John. 1996 [1984]. *Reading the Old Testament: Method in Biblical Study*. London: Darton, Longman and Todd.
Sherwood, Yvonne. 1996; 2nd edn 2004. *The Prostitute and the Prophet*. London: Continuum.
——. 2000. *A Biblical Text and Its Afterlives: The Survival of Jonah in Western Culture*. Cambridge: Cambridge University Press.

Appendix: Abstracts

beginnings

Lee Danes, Between Genealogy and Virgin Birth: Origin and Originality in Matthew

This essay examines the biblical problematic of authority in terms of the interrelationship of origin and originality in Matthew. From the very opening of his Gospel, Matthew stages the drama of the relationship of what we have come to call Judaism and Christianity in terms of a dialectic of old and new, origin and originality. This essay explores the aporia between Matthew's genealogy of Christ and his account of the Virgin Birth, and proposes a Derridean reading strategy to explicate that aporia. It is the essay's contention that Matthew posits the Gospel's singular authority in and through a radical discontinuity between its opening genealogy of Jesus (traced through Joseph back through David to Abraham) and the Virgin Birth (traced through Mary to the Holy Ghost). The Gospel opens, then, with a double positing of authority. In so doing, it produces a gap (about which it is silent and secret) between authority located in the traditional manner of genealogical lineage and authority located in the supernatural manner of a god's impregnation of a human woman. Matthew constructs Jesus' authority such that, although itself a product and producer of the biblical tradition, it negates and reinstantiates the tradition. Yet, from the beginning, the Jewish and Christian Bibles and their traditions involve and express an ongoing process of negation and reinstantiation as the very standard of their justice and authority.

writing, posting, erasing

Mark Brummitt, Of Secretaries, Secrets, and Scrolls: Jeremiah 36 and the Irritating Word of God

The secretary, writes Derrida, is one "who conceals." Jeremiah 36 is a chapter peopled with secretaries—the king's officials, the scribes within the temple courts, and of course the scribe who transcribes the words of the prophet—representatives of the structures (systems) of temple and court. By means of secretaries a scroll makes its way through these institutions from prophet to king: a journey marked by a series of openings, recitations, closings and concealings. And on its journey, it clearly disturbs those with whom it comes into contact. When the scroll *is* opened, it is in the hands of secretaries who keep their backs to the readers: seemingly it is enough to know that the book exists, we do not need to know—or *now* cannot know—its content. One glimpse is granted, a peek at what proves to be prophetic cliché and which effectively maintains the hiddenness of the content. By reading Jeremiah 36 alongside Derrida's *A Taste for the Secret*, this essay considers the acts of transcribing and transmitting speech as an act of concealment. The scroll then, is the locus of secrecy (in the hands of secretaries) and of secrets (its content).

Robert Paul Seesengood, Postcards from the (Canon's) Edge: The Pastoral Epistles and Derrida's *The Post Card*

The debate over the authorship of 1 and 2 Timothy and Titus has involved meticulous reconstructions of ancient layers of Christian history, painstaking linguistic analysis and powerful ideological argument. Despite the most vigorous and technical efforts of scholarship, there is not yet any clear consensus as to whether Paul or a student of Paul wrote the Pastorals. Ironically, these letters are obsessed with issues of authority, sound doctrine, and community governance and are perhaps the most intimate of the writings attributed to Paul. The "preface" (*envois*) to Derrida's *The Post Card* explores writing and identity, noting that written communication is fragmentary and mediated by a "post" that both delivers and (occasionally) misdirects messages. Reading Derrida alongside Paul (and Paul's would-be interpreters) reveals critical scholarship (and reading in general) failing at the precise point of intersection and transforms criticism into autobiography and aesthetics.

Brian M. Britt, Erasing Amalek: Remembering to Forget with Derrida and Biblical Tradition

This essay traces two traditional discourses of erasure: one originating in the curse on Amalek in Exodus 17 and Deuteronomy 25 and the other associated with Jacques Derrida. In response to several works exploring the intersection of deconstruction and negative theology, this essay suggests some points of contact between deconstruction and biblical tradition, in that both "traditions" of erasure evoke categories of writing, memory, and being. By way of a detour through the work of Emmanuel Lévinas, I propose that Derrida's conceptions of erasure and negative theology *do* resonate with biblical tradition, despite the divergent ontological and metaphysical categories of biblical tradition and poststructuralism.

specters and messiahs

Alastair G. Hunter, The Missing/Mystical Messiah: Melchizedek Among the Specters of Genesis 14

Historical study of Genesis 14 has failed to identify any plausible archaeological context; classic biblical criticism reveals structures of a complexity that defies tidy solutions; linguistically the chapter appears to be parasitic on a wide range of exotic biblical sources; stylistically the text is replete with puns and archaisms, together with a nested narrative structure of overlapping events and people and episodes inserted within episodes; as a character, Abram stands in stark contrast to the figure described elsewhere in Genesis; and the chapter finally is dominated by the mysterious and elusive Melchizedek. He plays an important minor role in the Jewish and Christian literature of the period from 200 m B.C.E. to 200 C.E., where he is presented as a priestly, messianic and eschatological presence. The Christian book of Hebrews in particular reinterprets him to the advantage of a supersessionist view of Jesus as Messiah.

A key term in the chapter is *melekh*; yet the one figure never thus characterized is Abram, though he is presented in many ways in regal (dis)guise. The chapter both effects a deconstruction of the meaning of "king," and simultaneously reinstates the term *in absentia* as the one word we are driven to use of Abram—though he himself appears ambivalent as to its propriety. Abram's meeting with Melchizedek is profoundly ambiguous—it is unclear who is the superior, to whom blessings are given, and (above all) whence this mysterious (messianic) figure comes.

In questioning the messianic in the context of the naming and unnaming of kings I draw upon Derrida's work on the proper name and the messianic in order to inform my reading of what is a puzzling and provocative text. The mystery of Melchizedek is in many ways the point: the only other reference in Tanakh is in Psalm 110:4, where the name may be nothing more than a phantom conjured from an imaginative etymology. Thus Abram's acceptance/rejection of the role model "Melchizedek" introduces a profound uncertainty at the heart of the Christian messianic rhetoric of the book of Hebrews, and opens up to an exploration of a more elusive messiah who subverts the claims of all three 'Abrahamic' religions.

David Jobling, Jerusalem and Memory: On a Long Parenthesis in Derrida's *Specters of Marx*

Despite the extensive response by biblical and religion scholars to many of Derrida's writings, there has been a curious neglect of *Specters of Marx*, Derrida's major work on Marx and Marxism. This is particularly unfortunate in that it tends to prevent conjunction between the "Derrida and religion" debate and liberation theologies. This essay takes off from an extraordinary four-page parenthesis (58–61) that Derrida inserts into his argument about the enormous energy expended since 1990 on "forgetting" Marx, a parenthesis which sees the current situation in the Middle East as the very center of this dynamic of "forgetting": "The war for the 'appropriation of Jerusalem' is today the world war." Building on my own earlier work (*1 Samuel*, 1998), and on other work on remembering and forgetting in the Hebrew Bible, I explore Jerusalem in the Bible as a figure for the programmatic "forgetting" of Israel's defining past, and relate the biblical dynamic to the current political situation.

boundaries/hyphens/identity-markers

Frank Yamada, Shibboleth, and the Ma(r)king of Culture: Judges 12 and the Monolingualism of the Other

In *Monolingualism of the Other; or, the Prosthesis of Origin*, Jacques Derrida takes up the topics of autobiography, cultural identity and the ways in which language is always differing from itself while always referring only to itself. Identity, cultural or otherwise, is complicated by the fact that language for Derrida is always the language of the other, and yet it is the only language one has. Thus, he proposes that "*we only ever speak one language*" and "*we never speak only one language*" (7). Judges 12:1–6 is a text about the ways in which language inscribes cultural difference through exclusion. The term, "shibboleth," which becomes a code word used by the men of Gilead to distinguish themselves from the Ephraimites, demonstrates the potential within language to both mark the identity of a group and divide a nation against itself. When one reads these texts, looking for what Homi Bhabha has identified as the emergence of culture at the interstices, a cultural identity surfaces that resists fixed categorizations of culture, preferring complex and conflicting hybridities. It is a cultural identity that results from the negotiation of difference "in-between"—a cultural *différance*.

Dmitri M. Slivniak, The Book of Esther: The Making and Unmaking of Jewish Identity

One of the central themes in recent work by Derrida is that of identity: its paradoxical character, essential instability, and violence. Derrida elaborates, in particular, on Jewish identity, which has become particularly paradoxical in the last two hundred years.

In contemporary Israel, the Law of Return was intended to assure the Jewish identity of the state while giving immigration rights to Diaspora Jews. But paradoxically it has led to a mass immigration of non-Jews and people who do not qualify as Jews according to the religious law.

The most "Jewish" of all the books of the Hebrew Bible is perhaps the book of Esther: the fundamental opposition underlying it is that of "Jews"—"Gentiles." The "secular" character of the book, where God and Temple are not mentioned, makes it appealing to Jews of all backgrounds and worldviews. On the other hand, Esther is perhaps the only book in the Hebrew Bible that has often been perceived in an antisemitic fashion—it was intuitively felt to be "too Jewish."

Using Bakhtin's theory of carnival, which resonates with the writings of Derrida, I analyse how the "wise" characters (Mordechai, Esther) and the "foolish" characters (Vashti, Haman, Assuerus) imitate and mutate into one another, so contesting the principle of monolingualism and stable identity. Read this way, the book of Esther resonates with the identities of Jew, Israeli, non-Jewish Israeli, and so on. And identity, not unlike God in negative theology, becomes not what one is but what one is not.

responsibilities, secrets, gifts

R. Christopher Heard, Triangulating Responsibility: How and Why Abraham, Isaac, and Ishmael Offer and Refuse the Gift of Death, and to/from Whom

Derrida's *The Gift of Death* includes an extended meditation on Kierkegaard's *Fear and Trembling*, itself a meditation on the biblical story in which God asks Abraham to sacrifice "his only son." As both the Bible and Qur'an testify, however, Abraham actually had *two* sons at the time God issued this request. Judeo-Christian tradition identifies Isaac as the son targeted for sacrifice; one stream of Islamic interpretation identifies Ishmael as the intended victim. Recognition of Ishmael's existence complicates Derrida's reading of Kierkegaard and Kierkegaard's reading of Genesis, setting Abraham's response to God's request into a context of potential competition between the two sons for the right to inherit from Abraham. In the interpretive tradition, however, the sons compete not to live and inherit, but to die and cede the inheritance to the other son. The mutual displacement of Ishmael and Isaac from Abraham's altar powerfully suggests that rejection of the gift of another's death may be an ethical imperative.

Oona Eisenstadt, Preferring or not Preferring: Derrida on Bartleby as Kierkegaard's Abraham

Derrida's main aim in chapter three of *The Gift of Death* seems to be to mediate between Lévinas and Kierkegaard. As part of this endeavour, he reminds us of certain parts of Kierkegaard's interpretation of the akedah, and compares them to elements in Herman Melville's story "Bartleby." The reading of "Bartleby" is, however, problematic. I argue that Derrida deliberately leaves holes in that reading in order to point to holes in Kierkegaard's understanding of the akedah—holes that point in turn back to Lévinas and to his difference from Kierkegaard. Derrida's main intention, I conclude, is to suggest that it is all but impossible to mediate between Lévinas and Kierkegaard, and that it might be folly to attempt to mediate between the traditions of reading they represent.

Theodore W. Jennings, Jr, Justice as Gift: Thinking Grace with the Help of Derrida

Paul's complex argument in Romans regarding justice can be helpfully illuminated by a reading of the work of Jacques Derrida. This may be illustrated by relating Derrida's reflections on gift to Paul's attempt to think gift or grace as the basis of a justice that stands outside the law. For Derrida, justice must be thought on the basis of gift. Yet the thought of gift is, in a certain sense, impossible since it tends inevitably to fall back into an economy of exchange from which it is both heterogeneous and indissociable (much as is justice in its relation to law). In thinking of the gift as the basis of an indeconstructible justice, Derrida acknowledges that he is interested in the gift "in the Christian sense." For Paul it is also the case that grace may be understood as the "gift of justice"; a justice which although it is not "under the law" nevertheless claims our "members" as instruments of justice. For both Derrida and Paul the heterogeneity of gift to economy ("works" in Pauline terms) seems to be indicated by a certain excess which also exceeds knowledge. For both thinkers, although in importantly different ways, justice based on gift stands outside the law even as the law makes evident and effective the claim of justice.

Andrew P. Wilson, Trembling in the Dark: Derrida's *Mysterium Tremendum* and the Gospel of Mark

This paper takes its lead from Derrida's *The Gift of Death*. A key concept in *The Gift of Death* is that of the *mysterium tremendum* which Derrida describes as a "frightful mystery, a secret to make you tremble" (53). Within the gospel of Mark, moments which can be described in these terms occur with some frequency: two key moments being at the Transfiguration and in the Empty Tomb. Traditional scholarship reads the Markan Transfiguration as brimming with presences: light, clarity, vision, voice, and so on . The Empty Tomb, by contrast, is marked by a conspicuous absence and a puzzling abruptness: Jesus's body is missing and the Gospel ends mid-sentence. Although contrasting in theme and imagery, the distance between the Transfiguration and the Empty Tomb is bridged by more than a homogenising metaphysics of presence. There is a fearfulness that pervades both these scenes, a primal fear that marks them as encounters with something wondrous and at the same time terrifying, a fear shared by both the disciples on the mountain and the women in the tomb. A Derridean reading of these two contrasting episodes will involve consideration of this fearfulness as a moment when traditional formulations of these texts are radically subverted . . . By engaging with the fear, the experience of the disciples and the women is seen to be an expression of fear of an unspeakable ungraspable subversion, an infinite lack in both subject and spectacle.

Marie Turner, Death At The Gate: Who Let Him In? Responsibility for Death in the Wisdom of Solomon and Derrida

Biblical writers are swift to praise God for the glories of creation but shy away from attributing death and decay to that same creator God. Derrida's insight on the way the devil exculpates God in dualistic theology is relevant to this question of theodicy. In the Wisdom of Solomon, a deutero-canonical book written in Alexandria sometime between the middle of the second century B.C.E. and the first decades of the first century C.E., the sage sees death and decay as radically evil and inimical to creation. He blames its presence on ungodly human beings and an envious devil whom they have invited on to the earth. My article argues that Sophia/Wisdom, image and reflection of God, is the agent of creation and responsible for immortality because her immortal spirit is in all things. She must therefore have power over life and death. When the ungodly bewail the transience of life and the passing even of memory, this is not the cause of their annihilation and death's entry into the world, as the sage claims. Death was already in creation, as symbolized by the rosebud that withers. The paper will conduct its investigation of a too-easy theology of immortality in dialogue with some of Derrida's later writings on death. These include *The Work of Mourning, The Gift of Death, A Taste for the Secret* and *Adieu, to Emmanuel Lévinas*. Derrida can be compared with the "ungodly," but only in the very limited sense that he claims that he "rightly passes for an atheist." But where the ungodly of Wisdom can be accused of nihilism and the exploitation of creation, Derrida's writings resonate with life and responsibility towards the "other."

endings

Francis Landy, The End of the World: *Archive Fever*, Qohelet 12.1–7, and Lamentations Rabbah

Archive Fever, originally a lecture delivered at the opening of the Freud Archives in London, is one of Derrida's most sustained reflections on memory, messianicity, anarchic violence, and hope, in the context of a critical dialogue with Yosef Hayyim Yerushalmi's *Freud's Moses: Judaism Terminable and Interminable*. Derrida's essay is contrasted with two texts that concern the themes of messianicity, memory, and desire. Qohelet (Ecclesiastes) 12:1–7 is a text about the end of the world, under cover of an extended simile about old age. It is, however, an anti-apocalyptic text, in which the world slowly fades out, its music dying away together with the poem. Proem 23 of *Lamentations Rabbah* is a protracted though parenthetic commentary on Qohelet 12:1–7. In it the cosmological imagery of Qohelet is transferred directly to Jerusalem and the fallen Israelite polity; Jerusalem is the cosmos, and its fate is that of the world. However, the destruction of Jerusalem is itself a symbol of a much more pervasive disaster, one symptom of which is the forgetfulness of Torah. Proem 23 is a beautifully constructed composition at the centre of which is the implacable but ultimately appeased blood of the prophet Zechariah, and the conversion of the conqueror Nebuzaradan. Proem 24, which is an enormously elaborated antithesis of Proem 23, focuses on the irreconcilable gap between God's inconsolable grief and his utter indifference; God is ultimately bereft of language, Torah, creation and history, and only the uncanny voice of Rachel, impersonating Leah's orgasm and vice versa, evokes an albeit deferred response. Rachel's voice, however, is inseparable from those of the women in the Midrash who challenge any possible theodicy. For them, and for at least one voice in the Midrash, suicide is the only viable option. The text is a centrifuge in which meaning is destroyed. On the other hand, there is an evocation of a Messiah, whose birth coincides with the catastrophe, and who is no sooner born than he disappears.

Jennifer L. Koosed, Decomposing Qohelet

This article presents the book of Qohelet as an exploration of the limits of signification, limits imposed on meaning through the gift of death. Death in Qohelet entails two themes: (1) the loss of memory, and (2) the leveling of differences. At the level of the physical body, no one is remembered after death and there is no differentiation made in death between the wise and the foolish, or even between the human and the animal. Death comes for all. Qohelet then enacts this inevitable decay of the body through a decay of the text. The physical body and the body of the book are intertwined. At the level of the textual body, meaning requires both repeatability and differentiation (Jacques Derrida's concept of "iterability"), two things extinguished by death. Qohelet enacts this through an incoherent structure, the positioning of "a time to die" in Qohelet 3:2–8, and the puzzling final poem in Qohelet 12:1–8. Finally, what is left after the disruption of death in life and in the text? Using Derrida's analysis of the gift of death, this article argues that what is left is responsibility.

Yvonne Sherwood, And Sarah Died

The "sacrifice" of Isaac (Genesis 22)—a biblical narrative that fascinates Derrida—is followed by a curious sequel that begins "And Sarah died." In this essay I explore some of the implications of Derrida's two brief commentaries on this scene where Abraham *mourns* and Abraham *pays*. I then show how these are radically amplified, beforehand, by ancient Jewish interpreters as they allow the "and" (Hebrew *waw*) to become a dissenting "*But* Sarah died." The multiple possibilities of conjunction between the two narratives raise questions of awkward relationships between virtual death and real death, sacrifice and disaster, and between the "Abrahamic" and the figures of the woman and the foreigner with whom he seems to be in "guilty" (?) negotiation from the first. By way of appendix I consider the awkwardly appended, but necessary, supplement Hagar (Genesis 21) whose story lies on the other side of Mount Moriah to the death of Sarah and functions as a complicating surrogate for the Abrahamic "sacrifice." I end by asking *why* this narrative of very tangled geneses begins in scenes of obligation, debt and mourning, and conceives (of) itself as passing through the womb of a foreign slave.

Author Index

Reference Index